THE LIFE OF
FRANÇOIS RABELAIS

PLATE I

PORTRAIT OF RABELAIS
(Museum of Versailles, No. 4046)

THE LIFE OF FRANÇOIS RABELAIS

BY

JEAN PLATTARD

PROFESSOR IN THE FACULTY OF LETTERS OF THE
UNIVERSITY OF POITIERS

LONDON
GEORGE ROUTLEDGE & SONS, LTD.
BROADWAY HOUSE: 68–74 CARTER LANE, E.C.
1930

Translated by

LOUIS P. ROCHE,

M.A., H. DIP. IN ED. (N.U.I.)

*Docteur de l'Université de Poitiers. Former Travelling Student
of the National University of Ireland.*

Printed in Great Britain at
The Mayflower Press, Plymouth. William Brendon & Son, Ltd.

CONTENTS

v

LIST OF ILLUSTRATIONS

PREFACE

" WOULD to heaven the life of Rabelais could be written ! "
wrote Michelet[1], about 1860. " It is impossible ! " he added,
discouraged by the penury of authoritative documents then
available as a basis for this biography.

The number of such documents has since appreciably increased. The inventory of them drawn up at the beginning
of the critical edition of *Gargantua* published under the direction
of M. Abel Lefranc[2], shows us that from the 4th of March, 1521,
to the 9th of January, 1553,—that is, from the time Rabelais
enters into relations with Guillaume Budé until his resignation
of the *cures* of Meudon and of Saint-Christophe-de-Jambet,
on the eve of his death,—there are very few years for which all
testimony to the man or to his work is completely absent.

True, the scope of this documentation is very unequal ;
it does not always inform us of significant facts. But, at least,
information is not now wanting about the circles in which
Rabelais lived, the Masters he acknowledged, his friends and
patrons. The formation of his mind, his culture, even his
character are made clear thereby. Of his attitude—whether
daring or cautious—in the conflict between the theologians of
the Sorbonne and the humanists and reformers we can now
judge, thanks to the precision which the researches of scholars
have introduced into the chronology of his works, the circumstances of their publication, the influence of his protectors
or enemies with the King, or the aspects of royal policy.

Michelet imagined Rabelais' existence as " unsettled, wandering and fugitive, that of the poor hare between two furrows."
A wandering existence it indeed was, but often so as a result
of the unsettled and roving temperament of Maître François.
If he was molested for having ridiculed the Sorbonne, he was

---

[1] *Histoire de France*, ed. Flammarion, vol. VIII, p. 361.
[2] *Œuvres de François Rabelais*. Edition critique, publiée par Abel Lefranc,
professeur au Collège de France, Jacques Boulenger, Henri Clouzot, Dr. Paul
Dorveaux, Jean Plattard et Lazare Sainéan. Paris, ed. Champion, vol. I,
pp. cxxviii–cxliii.

also in danger of imprisonment and, on two occasions, for reasons quite outside the domain of Theology. In any event, he was adept at avoiding his adversaries by providing himself with powerful patrons among those prelates given to the encouragement of letters. But, since the religious policy of the Government varied with the King's "good pleasure," a Cardinal's influence proved, betimes, an insufficient guarantee of complete security, and unexpected, if not dramatic, escapades are not wanting in his life.

It is, however, essential to rule out definitely those clownish anecdotes—fanciful creations of the 17th century—which tend to confound Maître François with Panurge. On the other hand, we may assume that the legend which represents him as a *bon vivant* is not a travesty, but merely an exaggeration of reality. That he was fond of wine to the point of drunkenness is the opinion of many of his readers, from Ronsard to M. Léon Daudet—but of this there is no proof. That he sought after pleasures, copious meals, an untrammelled existence, the company of cultured persons, and enjoyment in all its forms, is witnessed by numerous traits of his biography and all his work, which breathes the joy of living.

The most considerable addition which has been made to our knowledge of Rabelais since Michelet's despondent declaration is due to the *Société des Études Rabelaisiennes*, founded in 1903 by M. Abel Lefranc, at present professor of the *Collège de France* and *Membre de l'Institut*. For ten years, this society has centralised in its *Revue*—called since 1913 the *Revue du Seizième siècle*—nearly all the work done on Rabelais. It has reprinted several portions of the text of his works, and prepared a critical edition of which four volumes have already appeared ; it has stimulated research and created, outside its own body, a healthy and fruitful emulation. Having been associated with the activities of this Society from the outset, it is for me a pleasing duty to acknowledge that the present work owes much to its labours. It claims, very often, no other merit than that of bringing into line and presenting a synthesis of researches dispersed and scattered elsewhere, and often of a rather repellent technical nature.

A *Life of Rabelais* naturally called for a sketch of his literary work. Those who find that the space given to this study is too meagre may refer to the volume I devoted formerly to the literary art of *Gargantua* and *Pantagruel*[1] and also to the excellent work in which my colleague and friend, M. Pierre Villey, has accurately determined the particular aspects of each part of Rabelais' work and the general characteristics of his art and style[2].

J. P.

POITIERS,
   4th October, 1928.

[1] *L'Œuvre de Rabelais* (*Sources, Invention et Composition*). 1 vol. 8vo, Paris, H. Champion, 1910.
[2] Pierre Villey, *Les Grands Écrivains du XVIe siècle.* *Évolution des œuvres et invention des formes littéraires.* *Vol. I.* *Marot et Rabelais.* 1 vol. 8vo, (*Bibliothèque littéraire de la Renaissance*), Paris, ed. Champion, 1923.

LIFE OF FRANÇOIS RABELAIS

CHAPTER I

BIRTH AND EARLY EDUCATION

HOWEVER little one's acquaintance with our *literati* of the first half of the 16th century, one is struck by the contempt which they profess for all the productions of the art and thought of the Middle Ages. No generation in our literary history appears more proud of its originality than that of the Renaissance. It would seem that, previous to it, there was nothing but ignorance, and that the darkness of what our Humanists called the " Gothic night " had overspread France until the dawn of their century. That they were thus contemptuous of the culture of the Middle Ages is due to the fact that the greater part of them were acquainted with it only through the teaching of the colleges. Having reached adolescence, they were all fascinated by the literature of Greece and Rome which the works of scholars, translators, poets and artists had just placed within their reach. In comparison with the " *lettres humaines* " and the poetry, the eloquence, the philosophy of the Ancients, what value had in their eyes that scholastic philosophy, of which the creators,—Saint Thomas Aquinas, Alexander of Hales, Saint Bonaventure, and Duns Scotus,—are for us the glory of an epoch ? They possessed of their teaching only a degraded, narrowed and deformed idea, that which the " regents " of the colleges had given them. It evoked for them merely the painful memories of their early education, in utter contrast to that of which the new culture was drawing up the plan.

No writer has felt or expressed more vigorously than Rabelais this disdain for the educational methods which had fashioned his youth. He speaks in quivering anger of these masters, whose methods were in danger of debasing noble youth[1]. Nevertheless, it is likely that his early education had been sound : our vouchers for it are the situation of his family and his father's status.

The painstaking investigations of contemporary scholars[2] have thrown some light upon his origin, which had been for long surrounded by legends. One of the few real traits which has not been falsified by legendary tradition is that François hails from the *Chinonais* district. Indeed, as far back as 1457, one Guillaume Rabelais figures in an official document as tenant of the Abbey of Seuilly, a good league to the south of Chinon[3]. At the end of the 15th century, the head of the family, our author's father, is named Antoine Rabelais. He is neither an innkeeper, nor an apothecary, as has been supposed even quite recently, but an advocate at the *siège royal* of Chinon[4], a licentiate of laws. He will even have the honour, in 1527, of acting for the *Lieutenant général et particulier* and, in his absence, directing the procedure, in his capacity of assessor, being the senior advocate of the Court. Thus, François Rabelais, on his father's side, belongs to the legal world, one of the most enlightened classes in French society of the time. Consequently, he will be quite ready, in his adolescent days, as we shall see, to enter into relations with a group of magistrates and advocates. He early becomes familiar with the terms of legal procedure and disputation. Perhaps even to this origin can be ascribed his handwriting, elaborate and full of parasite letters, which was, as has been remarked, that of the legal practitioners, whose tradition it was to multiply the

---

[1] " Their knowledge was nothing but loutishness, and their wisdom but blunt foppish toys, serving only to bastardise good and noble spirits, and to corrupt all the flower of youth." *Gargantua*, ch. XV. Cf. Marot's declaration :

> " En effect, c'estoient de grandz bestes
> Que les regens du temps jadis :
> Jamais je n'entre au paradis,
> S'ilz ne m'ont perdu ma jeunesse ! "
>
> Ep. 44 (*Deuxième espistre du Coq en l'asne*).

("Indeed, they were great dolts, the schoolmasters of former days : May I never enter paradise, if they did not waste my youth ! ")

[2] In particular, the researches of M. Grimaud and those of M. Abel Lefranc. Cf. *R.É.R.* (*Revue des Études Rabelaisiennes*), III, 48.

[3] Rabelais' name, which is found as a place-name in many parts of France, seems to be derived from *érable* (a maple tree) : a *rabelais* would be a place planted with *érables*. Other forms of our author's name are : Rabellais, Rabellet, Rabaillais, Rabeles. Cf. *R.É.R.*, III, 48 and 157, note 3.

[4] An original deed preserved in the archives of a notary's office in Tours, refers to him as " *conseiller et avocat au siège de Chinon*."

capitals and superfluous letters in order to add to their scrolls[1].

Antoine Rabelais is not only an advocate esteemed in his small town, he is a landed proprietor. He possesses at Chinon one of the big houses of the *rue la Lamproie*[2]. He owns, in the parish of Seuilly, a farm—*La Devinière* which he uses as a country residence, brought to him by his wife, in 1505, as also the *Chastel* and "noble house"[3] of *Chavigny-en-Vallée* (in the township of Varenne-sur-Loire, department of Maine-et-Loire), its appurtenances and dependencies, two acres of land situated near the *Moulin du Pont*, at Seuilly, some *chénevreaulx* and all the lands of *La Devinière*.

He is allied to good families, the Frapins, the d'Aquins, the Dussouls, the Delopiteaux. He is himself father of a daughter and three sons : Janet, Antoine and François[4].

Upon what date was the last son born ?

We do not possess any document which would allow us to state the exact date. The indications furnished both by authoritative documents and by old traditions are contradictory. In a manuscript collection of epitaphs in Saint Paul's Church, Paris[5], composed later than 1739, we read, beside three epitaphs upon Rabelais, the following mention : "François Rabelais, deceased, at the age of 70 years, rue des Jardins (Saint-Paul), 9 April, 1553, was interred in Saint Paul's Cemetery." If Rabelais died in 1553, at the age of seventy, the year of his birth would be 1483.

---

[1] Rabelais calls this (*Third Book*, ch. VII) "lengthening the ss" (i.e. changing the *s* (sols) into *f* (francs)). Cf. Charles Beaulieux, *Histoire de l'Orthographe française*, Paris, É. Champion, 1927, vol. I, p. 134.

[2] At present no. 15 in this street. About 1590, an hostelry, called *de la Lamproie*, was opened in the Rabelais' dwelling. This is, no doubt, the origin of the legend which later made Rabelais an innkeeper's son. This hostelry was transferred in the beginning of the 18th century to another house in the same street, at present no. 2. Cf. *R.É.R.*, III, 53.

[3] The Rabelais family have a coat-of-arms in the 17th century—argent, with three rabbits sable, each placed on a small sinople background, a prior's staff pale behind the shield. Cf. *R.É.R.*, III, 51.

[4] We possess an analysis of the deed of the division of his estate, which took place January 26th, 1534. Cf. *R.É.R.*, III, 49. François, being a religious and hence dead in law, is not mentioned, cf. *R.É.R.*, I, 67 and 153, and, in the *Revue du XVIe siècle*, 1920, p. 182, an extract from the *Coustume du duché et bailliage de Touraine*, with regard to rights of inheritance. "Man or woman, noble or commoner, who enters an approved religious community, after they have made express and valid professions, without force or constraint, are excluded from all inheritances past or to come, which inheritances shall pass to their parents, *as though they were deceased*, and in such wise that the aforesaid persons shall hereafter have no share in such heritages."

[5] Preserved in the Historical Library of Paris, no. II, 939, A.

Now, this date is incompatible with the terms of a letter of 1521, in which Rabelais alludes to himself as *adulescens*[1]. This word was applied by the Romans to the third age of life, which stretched from the fourteenth to the twenty-eighth year[2]. Rabelais was too well versed in Latin usages to call himself *adulescens* at thirty-eight, which would have been his age in 1521 were he born in 1483. A little later, in 1524, a friend praised him as shining forth by learning beyond his years : the compliment would have been pointless if addressed to a man of forty-one. These two texts do not, then, admit the date of 1483, taken from the epitaph-book of Saint-Paul's. They would more readily admit the date 1490 which Guy Patin gives ; but in all likelihood we must come down still further[3] to the year 1494.

We are not informed in any more certain manner of François Rabelais' birthplace. He placed after his name in certain official documents, for example in the matriculation register of the Faculty of Medicine, in Montpellier, the qualification *Chinonensis*, Chinonais. Hence the writers of the 16th and 17th centuries, Pasquier, Brantôme, J. A. de Thou, Scévole de Sainte-Marthe, Tallemant des Réaux, André du Chesne, gave Chinon as his birthplace. But *Chinonensis* and *Chinonais* may mean : native of the region of Chinon and not only of the town of Chinon. Indeed, a local tradition placed the birth of Rabelais at *La Devinière*, his father's farm. The traveller Roger de Gaignières, in 1699, after having had two views of Rabelais' reputed home in Chinon executed by his draughts-man, Boudan, repaired to the Benedictine Abbey of Seuilly, and on the edge of a sketch of *La Devinière*, he wrote the following note : " La Devinière, a good league from Chinon, two gun-shots from the Abbey of Sully (Seuilly) and almost opposite La Roche-Clermaut is the place where was born Rabelais, of the parish of Saint-Pierre de Sully in Touraine "[4].

[1] Cf. the text of this letter, with a translation and commentary, in an article by Abel Lefranc, *R.É.R.*, III, 338.

[2] According to Isidore of Seville, *Orig.*, II, 3, 4 : " Tertia ætas est adulescentia ad gignendum adulta, quæ porrigitur a decimo quarto usque ad vigesimum octavum annum."

[3] Cf. in the *R.É.R.*, III, 53, VI, 265–270, and IX, 73, the arguments put forward by M. Abel Lefranc in support of the dates 1494 and 1495.

[4] Cf. *R.É.R.*, III, 54 ; VI, 75–76 and VII, 47. M. H. Clouzot has published in the last-named volume an enumeration, from a survey, of the property of Seuilly Abbey, in the parishes of Seuilly and Cinay, in the 17th century.

A half-century later, a Benedictine scholar, usually well-informed, Fr. Arcère, in his *History of La Rochelle*[1], recalled, apropos of Rabelais' sojourn at Maillezais, that he was born at *La Devinière*, near Chinon. Finally, in 1802, the *Annuaire d'Indre-et-Loire pour l'an X* gives the farm of *La Devinière* as the birthplace of " the incomparable Rabelais "[2].

This very persistent tradition has found favour in our time since M. Abel Lefranc has shown the exceptional place which *La Devinière* occupies in Rabelais' books[3]. It is mentioned as often as the town of Chinon, and whereas the latter plays no part in the events narrated, we remark that, on the other hand, *La Devinière* is in *Gargantua* not only the home of the Giant's family, but, further, the general headquarters and the centre of operations of the Picrocholian war.

This predilection of Rabelais for *La Devinière* is easily explained if we admit, with the local tradition preserved by Gaignières, that it was there he had first seen the light.

It is to this little patch of ground that his souvenirs of childhood went back. Vineyards, meadows, lands shaded by chestnut and walnut-trees, old wall enclosures, whose white stones are sheathed in ivy, pines and oaks ; on the heights, the villages grouping around the belfry-tower, their high-topped roofs covered with flat russet tiles, sometimes with slates—these are the essential traits of the Chinonais landscape. It is a " good country "[4], hardly picturesque. But the hamlet of *La Devinière* held for Rabelais that unique and sovereign charm of the native sod, which is that of calling up to our maturity the sensations of childhood, and there lies the secret of his willingness to travel back in imagination to these places, where formerly his life was " new." He thus evokes the garden with its " Chichling peas, cabbages and lettuces," its young walnut-tree,[5] the farm's excellent white wine[6], Jean Denyau the Wheelwright's workshop[7], the grove of willows[8], the broad highway[9]. The surrounding country appears in his books drawn in bold outline as in the miniatures of old manuscripts, and serving as a

---

[1] Published in 1756, in 2 vols. in 8vo.   [2] Cf. *R.É.R.*, VII, 516.

[3] Cf. *R.É.R.*, III, 57–60. Jacques Boulenger has again studied the question in an article *Au Pays de Rabelais*, in the *Revue des Deux Mondes*, November 15th, 1921.

[4] Rabelais praises the richness of the country. Cf. *Gargantua*, ch. XIII : " the good country of Verron."

[5] *Gargantua*, ch. XXXVIII.   [6] *Ibid.*   [7] *Ibid.*, ch. VII.

[8] *Ibid.*, chs. IV and V.   [9] *Ibid.*, ch. XXV.

framework for the tasks and games of rustic life in their simplest form : the winter evenings spent at the fire, " Drawing scratches on the hearth, with a stick burnt at the one end "[1], the salting of meat[2], hawking[3], the sowing of hemp " at the first coming of the swallows "[4], harvest time[5], quarrels between the lads of neighbouring villages[6], nut-gathering[7], and the hemp-picking " when the grasshoppers begin to be a little hoarse "[8]. Sometimes, in these descriptions, we find certain details which refer precisely to the child's own life. Thus, having explained how hemp is prepared by separating the fibres from the woody part, Rabelais adds, mindful of a pastime of his youth, that this stem is useless, " except to make a clear and glistening blaze, to kindle the fire, and *for the play, pastime and disport of little children, to blow up hogs' bladders* "[9].

The house where Rabelais was born is still extant : it is small. It seems to have been built at the end of the 15th century. On the outside, stone steps, bordered with cylindrical pillars upon which rests a prolongation of the roof, like a penthouse, lead to a very low-ceilinged room—Rabelais' room. In the solitary window-recess a stone bench has been placed. From this seat the master could overlook some of his properties. On the wall, figures, effaced letters, Greek characters—a tribute from some cultured visitor to the Humanist's memory. There are other inscriptions scratched on the stone of the walls of the loft, but these are quite crude ; they consist of lines and marks made during the division of the harvest between the proprietor and his tenants. Another room, adjoining Rabelais', is also decorated with a window and stone-seat. Above it is the loft. On the ground floor a large room with a beautiful old fire-place. Around the house, the usual dependencies of a country residence—a kerb-protected well, a *timbre* or trough, cellar, pigeon-house, bakehouse, recesses and caves hollowed in the rock, and an underground passage now blocked up, by which tradition has it Rabelais once took flight to evade arrest.

Not far from these, " at two gunshot ranges", the Benedictine Abbey of Saint-Pierre de Seuilly, enclosed by low walls,

[1] *Gargantua*, ch. XXVIII.   [2] *Ibid.*, ch. IV.
[3] *Ibid.*, end of ch. XXXIX.   [4] *Third Book*, ch. XLIX.
[5] *Gargantua*, ch. XXV.   [6] *Ibid.*
[7] *Ibid.*   [8] *Third Book*, ch. XLIX.   [9] *Ibid.*, ch. L.

PLATE II

VIEW OF CHINON IN THE EIGHTEENTH CENTURY
(Library of Tours, Touraine Album, No. 177)

[face p. 6

grouped together its claustral buildings, its church, its hospital, where the " rascally beggars " received liberal charity on feast days[1]. This monastery, founded towards the end of the 11th century, was a dependency of the monks of Maillezais in Bas-Poitou. Even to-day the dimensions of the cellars bear witness to the extensive vines of their vineyards, which gave Friar Jean des Entommeures his first chance of displaying his bravery by stemming the invasion of Picrochole's followers.

A local tradition supposes that the Benedictines of Seuilly taught young François Rabelais his elements. The fact is not impossible, but it is equally probable that Maître Antoine Rabelais kept his son with him during the greater part of the year at Chinon, where his legal practice held him.

The old town, squeezing in its two parallel streets, crossed transversally by some smaller ones, between the low bank of the River Vienne and the sharp slope of the hill, was also the scene of his youthful life. Chinon has maintained even to the present day its ancient appearance[2]. Few French towns offer the stroller the spectacle of such a rich *ensemble* of old houses built in mediæval or Renaissance style : octagonal towers, serving as a framework for spiral staircases, buttressed gables decorated with crockets or *persillages*, red-brick walls framed by fashioned beams, mullioned windows, corbelled out storeys, spacious lofts with their skylights on a level with the roof, supporting from the arch above the street a solid pulley. Some dwellings clinging to the hill-side still have their out-buildings, their cellars and stables hollowed out of the chalkstone, as in the time when the sire of Painensac's steward knew of stables placed in the top of certain Chinonais dwellings[3]. Innocent-the-Confectioner's shop, at the north-east corner of the *rue du Grenier-à-sel*, remained a delightful souvenir in the memory of the youthful François : it has now disappeared, just as the painted cave[4] and the Nun's Bridge (*Pont de la Nonnain*) in the south of the town have changed. Of the fortified castle which at that time reared upon the hill its towers, fortified curtains and extensive roofs, there remain since Richelieu's day only ruins. It is there that Joan of Arc had seen for the

[1] *Fourth Book*, ch. L.
[2] M. Gabriel Richault's *Histoire de Chinon* (1912, republished 1926) is the best study we are acquainted with on the past history of this town.
[3] *Gargantua*, ch. XII.
[4] *Fourth Book*, ch. XX, and *Fifth Book*, ch. XXXIV.

first time and recognised, from amongst many excellently dressed lords, the poor King of Bourges, Charles VII. There, on the 18th December, 1498, Louis XII had received a messenger of another sort—Cesare Borgia, commissioned by Pope Alexander VI to bring him the Bull annulling the King's marriage with Jeanne de Valois and leaving him free to marry Anne, Duchess and heiress of Brittany. Mayhap young François gazed with his own eyes upon the sumptuous retinue of the Italian prince as Brantôme describes it[1]—the silver trumpets, seventy mules richly caparisoned in yellow satin and cloth of gold, the sixteen coursers held in check by the hand, the eighteen pages clothed in crimson velvet and embroidered cloth of gold, the thirty gentlemen attired in gold and silver, and finally the Duke, on horseback, in a costume of red satin and cloth of gold, covered with precious stones and pearls, a collar of thirty thousand ducats around his neck, and behind him a long convoy of valuable baggage.

As usually happens, the treasure of Rabelais' childhood reminiscences of Chinon was constituted by local particularities, witty sayings, tales, anecdotes[2] and, perhaps, some aspects of the family house : the advocates' office with the *dossiers* in labelled " sacks," invaded by litigants bringing chickens, pigeons, game, eggs and other presents.

His souvenirs of childhood and of youth are attached likewise to Angers. His mother's family, the Frapins, resided there. He himself tells us that his uncle Joseph was fond of composing beautiful and joyous carols, in Poitevin dialect. It is in his " house on Saint-Laurent's mound," an inn, that the youthful Rabelais, having noticed on the walls of the " low hall " paintings representing magpies and jays, and informed himself as to their meaning, learnt the history of the jay Goitrou, which was a great pet of his Uncle's because he never ceased urging callers to drink.

On a fine day in 1486, seeing a flight of jays passing over the town, Goitrou joined them. These jays gave battle to a flock of magpies and defeated them at the Malchara cross—presage of

---

[1] *Vie des grands capitaines étrangers, César Borgia,* Lacour's edition, vol. II, p. 214.

[2] Cf. in the prologue to the *Fourth Book,* the anecdote of the poor villager, a native of Gravot, wood-cutter and log-merchant, who lost his axe one day. Gravot is a hamlet in the *commune* of Bourgueil, on the borders of Anjou and Touraine, in which the Rabelais family owned several properties.

ill-omen for the Bretons whose arms include ermines (stoats) resembling exactly magpies' tails ! And, indeed, on the following day, their Duke, François II, in revolt against Charles VIII, was beaten by the royal army at Saint-Aubin-du-Cormier. Goitrou, however, returned to Angers " incensed " by the wars and with a bruised eye. The populace, the fashionable people, the students flocked in a crowd to see the sad plight of the one-eyed Goitrou. And the jay urged them in his customary manner to drink, adding at the end of each exhortation : " Gobble up the Magpies," doubtless the watchword of the battle-day. From this came the common proverb : " to drink deeply and with lengthy draughts is in sooth to gobble up the magpies "[1].

This savoury anecdote and many other stray touches in his work prove that Rabelais resided at, or frequently came to Angers between 1515 and 1518 : here, the mention of cattle-houses hollowed in the rock on a level with the roof at the convent of La Baumette[2] ; or again, a reference to one of the epidemics which ravaged the town in 1515 and 1518[3] ; or a humorous note on the origin of the chain which the King caused to be stretched across the River Maine, in 1518, to prevent the passage of contraband salt makers and regulate navigation[4]. Does it not follow that he had studied there ? What town in the neighbourhood of Chinon could offer Maître Antoine Rabelais greater facilities for his son's education than Angers, in which there was a flourishing University ?

An Angevin lawyer, of the beginning of the 17th century, Bruneau de Tartifume, states that Rabelais was in his youth a novice in the Franciscan monastery of La Baumette, founded towards the middle of the 15th century at the gates of Angers, by the " good King " René of Anjou, in memory of Saint Baume, a famous sanctuary of Provence, his apanage.

[1] Old prologue to the *Fourth Book*.
[2] *Gargantua*, ch. XII. A century later the monks still housed there the ass which brought from the town the alms in kind which were given them.
[3] *Pantagruel*, ch. V. : " After that . . . he came to Angiers, where he found himself very well, and would have continued there some space, but that the plague drove them away."
[4] *Ibid.*, ch. IV. This is one of the chains used for tying Pantagruel into his cradle.

Although we have no proof of this assertion[1] it is not entirely untrustworthy[2]. Rabelais may have undergone with the Franciscans of La Baumette the course of studies indispensable for entering upon the clerical state.

Whether he was the good scholar, well-groomed, " neat and trim " who arrives " with his cap in his hand, a clear and open countenance, beautiful and ruddy looks, his eyes steady " and his looks fixed, " with a youthful modesty " upon his inter-locutor, or, on the other hand, the timid and awkward youth, who sings dumb to even the kindliest of questionings and "hides his face with his cap "[3], we cannot say. But through himself and some contemporary men of letters we are acquainted with the essential features of the course of studies he presumably followed. A future cleric must, in the first place, speak Latin, and the whole working of the schools aimed at the teaching of Latin. At table, and even during recreations, the use of Latin was prescribed : has not a pedagogue of the period put on the same footing, among the faults of the schoolboys, swearing, lying and the use of the vernacular[4] ? The good student should be scrupulous about talking French, even to his mother[5], and Rabelais did not fail to scoff at these provisions

[1] It was at La Baumette that he is supposed to have met the brothers Guillaume and Jean du Bellay, who were later to become patrons of his. The Du Bellays' arms are still to be seen on the windows of the convent-chapel (Cf. *R.É.R.*, VI, 277), a proof of the interest they took in this house. But in 1506, Guillaume was pursuing his studies in Paris. (Cf. Bourrilly, *Guillaume du Bellay, seigneur de Langey*, Paris, 1905, in 8vo, p. 6.) Hence, it is hardly likely that Rabelais knew him at La Baumette.

[2] Cf. V. Dauphin, *Rabelais à La Baumette*, in the *Rev. XVIᵉ s.*, 1913, p. 477. Bruneau de Tartifume's testimony is more valuable than that of Pierre Guillebaud, called Pierre de Saint-Romuald, a monk in the Order of St. Bernard, who, in his *Trésor chronologique* (3 vols. in folio published in 1642–1647), includes among the events of the year 1511 Rabelais' entry into the Franciscan Order at Fontenay-le-Comte. We shall see that this date is certainly erroneous, as is the profession of hotel-keeper which P. de Saint-Romuald assigns to Rabelais' father.

[3] Portraits of the scholars Eudémon and Gargantua in the XVth ch. of *Gargantua*.

[4] Maturin Cordier, in the notice at the end of the *De corrupti sermonis emendatione* (1530) : " Nunquam jurat, mentitur numquam, vernacule numquam loquitur, nemini unquam maledicit (probissimus adulescens)." Cf., on Maturin Cordier, Jules Le Coultre's excellent work, *Maturin Cordier et les origines de la pédagogie protestante dans les pays de langue française* (1530–1564), Mémoires de l'Université de Neuchâtel, vol. V, 1926.

[5] " Eosque pudeat vel cum ipsis matribus uti lingua vernacula, nec nisi maxime inviti hanc usurpare velint "—Maturin Cordier, preface to the *De corrupti sermonis emendatione*. Cordier has the great merit of having attempted to reform school Latin ; but his recommendations with regard to the use of Latin in school are as uncompromising as those of the mediæval pedagogues.

of the scholastic rule : hardly has the young Gargantua been initiated in the rudiments when he sets to proving " on his finger-ends to his mother that *de modis significandis non erat scientia* "[1].

Like young Gargantua under the educational system of the Theologian-masters, Rabelais, then, learnt Latin in those treatises which, for centuries, generations of schoolboys had copied and learnt by heart, to the point of being able to recite them backwards[2]. He has made a list of them in *Gargantua*[3]. They included the *Donatum*, by the grammarian Aelius Donatus (4th century) ; the *Partes* (in French *les Pars*[4]) ; the *Quid est*, a sort of catechism which taught by questions and answers the grammar of the eight parts of speech ; the *De modis significandi*, a treatise on speculative grammar which a Venetian edition of 1488 attributes to Duns Scotus, the subtle doctor, one of the celebrities of the Franciscan Order[5] ;—the *Doctrinale puerorum*, grammatical elements put in hexameters by Alexandre de Villedieu, which had supplanted the manuals of Donatus and of Priscian because, being written in leonine (that is, rhyming) verse, it was easier to memorise. Of the same type were the vocabularies then in use in the schools : the *Liber derivationum*, or *Hugutio*, a sort of garden of Latin roots, composed in the 12th century by a bishop of Ferrara, Ugutio of Pisa, after the glossary of Papias ;—the *Grécisme* of Everard of Béthune (13th century), thus called because the first eleven chapters are devoted to Latin words which come from Greek ; and, finally, the *Mammotreptus*, of which the peculiar name will bring to the mind of the author of *Pantagruel* the image of " the movement of the chaps peculiar to monkeys "[6] : it contained the vocabulary special to the Scriptures and was in especial honour among Franciscans, being the work of a Friar, Marchesinus, of Reggio.

Like all the young clerics of his day, Rabelais was trained in the manners and polite behaviour of youth by the *Facet*

---

[1] *Gargantua*, ch. XIV.

[2] " To try masteries in school disputes with his condisciples he would recite it by heart backwards." *Gargantua*, ch. XIV.

[3] Ch. XIV.

[4] A school proverb ran : " qui nescit *Partes* in vanum tendit ad artes."

[5] Cf. *Rabelais, selected readings*, by W. F. Smith (Cambridge, 1920), Appendix A.

[6] *Pantagruel*, ch. VII : " *Marmotrectus de Baboinis et Cingis, cum commento d'Orbellis*." Nicolas des Orbeaux (d'Orbellis) was a Franciscan who taught at Poitiers towards the end of the 15th century.

(Facetus)[1], which prescribed, for instance, that one should not blow one's nose in the tablecloth nor pick one's nose with the fingers during meals. He learned the correct behaviour for mealtimes in the *De moribus in mensa servandis*[2]. For the inculcation of good morals he was made recite the distichs of the *Catonet* (*Libre Cathonis*), a famous third century collection attributed to Cato the Censor, and also the *Treatise of the four ordinal virtues* (*De quatuor virtutibus ordinalibus*), whose author, a Portuguese Bishop of the 6th century, had commended the book, which he attributed to Seneca. The *Théodolet*, wrongly ascribed to Theodulus, Bishop of Syria in the 5th century, showed him how the fables of mythology agreed with the truth of the Scriptures. The *Liber Parabolarum*, composed in the 13th century by Alain de Lille, doctor of the University of Paris, further supplied him with a notable contingent of moral distichs and quatrains for memory drill and disputations.

For, besides the "memorisations," debates constituted the principal school exercise. They were imposed upon the scholars from an early stage in order to familiarise them with Latin. The subjects for these discussions were drawn from the grammatical or moral treatise which had been explained by the master, and they afforded for the young logic-choppers an occasion of displaying their scholarly attainments and an exercise in speaking Latin. In truth, their language was a peculiar jargon and the profit they drew from these discussions was not a sound mental discipline. The pedagogues of the time have often described for us these altercations[3] : on one side the *Propugnator* or upholder of a thesis, thin and pale as a result of his nightly labours, now making frantic endeavours to refute one of those irrefutable arguments which were styled *Achilles* (*Achilles invincibiles*)[4], now subtly evading the point at issue ; on the other, his attackers, some arguing without forcefulness, others persisting doggedly, shouting in hoarse

[1] This is one of the treatises known in the Middle Ages under the name *Auctores morales octo*. The complete title is : *Facetus quidem liber metricus a magistro Faceto editus, loquens de præceptis et moribus a Cathone in sua ethica omissis. Et dicitur facetus propter etymologiam quasi favens cetui, id est placens tam in dictis quam in factis populo.*

[2] By an Italian of the late 15th century, Sulpizio de Veroli.

[3] Cf. for example, in Vivès' *Linguæ latinæ exercitatio* (Lyons, Seb. Gryphius, 1543) the amusing dialogue on pp. 55–59.

[4] *Gargantua*, ch. XIX.

tones and refusing to give way before the defender's answer
or the chairman's decision.

These exercises, at least, left imprinted for long in the
memory the substance and the letter of the school handbooks.
Rabelais will scoff at these antiquated works, but he will not
forget them. He will readily include in his facetious remarks
here a joke about noses, perpetuated by a schoolman's gloss
on the *Liber Thobiæ*[1], there a maxim from the *Facet*[2], and
elsewhere reminiscences of the *Catonet*[3].

The study of these manuals, augmented by supplements and
by " supplements to the supplements ", *supplementum supple-
menti*, was crowned for the cleric preparing for the priesthood
by his initiation to Scholastic Philosophy and, then, Theology.
Now, François Rabelais received minor and major orders.
He was a priest, whether he was prepared for the priesthood
by the Franciscans of La Baumette or in another convent, he
studied scholastic theology.

In what did this teaching consist ? Of the various systems
created by mediæval philosophy[4], only two found favour at
at the end of the 15th century ; the Terminism of William
Occam and Scotism. The latter, conceived by Duns Scotus,
who was, in the 14th century, the glory of the Franciscan
Order, as Saint Bonaventure had been in the 13th, was naturally
supreme in all the convents of this Order. It is true, that it
was not there studied in the original works of its creator, but

---

[1] *Pantagruel*, ch. I. " Naso and Ovid had their extraction from thence,
and all those of whom it is written, *Ne reminiscaris* " ; and the distich :

> " *Ne reminiscaris* servi delicta parentum
>   Sint peccata licet multa, remitte reis ".

[2] " *Fortunam reverenter habe*, quæcumque repente Dives ab exili pro-
grediere loco ", becomes in *Gargantua*, ch. XXXV : " It becomes all cavaliers
modestly to use their good fortune ".

[3] Here are some of Cato's verses met with in Rabelais, quoted from the
excellent edition of the *Catonis Disticha* published by Joseph Nève, at Liége,
in 1926.

     I.   10.—Sermo datur cunctis, animi sapientia paucis,
                                   Third Book, ch. XLI.
         39.—Cum labor in damno est, crescit mortalis egestas,
                                   Ibid., ch. XLII.
     II. 26.—Fronte capillata, post est Occasio calva,
                                   Gargantua, ch. XXXVII.
        " Occasion hath all her hair on her forehead . . .
        she is bald in the hinder part of her head ".
     III.   6.—Interpone tuis interdum gaudia curis,
                                     Third Book, ch. XL.

[4] Cf. Étienne Gilson, *La philosophie au moyen âge*, 2 vols., in the *Collection
Payot* (1922).

in those of his commentators. The most famous was Brulefer[1], who had composed some elucidations of Duns Scotus's commentaries on the fourth book of the *Sentences* of Pierre Lombard, and Pierre Tateret, a secular, who was Rector of Paris University in 1490, and had written a book of questions, " very subtle and useful "[2], on Logic.

It is these works of two Scotist doctors which initiated Rabelais to scholastic philosophy. He was, moreover, not slow to take a dislike to this system, and to turn it and its exponents to ridicule[3]. He accused Scotus, the " Scotists " and the " Scotist sentences "[4] of all the nonsense which the humanists denounced in scholastic philosophy. Subtle questions on " secondary instructions," formalism in their logic, *baraco* and *baralipton*, these are the *Barbouillamenta Scoti* which Pantagruel discovers among the " fine books " in the library of Saint Victor's Abbey[5].

Nevertheless, even at the time when Rabelais professed scorn for scholastic philosophy, its influence upon him was still apparent. In the first place, the technical language of this philosophy finds its way into his book, not only in the author's talk, but even in the conversations of his characters. The good people of Seuilly whom he pictures stretched on the thick grass of the willow-grove among flagons, jugs, goblets and " gammons "[6], punctuate their joyous drinkers' jokes with axioms of Thomistic philosophy and humorous allusions to the scholastic definition of eternity.

Besides, Rabelais will unconsciously keep more than one essential feature of this traditional education, even when ridiculing it and opposing to it a new education, in conformity with humanistic tastes and ideas. Ponocrates, the ideal pedagogue whom he gave Gargantua, will often go upon the lines of the " *sorbonagre* " teachers. Like Maître Thubal Holopherne,

[1] On scholasticism in Paris at the beginning of the 16th century, cf. A. Renaudet, *Préréforme et humanisme à Paris* (1494–1517), Paris, 1916.
[2] *Questiones admodum subtiles et utiles . . . super libris Logices Porphyrii et Aristotelis.*
[3] Cf. *Pantagruel*, ch. VII: " *Poiltronismus rerum Italicarum autore magistro Brulefer ;* Tartaretus, *De modo cacandi* ".
[4] *Gargantua*, ch. VII and XII ; *Third Book*, ch. XVII ; *Fifth Book*, prologue.
[5] *Pantagruel*, ch. VII.
[6] *Gargantua*, ch. V. On the scholasticism of Rabelais. Cf. Gilson, *Rabelais franciscain* in *la Revue d' histoire franciscaine* (1924) and *Notes médiévales au Tiers Livre* (*ibid.*, 1925).

he will assign pride of place in education to memory-work;
like the theologian-teachers, he will explain and commentate
treatises and texts, without ever giving his pupil practice in
the writing of compositions, imitations or amplifications of the
model. Like these, he will consider the vulgar tongue incapable
of expressing the lofty conceptions of philosophy, and young
Gargantua will have all his classes in Latin.

To the scholastic tradition, Rabelais will even owe one of the
favourite exercises of his mind—paradoxical argument. It
is not for nothing that young François is destined several
times a week for years to be trained in the practice of argument.
When he comes to recount " the horrible deeds " of Pantagruel,
he will ascribe to his Giant as his first deeds of prowess, his
successes in academic argumentations, and the story-teller
himself will revel in his hair-splitting paradoxes, laughing
maliciously like Panurge, when he disconcerts reason or common sense by his reasoning[1].

[1] Cf., for example, Panurge's apologia of extravagance and of debts, chs.
II–IV of the *Third Book* ; or, again, *Gargantua*, ch. X, a development based
upon a rule of Aristotelian logic.

CHAPTER II

THE YEARS OF MONKHOOD AT FONTENAY-LE-COMTE

WITH the year 1520, we come to the end of the period of
Rabelais' life which still remains the most obscure for us—his
childhood and youth, of which our knowledge is obtained from
conjectures, analogies and clues, which are often doubtful. His
figure emerges at last from the penumbra which hitherto
obscured it. An authentic document—a letter written in
his own hand, the 5th March, 1521, and sent from the Franciscan monastery of Fontenay-le-Comte[1], in Bas-Poitou, to
Guillaume Budé, attests that at this date he is a Franciscan
monk[2]. If he is not yet a priest, at least he will soon be[3].
In any event, as a Friar Minor, he has taken a vow of poverty,
he has put on the ash-coloured habit of rough serge, his loins
are girt by a rope, his feet bare or sandalled. Thus he makes his
appearance in his twenty-sixth year.

The fact that Rabelais entered religion, and particularly the
Order of the Friars Minor, whom the *literati* of the period denounce as the most ignorant of monks, is a surprising fact for
whoever knows, from his works, the nature of his tastes and
his temperament. It may be urged that at the moment of
pronouncing the monastic vows he did not yet realise to what
extent his independent nature would render their observance
difficult. But is it possible that he apprehended in the Franciscan life nothing which might become a constraint upon this
appetite for knowledge which was to be his most striking mental
characteristic? Doubtless, the Order of Saint Francis prided
itself upon having given to the Church some of its greatest

---

[1] Capital of La Vendée.

[2] This letter was first published in 1860, by Auguste Scheler, in the *Bulletin
du bibliophile belge*. It is reprinted in Marty-Laveaux' edition of Rabelais,
vol. IV, pp. 367–370. As to its history and its authenticity, cf. M. Abel
Lefranc's article on the autographs of Rabelais, *R.É.R.*, III, 340–349. This
letter is now in M. Henry Fatio's fine collection of autographs, at Geneva,
where I have been able, through his courtesy, to examine it. He acquired it
at the sale of the Morrison Collection in London.

[3] According to a letter of Guillaume Budé which we quote later : " Sacer-
dotem te esse oportere fidei haud benignæ ". Marty-Laveaux's edition, vol.
III, p. 291.

thinkers—Alexander of Hales, the *Doctor irrefragabilis*, Saint Bonaventure, called the Seraphic Doctor, Roger Bacon and Duns Scotus. But these were doctors of scholastic philosophy which, attacked and decried by the Humanists, no longer exercised, at the beginning of the 16th century, any appeal upon minds avid for learning. Could a man like Rabelais risk the hazard of entering the Friars Minor with the intention of there devoting himself to study ?

Thus do we reason, influenced by the invectives of the humanists, and particularly of Erasmus, against the Franciscans. The people of the time were, as a matter of fact, far from drawing such a sharp contrast between intellectual culture and the monastic life. To be convinced of this, one need only read the two letters which, just at this time, in 1520 and 1521, Guillaume Budé sent to a young Franciscan, Pierre Amy[1], who was later to be Rabelais' friend at the convent of Fontenay-le-Comte.

Of course, Budé is too fascinated with the culture of the ancients to make of scholastic philosophy the privileged object or the crowning end of study. But, like all French humanists of the time, he is profoundly religious. He conceives study as the search after truth, as a progress towards the perfect Christian life. And, are there any conditions more propitious to intellectual labour than the monastic life ? The solitude inviting reflection, freedom from the worries of civil life, the recollection of divine things associated with the acts of the day, the remoteness of family affairs, the absence of liberty, these are so many privileges by the aid of which monks quickly outstrip laymen on the road of knowledge and of philosophy[2]. It was, thus, vain for Pierre Amy to complain that the worries and duties of

---

[1] Both these letters are in the first collection of Guillaume Budé's correspondence, published at Bâle, by André Cratander, in 1521. The first is dated February, the second May, with no mention of the year. But there is hardly any room for doubting that they date from 1520.

[2] " Quocirca magnus jam hic gradus vobis ad Philosophiam factus, lata jam via munita et perpurgata ad veritatem investigandam iter contendentibus. Accedit solitudo invitatrix mentium ad commentandum, feriæque (ut ita dicam) perpetuæ et immunitas turpium animi affectionum aut alias abhorrentium a contemplatione commentationeque sanctiore. Adjuvat assidua rerum divinarum recordatio atque inculcatio veritatis, in omni parte functioneque vitæ, vestræ professionis scitis astrictæ, connexa et implicata. Quo fit ut vestræ istæ piæ sodalitates non modo bonis imaginariis fortunæque cedentium ipsa professione, sed etiam tribus rebus animum abdicantium, quæ maxime cujusque sunt propriæ, civitate, cognatione, libertate mihi velut seminaria esse videantur animarum beatarum . . . ". *Gulielmi Budæi regii secretarii epistulæ* (Bâle, 1521), pp. 154–155.

C

his religious profession, the habits and rules of his order, kept him from the cult of letters[1]. Budé holds that in spite of these obstacles monastic life is favourable to study.

If such was Budé's opinion, why should we be surprised that Rabelais sought refuge in the peace of a Franciscan cloister for a life which, apparently, his tastes directed towards intellectual effort ? Is it because the latent hostility between the Sorbonne and Humanism was soon going to render difficult certain branches of study, like the study of Greek ?—But did Rabelais know when he entered the Friars Minor that his interest was going to be particularly captivated by Hellenic studies ? and how, in 1520, could the approaching conflict between the Paris Theological Faculty and Humanism have been foreseen ? Might not one have hoped that the theologians would rally to the cause of " good letters " like the great Italian prelates ? Did not Guillaume Budé, some years later,[2] write that the Sorbonne and the Collège de Navarre, these two gateways of orthodoxy, these two oracles of scholastic philosophy, at last welcomed the Attic as well as the Latin Minerva, and admitted them to sit and even to speak among the Theologians ?

Thus, even if Rabelais, at twenty-five years of age, considered before all else the future of his intellectual effort, even if he already had a taste for the letters of the ancients, there was no reason why he could not enter the order of these Friars Minor, from whom he had received his first lessons at La Baumette. A vocation to Humanism, at this period, might not have seemed incompatible with the Franciscan life.

It is more difficult to state with certainty for what reasons we find him at this particular convent of the Puy-Saint-Martin, at Fontenay-le-Comte, in 1521. This monastery[3] was one of the oldest of the Franciscan province of Pictavian

---

[1] These are his own words for describing Amy's woes : " Distrahentibus te curis et officiis tuæ professionis, in diversumque trahentibus a literarum bonarum cultu moribus et institutis sodalitatis vestræ ". Budé's first letter to Pierre Amy, 11 February, 1520, same collection, p. 99.

[2] In *De Studio litterarum recte et commode instituendo* (1527) :
" Nunc porticus duæ orthodoxiæ Sorbona et Navarra et philosophiæ theologicæ tanquam oracula duo nominatissima, qua fines cumque patent nominis christiani et latinæ jam et atticæ Minervæ non modo sedendi locum, sed etiam loquendi inter disputantes dederunt ".

[3] It was ruined by the Protestants in 1568, and nothing now remains of it. It was situated on the road to Le Gros-Noyer, between the R. Vendée and the hill overlooking Fontenay to the west, on the site of the present Hôtel de Ville. Cf. H. Clouzot, *Rabelais à Fontenay-le-Comte, R.É.R.*, V, 413.

Touraine, having been founded in 1321. Perhaps it owed to its antiquity a special reputation, and its fame on this account might be the explanation of our Chinonais entering it, rather than another Franciscan house, nearer his native district, such as Cholet, Clisson or Mirebeau.

He had been there for only a short period when he wrote to Budé, the 4th March, 1521. Indeed, in an earlier letter which Budé sent Pierre Amy, 10th February, 1520, the philologist sympathises with his correspondent on being alone among his community in his devotion to the cult of letters[1]; and a second letter, of the end of April of the same year, makes no reference to Rabelais' presence in the convent[2]. Now, his arrival at the Puy-Saint-Martin will be for Pierre Amy a notable event in his life as a monk. If, then, Budé has not yet heard of Rabelais at the end of April, 1520[3], the reason is that the latter's entrance into the monastery of Fontenay-le-Comte took place in the second half of 1520.

Henceforward, and for long years, his existence will be subjected to monastic rule. He will " guide and direct his courses by the sound of a bell "[4], by which everything will be " compassed, limited and regulated by hours "—the morning awakening, assistance at offices, meals eaten in common and recreations. It is to these years of monkhood that we owe the picturesque description of the *gent monacale* which he has left in his work. We know from him, better than any contemporary writer, the life of the religious : their language, their sayings and proverbs[5], which often have reference to

[1] "῍Ην [φιλοσόφιαν] δὲ σὺ μόνος, ὡς οἶμαι, ἐν ταύτῃ τῇ ἑταιρείᾳ ἀσπάζει τὲ καὶ καταφιλεῖς."

[2] It may be remarked that these letters give no year in their date. The collection was published at Bâle in Feb. 1521 ; various clues point to the date 1520.

[3] As H. Clouzot has shown, the two documents which, according to Benjamin Fillon, *Lettres écrites de la Vendée*, prove that Rabelais resided at the Puy-Saint-Martin before 1520—namely, his signature to a deed of purchase of the half of an inn, and a receipt given by a traveller of Henri Estienne's establishment for books supplied to the Bishop of Maillezais—can be taken as not genuine. Cf. H. Clouzot, *Rabelais à Fontenay-le-Comte et le prétendu acte de 1519, R.É.R.*, V, 413.

[4] He seems to have ill borne this division of time by the ringing of bells : " Nor can there be any greater dotage in the world than for one to guide and direct his courses by the sound of a bell, and not by his own judgment and discretion ". *Gargantua*, ch. LII.

[5] " To sing Magnificat at Matins ", *Gargantua*, ch. XI. The *Magnificat* is sung at Vespers ; hence " To sing *Magnificat* at Matins " means to do something at a wrong or unsuitable time.—" To know, or say right up to the *Tu Autem* ". *Tu autem, Domine, miserere nobis*, is the formula which ends every

meals[1], their "metaphors extracted from the claustral kettle",
and even their favourite choruses[2]. As soon as Rabelais takes
his pen to set down the flights of his fancy, reminiscences of the
Bible, which the duties of his state in life had obliged him to
read, crowd to his memory. There are nearly forty of them
in the thirty-four chapters of *Pantagruel*, a dozen more in
Gargantua. The breviary, which he had thumbed so much, is
familiar to him. As to religious literature, he cites readily the
mediæval commentators, like the Franciscan Nicholas of Lyra,
whose *Postillæ*, or glosses on the Bible, commonly figured on
the margin of psalters, books of hours and breviaries. He
exhibits his curiosity for the Fathers of the Church,—Saint
Augustine, Saint Jerome, Saint Cyprian, the pseudo-Arnobius,
Saint Hilary, Saint Irenæus, Saint John Chrysostom,—who
were then for numerous *literati*, and in particular for Erasmus,
an object of diligent study.

The fact is that he was hardly in the convent a few months
when he showed (his letter of the 4th March, 1521, to Guillaume
Budé proves it) a marked taste for profane knowledge, in
particular for Greek literature.

It was at that time in France, an arduous task to learn
Greek. Hellenism was in its infancy. Professors and books
were scarce. Towards the end of the 15th century, two professors came from Italy, George Hermonymos and Janus
Lascaris, and had given some Greek lessons in Paris. Then,

---

lesson of the priest's office. To know a question down to the *tu autem*, is to
know it to the very end, to know it thoroughly. Cf. *Pantagruel*, ch. XI:
" Then, said Pantagruel, my friend, is this all you have to say ? . . . Yes,
my Lord, for I have told you all the *Tu autem*"; and *Gargantua*, ch. XIII:
" I was coming to it, said Gargantua, and by and by shall you hear the *Tu
autem*".—" To have the *miserere* as far as *vitulos*". Cf. *Third Book*, ch.
XXIII. " And if ever hereafter I may but lay hold on thee within the limits
of our chancel at Mirebeau, thou shalt have the *miserere* even to the *vitulos*".
When the monks used the discipline, the scourging was usually accompanied
by the singing of the Penitential Psalms ; so Friar Couscoil (Crankcod) means
a scourging which will last the whole length of the *Miserere*, *vitulos* being the
last work of this Penitential Psalm. " Tunc imponam in altare tuum *vitulos*".
    [1] *Third Book*, ch. XV. *De missa ad mensam* (From Mass to table).
Gargantua, ch. XXVII. " It is a monastical apophthegm", declares Friar
Jean, " that never yet did a man of worth dislike good wine"; *ibid.*, ch. XLI,

Brevis oratio penetrat cœlos
Longa potatio evacuat scyphos,

and *Third Book*, ch. XV: " I prefer the soups . . . always accompanied with
a round slice of the Nine-lecture-powdered labourer. I know thy meaning,
answered Friar John ; this metaphor is extracted out of the claustral kettle".
    [2] Cf. *Gargantua*, ch. XLI: " Ho ! Regnault, réveille-toi ! " (Ho ! Reg-
nault, awake !)

from 1508 to 1512, Jerome Aleander had taught this language in a college of the University. But the group of Parisian Hellenists remained restricted to about ten professors, magistrates and doctors. The indispensable books, texts and grammars, had to be imported from Italy at great expense. From 1508 to 1512, hardly two dozen Greek works had come from the presses of Gilles of Gourmont, the only printer of Greek in France.[1]

In the provinces we can find traces in different towns, at Lectoure, Agen[2], Lyons and Dijon[3], of professors who taught the humanities and explained the poets. These lessons were ephemeral. Nevertheless, this teaching, however uncertain, had created a taste for the works of the ancients and sometimes excited great interest in Greek literature. Although it is a fact that between 1520 and 1530 some Hellenists are to be met with in small towns like Saint-Jean d'Angély and Fontenay-le-Comte, it is none the less true that a young Franciscan friar would need an ardent appetite for knowledge to undertake the study of Greek.

Happily the bonds of brotherhood promptly drew together the adepts of the cult of the Attic Minerva, as Guillaume Budé named them. Hardly was Rabelais initiated into Hellenism when he found encouragement and support from other Hellenists : Pierre Amy, his companion of the Puy Saint-Martin, Guillaume Budé and some cultured lawyers of Fontenay-le-Comte.

Pierre Amy[4] belonged apparently to a family of Orleans. In this town, in 1510 and 1511, the Italian Jerome Aleander had taught the Greek tongue to two dozen pupils[5] and the taste for Hellenic culture had remained living there after his departure. Obliged by his father, for reasons which remain obscure, to enter the Franciscans[6], he profited of the leisure

---

[1] Cf. Delaruelle, *L'étude du grec à Paris de* 1514 *à* 1530, in the *R. XVIᵉ siècle*, vol. IX, pp. 51 *seqq.*

[2] L. Delaruelle, *Un enseignement des humanités à Agen en l'année* 1515, *Annales du Midi*, January–April, 1925.

[3] Cf. A. Lefranc, *Histoire du Collège de France*, pp. 96–98.

[4] Not Pierre Lamy, as is sometimes written. Rabelais, *Third Book*, ch. VII, writes Pierre Amy.

[5] Cf. Cuissard, *Un cours de grec à Orléans*, in the *Bulletin de la Société archéologique et historique de l'Orléanais*, vol. XII (1898), p. 182.

[6] " Tum illud præcipue contigit ut in utriusque linguæ officinis egregie inchoatus, reclamante (ut memini) parento tuo, faceres ut in istam sodalitatem dares nomen primum, deinde profiterere . . . ". Gulielmus Budæus Petro Amico sodali franciscano. *Epistulæ*, 1521 edition, p. 155.

afforded by monastic life to devote himself ardently to the study of Aristotle's metaphysics and of philosophy[1]. Early in 1520, the Humanist Deloynes, professor of law at Orleans University, put him into relations with the first scholar of the kingdom, this Guillaume Budé, towards whom all Frenchmen interested in ancient literatures were turning their eyes[2]. We have seen how Budé in two long letters encouraged Pierre Amy to persevere in the study of philosophy.

Rabelais was not long in earning Pierre Amy's esteem by his application to work. By the month of October, 1520, the latter judged that his companion in study could make himself known to the learned Guillaume Budé and he persuaded him to recommend himself to him by letter. The young Greek student at first hesitated. To risk such a step should he not wait till he had achieved greater facility at writing elegantly in Latin ? Amy pointed out to him that Budé was interested in whoever had a taste for literature, and Rabelais yielded to his companion's persuasion, composed a letter and sent it. It is now lost, and we know of it only by the one which followed it ; doubtless the new Hellenist had wished to exhibit therein some specimen of his learning, and it concluded by an entreaty in Greek verse[3].

Budé was at this time Royal Secretary and, at times, extremely taken up by his duties. But he let pass no occasion of awakening or encouraging the curiosity of young students for the literature of the ancients. His correspondence for 1516–1522 (four books of Latin, and one of Greek letters) gives a high idea of the activity he displayed in his zealous encouragement of philosophy. He sent word to Rabelais by Pierre Amy that he had received his letter.

It was for Rabelais a great joy to see himself recognised by the Prince of Hellenists. In a second letter, dated 4th March, 1521, he hastened to excuse his boldness in taking such a step, and express joy at its success.

---

[1] According to Guillaume Budé in his letter *cit. supra*.

[2] On Guillaume Budé consult especially L. Delaruelle, *Guillaume Budé, les origines, les débuts, les idées maîtresses*, Paris, 1907 (fascicule no. 162 of the Bibliothèque de l'École des Hautes Études) and *Répertoire analytique et chronologique de la correspondance de Guillaume Budé* (Champion, 1907). I have given a sketch of his life and work in *Guillaume Budé* (1488–1540) *et les origines de l'humanisme français* (Paris, Les Belles-Lettres, 1923).

[3] All these details are taken from the letter sent by Rabelais to Budé on 4th March, 1521.

Some time later, he had the honour of receiving a long epistle from Guillaume Budé. It was sent from Villeneuve-sur-Vingeanne, in Burgundy, where the Royal Secretary had accompanied François I. Amid the worries of Court life he envied, so he declared, the leisures, the liberty, the youth of Amy and of Rabelais entirely devoted to their pursuit of Philosophy. Incidentally, he praised his correspondent for his proficiency in both the Latin and Greek tongues[1].

In the subsequent two years (1522–1523) Rabelais wrote several times to Budé. His missives did not all reach their destination and the collection of Budé's letters contains only two answers of the great Humanist to Rabelais.

What information can be gleaned from this correspondence about the studious occupations of Rabelais at the convent of the Puy-Saint-Martin ? He naturally shows himself anxious to give his learned patron a favourable idea of his erudition. He intersperses his Latin with long passages of Greek. Two of his letters end up by Greek verses of his own composition. He quotes textually a verse of Homer. Besides, he is fond of a joke. He ridicules, for example, the rich ignoramuses who abound at Court, and tosses off a Greek epigram against their idol, the blind Plutus, whose eyes Budé only could open to the beautiful light of day. He jestingly again threatens Pierre Amy with an action at law, *de dolo malo*, for having urged him to take the bold step of corresponding with Budé.

The latter also mixes with his Latin long fragments in Greek. But, being too far apart from Rabelais to direct his studies in a practical manner, he gives him no advice. He limits himself to congratulations and encouragement. To the monk's learned pleasantries he replies no less ceremoniously. He points out to him that he is mistaken in the kind of legal action applicable to Pierre Amy's crime, and adds : you, who have studied law, know that[2].

Rabelais, was then, at this period, versed in the knowledge of Roman law. The reason is that he was then experiencing an influence more direct and more efficacious than Budé's

---

[1] " *Epistula tua . . . utriusque linguæ peritiam singularem redolens* ". The text of this letter has been printed by Marty-Laveaux in his edition of Rabelais' works, vol. III, p. 289, and analysed and annotated by Delaruelle, *Répertoire . . .* , p. 140.

[2] " *Ut nosti, qui juris studiosus fuisti* ".

distant encouragements—that of a group of lawyers which he frequented at Fontenay-le-Comte. By a stroke of good fortune singularly favourable to our humanist's vocation this humble city was then one of the centres of the new culture in France ; it had several lawyers initiated to Hellenism.

Fontenay-le-Comte, an old Feudal town, which formerly belonged to the Counts of Poitou (whence its name), had been successively in the possession of the King of France, of the English, of Duke Jean de Berry, and of the Duke of Brittany. Its ramparts, and its Castle, fortified by five great towers and a keep, made of it during the whole of the Middle Ages a solid fortress[1], of which imposing remains are still extant.

It had been finally united to the Crown by Louis XI. This king, who brought back prosperity to his country by favouring commerce and industry, made Fontenay a *commune*. Henceforward, the town developed and became rich. Corporations of cloth merchants and of tanners flourished there. The markets, built in wood, and ornamented with a fine sculptured façade, housed three important fairs yearly. The city, originally confined to the slope overhanging the right bank of the Vendée, saw its suburbs extend. Two churches, Saint-Nicolas and Saint-Jean, the latter still standing, were reconstructed. The church of Notre-Dame reared aloft, above the clustered roofs of the old quarters, the elegant pyramid of its Gothic belfry, which is still admired by connoisseurs, even after the restoration it has undergone in the 18th century. To establish definitely the importance of this capital of Bas-Poitou, Louis XI gave it the jurisdiction of a *siège royal*. The *siège royal* consisted of an assessor or lieutenant-seneschal of Poitou, a *lieutenant criminel et particulier*, councillors, advocates, procurators, that is, solicitors and clerks of Justice.

At the time of Rabelais' entry into the convent of the Puy-Saint-Martin, a great fever of learning reigned in this group of lawyers. The juridical sciences were studied according to the methods recently put into favour by the humanists Lorenzo Valla, of Italy, and Guillaume Budé. In addition, these lawyers were interested in the "letters of humanity"—the history, philosophy and poetry of the Ancients.

---

[1] On Fontenay-le-Comte, cf. an article by Vallette in Robuchon's *Sites et monuments du Poitou*, and a *causerie* by André Hallays in the *Journal des Débats*, 4 Oct., 1912, reprinted in *En flânant. À travers la France. De Bretagne en Saintonge*, Perrin, 1914.

The most widely-known amongst these were the *lieutenant criminel et particulier*, Artus Cailler, and his son-in-law, the advocate André Tiraqueau. It is at the latter's house they usually assembled, in the garden or under a laurel arbour. The discussions of this little society treated of law, ethics, philosophy and poetry. It was not a *salon*, women being absent, but a meeting of men of the world, which were to give to Brothers Amy and Rabelais insights into the world of their day. The learned conversations of their friends, the legists, taught them many things which neither their monastic life, nor their books gave them an opportunity of studying. For instance, there was a certain period during which the greater part of these conversations treated of marriage and of women[1].

Tiraqueau, indeed, had achieved a certain notoriety through having published at the age of twenty-four two treatises on marriage (1513). One was a re-editing[2] of a Latin work by the Italian Francesco Barbaro, *De re uxoria*, which had had a success on the other side of the Alps, witnessed to by three editions and an Italian translation.

The other was an original work[3]. It was intended as the first part of a commentary which Tiraqueau projected writing on the common law of Poitou, for the enlightenment of his compatriots, the Poitevins, a race, he added, which is neither dull nor stupid, *gentem alioquin nec bardam, nec stupidam*. He opened this commentary by the examination of Title XV of the *Coutumier du Poitou*, codified at Parthenay[4], in 1457 : "*Of the husband's power and administration.*" He entitled his work *De legibus connubialibus* (Marriage Laws). By *Leges* he means, not the clauses of the *Coutumier*, the civil laws, but moral precepts which he himself formulates in lordly and concise Latin.

The work was dedicated to Artus Cailler, his father-in-law : it contained a programme of married life which Tiraqueau adopted at the time of his marriage, just as the *De re uxoria*

[1] On this question cf. J. Barat, *L'Influence de Tiraqueau sur Rabelais*, R.É.R., vol. III, pp. 138–253.
[2] Paris, Josse Bade, 1513.
[3] *Andreæ Tiraquelli Fontiniacensis judicis ex commentariis in Pictonum consuetudines sectio de legibus connubialibus*, Paris, Josse Bade, 1513. For a bibliographical description of these two works, cf. M. L. Polain, R.É.R., vol. III, p. 271.
[4] On this *Vieux Coustumier du Poitou* cf. Maurice Lacombe, *Essai sur la coutume poitevine du Mariage au début du XVe siècle*, Paris, 1910.

represented the rules of conduct which he recommended to Marie Cailler, his very young wife[1].

An identical spirit dominated the two works. The *De re uxoria* of Francesco Barbaro enjoins upon women the observance on all occasions of a prudent reserve. It forbids them severely anything which might be a mark of frivolity : an excessively quick gait, agitations of the hands, mobility of looks. To laugh loudly, he declares, is indecent in a woman. He does not condemn ornament, but limits it to solid and lasting articles—gold, precious stones, jewels—which do not need incessant renewal, like delicate stuffs and trinkets. All his recommendations tend to confine woman to her duties as a wife and the care of the household.

Tiraqueau's conjugal precepts come from the same conception of woman's rôle in marriage. Title XV of the Common Law of Poitou stipulated that "the wife is in the power of (subject of the authority of) her husband". Commentating this text, Tiraqueau thus formulates his first matrimonial law :

> Viri uxoribus imperanto
> Uxores viris obediunto.

The eleven precepts which follow all proceed, more or less, from this principle. They are corroborated by numerous quotations, taken mainly from jurists. All these "laws" are founded upon this undisputed axiom, that woman is by nature a weak creature. They all uphold the strictest tutelage on the husband's part, of which even the abuses did not then shock either custom or opinion. Thus, in the question, so often debated during the Middle Ages, as to whether the sexes are equal, Tiraqueau sided against woman, whom he considered man's inferior[2].

His work caused some stir. A Metz lawyer, Claude Chansonnette, plagiarised it. Tiraqueau resolved to publish a second edition, augmented by all the Latin, Greek and Italian texts which his reading supplied him with in support of his theses.

---

[1] She was not yet twelve when he married her. He was twenty-four (according to Barat, *art. cit.*, p. 139). Girls were then married when they had emerged from childhood. Guillaume Budé, for example, in his thirty-eighth year, married Roberte le Lieur, who was barely fifteen. He had seven children by her. Cf. Delaruelle, *Guillaume Budé*, p. 89.

[2] On this question cf. Abel Lefranc's article, *Le tiers livre du Pantagruel et la querelle des femmes*, R.É.R., vol. II, pp. 1–78.

He put to advantage, seemingly, not only his reading but also that of his friends of Fontenay-le-Comte, and the questions relative to woman and marriage were often discussed, in the laurel-grove, in presence of Amy and Rabelais.

While he was thus preparing the second edition of his *De legibus connubialibus*, there appeared in 1522, at Paris, and issued by his own publisher, Josse Bade, an apology of the feminine sex, written in Latin. The Greek title : Τῆς γυναικείας φυτλῆς *apologia*, showed it to be the work of a humanist. It was, in fact, the work of a magistrate, renowned for his Greek and Latin culture, Amaury Bouchard, lieutenant general of the Seneschal of Saintonge at the *siège royal* of Saint-Jean-d'Angély[1].

The book opened with a Latin epistle from Friar Pierre Amy to Tiraqueau. The monks of the Puy-Saint-Martin must not have been strictly obliged to residence, for it is from Saintes, where he lived with Bouchard for some time past, that Amy writes to Tiraqueau. He entrusts him with affectionate messages for his companion Rabelais, "the most erudite of the Franciscans," and expounds with some caution the object of the book—it is a plea for woman, whom Tiraqueau has somewhat discredited. Henceforward, he declares, a combat is in progress between the two friends[2].

In this duel, Bouchard had the advantage of courtesy. He did not overestimate the scope of his book. While unoccupied at Bordeaux, where he was awaiting the termination of a lawsuit, he had amused himself by writing as a pastime this refutation of the *De legibus connubialibus*. His apology

---

[1] Saint-Jean-d'Angély, like Fontenay-le-Comte, had its group of *literati*, as we learn from an *Epistle to the reader* with which a certain Pierre Valla accompanied a collection of psalms set to Latin verse by François Bonade, a priest of Saintonge : *Eximii prophetarum antistitis regis Davidis oracula, per Franciscum Bonadum Angeriæ presbiterum Santonensem Aquitanum ad Psalmorum seriem centum quinquaginta numeris poeticis exarata.* (Paris, Christian Wechel, 1531, 16 mo.). There were three Hellenists in this group, Amaury Bouchard, Briand Vallée—of whom we shall say more later—and a poet who cultivated both the Greek and Latin Muses, Mathurin Aumand (Mathurinus Almandinus). In addition, we know from some poems printed at the end of Bonade's work that a physician, Pierre Hilairet, a priest, Martial Labbé, and a certain Pierre Aymery were also able to write Latin verse.

On Amaury Bouchard, cf. *Un diplomate poitevin du XVIe siècle, Charles de Dauzay, ambassadeur de France en Danemark*, by Alfred Richard, in the *Mémoires de la Société des antiquaires de l'Ouest*, 1909.

[2] It was clear from the full title of Bouchard's work : *Almarici Bouchardi Angeliaci Sanctorum præsidis . . . adversus And ream Tiraquellum Fontiniensem.*

of the feminine sex was merely an exercise of dialectic and of style, and he spoke of it with a certain disinterestedness.

On the contrary, Tiraqueau, whose vanity was ticklish, did not consider his anti-feminist thesis a matter for trifling. When, nearly two years later, he at last published the second edition of the *De legibus connubialibus*, revised and with additions, he launched out into recriminations against Amaury Bouchard who, to act the gallant and capture the good graces of the feminine sex, had not hesitated to tear to pieces, defame and trample under foot a book written by a friend ! He grudgingly admitted that Bouchard's work was not without charm, although the ideas were confused and their expression obscure. In fine, he adhered to his thesis, contenting himself in this second edition with confirming and developing the ideas which his adversary had tried to demolish and refute.

This confirmation of his theses consisted in citations of authorities as numerous as they were varied. Tiraqueau quoted pell-mell philosophers and poets, historians and orators, Livy and Cicero, Plato and Petrarch, Ezechiel and Propertius. The work became thus considerably enlarged. From the 27 pages which composed the original edition it had grown to 276.

Thus did the lawyers dispute among themselves ! During this time what were our two monks, Friar Pierre Amy and Friar Rabelais, doing ? Attached to both adversaries, they admired them equally and did not consider themselves obliged to take sides for one or the other of them. Rabelais will later dedicate one of his learned publications to Amaury Bouchard[1]. In the meantime he composed four Greek verses in honour of Tiraqueau. If these laws, asks this quatrain, which appears at the head of the second edition of the *De legibus connubialibus*, if these laws formulated by a Poitevin jurisconsult were Plato's would there be among men a more illustrious person than Plato ?

And Brother Amy, in a Latin quatrain, repeated this eulogy, proclaiming at the same time his admiration for Rabelais' learning[2]. " He whom you praise ", he affirms, " cannot be

---

[1] *Vide infra*, ch. VIII.
[2] " Quem, Rabelæse, probas, graio latinoque polite
　　Eloquio, rerum qui monumenta tenes,
　　Doctum quis esse neget ! Probe mihi cognitus idem
　　Doctior hoc multo est, quod, Rabelæse, probas."

other than learned. He is so all the more since it is you, Rabelais, who praise him."

On his side, Tiraqueau introduces among his quotations and references his praises for the learning of Rabelais and of Amy. Incidentally, he informs us of the pursuits to which Rabelais devoted himself in his cell of the Puy-Saint-Martin. He was there translating the second book of Herodotus, doubtless into Latin, since he proposed to fill in a gap in the Latin translation undertaken but left unfinished by the Italian Humanist, Lorenzo Valla. In any event, this translation was elegant, and Tiraqueau, in this respect, pays the following homage to Rabelais—that his erudition in Greek and Latin was far above what could be expected from a man of his age and, especially, from a Franciscan monk[1].

Rabelais owes a part of this learning, which was to become encyclopædic, to the *cénacle* of Fontenay. There were not then any definite lines along which French Humanism was being directed. It was at the hazard of circumstances and of acquaintances that our scholars chose for study, in the treasury of ancient literatures, the poets, philosophers, or the historians. At Fontenay-le-Comte, Plutarch and Lucian were in particular favour. They will later be Rabelais' favourite authors, with Plato, who, among the philosophers, was Amaury Bouchard's[2] intellectual guide. We can go further : it has been shown that a great amount of the knowledge of women and marriage displayed by Rabelais in the third book of *Pantagruel* is already to be found in this *De legibus connubialibus*, which our two monks had seen grow and develop during the discussions of Tiraqueau with his familiars of Fontenay-le-Comte[3].

The meeting with these lawyers, friends of the Ancient literatures, was, then, for Rabelais a happy chance. Stimulated by them, praised by Tiraqueau, encouraged by Guillaume Budé, he practised the use of the Greek tongue by translating Herodotus, and, doubtless, aspired only to a better knowledge of Greek and Latin writers, when an unforeseen event came to

---

[1] " Franciscus Rabelæsus Minoritanus, vir supra ætatem præterque ejus sodalicii morem, ne nimiam religionem dicam, utriusque linguæ omnifariæque doctrinæ peritissimus ". Folio LXXIV, *verso*.

[2] He has left a manuscript work on the immortality of the soul according to Plato's *Timaeus*, which is preserved in the Bibliothèque Nationale at Paris, *Manuscrits français, ancien fonds*, no. 1995.

[3] This has been shown by Barat, *art. cit.*, p. 25, n.1, but his demonstration can be accepted only with reservations on some points.

trouble this hard-working existence : in pursuance of a decision of the Faculty of Theology of Paris, the superiors of the Puy-Saint-Martin confiscated the Greek books of Amy and of Rabelais.

This was about the end of the year 1523. The publication of Erasmus's *Commentaries* on the Greek text of the Gospel according to Saint Luke had alarmed the Theological Faculty, or, as it was then called, the Sorbonne, from the name of the college where the Council of this Faculty ordinarily met.

It beheld with horror the growth of the spirit of investigation among the Humanists. It noticed numerous affinities between Lutheranism, which was beginning to appear in France, and the ideas which were propagated by Jacques Lefebvre d'Étaples, the doyen of French humanists. He upheld that the Bible is the only foundation for Christ's doctrine, that dogmas are the work of man and that it was necessary to abandon many religious institutions authorised by Catholic tradition to return to the pure Gospel. Hence the name of *Evangelism*, which has been given to the whole body of the aspirations and ideas of the French pre-Reformation.

In order to combat these new ideas the Sorbonne in its surprise had at first resorted to the arsenal of scholastic philosophy. Alas ! this philosophy was decried among Humanists. They ridiculed it, thereby merely irritating the theologians, and passing for rebels. They were, however, good Christians who did not think of leaving the Church, but who admitted exclusively recourse to the examination of the original texts (of the Bible) to verify the claims of dogma upon their acceptance. In this philological study they surprised the theologians who were ignorant of Greek, and that is why the Sorbonne, having recourse to force and not to persuasion, decided to forbid the study of Greek in France.

The confiscation of the books of Rabelais and of Pierre Amy was a repercussion of the conflict which had arisen between the spirit of investigation and the authority charged with preserving the integrity of dogma. Is it in this light that this measure was visible to our Hellenists ? It is very doubtful, and if there was then a crisis in Rabelais' conscience it was probably less tragic than some of his biographers have pictured it. For him there was no question of choosing between the spirit of the Renaissance and the Faith, nor even between Greek and the religious habit. He was exposed to the suspicion and, perhaps, to the affronts of the monks of his convent, for having learned Greek ; it was a trial, which he could only consider as a passing one. There is not, in fact, a humanist who, at this time, doubted the final triumph of knowledge over ignorance. What did they all do, by their recourse to free investigation, but yield to a reasonable need : that of finding for the accepted religious doctrine a more solid foundation than popular traditions, or a philosophy which had degenerated into vain sophistical subtleties ? How could they have supposed that this spirit of research, favoured by the manifest progress of literary studies, would not win over, one day or another, the defenders of the traditional faith ? " What an outrage has been committed against the Muses ", wrote Guillaume Budé to Pierre Amy to console him, " by persecuting you for the zeal you bring to the study of Greek ! How one would like to chastise these convent superiors who cultivate ignorance under the name of orthodoxy ! . . . It is Erasmus's latest works which have provoked this assault of the theologians against the Greek tongue. Happily they have no longer any credit at Court, and nothing henceforth will arrest the renaissance of letters "[1].

All Humanists thought likewise—with the support of the King " good letters " were bound, sooner or later, to triumph over ignorance. The struggle in their eyes was not between heresy and the Faith, the Evangelicals not being hostile to the Church, but between Learning, desirous of basing religious life upon enlightened conviction, and the apathy of Theologians who opposed to the new aspirations and questionings merely outworn formulæ, authority or force.

In their tribulations, the two Hellenist monks asked themselves if they would not find some religious order less docile to the instructions of the Sorbonne, or less rigorous than the Friars Minor towards the poor brethren guilty of being interested in Latin and Greek literature. They both thought of the Benedictines. Before leaving the Puy-Saint-Martin, Pierre Amy, following a usage borrowed by the humanists from the

---

[1] This letter is dated Feb. 24 ; Mr. A. Tilley has shown that it must be assigned to 1524, contrary to M. Delaruelle's opinion (*Répertoire* . . . p. 199) who proposed 1523.

Ancients, consulted Virgil to know the future[1]. Having opened
the book at random, he chanced upon this verse from the third
book of the *Æneid* :

> Heu ! fuge crudeles terras ! fuge littus avarum.

In his impatience to resume his Greek studies he followed the
advice of Virgil's line, ran away, " escaping safe and sound
from the ambush of the hob-goblins ", that is, of the Friars
Minor, and took refuge in the Benedictine convent of Saint-
Mesmin, near Orleans, where he again immediately set about
translating from Greek into Latin[2]. Some months later, the
7th October, he was at Lyons[3] in company with personages
who were nearly all later to pass over to the side of the Reformation, and who, by reason of his Evangelical faith, professed
great esteem for him. Then we lose sight of him.

What meanwhile was Rabelais' attitude ? We have neither
any document nor any declaration as to his sentiments during
the height of this crisis. It is probable that he bore his hardship
patiently and bent his back to the storm. The trial, in any
event, did not last. After a certain time, his books were returned
to him. But, fearing, doubtless, for the future of his studies
did he remain with the Franciscans, he solicited and obtained
from Pope Clement VII an indult authorising him to transfer
to a monastery of the Order of Saint Benedict, at Maillezais,
in the neighbourhood of Fontenay-le-Comte[4].

[1] This information is supplied by Rabelais himself, *Third Book*, ch. X.
The custom of consulting Virgil to know one's fate remained in vogue among
humanists until the end of the century, as is shown by a curious letter of
Nicolas Rapin to D'Aubigné, which I published in an article upon Rapin's
unpublished poems—*Poèmes inédits de Nicolas Rapin* in *la Rev. XVIe siècle*,
1922, p. 277.

[2] " Intellexi eum non amplius apud Minoritas agere, sed indutum cucullo
nigro, in quodam cœnobio magni eleemosynarii degere, nescio quæ ibi e græco
latine faciens ".—Letter from Lefèvre d'Étaples to Guillaume Farel, July 6th,
1524, in Herminjard's *Correspondance des Réformateurs*, vol. I, p. 225.

[3] On his stay in Lyons cf. N. Weiss, *Bulletin de la Société d'histoire du
protestantisme français*, 1921, p. 210.

[4] We know this from the *Supplicatio pro apostasia* which he sent in 1535
to Pope Paul III (*v. infra* ch. XII). He recalls at the outset of his request
that he had been regularly transferred from the Franciscan to the Benedictine
Order.
" Cum alias postquam devotus Orator Franciscus Rabelais Presbyter
Turonensis Diocœsis tunc Ordinem Fratrum Minorum de Observantia pro-
fessus, sibi quod de Ordine Fratrum Minorum . . . ad ordinem S. Benedicti
in Ecclesia Maleacensi dicti ordinis se libere transferre per fælicis recordationis
Clementem Papem VII Prædecessorum Vestrum Apostolica obtinuerat autori-
tate concedi seu indulgeri ". For the text of this document cf. Marty-
Laveaux, vol. III, pp. 336–339 ; on its origin and authenticity cf. *ibid.*, vol.
IV, p. 381, and Jacques Boulenger, *La supplicatio pro apostasia et le Bref de
1536, R.É.R.*, II, 110–134.

Saint-Pierre was Bishop of Maillezais and his monks became canons of the cathedral[1].

Up to 1516, the Bishop-abbot was elected by the Abbey Chapter. At this date, the Concordat entered upon between Leo X and François I gave the King the right of nominating the Bishops of France. Reasons foreign to the spiritual interests of the Church dictated the greater part of his choices. It is thus that the first concordatory Bishop of Maillezais, Geoffroy d'Estissac, was raised to the episcopacy less in reason of his piety or virtue, than by the privilege of his birth[2].

He had the double good fortune to belong to a good family of Périgord, the Madaillans, and to have an elder brother, Bertrand, who had by his military valour established his claims upon the gratitude of our Kings. Bertrand d'Estissac had accompanied Charles VIII to the conquest of the kingdom of Naples, as esquire. Later he had again crossed the Alps with Louis XII and taken part in the siege of Alexandria (1499). He had again distinguished himself before Salces, in Roussillon. As a reward he had been appointed successively seneschal of Agenais, seneschal of Périgord, lieutenant-governor of Guyenne, and, after his marriage with the niece of the powerful Cardinal Philippe de Luxembourg, mayor and captain of Bordeaux. Honours and offices were showered upon him. He distributed them lavishly among his family and especially upon his brother Geoffroy.

The latter, at the age of twenty-six, was appointed Prior of Ligugé, near Poitiers. A year later, in 1504, at Bertrand's request, King Louis XII himself wrote a letter to the Chapter of Saint-Hilaire de Poitiers, asking them to elect Geoffroy d'Estissac their dean. In 1515, Geoffroy was preferred to two other ecclesiastical benefices, the Abbeys of Cadouin, in Périgord, and of Notre-Dame-de-Celles, in Poitou. Finally, in virtue of his rights under the Concordat, François I made him Bishop of Maillezais in 1518.

Geoffroy was not an unworthy churchman. If his merit was

---

[1] Cf. Charles Arnaud, *Histoire de Maillezais*, Niort, 1840, and an article by Bourlaton in the Introduction to Robuchon's *Sites et Monuments du Poitou*.

[2] The greater part of this information about the D'Estissac family is taken from Maurice Campagne's work, *Histoire de la maison de Madaillan*, 1076 à 1700 (Bergerac, 1900). There is a short account of Geoffroy d'Estissac in the *Mémoire pour l'histoire de l'abbaye et évéché de Maillezais*, manuscript no. 545 (18th century) of the Municipal Library of Poitiers.

beneath his titles and functions, he, at least, unlike many prelates of the time, did not disinterest himself from his diocese.
He rarely went outside it ; he lived in Poitou, whereas the
bishops of Poitiers, for example, in the course of the 16th
century, only made very few appearances in their episcopal
town.

There is some question as to how Rabelais had made himself
known to him : the young monk's culture had doubtless recommended him to the prelate who liked to surround himself with
learned people.　In any case, one fact is incontestable : very
rapidly the new Benedictine entered Geoffroy d'Estissac's
service.　In what capacity ?　As secretary, and also, perhaps,
as tutor to Louis d'Estissac, Bertrand's son, placed since his
father's death (1522) under his uncle's guardianship[1].　During
at least three years Rabelais will be one of the household of the
Bishop of Maillezais.　In his mental development, the widening
of his culture and experience, his capacity of Benedictine monk
counts for little : but he will owe much to his situation as an
intimate of Geoffroy d'Estissac.　For him there begins a new
life, free and varied, which gives him facilities for study,
provides him with learned conversation, gives him numerous
chances of observing the different "estates of the world",
and brings him into contact with the things and people of the
province of Poitou.

The Abbot of Maillezais rarely resided in his Benedictine
Abbey.　He was continually in movement, superintending
in person the temporalities of his abbeys and priories.　Like
many great lords of his time, he had a taste for building.　He
built or restored the choir and transept of the church at
Maillezais, the deanery of Saint-Hilaire[2] at Poitiers, and the
porch of the church and the priory of Ligugé ; and at L'Hermenault, three leagues north of Fontenay-le-Comte, the buildings of a priory, which was used as a summer residence by the
bishops of Maillezais.　He had inherited from his father the
property of Coulonges-les-Royaux (to-day Coulonges-sur-

---

[1] We learn these facts from Jean Bouchet's *Épître* to Rabelais which we
treat of later, ch. IV.　For the text of this epistle cf. Marty-Laveaux, *op. cit.*,
vol. III, p. 305 ; and Abel Lefranc, *Rabelais secrétaire de Geoffroy d'Estissac* ...,
R.É.R., VII, pp. 411–413.
[2] Now a training college for primary teachers.　The main doorway, with
its depressed arch, flanked by carved storing-races, still bears traces of this
reconstruction.

l'Autize) half-way between Fontenay and Niort[1]. He had built there a magnificent dwelling, ornamented by a porch with pilasters, carved compartment-ceilings, and, later on, a monumental chimney-piece, all of which are still to be seen at the Castle of Terre-Neuve[2], near Fontenay-le-Comte.

These constructions and embellishments on his domains entailed constant travelling for Geoffroy d'Estissac. Rabelais used to accompany him. He wandered thus during several years across Poitou. He went over it in every direction, from west to east and north to south, from Maillezais to Montmorillon and from Parthenay to Charroux. Of reconstituting these peregrinations there can be no question. He has himself, in a chapter of *Pantagruel*, marked the stages of these itineraries. The giant, having to go from Poitiers to La Rochelle, instead of following the ordinary road, goes away from it, now to the right, now to the left[3]. He passes through Ligugé, Lusignan, Sanxay, Celles, Saint-Ligaire, Coulonges, Fontenay-le-Comte. Now, each one of these names represents either properties or convents belonging to, the Bishop of Maillezais—as Sanxay, Celles, Saint-Ligaire and Coulonges-les-Royaux,—or localities where he had friends, whom Rabelais mentions with a word of praise.

He has in this manner cited in *Pantagruel* and *Gargantua* more than 50 Poitevin place-names[4], of which some designate obscure small towns which only the chance of his travels could have called to his attention.

This acquaintance with the topography of Poitou is merely a part of the store of information that his work gives us on the flora, fauna, productions, customs, traditions, legends and even the speech of this province of Poitou.

His enumerations of eatables, the menus of the meals which he composes for his Giants, consist of products of the land of Poitou, whose fame did not go outside the frontiers of the province : the wine of Ligugé[5], or that of La Faye-Monjault[6], capons of Loudunois[7], chestnuts from the wood of Estrocs[8],

---

[1] Work was carried out there from 1523 to 1528. Later, this dwelling was ruined by the Protestants.
[2] Brought thither, forty years ago, by Octave de Rochebrune.
[3] Cf. *Pantagruel*, ch. V.
[4] Cf. H. Clouzot, *Topographie rabelaisienne*, R.É.R., II, pp. 143 and 227.
[5] *Third Book*, ch. XLI.
[6] *Gargantua*, ch. XXXVII.
[7] *Ibid.*, ch. XL.   [8] *Ibid.*

in the neighbourhood of the episcopal house at L'Hermenault. His catalogues of fishes and birds include some terms current only in Poitou[1]; here, river-birds very plentiful in the *Marais poitevin*[2], there, sea fishes which mounted the water-courses as far as Maillezais and which he could have seen on fast-days on the fish-merchants' stalls or on the convent table.

Of every canton, of every town in the province he knows the particularities and special productions. He quotes the Mirebalais for its asses, still famous to-day, for its windmills[3], for its " walnut-tree tapers ", a sort of pounded chestnut paste, from which protruded a hempen wick[4]. He brings from Châtel-lerault, whose principal industry was cloth-making, the 900 ells of stuff necessary to manufacture Gargantua's shirt[5]. He has gone right to the confines of the province, even to the edges of the Ocean. At Olonne-en-Talmondois, he has noted that the hemp exceeds the length of a lance, by virtue of the " sweet, easy, warm, wet and well-soaked soil "[6]. At La Rochelle, the great port of the West since the discovery of the New World, he has noticed the thick chain which was stretched between the two towers of Saint-Nicolas and of the Chain, which stand at the entrance to the harbour[7]. He admired the Gothic lantern which sheltered at the summit of a tower the beacon designed to guide ships in search of haven[8]. How did Rabelais gather all these local traditions ? Dressed in his Benedictine's habit, he mixed with the people more than any writer of his time. He knew the art of loosening the tongues of the cattle-drover in the field, the artisan in his workshop, the merchant in the inn. He can, on occasion, make use of

---

[1] Such as *la meuille* (mullet), *la moulue* (cod), *le papillon* (skate), *le butor* (bittern), *le corbigeau* (curlew), *le hegronneau* (young heron), *le pouacre* (grey heron), *le tyranson* (sandpiper), *le bitard* (young bustard), *le chardrier* (gold-finch), *la duppe, la pupu* (lapwing), *le huteaudeau* (young capon). Cf. Sainéan, *L'Histoire naturelle dans Rabelais*, in the *Rev. XVIᵉ siècle*, 1913–1918.

[2] Cf. Ét. Clouzot, *Les Marais de la Sèvre-Niortaise et du Lay, du Xᵉ à la fin du XVIᵉ siècle.* (1903.)

[3] *Gargantua*, ch. XI ; *Third Book*, ch. XX.

[4] *Pantagruel*, ch. XIII ; *Fifth Book*, ch. XXXII.

[5] *Gargantua*, ch. VIII.

[6] *Third Book*, ch. XLIX, the description of hemp under the name of Pantagruelion.

[7] *Pantagruel*, ch. LV.

[8] *Fifth Book*, ch. XXXII : " There Pantagruel discovered, on a high tower, the lantern of (La) Rochelle ". The *Brièfve déclaration* . . . quotes as types of lighthouses those of La Rochelle.

their dialect[1], their familiar metaphors[2], their customary swear-words. The characters in his book readily invoke the Saints who were honoured in Poitou. Here, for example, it is Saint Jago de Bressuire[3], Saint James, who had under his protection in this town an almonry for the poor sick and for pilgrims to Compostella; there, it is the "arm of Saint Rigomer"[4], a reliquary preserved in the Church of Maillezais since the beginning of the 11th century and venerated throughout Poitou; again, it is the venerable Goderan[5], Abbot of Maillezais in the 11th century. The more popular swear-words[6]: *M'arme!* (*par mon âme*, by my soul), *mer dé!* (by the Mother of God), *merdigué!* (an attenuated form of the same oath), *pé le quaudé!* (by God's body); and some verses of a Poitevin carol[7] give evidence of Rabelais' acquaintance with the country-folk.

We can easily picture him mingling with the throng of rustics at the fairs of Niort, Saint-Maixent, or Fontenay, which he has mentioned in his book[8], observing as an artist delighting in movement and colour, the people and the animals, noting the manœuvres of the merchants and the keen bargaining of the purchasers. One of the most truculent figures in his work, Dindenaut, the cattle-merchant[9], has doubtless been drawn from memory, after some individuals whom he met on

---

[1] Poitevin terms familiar to Rabelais are—*acimenter* (to season), *acroué* (crouched), *aiguë* (mixed with water), *appigret* (seasoning), *becgueter* (to stammer), *billevezée* (nonsense; literally, an empty gut, something hollow), *biscarié* (damaged), *burgot* (drone), *chalupper* (to pick nuts), *chenin* (variety of grape), *coireaux* (fattened oxen), *cormé* (drink made from sorb-apples), *foupi* (tattered), *fournées* (for *enfourné*, put into the oven), *gaudebillaux* (tripe), *guimaux* (meadows bearing two crops yearly), *hugrement* (briskly, quickly), *jadeau* (platter), *oince* (phalanx, *anat.*), *pibole* (flute with a mouthpiece and three holes), *poysard* (pea-stalk), *quecas* (sort of nut), *rebindaine* (head over heels), *rimer* (to stick to the pan, of food which is slightly burnt), *sallebrenaux* (elegant), *sublet* (a whistle), *vèze* (bagpipes), *vimère* (damage caused by storm). Cf. Sainéan, *La langue de Rabelais*, vol. II, pp. 337–340.

[2] *Les ferremens de la messe* (tools of the Mass), for the ornaments; *le manche de la paroisse* (handle of the parish), for the church-steeple (*Fourth Book*, ch. XVI); the *croix hosannière* (Hosanna-cross), where *Hosanna filio David* is sung on Palm Sunday (*ibid.*, ch. XIII). Cf. The *Brief declaration of some more obscure sayings* appended to the *Fourth Book*.

[3] *Third Book*, ch. XXXI.

[4] *Ibid.*, ch. XXVII.

[5] Friar Jean des Entommeures makes him a Saint. Cf. *Gargantua*, ch. LVIII.

[6] Studied by Sainéan, *La langue de Rabelais*, vol. II, p. 337.

[7] *Fourth Book*, ch. XXII. The full text and music of this carol can be found in the collection of H. Lemaître and H. Clouzot, *Trente Noëls poitevins du XVᵉ au XVIIIᵉ siècle* (1908).

[8] *Third Book*, ch. XIII, and *Fourth Book*, ch. XIII.

[9] *Fourth Book*, chs. V–VIII.

fair-greens. The conceited bragging of this big merchant who acts in high-handed fashion towards suspicious-looking clients like Panurge, his formulæ of rustic politeness, his quibbles, his jokes, all these traits which we do not meet with in any previous description of a merchant, must have been drawn from personal observation.

Rabelais also mingled in other no less noisy gatherings—those who swarmed around the booths where mystery-plays, farces or moralities were staged. The first quarter of the 16th century saw the apogee of this dramatic art which was one of the most original creations of the Middle Ages. Theatrical performances were then numerous in Poitou, those of Mont-morillon, of Saint-Maixent and of Poitiers were famous[1]. They awakened great interest in all classes of society. Churchmen, as well as lay-folk, considered it an honour to play in the mysteries ; some of them even took comic parts in the farces, and the ecclesiastical authorities had to recall them to a sense of their dignity[2].

Indeed, it is in Poitou that Rabelais most likely developed a taste for those dramatic performances to which he will make frequent allusions in *Pantagruel* and *Gargantua*[3] and which he can describe, if necessary, in the terms of the profession[4]. He enumerates the most notable of the Poitevin *diableries*, those of Montmorillon, Saint-Maixent and Poitiers[5]. He recounts a scandalous scene which took place at Saint-Maixent

---

[1] *Fourth Book*, ch. XIII.

[2] Cf. H. Clouzot, *L'ancien théâtre en Poitou*, 1 vol. 8vo, Niort, 1900, ch. I.

[3] Cf. Gustave Cohen, *Rabelais et le théâtre*, R.É.R., IX, 16.

[4] *Third Book*, ch. XXVII. " The prompter (*portecole*) forsook his copy ; he who played St. Michael's part came down from his perch (descendit par la *volerie*) ; the devils issued out of hell and carried along with them most of the pretty girls that were there ; yea, Lucifer got out of his fetters. In a word, seeing the huge disorder, I disparked myself forth of that inclosed place (je *déparquay* du lieu) ".

The scene is described with technical accuracy worthy of remark. The *parc* or *parquet* was the *inclosed place* where the spectators were, some standing, others seated in the galleries ; Panurge, on leaving *disparks* (*déparque*) from the place—the expression is accurate. The *portecole*, who starts off the disorder, is the prompter-director who, text in hand, stayed upon the stage to regulate the actors' entrances and movements and remedy their defects of memory. The *volerie*, from which St. Michael hurriedly comes down, is the whole array of machines, ropes, pulleys and trap-doors by which the angels, perched upon the scaffolding of " Paradise ", were let down to earth. Cf. Gustave Cohen, *Le livre de conduite du régisseur* and the *Compte des dépenses pour le mystère de la Passion joué à Mons en* 1501. Strasbourg, Publications of the Faculty of Letters, fasc. 23 (1925), p. liii.

[5] *Fourth Book*, ch. XIII.

the day of the production of the mystery of the Passion[1]. He himself describes a " diablerie ", that is to say a devil's procession, with extraordinary accuracy[2], and places the scene at Saint-Maixent, where he had had no doubt the occasion of seeing it. Hence, he owes to Poitou his initiation into theatrical matters.

He liked equally well collecting racy tales and local anecdotes. Such as, for example, the story which represents the poet, Villon, " in his old age retired to Saint-Maixent ", and there producing the *Passion*, in Poitevin dialect, after the fairs of Niort. As he was endeavouring to procure costumes suitable to the characters, Friar Étienne Tappecoue, secretary of the local Friars Minor, refused to lend him a cope and stole, required to dress up an old peasant taking the part of God the Father. Villon, indignant at his refusal, decided to wreak vengeance upon him. " On the Saturday following, he had notice given him, that Tickletoby (*Tappecoue*), upon the filly of the convent, so they call a young mare that was never leaped yet—was gone a mumping to St. Ligarius, and would be back about two in the afternoon. Knowing this, he made a cavalcade of his devils of ' The Passion ' through the town." Then he led his grotesque crew to a country-house on the road to Saint-Maixent. Hardly had Tappecoue arrived, than all the devils, screaming, beating their cymbals, and " throwing fire from their squibs and burning sticks " threw themselves in his path.

" The filly was soon scared out of her seven senses, and began to start, to funk it, to squirt it, to trot it, to fart it, to bound it, to gallop it, to kick it, to spurn it, to calcitrate it, to wince it, to frisk it, to leap it, to curvet it, with double jerks, and bummotions ; insomuch that she threw down Tickletoby, though he held fast by the tree of the pack-saddle with might and main. Now his straps and stirrups were of cord ; and on the right side, his sandals were so entangled and twisted, that he could not for the heart's blood of him get out his foot. Thus he was dragged

---

[1] *Third Book*, ch. XXVII.
[2] *Fourth Book*, ch. XIII : " Knowing this, he made a cavalcade of his devils of ' The Passion ' through the town. They were all rigged with wolves', calves', and rams' skins, laced and trimmed with sheeps' heads, bulls' feathers, and large kitchen tenterhooks, girt with broad leathern girdles ; whereat hanged dangling huge cow-bells and horse-bells, which made a horrid din. Some held in their claws black sticks full of squibs and crackers : others had long lighted pieces of wood, upon which, at the corner of every street, they flung whole handfuls of rosin-dust, that made a terrible fire and smoke ".

about by the filly through the road, scratching his bare breech all the way ; she still multiplying her kicks against him, and straying for fear over hedge and ditch ; insomuch that she trepanned his thick skull so, that his cockle brains were dashed out near the Osanna or high-cross. Then his arms fell to pieces, one this way, and the other that way ; and even so were his legs served at the same time. Then she made a bloody havoc with his puddings ; and being got to the convent, brought back only his right foot and twisted sandal . . . "[1]

This picturesque story is founded upon a tradition of doubtful authenticity : Villon being dead at thirty-three could not have retired *in his old age* to Saint-Maixent, and from the fact that he declares in his *Testament* that he speaks *a little Poitevin*, it does not follow that he was capable of writing in this dialect the few thousand verses that the Passion play would have contained. But it shows to what a degree Rabelais had familiarised himself with the places and the customs of Poitou. Saint-Ligaire, at some distance from Saint-Maixent, was an abbey dependent on the Bishop of Maillezais. The crosses called *hosannières* (there are some of them still extant) are those to which the procession came on Palm Sunday to chant " Hosanna filio David ". Finally, it is probable that Tappecoue's accident had some connection with the name of a fief adjoining Saint-Maixent : the fief of the " dead monk ".[2]

Rabelais also heard the old legends of the district being told. The most famous was that of Mélusine, the woman-serpent of Lusignan, who on Saturdays, at evening time, returned sometimes to bathe in the Font-de-Cé, disappearing as soon as she was seen[3].

This legend was very ancient. It would seem that Mélusine was originally a Celtic divinity, protectress of a well which issues forth from the side of the hill of Lusignan[4]. Christianity did not succeed in banishing the memory of this beneficent divinity. In the Middle Ages, a great feudal family, the

---

[1] *Fourth Book*, ch. XIII.
[2] Cf. H. Clouzot, *L'ancien théâtre en Poitou*, pp. 18–26.
[3] That is what the people of the district told Catherine de' Medici when she visited the ruins of Lusignan Castle, according to Brantôme, *Œuvres*, ed. Lalanne, vol. V, pp. 16–22.
[4] Cf. Léo Desaivre, *Le mythe de la Mère Lusine*, Poitiers, 1883. A complete bibliography of the Mélusine myth will be found in the magnificent facsimile edition of *L'histoire de la belle Mélusine, de Jean d'Arras*, from the Geneva edition printed by A. Steinschaber in 1478. (Paris, published by Champion, 1924.) Michelet makes Mélusine " a combination of divers natures ", a symbol of Poitou.

Lusignans, who won fame at the Crusades, cleverly exploited this legend by making Mélusine the founder of their family. In popular imagination the myth had taken other shapes. Mélusine was credited with the power of building at night with magical rapidity. The most imposing constructions of the region were attributed to her : the Amphitheatre of Poitiers, for instance, and especially the feudal fortresses of the Lusignans and their allies. The *Guide des chemins de France* (1552) recommends the traveller to admire the castles of Lusignan, Vouvent and Mervent (the latter two to the north of Fontenay-le-Comte), which are Mélusine's handiwork. She had, in addition, built the towers of Parthenay, ruined under Charles VIII. The fortress of Pouzauges, in Bas-Poitou, was the last thing she built. Surprised at her work, in the depth of night, by the gaze of an unwary watcher, she uttered a curse upon her works :

> Pouzauges, Tiffauges, Mervent, Chateaumur et Vouvant
> Iront chaque an, je le jure, d'une pierre en périssant[1].

It is in some one of these localities that Rabelais had heard of the woman-serpent : " Visit," he says, " Lusignan, Parthenay, Vovent, Mervent and Pouzauges in Poitou. There you will find a cloud of witnesses, not of your affidavit men of the right stamp, but credible, time out of mind, that will take their corporal oath . . . . that Melusina, their founder, or foundress, which you please, was woman from the head to the prick-purse, and thence downwards was a serpentine Chitterling, or if you will have it otherwise, a Chitterlingdized serpent[2]."

Of the race of Mélusine was Geoffroy II de Lusignan, seigneur of Vouvent in the neighbourhood of Fontenay-le-Comte, nicknamed Geoffroy-of-the-Big-Tooth, of whom Rabelais had made the " grandfather of the beautiful cousin of the elder sister of the aunt of the son-in-law of the uncle of the daughter-in-law of the mother-in-law " of Pantagruel[3]. He lived at the beginning of the 13th century, and made himself famous for his acts of violence. As a result of differences which arose between himself and the Abbot of Maillezais, the buildings of the Abbey

---

[1] " Pouzauges, Tiffauges, Mervent, Chateaumur and Vouvant,
    Will perish, disappearing, I swear, by one stone each year ".
[2] *Fourth Book*, ch. XXXVIII.
[3] *Pantagruel*, ch. V.

were pillaged and burnt[1], the monks put to flight and pursued by Geoffroy's followers. The Pope pronounced the excommunication of the author of these crimes. Then Geoffroy went in penitence to Rome and, having gained pardon of his guilt, sealed his peace with the Abbey of Saint-Pierre-de-Maillezais by rich gifts. When he died, the monks, remembering only his penance and the generous reparation of his outrages, erected in his honour, in their Abbatial church, a cenotaph adorned with his effigy carved in the stone. Geoffroy was interred at Vouvent. But, with the lapse of time, it came to be commonly believed that the tomb in the Church of Maillezais contained his remains, as is seen from these verses of the poet, Couldrette, at the end of the 15th century :

> " Encore y est ensevelis
> Geoffroy le chevalier gentils ;
> Là q'est Geoffreoy et là repose,
> Je l'ai veu, bien dire l'ose
> Pourtrait en une tombe en pierre,
> Dessoubs celle fu mis en terre[2]."

It is this grave that the young Pantagruel, while a student at Poitiers, came to visit one day[3]. Rabelais tells us that the Giant was " somewhat afraid looking upon the picture " of Geoffroy ; for he is there " set forth in the representation of a man in extreme fury, drawing his great Malchus Faulchion[4] half-way out of his scabbard."

Thus, the artist who had carved this image had represented the defunct not in an attitude of repentance, but under that

---

[1] In the picture of Hell painted by Epistemon in ch. XXX of *Pantagruel*, Rabelais makes Geoffroy-with-the-Great-Tooth, in memory of this fire, " a tinder-maker and seller of matches."

[2] The poem of *Mélusine*. (" Here is buried, besides, Geoffroy the noble knight ; it is there that Geoffroy is and there he rests, I have seen him, I well dare to say it, portrayed in a stone tomb ; beneath this was he interred ".)

[3] In this connection may be remarked the interest displayed by Rabelais in the monuments of our national history. It is the Renaissance which first considered these remnants of the past as objects worthy of study. François I himself took an interest in them. He had, says M. Jullian (*Revue bleue*, Jan. 6th, 1906), " a rival or an associate in these voyages of enquiry in the person of Pantagruel. . . . Of the two travellers, Pantagruel had the wider appreciation, for he was able to visit on a single occasion a dolmen, a Roman aqueduct, and *the graves of Knights*. He comprises the three ages of our national antiquities ".

[4] A sword with curved blade. Malchus is the name of the man whose ear St. Peter cut off, when attempting to protect Jesus, in the Garden of Olives. The people " had taken his name from him to give it to a sort of sword ", Henri Estienne tells us in his *Apologie pour Hérodote*, ed. Ristelhuber, vol. II, p. 146.

aspect of a raging warrior which the surname of Geoffroy-of-the-Big-Tooth had fixed in popular memory. Of this horrific " portraicture ", there subsists to-day only the head which was discovered, in 1834, in the ruins of Maillezais Church and brought to Niort Museum[1]. The knit brows, the hard and fixed look, the bristling moustache, the open mouth, the sharp teeth, everything in this face naïvely expresses anger, and we understand the terror of young Pantagruel and his reflection before this effigy of his ancestor : doubtless, he says, " there was some wrong done him, whereof he requireth his kindred to take revenge. I will inquire further into it, and then do what shall be reasonable."

These souvenirs of Poitou, so varied and so precise, are met with in books that Rabelais wrote five, seven, and even twenty years after he had ceased to live in this province. Besides, it is for modern commentators a surprising fact that he evokes Poitou in his work no less frequently than his native district of Chinonais. The vividness of his impressions around his thirtieth year is equal, then, to that of his childhood days, as if his senses had joyously opened out to life at the time of his wanderings in Poitou, after he had left his hard-working novitiate as a humanist at Fontenay-le-Comte. He did not, besides, neglect Latin and Greek literatures ; but his study seems to have been situated not in the Benedictine monastery of Saint-Pierre-de-Maillezais, but in the priory of Ligugé, scarce two leagues south of Poitiers.

[1] A replica of it has been aptly placed in Lusignan railway station, among the grotesque figures which adorn the entrance on the side giving upon the railway line.

CHAPTER IV

AT THE PRIORY OF LIGUGÉ

THE first in date of the French writings of Rabelais which we can read to-day was composed at Ligugé between 1524 and 1527. It is a familiar letter of one hundred decasyllabic verses addressed to a friend, Jean Bouchet, who published it in the collection of his own epistles[1], in 1545, under the following title : *Epistre de Maistre François Rabelais, homme de grans lettres grecques et latines à Jehan Bouchet, Traictant des ymaginations qu'on peut avoir touchant la chose désirée.*

That a Hellenist, who had translated the second book of Herodotus into Latin and who was, as his correspondent states, " a man of great (learning in) Greek and Latin letters ", that a scholar should have composed French verses, is a surprising thing for anyone who knows the prejudices of the learned of that time against the vulgar tongues[2]. The mother-tongue was not a tongue worthy of *savants*. A certain humanist who wrote numerous French verses excused himself for it and confessed his predilection for Latin : " Better I like of Latin the sweet sound "[3]. In the preliminary verses recommending the treatises published by Tiraqueau and Amaury Bouchard, the Fontenay jurisconsults, there did not appear one piece in French. The epistle composed at Ligugé by Rabelais offers

[1] P. xxxv, *verso*, of his *Épîtres morales et familières du Traverseur*, published by Jacques Bouchard, Poitiers, 1545, in-folio. This epistle is reprinted by Marty-Laveaux, *op. cit.*, vol. III, p. 299, along with Jean Bouchet's answer, p. 303.

[2] These prejudices were still alive in the latter half of the century, after the publication of Joachim du Bellay's *Deffence et illustration de la langue françoise ;* cf. Estienne Pasquier's complaint against M. de Tournebu, (Turnèbe), King's professor of Greek Letters in the University of Paris, who considered " that our language is too lowly to receive noble thoughts, and is fitted only for the purpose of homely matters ; so that if we conceive anything of beauty within our hearts we must express it in Latin ". *Les Lettres d'Estienne Pasquier conseiller et advocat general du Roy en la chambre des comptes de Paris*, Avignon, 1590, small 4to, p. 4.

[3] From *Dixain* LXV in *Les Trois Centuries* by Jean de Boyssonné, pub. Jacoubet, Toulouse, 1923, p. 118. We speak further on of this humanist who was a friend of Rabelais.

us, then, a new and unexpected aspect of his culture. From the years 1524 to 1527, he is not only a scholar devoted to learned pursuits. In his hours of relaxation, he writes in the vulgar tongue. He is not the humanist who spurns everything foreign to Ancient Literatures—he practises French versification. Of this initiation to the " art of second rhetoric ", as poetry was then called, it seems assured that the merit is due to his Poitevin friend, Jean Bouchet[1].

This *Grand Rhétoriqueur*,—who strikes us as so touching to-day by the zeal with which he endeavoured to apply his versifier's talent to the good of souls, and as so ridiculous by the conception he had of a poet's work—was then somewhat of a personage in Poitiers.

He exercised his profession of *procureur*, that is to say, attorney, at the Courts of Poitiers and was, at the same time, *receveur*[2], that is, agent of the powerful family of La Trémoïlle. He had acquired a respectable competency, possessed in town the *Hôtel de la Rose*, where Joan of Arc had once stayed, and, in the county, in the parish of Chauvigny, on the banks of the Vienne, the *Villette* (little villa) of the Bois-Sénebault. He was a very active practitioner and found time to write not only a treatise of judicial practice[3], an historical compilation—the *Annales d'Acquitaine* ; a collection of prayers—the *Cantiques et oraisons contemplatives de l'âme traversant les voies périlleuses du monde*[4], but numerous volumes of verse besides. In his perfectly regulated life he had decided to devote to poetry all the moments of respite which the chicanery of law and the cares of his numerous family left him : for he had eight children, four boys and four girls, of whom one daughter entered religion at the Abbey of Sainte-Croix at Poitiers at the same time as a

---

[1] Cf. on Jean Bouchet, Auguste Hamon, *Un grand Rhétoriqueur poitevin, Jean Bouchet* (1476–1557), Paris, 1901 ; Guy, *La poésie française au XVIᵉ siècle*, vol. I, and A. Richard, *Notes biographiques sur les Bouchet imprimeurs et procureurs à Poitiers au XVIᵉ siècle*, Poitiers, 1912.

[2] He himself gives this definition of the words *procureur* and *receveur*. " In civil law, they are called *Procureurs* who are entrusted not only with lawsuits and cases, but with the business and ordinary affairs of the household, whom in common speech we call *Receveurs ;* but at present we style *Procureurs* those who are engaged upon nothing else besides the conduct of law cases and suits ". *La forme et ordre de plaidoierie en toutes les courts Royales et subalternes de ce Royaume, régies par coustumes, stiles et ordonnances royaulx*, quarto, Paris, 1566, p. 15.

[3] This work was not published until after his death, in 1566.

[4] Cf. an article on this work which I published in the *Rev. XVIᵉ siècle*, vol. IX, p. 80.

sister of Ronsard, thus bringing the *Grand Rhétoriqueur* into relationship with the humanist-poet's father. He versified in his leisure hours, that is to say, from time to time on working days[1], Sundays and holidays, and during the law vacations, at harvest and vintage seasons. After thirty years he calculated that he had thus given to the Muses " ten times one thousand nine hundred and fifty hours " and he congratulated himself on these recreations so wisely employed—was it not better than to have been at the tavern " tippling between glasses and cards " ?

At the period that Rabelais met him, he had just published his *Annales d'Acquitaine* (1524) and had gained fame among the *Grands Rhétoriqueurs* by composing some allegorical poems, like the *Chappelet des Princes* dedicated to Charles de la Trémoïlle, son of Louis II, the " knight without reproach ", the *Temple de bonne renommée* and the *Labyrinthe de Fortune*, which contains a lament upon the death of Artus Gouffier, Grand-Master of France. He enjoyed the favour of the great, whom he knew how to praise in the style approved by fashion, and was well received by men of learning, for whom he professed his respectful admiration. He liked being in their company, trying to get from their learning the means of improving his French verses, staying modestly in his place[2]. Deferent, obliging, of equable character, besides being well-acquainted with the history of his province and interested in all branches of learning, the worthy *procureur* had gained the good graces of Geoffroy d'Estissac if we may judge from Rabelais' letter. With what impatience did the prelate, his nephew and his

----

[1] As can be seen from several of his epistles which are dated Saturday evening :

" Escript soudain ce samedy bien tard
Lorsque j'estois de practique à l'escard ".

(" Written in haste late this Saturday when I was freed from legal work ".)

Ep. XXX, p. xxviii *verso*.

[2]   " Desquelz parfois quelques mots je soubstraitz
Qu'a mon *vulgaire et maternel* j'atraiz
Tout en ce point que je les puis comprendre
Selon mon sens et mon petit entendre,
Non *haultement*, car des infimes suis,
Le naturel seulement je poursuis ".

(" From whom, betimes, I take some words, adapting them to my own *vulgar mother tongue*, provided that I can understand them with my small sense and understanding, and *not in order to enoble my style*, for I am of the very humblest and aim only at naturalness ".)

Ep. XXX, p. xxviii *verso*, to the Abbot of Fontaine-le-Comte.

secretary await Bouchet at Ligugé priory ! He had left seven
days previously, saying he would return by the end of the week,
and he did not come back ! The hours seemed days, the days
years, the week a century ! The " thing desired ", which
prompted wild " imaginings " and " reveries ", was his visit.
Why did he put off leaving his " study ",

> A différer ceste sollicitude
> De litiger et de patrociner[1],

to take the winged-heels " of his patron Mercury " and fly to
Ligugé on the wings of " gentle and sweet Zephyr ! " Was he
not assured of there finding great lords willing to forget their
exalted rank to pamper him ! Did he then ignore the charm
of his writings " so sweet and mellifluous ", so fitted to banish
worries and squabbles, so full of " sweetness " and of " discipline " ? Rabelais entreats him to come and let them hear

> " Ceste faconde et eloquente bouche
> Par où Pallas sa fontaine desbouche
> Et ses liqueurs castallides distille "[2].

Let him first send a " line of letter " and then come to see the
company
> " Qui de par moy de bon cœur t'en supplie "[3].

And the following four verses dated and signed this amiable
letter :
> " A Ligugé, ce matin de septembre
> Sixième jour, en ma petite chambre,
> Que de mon lict je me renouvellais
> Ton serviteur et amy Rabellays "[4].

Upon receipt of this missive Jean Bouchet sent his correspondent an *épître responsive*, which in the collection of 1545, is
presented as containing " the description of a beautiful dwelling
and praises of My Lord d'Estissac ". He first excuses himself
for having broken his promise ; the explanation being that by
his profession he is at the command of several people. If he
has been prevented from returning to see Messieurs d'Estissac

---

[1] " Postponing his eagerness for litigation and argumentation ".
[2] " That ready and eloquent mouth, through which Pallas pours forth her
fountain and distils her Castalian essences ".
[3] " Which through me right heartily invites thee ".
[4] " At Ligugé, in my little room, this September morning, the sixth day,
on which I again signed myself your servant and friend, Rabellays ".

E

it was by the " despicable jobbery of pleadings, lawsuits and causes " on which is founded his own sustenance, and that of his wife and children,—

> " Car si n'estoit le labeur de practique,
> Auquel pour vivre il fault que je m'applique,
> De trois jours l'un irois voir Ligugé "[1] ;

and he enumerates all the motives which would entice him to leave the Law Courts to go to Rabelais' retreat. First, and mainly, the charm of its situation—the banks of the Clain, gentle river, where " in green and humid meadows " the Nymphs, Naïads and Hymnides disport themselves ; the wooded slopes where the voices of Dryads, Hamadryads and Oreades re-echo, the fountains and streams of the " gentle Napæae " ; also, the " very pleasing " church of Saint-Martin ; the richness of the table, supplied with " good fruits and good wines,

> Que bien aymons entre nous Poictevins." [2]

Especially the welcome of the reverend Bishop of Maillezais,

> " Prélat dévot, de bonne conscience
> Et fort savant en divine science
> En canonique et en humanité . . ."[3].

Bouchet then proceeds to vaunt also the virtues of his nephew, a " very daring warrior " and so restrained in his manners, so " well-gifted with simple eloquence, that he is everywhere acceptable ". What a difference between the pleasant company of these persons of good family and the arrogance or boorishness of those who frequent the Law Courts, judges and clients,

> " Des palatins et gros bourgeois de ville ! "

May we always enjoy their good graces ! It is with this wish that the letter, dated September 8th, ends.

Thus, Rabelais' letter being of the 6th, to write this answer of one hundred and eight verses, Bouchet had taken less than two days ! The reason is that the themes developed in it were those which his rhetoric treated the most readily. Already, in

---

[1] " For were it not the toil of legal practice to which I must apply myself for a living, one day out of every three would I go to Ligugé ".

[2] " Which we Poitevins like well ".

[3] " A devout and conscientious prelate, very learned in Divine science, Canon Law and the humanities ".

This text is the earliest example of the use of this word *humanities*, in the sense of *humaniores literæ*. The subsequent triumph of Humanism has perpetuated its use.

another epistle to a friend, on *le plaisir des champs* (Rustic pleasures), Epistle VI, he had evoked the Hymnides, Napæae, Oreades, Naïads, Hamadryads and rustic divinities. Besides, this commonplace suited the character of the Ligugé countryside, a cool valley, watered by the Clain and girt by wooded hills[1]. Nor were his complaints about the exigencies of the legal profession which kept him from communing with the Muses, nor his regrets at being unable to enjoy more frequently the society of the Bishop of Maillezais and of Rabelais, any less sincere. We find in his verses, mixed with conventional eulogies, some information about the tastes and existence of these latter. We learn that Geoffroy d'Estissac liked cultured persons, learned in Greek and Latin, and able to discuss history or theology in French. It is for this reason that he attached to himself Rabelais, "expert in all learning", and Bouchet adds, revealing to us doubtless a wish of his learned friend :

> " Tu ne pouvais trouver meilleur service
> Pour te pourvoir bien tost de bénéfice "[2].

On one point Bouchet's epistle does not satisfy our curiosity and does not come up to the promise of its sub-title : we look in vain in it for the " description of a beautiful dwelling ". The site is described : the " very pleasing " Saint-Martin's church is merely referred to, Bouchet being deficient in the vocabulary needed to describe the charming doorway in flamboyant gothic with deep covings and spirals of slender pillars[3] ;

[1] This landscape, like nearly all those of the Poitou countryside, is by no means grandiose, but it is gay and fresh. Huysmans commented upon it when he paid a visit to Ligugé in 1898. He described the " sinuous " and " loitering " River Clain thus—" It trifles along its course, amusing itself by dividing and reuniting, traversing a wide valley whose horizons are made pleasing by bright hills, passing between rows of poplars whose foliage, on a windy day, makes a noise like the sea breaking upon a shore ". Article in the *Revue encyclopédique Larousse*, 24 Dec., 1898. He later resided for a while at Ligugé, where he was admitted as a Benedictine lay-monk in 1901. Upon the departure of the Benedictines, in the end of the same year, he abandoned Poitou, " that horrible Poitou ", as he called it. He did not know it well. He had only twice walked in the country and had returned home " so disgusted with the trees which were dwarfed, the hills which were ridiculously low, the streams which were muddy, the birds which did not sing and the peasants who sang too much ", that he swore never to leave his garden and never to take any other road than that which led to the Monastery. Cf. Raoul Aubry, *Les Travaux de M. J. K. Huysmans, oblat*, in the *Temps*, 8th Jan., 1902.

[2] " You could not find better service
To provide you soon with preferment ".

[3] There are, on either side of the doorway, prismatic stone columns, tapering and surmounted with small fleurons, which Rabelais calls *lardoires* (" larding-sticks ") on account of their resemblance to cooking-spits. *Fourth Book*, ch. XXIX.

but nothing is said of the dwelling-house proper. Presumably it was very modest.

The Priory of Ligugé[1], founded by Saint Martin, attached in the 12th century to the Abbey of Maillezais, had been transformed into a fortress by the English during the Hundred Years War. In 1359, the inhabitants of Smarve and other neighbouring towns, taking advantage of the absence of a garrison, demolished this abode of soldiers[2]. The religious who came back to settle down in the ruins of the conventual buildings (the dormitory and refectory which had been big and sumptuous, says Bouchet, had been knocked down) were long unable to repair them. Abbot Jean d'Amboise, to whom, as Bishop of Maillezais, the Monastery reverted in 1475, undertook the reconstruction of Saint-Martin's church and to him are due, most probably, the present belfry and great door, completed perhaps on his translation to the episcopal see of Langres (1481). But there is no indication of his having given the same care to repairing the ruined or dilapidated buildings. It is thus likely that the Priory of Ligugé, in Geoffroy d'Estissac's day, had nothing of the pleasing aspect or of the rich decoration of his dwellings of L'Hermenault or Coulonges-les-Royaux. We have some idea of the plan of this monastery : its general disposition was the same as it is still to-day, with this difference, that to the north was a forest of full-grown trees " where *Trut* was played ", says an 18th-century text[3]. But the accurate appearance of the buildings is more difficult of reconstitution. Perhaps the Priory had still that fortress-like appearance that so many monasteries in Poitou had taken on during the Hundred Years War. In the northern portion of the outside walls, a round, squat tower is inserted, which is still called " Rabelais' tower " (*tour de Rabelais*), a very old name for it, already found in a manuscript memoir upon Ligugé composed at the beginning of the 17th century[4]. Is it there was placed

---

[1] Dom Chamard has written a monograph thereon, *Saint-Martin et son monastère de Ligugé* (Poitiers, 1873), of which a second, revised and corrected edition is being prepared by Dom de Monsabert, and will shortly appear.

[2] Jean Bouchet, *Annales d'Aquitaine* (Monnin's edition, 1644), p. 208.

[3] *Le livre des plans du prieuré de Saint-Martin de Ligugé et des fiefs en dépendant*, Archives de la Vienne, pp. 72, 75. Rabelais mentions (*Gargantua*, ch. XXII) two children's games of which the names contain this word *tru* : *l'aiau tru* and *l'archer tru*. It is not known what they consisted in.

[4] " Turrim quoque Rabelæsi nomine denotavere, quippe in ea dictus Rabelais libros conscripsit nugacium calculos multi faciendos ". Note by Dom Estiennot, in Dom Fonteneau's Registers, Municipal Library of Poitiers.

this "little chamber" from which Geoffroy d'Estissac's secretary wrote in bed, on a September morning, to Jean Bouchet ?

The beauty and decoration of this Priory were, next to its situation, the gardens placed to its south ; they were rich in vegetables and fruit-trees of every sort. Horticulture seems to have been one of the Bishop of Maillezais' favourite pastimes. Like the Bishop of Le Mans, René du Bellay, who, at the same period, acclimatised in the gardens of Touvoie, his summer-residence, ebony-trees, pistachio-trees, and other exotic plants[1], Geoffroy d'Estissac delighted in enriching and embellishing his gardens of L'Hermenault and of Ligugé. We shall see how Rabelais will play up to this whim of his protector by sending him from Rome the seeds of salads, artichokes, carrots, melons and various ornamental plants. It is the setting of these gardens of Ligugé, regularly mapped out in the style of the time, under the trellis-archways, between the flower-beds edged by narrow box borders, that we most readily figure Maître François Rabelais conversing with the Bishop of Maillezais and his guest, the *procureur*, Jean Bouchet.

Quite near Ligugé, hardly a league distant, another monastery received frequent visits from Bouchet and Rabelais. This was the Abbey of Fontaine-le-Comte. Founded in 1127, by Guy de Loroux, or Loriol[2], in the middle of woods and waste lands which William VIII, Count of Poitiers, had granted to him, this Abbey of Augustine monks had undergone the same fate during the Hundred Years War as Ligugé Priory. Sacked by the English, it had been ruined by the inhabitants of Poitiers, who thus prevented the enemy from transforming it into a fortress. It subsequently found a protector in the person of Jean, Duc de Berry. Its church was restored in the 15th century by Abbot Guy Dousset who "had it much repaired",

---

Dom de Monsabert, a fellow-member of the *Société des Antiquaires de l'Ouest*, has suggested to me that readers of Bouchet's epistle probably hit upon the smallest room in the monastery as being Rabelais' study, viz. the one in the narrow northern tower. Hence the name *Rabelais' tower*.

[1] Cf. *La Vie aventureuse de Pierre Belon*, by Dr. Delaunay, Paris, Champion pub., 1926, pp. 86 *seqq.*

[2] On the Abbey of Fontaine-le-Comte cf. Rédet, *Notice historique sur l'abbaye de Fontaine-le-Comte près Poitiers* (Mémoires de la Société des Antiquaires de l'Ouest, t. III, pp. 226–231) ; Brutails, *Geoffroi du Louroux et ses constructions* (Bibliothèque de l'École des Chartes, janvier-juin, 1922) and Salvini, *L'Abbaye de Bonnevaux et l'architecture monastique au début du XIIe siècle dans la région de Poitiers* (*Bulletin de la Société des Antiquaires de l'Ouest*, du 2e trimestre de 1923).

says an inscription carved on the façade, and by Ardillon, first Abbot of the name, whose arms, three buckle-tongues, can be seen on a crest forming a keystone in the transept. The monastery buildings were to be again ravaged by the Protestants. Only very small portions of them are still remaining : sombre old dwellings, a door surmounted by a chiselled shield, and crowned with machicoulis. The church, Romanesque in style, still shows by its vast proportions how great was formerly the importance of the monastery.

In François I's time, this Abbey had at its head Antoine Ardillon whom Rabelais mentions twice in his works[1]. He observed strictly the rule of residence, but willingly opened his house to cultured clerics and layfolk. Already in 1517, we find him in touch with Jean Bouchet[2], who has preserved for us in his *Épîtres* the names and professions of some of his guests. There were Messire Jacques Prévost, doctor of Theology, regent in the University of Poitiers ; Nicolas Petit, licenciate in Laws ; the Franciscan Trojan ; another religious, Quentin, a great traveller ; Jacques de Puytesson, canon of the collegiate church of St. John the Baptist at Ménigoute[3] ; and sometimes, no doubt, Jean d'Auton, Abbot of Angle-sur-Anglin. Upon one occasion it was a group of students, of " scholars lovers of the Muses "[4]. From the depths of his lawyer's office piled up with bags of legal documents, Jean Bouchet dreamed of this learned company assembled in Fontaine's fresh valley :

" Clers ruisseaux,
Boys verdoyans et petits arbrisseaux !
Où bien souvent se trouve, au cler matin,
Ce Rabelay, sans oublier Quentin,
Trojan, Petit, tous divers en vesture
Et d'ung vouloir en humaine escriture "[5].

However motley this group of Augustinians, Franciscans and

---

[1] *Pantagruel*, ch. V ; *Third Book*, ch. XLIII.

[2] The *Labyrinthe de Fortune* is preceded by a Latin epistle of Ardillon's, *Johanni Boucheto, viro eruditissimo atque humanissimo*, and Bouchet's reply. Bouchet dedicated his *Annales d'Aquitaine* to Ardillon.

[3] In the arrondissement of Parthenay (Deux-Sèvres). It had been founded in 1324, and the right of presenting to its canonical benefices belonged to the barony of La Mothe-Sainte-Héraye.

[4] Information given in nos. I, XXX and LXXXV of the *Épîtres familières*. A neo-latin poet, whom we later mention, Salmon Macrin, of Loudun, dedicated one of his odes to Ardillon.

[5] Ep. XXX. (" Clear streams, verdant woods and young trees ! Where often in the clear morning is to be found Rabelais, not forgetting Quentin, Trojan and Petit, all different in vesture, but of one will in the study of the humanities ".)

Benedictines, " different in dress ", may have seemed to Bouchet, they were, indeed, only religious, teachers, theologians and canons. Laymen were rare, and, at Fontaine-le-Comte, as at Ligugé, the circle in which Rabelais lived seems to us rather narrow. They rarely leave the cloister and the conversation in the " verdant woods " is between persons who have nearly all professed to renounce the world.

The close reading of Bouchet's epistles and the examination of the preliminary verses to his works, written by his friends, show us, however, that Rabelais' companions were far from being shut off from the world. Some of them, like Quentin, D'Auton and Bouchet, had travelled in France and abroad. Bouchet was in correspondence with poets in Dieppe and Rouen, with an advocate of Tours, with Messire Louis de Ronsard. Antoine Ardillon was in relations with a poet-humaniste, Nicolas Bourbon of Vandœuvre[1]. All, or nearly all, of them had some knowledge of " *l'humaine écriture* ", as Bouchet puts it, that is to say of profane literature. The names of Sallust and of Cicero, of Horace and of Virgil, are quoted in their letters.

They have read the poetry of the rhymers then in vogue, the *Grands Rhétoriqueurs*. Ardillon, in the preliminary epistle to the *Labyrinth of Fortune*, extols the talent of the principal masters of this school : André de la Vigne, Octovien de Saint-Gelais, Guillaume Crétin. Jean Bouchet, for his part, extolled Chastellain, Meschinot, Jean Lemaire de Belges. The *Illustrations des Gaules et singularités de Troie*, the *magnum opus* of this last, excited Jean Quentin to transports of admiration[2]. " What naturalness ! " he cries in a Latin epistle placed in front of the *Annales d'Aquitaine*, " and what learning ! It is the greatest glory and finest ornament of our time ! "

Even Italian literature was not entirely unknown to this group of Poitevins. Jean d'Auton had formerly accompanied King Louis XII to Genoa and Lombardy, as his historiographer-royal. Jean Bouchet had lived at Lyons in 1497,

---

[1] The *Nugæ* of this neo-latin poet (Lyons, Gryphius, 1538) contain a poem (VIII, 18) dedicated to Ardillon.

[2] " Amplissimæ nostri temporis gloriæ maximo est ornamento vir dignus, quem in numero veterum præcipuum loces, Joannes Marius Belga, vir, o Musæ, quanti candoris ! quam multarum litterarum ! qui a primis nascentis mundi cunabulis, in sua usque tempora, perpetuo historiæ filo, acute simul, et accurate res gallicas deduxit : in quo eloquentiæ multum, est enim in narrando miræ jucunditatis, sed longe plus scientiæ reperies ". He declared it to be superior to Livy in its richness, *lactea ubertate*.

that is, after the return of the first Italian expedition, at the time when the second town in France, peopled by bankers and merchants from beyond the Alps, was beginning to undergo the influence of the Italian Renaissance. Antoine Ardillon, in this same Latin epistle, which opens the *Labyrinth of Fortune*, cites Dante and another Italian, Francesco Philelpho, whose treatise on education, *De educatione puerorum*, had been published at Poitiers, in 1500, by a *maître* of Bouchet's, Julien Tortereau[1]. They talked then, of Italy, and appreciated the Italians, in this circle at Fontaine-le-Comte ; it is there, perhaps, that Rabelais conceived his ardent desire of visiting Rome which he was to satisfy some years later.

Discussions on profane literature were not the only glimpses of the outside world that Ardillon's guests had. All Christendom was resounding with Luther's daring.

How could these religious and devout laymen have abstained from talking of the Church's woes and of the projects for reform which then preoccupied all thinking minds ? What did they, who delighted in the *lettres humaines*, think of the Sorbonne's hostility towards the humanists ?—Rabelais, who, at the Puy-Saint-Martin, had suffered from this conflict, must have been anxious to know the opinions his new friends held about the Faculty of Theology. Jean Bouchet, it is true, reproved the errors of "that poor and imprudent Luther" ; he was aggrieved at the blasphemies of his sectaries " for which good Christians should have tears in their eyes[2] " ; but he was none the less saddened to see theologians adhering to scholastic philosophy and losing themselves in subtleties instead of meditating upon the Scriptures :

> " Quand nous parlons de l'Écriture Sainte
> C'est seulement la Bible où n'y a feinte,
> Fard, ne mensonge : à elle croire il faut,
> Quant aux docteurs, souvent y a deffaut
> En aucuns dicts et souvent se discordent . . .
> L'opinion des hommes n'est pas sûre
> Si du haut Dieu ne vient, qui seul l'assure.
> Mais ce qui est dedans la Bible écrit
> Est inspiré du benoit Sainct-Esprit "[3].

---

[1] A. Hamon, *Jean Bouchet*, p. 87, note.

[2] Cf. *Annales d'Aquitaine*, ch. XIII.

[3] *Épîtres morales*, III, *A Messieurs les Prédicateurs, concionateurs et déclamateurs du verbe divin* . . . composed between 1521 and 1528, published in 1545. (" When we speak of Holy Scripture, it is solely the Bible where there

He professed the greatest respect for ecclesiastics : " for a layman should not speak ill of them ", he said ; he declared that there are, " keeping in the shade ", much more good people than is commonly believed : but he was indignant at the ignorance, the impudence, and the hypocrisy of certain monks, exploiters of the credulity of the mob, sellers of false relics, who

> " Font accroire aux simples imbéciles
> Pauvres d'esprit, à croire trop faciles,
> Qu'ils s'en iront au Paradis tout droict,
> Si leur devoir font de payer le droit,
> Par eux mis sus, de quelque confrarie "[1].

Rabelais will not find more violent terms to stigmatise the practices of these bad monks, whom Bouchet, before him, calls *cafards* and *chattemittes*.

It is the Church herself which should reform these abuses. Bishops should visit the monasteries twice yearly, superintend the parochial clergy and the monks, and not tolerate ignorance among their priests.

Thus, it was not on the Pope that Jean Bouchet counted to cure the ills of the Church. Among the group at Fontaine-le-Comte eyes were not turned towards Rome. The memory of the last conflict of the Holy See with the King of France, during which two of Antoine Ardillon's intimates had taken up the pen for the French cause, was still alive there. That was in 1511. King Louis XII, on the point of declaring war on Pope Julius II, who was leaguing Italy against France, had endeavoured to reassure the French Catholics' conscience. He had caused the temporal ambitions of the Holy See to be condemned by the Council of Tours and endeavoured to influence public opinion through writers. Pierre Gringore had held up the Pope to ridicule on the boards of the market-place, in the *Jeu du prince des Sotz*. Jean Lemaire de Belges had exposed and upheld the policy of the King of France in the *Traité de la différence des schismes et des conciles*. Jean d'Auton had

is neither pretence, hypocrisy nor falsehood : we must believe it. As to the Doctors there often are defects in some of their sayings and they often differ. . . . The opinion of men is not sure unless it come from the High God, who alone makes it trustworthy. But that which is written in the Bible is inspired of the blessed Holy Ghost ".)

[1] Epistre III. (" Who make simple fools, poor of wit and too easily credulous, believe that they will go straight to Paradise if they acquit themselves of the payment of an offering to some confraternity, which they themselves have imposed ".)

published an *Épître élégiaque pour l'Église militante*[1] (1511) and Jean Bouchet, in his *Déploration de l'Église militante* (12 March, 1512) had implored the King not to abandon the Church. He advised him to assemble a Council. Come together, he said to kings and princes :

> " Vous efforceans faire faire ung Concile
> Au père Sainct, prélatz et Cardinaux ;
> Et cela faict, ne sera difficille
> De corriger par doctrine facile
> Les dictz abus, erreurs, crimes et maux "[2].

Louis XII, did, in fact, despite Pope and Cardinals, bring together at Pisa a Council whose aim was to suspend Julius II from all pontifical administration. But the fortune of arms turned against France. The Pope took advantage of it to rise up and set against her the King of Spain, the Emperor, and the King of England, Henry VIII. It is upon this occasion that Jean Bouchet composed a long fictitious epistle " from Henry VII to Henry VIII ", in which he attributes to the late King of England numerous arguments to dissuade the reigning King from going to war against Louis XII and joining the Pope's party. For, what faith can be had in this Julius II who does not hesitate to " put on harness instead of cope " and mingle with the soldiers ?

> " Faut-il que lui qui se dit Père Sainct
> Soit proditeur et homme double et fainct !
> Las ! faut-il voir la chaire de saint Pierre
> Teincte de sang ?   Quel horrible tonnerre !
> O quelle éclipse et scandalle en l'Église "[3].

Thus Rabelais found at Fontaine-le-Comte two writers who had made themselves the semi-official apologists of the royal cause in Louis XII's dispute with the Holy See ; and the two editions which Bouchet published in 1525 and 1526, of the

---

[1] Mentioned by H. Guy in his *Histoire de la poésie française au XVIe siècle*, vol. I, p. 274, note. Only one copy of this epistle is known—in the Library of Leningrad.

[2] (" Bending your efforts towards making the Holy Father, prelates and cardinals come together in a Council, and when that is done it will not be difficult to correct by clear teaching the said abuses, errors, crimes and evils ".)

[3] *Épîtres familières*, " Henry VII to Henry VIII ". [" Should he who calls himself the Holy Father be a traitor, double-dealer and hypocrite ? Alas ! to see the throne of Peter tinged with blood ! What a horrible thunderbolt ! What an eclipse and scandal in the Church ! "]

Déploration de l'Église militante perhaps revived sentiments of animosity against Rome, or, at the very least, recalled the attention of Ardillon's guests to the Gallican claims.

Rabelais will remember it some years later, when, in a chapter of *Pantagruel*, he shows us Jean Lemaire de Belges, in Hell, mimicking the Pope's ritual gestures[1], while Julius II shorn of " his great buggerly beard "[2], reduced for a living to selling pudding-pies, is whipped by his master, the pastry-cook, for having let himself be defrauded of his wares by Pathelin.

We can, therefore, get an idea of what Rabelais' discourses were with Abbot Ardillon's *habitués* at Fontaine-le-Comte. Among his companions, there is one who was openly to pass over to heresy, the Friar Minor, Jean Trojan, who, in 1537, preached Calvinism to the students of Poitiers[3]. The others, for the greater part, will belong to that third party which, while remaining in the bosom of the Catholic Church, will keep at equal distance from the uncompromising traditionalists,—like the Sorbonne theologians,—and the heretics, Lutherans and Calvinists. The Council of Trent was later to satisfy their desire for reforms. Towards 1525, they were speaking of it among themselves. The ideas which Rabelais will set forth in his humorous books on superstitious practices, pilgrimages, the cult of relics and the ignorance of monks, were theirs. But he will give them another tone, often a different significance, and will mingle boldly with them the most pitiless ridicule of the defenders of orthodoxy, the Sorbonne Theologians.

[1] *Pantagruel*, ch. **XXX** : " I saw Master John le Maire there personate the Pope, in such fashion that he made all the poor kings and popes of this world kiss his feet ; and, taking great state upon him, gave them his benediction . . ."

[2] *Ibid.*, Julius II's contemporaries had been shocked at this Pope's reverting to wearing a beard, a custom which had long been abandoned by preceding Popes. Cf. Gringore, *Espoir de Paix* :
"Anacletus deffent porter en face
Longues barbes à tous prestres : mais quoy ?
Cil la porte, qui deust garder la loy ".
(" Anacletus forbids all priests to wear the beard long on their faces : but what ? he, who should observe the law, wears one ".)
In the *Fourth Book*, ch. XII, Rabelais returns to the " fury of Pope Julius the Second " against which " the Duke of Ferrara, with the help of the French, bravely defended himself " ; and, in ch. L, he recalls having seen Popes " not with their pallium, amice or rotchet on, but with helmets on their heads ".

[3] According to A. Lièvre, *Histoire des protestants et des Églises réformées du Poitou*, Poitiers, 1903, 1 vol. 8vo.

Thus the intellectual horizon of the monks and pious laymen with whom Rabelais associated at Ligugé and at Fontaine-le-Comte was less limited than might at first be supposed. Our Humanist seems, in addition, to have derived an unexpected advantage from his relations with Jean Bouchet. It is, seemingly, at the instigation of this copious *Rhétoriqueur*, who hardly allowed a week to elapse without rhyming, that he practised the art of versifying. Doubtless, his epistle from Ligugé does not attest any great skill: the rule of alternative masculine and feminine rimes which was beginning to be observed in the school, is not observed in it (no more, indeed, than in Jean Bouchet's answering letter). But Rabelais will improve in this art of " second rhetoric " and will rhyme on several occasions when writing his books in the vernacular.

Pantagruel, indeed, contains some poems intended to set off the narrations, such as the epitaph of Badebec, the *blason* of the licentiates of Orleans University, the *rondeau* sent by Panurge to the Parisian lady with whom he was in love, several distichs, two " *dictons victoriaux* ", inscriptions to commemorate the prowesses of Pantagruel and of Panurge in the War of the Dipsodes. *Gargantua* affords (besides some distichs and the two obscene short poems in ch. XIII) three pieces in verse of greater length: *The Antidoted Fanfreluches* (ch. II), the *Énigme trouvé aux fondements de l'abbaye de Thélème* (ch. LVIII), and the *Inscription set upon the great Gate of Thélème* (ch. LIV). If we except the *Fanfreluches* and the *Enigma*, which are (Rabelais himself tells us so for the latter of these poems) Mellin de Saint-Gelais'[1], the *Inscription* is the only one which shows a skilled hand in the poetic art of the period[2]. It presents certain characteristics which were then considered very distinguished. It is decorated with *rimes équivoques*, that is to say, " rich rimes ", and with *rimes batelées*, that is, repeated at the cæsura, at the end of the first hemistich. This fondness for numerous assonances and these reduplicated rimes seem to us to-day vain artifices of versification: they were the *Rhétoriqueurs'* glory, and it is certainly through them that Rabelais got his name as a poet; for Marot writing in 1537, his epistle to Sagon under the name of Fripelipes, his

---

[1] On the relations between Rabelais and Mellin de Saint-Gelais, cf. my article in *R.É.R.*, IX, pp. 90–108.

[2] For a study of Rabelais as a poet, I take the liberty of referring to an article which I published in *R.É.R.*, X, pp. 291–304.

valet, placed him among contemporary poets in very good company :

> " Je ne voy point qu'un Saint-Gelais
> Un Héroët, un Rabelais,
> Un Brodeau, un Sève, un Chappuy
> Voysent [aillent] escrivant contre luy "[1].

And Sagon, in his reply, was very careful not to dispute the talent or the authority of any of these poets :

> " On sait assez que ces huit ont renom
> Comme Marot, au mieux s'entendre en rime "[2].

Rabelais could have attributed his success as a poet to Jean Bouchet, from whom he had received his first lessons in versification at Poitiers, at his *logis de la Rose*, in the gardens of Ligugé, or again in the shaded woods of Fontaine-le-Comte.

He has never introduced the grave *Rhétoriqueur's* name into his humorous works. But, at least he amused himself by evoking the pen-name of *Traverseur des voies périlleuses*, which Bouchet had adopted after the publication of his book : the *Regnards traversant les voies périlleuses des folles fiances du monde.* Among Pantagruel's companions making ready for the country of *la Dive Bouteille*, Rabelais has placed one *Traverseur des voies périlleuses*, thus giving to the bold navigator the pseudonym of a timorous moralist who had seen only from afar the reef of the " fond trustings of the world "[3].

[1] " I do not notice Saint-Gelais, Héroët, Rabelais, Brodeau, Sève or Chappuy setting out to write against him."

[2] " It is well known that these eight have, like Marot, the reputation of being very proficient in poetry ".

[3] *Fourth Book*, ch. I ; " Xenomanes, the great traveller and traverser of perilous ways ". It is, besides, possible that the Xenomanes thus named by Rabelais, is to some extent modelled upon Jean Fonteneau, called Alphonse the Saintongeois, who had been Roberval's pilot on his voyage to Canada in 1542. M. Abel Lefranc expounds this theory in his *Navigations de Pantagruel* (Paris, Leclerc, 1905, 8vo), pp. 65–68.

CHAPTER V

VISITS TO POITIERS

From Ligugé, Rabelais could easily go to Poitiers, which was then, with Lyons, the greatest town in France, after Paris.[1] It is true that this town, for a good third of the territory enclosed by its boundary walls, resembled the country. Built upon a long ridge of hill, on a spur cut off to the south by the moats of La Tranchée and by a wall which descended the hill on both sides and encircled it at the foot, it was covered by houses only on the plateau. Practically all its slopes were given over to vines, meadows and cultivated land. The whole had a rustic appearance. Charles V, who passed through in 1539, called it a "big village" and, a century later, La Fontaine having visited it on his journey to Limousin, wrote : "Poitiers is what is properly termed a *villace*[2], which between houses and arable lands may have a circuit of two or three leagues ; a town badly-paved, full of students, abounding in priests and monks".

The geographer Mercator notes the "excellent structure of the buildings "[3] in this singular town, rich in vineyards and in tilled land. Rabelais mentions some of them : the "bourgeois' parlour ", that is to say, the Town Hall, where plays were sometimes produced[4], and the Law Courts[5], former palace of the Counts of Poitou, whose great hall, with its beautiful Romanesque arcatures, and the Gothic fire-place of Jean, Duc de Berry, then sheltered small mercers' stalls, like the famous Paris *Galerie du Palais*.

Another of Poitiers' monumental curiosities had attracted

---

[1] "Great and strong cities, not a jot less than Lyons or Poictiers ". *Pantagruel*, ch. XXXII.

[2] *Villace*, a large straggling, scarcely populated town. *Voyage en Limousin*, Letter VI.

[3] *Atlas*, 1609 edition.

[4] " I defy the devils of Saulmur . . . nay, by gad, even those of Poictiers, *with their parlour* ". *Fourth Book*, ch. XIII. Now the seat of the Société des Antiquaires de l'Ouest.

[5] *Third Book*, ch. XLI.

Rabelais' attention. In the midst of a carousal the giant
Pantagruel, wishing to have a bell hanging from his chin to
ring a peal " at the wagging of our chops ", fixes his choice
upon one of the biggest bells in France, that of Poitiers[1].
It was, in truth, a considerable mass, weighing 18,600 pounds.
It had been presented by Jean, Duc de Berry. To house it there
had been erected opposite the church of Notre-Dame-la-Grande
a massive tower in three storeys, surmounted by a framework with lead-roofed campanile, which, in the old views of
Poitiers, dominates all the other buildings in the town[2].

Poitiers offered numerous other " venerable " edifices : a
Roman amphitheatre, Romanesque churches like Saint-
Hilaire and Notre-Dame-la-Grande, private mansions such as
l'Hôtel Fumée, to-day the seat of the Faculty of Letters.
Even Renaissance architecture, which was to leave its imprint
on so many buildings, was already represented there by the
elegant dwelling of the financier René Berthelot. But another
building in similar style was to furnish Rabelais with themes
for " *pourtraicture* " or description ; it was the castle that
Messire Guillaume Gouffier, Admiral of France, brother of
Arthur Gouffier, the Grand-Master, had built four leagues from
Poitiers, at Bonnivet, between 1513 and 1525.

It is, without any doubt, the Castle of Bonnivet " one of
the richest in the kingdom of France "[3], which was Rabelais'
model for his description of the " manor " of the Abbey of
Thélème. The text of the early editions of *Gargantua* (1534–
1535, 1537) states so explicitly : " This same building, says
the narrator, was a hundred times more magnificent *than is
Bonnivet*. . . ." He will add later : " or Chambourg (Cham-
bord), or Chantilly "[4].

Of these three examples of the Franco-Italian architecture
of our Renaissance, Bonnivet is perhaps the only one which
Rabelais had been able to examine at the time when he was
composing *Gargantua*. " Monsieur l'Admiral " was a great
personage in Poitou. Through his influence, Jean Bouchet

---

[1] *Pantagruel*, ch. XXVI.
[2] As this belfry was falling into ruins, it was decided, in 1787, to knock it
down. It was finally demolished in 1815. On its site to-day stand the buildings of the Law Faculty and of the Municipal Library.
[3] Jean Bouchet thus describes it in his *Annales d'Aquitaine*, ed. Monnin,
1643, p. 372.
[4] *Gargantua*, ch. LIII.

tells us, the town of Poitiers had been exempted, in 1522, from providing soldiers for the campaign of Picardy[1]. And in this connection the annalist mentions this stately castle of Bonnivet, in the neighbourhood of Poitiers, as one of the glories of the province. It is probable that Rabelais and Geoffroy d'Estissac had occasion to visit this dwelling.

Bonnivet was destroyed in 1788. Of it there remain some fragments of sculpture placed in the Municipal Museum at Poitiers and in a hall belonging to the *Société des Antiquaires de l'Ouest*. Some drawings, executed in the 17th century, allow us to reconstitute it with sufficient precision. It was formed of several blocks of buildings, disposed according to a regular plan, and flanked at each corner with a round tower. These towers, by a desire for symmetry rare enough at the time, had all the same diameter and the same profile. In the middle of the main group of buildings, a staircase was placed in the building itself and no longer, following the custom of preceding centuries, in a special tower. It was lit by semicircular windows. The decoration, pilasters, medallions, cornices, and compartment-ceilings, were Italian in character.

Now, the general architectural features of the Thelemites' manor correspond to those of Bonnivet. " The architecture was in a figure hexagonal, and in such a fashion that in every one of the six corners there was built a great round tower . . . and were all of a like form and bigness. . . . Between every tower, in the midst of the said body of buildings there was a pair of winding, such as we now call lanthorn stairs, and one with the building itself. . . . In every resting place were two fair antique arches, where the light came in, and by those they went into a cabinet, made even with, and of the breadth of the said winding. . . ."[2]

Doubtless, these architectural arrangements are those of the greater number of the castles built under François I. Except for the regularity of the plan, which was exceptional for the time, they are characteristic of the Franco-Italian architecture of our Renaissance. It is none the less true that Bonnivet is the only castle of the time with which Rabelais at first thought of comparing his Abbey of Thélème. We

---

[1] *Annales d'Aquitaine, ibid.* Rabelais (*Gargantua*, ch. IX) refers to his motto—*Festina lente* with a dolphin on an anchor.

[2] *Gargantua*, ch. LIII.

should only perhaps seek in this famous manor a "*pour-traicture*" embellished, enriched and, especially, increased to gigantic proportions, of the castle of Monsieur l'Admiral. The description of Thélème, so noteworthy by reason of its rich-ness and precision of vocabulary, comes in part from the memory of an edifice which was the pride of the province of Poitou.

As in La Fontaine's day, and perhaps even much more so, Poitiers, in the time of Rabelais, was a town full of students. It could count four thousand of them according to the report of the Venetian ambassador, Andrea Navagero, who visited it in 1528, and this figure is confirmed by the testimony of a com-piler, Chasseneux, who lived there for three years about the same time.

This affluence of students was due to the reputation of its University which was then counted the second in France by reason of its valuable legal teaching[1]. Founded in 1431 by Charles VII, then "King of Bourges", to take the place in his Kingdom of the University of Paris, which had become English, the University of Poitiers counted four Faculties—Arts, Theology, Medicine and Law.

The Faculty of Arts was composed of seven colleges, of which the most famous were the colleges of Sainte-Marthe and of Le Puygarreau.

The theological faculty was undistinguished[2]. The Faculty of Medicine was not destined to become famous until the end of the century[3]. On the other hand, the Faculty of Law was long since celebrated[4]. It included the teaching of

---

[1] Some testimonies are worth quoting, especially Christophe de Longueil's : " Attamen arbitratus me egregium a litterarum studiis fructum percepturum, nisi juris etiam vestri (sc. romani) prudentia animum excolerem, contuli me Pictaviam, Aquitaniæ urbem, cum frequenti studiosæ juventutis cœtu, tum divini humanique juris professorum doctrina inter eas gentes haud igno-bilem ". *Christophori Longolii civis Ro. perduellionis rei defensio* (Rome, 1519) f. 7 ; and, then, those of the geographers Sebastian Munster (1550) and Mercator.

[2] Only one of its teachers has left a name—Nicolas des Orbeaux, author of an *Expositio in IV libros sententiarum*, published in 1498, and again in 1509, 1511 and 1515. He was a Scotist. In his catalogue of St. Victor's Library Rabelais represents him as the ridiculous commentator of a book on the mutterings of baboons and monkeys : *Marmotretus de Baboinis et Cingis, cum commento d'Orbellis.*

[3] Cf. P. Rambaud, *Bulletin de la Société des Antiquaires de l'Ouest*, 1923 : *L'ancienne faculté de médecine de Poitiers.*

[4] The origins and early history of this Faculty have been described by M. Audinet in the *Bulletin de la Société des Antiquaires de l'Ouest*, 1922, pp. 17–46.

F

ecclesiastical or canon law and of civil law, each having two chairs occupied by "regenting Doctors". The most eminent teacher of this Faculty was then a Scot, Robert Irland, whom Rabelais mentions under the name of "the most decretali-potent Scotch Doctor "[1].

Was he a pupil of his? Must we attribute to the narrator himself these declarations of two of the personages of his book, one of Judge Bridoye (Bridle-goose): "At the time when at Poictiers I was a student of law "[2], and the other of Panurge, "One day by chance I happened to read a chapter of them (the *Decretals*) at Poictiers, at the most decretalipotent Scotch Doctor's "[3]? Is it from Robert Irland, or at his lectures that he got this law student's witticism that the closed book which appears in the arms of the old University of Poitiers is none other than the *Decretals*[4]?

We have no document to attest Rabelais' matriculation as a student of the University of Poitiers[5]. But it is incontestable that from 1532 he was familiar with the works of law and juris-prudence commented in the law-schools: the *Pandects*, the *Code*, the *Institutes*, the *Decretum*, the *Decretals*. It is possible he acquired this knowledge at the hands of the professors of the University of Poitiers, so famous for legal studies[6].

[1] *Fourth Book*, beginning of ch. LII. Robert Irland professed for sixty years and had some distinguished pupils, one of them being the jurisconsult Eguinarius Baron. A son of his, Bonaventure Irland, was also a professor in the same Faculty. The house of this Irland family was situated in the street still named *rue des Écossais*. Battendier, a pupil and friend of Boyssonné, the humanist, naming all the best known professors of law and comparing them with Alciat, mentions the Scot among those who attracted students to Poitiers : "*Pictavi Scotum audivi*". Letter dated from Chambéry, Nones of June 1547 ; cf. *Rev. XVIᵉ siècle*, 1926, p. 240.

[2] *Third Book*, ch. XLI.

[3] *Fourth Book*, ch. LII.

[4] "I will discover you a great secret. The Universities of your world have commonly a book either open or shut in their arms and devices : what book do you think it is? Truly, I do not know, answered Pantagruel ; I never read it. It is the *Decretals*, said Homenas, without which the privileges of all Universities would soon be lost". *Fourth Book*, ch. LIII. The arms of the University of Poitiers were a closed book on which was painted a gilt crucifix, with the motto : *Crescentes in scientia Dei*.

[5] The University Registers for the 16th century are lost, with the exception of the Register of Graduates in the Faculty of Laws for the years 1576–1595, which is kept at the Municipal Library. Moreover, no academic qualifications, nor proofs of previous studies done, were asked for to gain admission to the Law Faculty.

[6] The lectures in Law hardly ever ceased. During the summer vacation there were, at least in the second half of the 16th century, extraordinary lectures (*prælectiones extraordinariæ*) in Canon Law, which were attended by all sorts of people—theologians and philosophers, disputing according to their

He knew well the life of the Poitevin students. He amused himself by connecting with the prowess of his giant Pantagruel some of their traditional rites. " So he came to Poictiers, where as he studied and profited very much, he saw that the scholars were oftentimes at leisure, and knew not how to bestow their time, which moved him to take such compassion on them, that one day he took from a long ledge of rocks, called then Passelourdin, a huge great stone, of about twelve fathom square, and fourteen handfuls thick, and with great ease set it upon four pillars in the midst of a field, to no other end, but that the said scholars, when they had nothing else to do, might pass their time in getting up on that stone and feast [there] with store of flagons, gammons and pasties, and carve their names upon it with a knife, in token of which deed till this hour the stone is called the Lifted Stone. And in remembrance hereof there is none entered into the register and matricular book of the said University (of Poictiers) [or accounted capable of taking any degree therein] till he have first drunk in the Caballine fountain of Croustelles, passed at Passelourdin, and got up on the Lifted Stone "[1].

Croutelles, a league from Poitiers, on the road that Rabelais had many times followed on his way from Ligugé to Fontaine-le-Comte, abounds in springs ; we are not certain as to the identity of the fountain which he calls " Caballine ", in memory of the fountain of Hippocrene that the shoe of the horse, Pegasus, caused to spring forth upon Parnassus[2]. Passelourdin is, to the south-west of the village of Saint-Benoît, rising above the right bank of the river Clain, a cornice of the rocky spur of Mauroc. Finally, the antique dolmen of the *Pierre Levée* (*Lifted Stone*), at present enclosed in a small, narrow garden between a paddock and a prison, and besides, broken across the centre, has neither the dimensions nor the imposing appearance which it had in Rabelais' day. It is even doubtful whether the grain of this stone, hard and rough, ever tempted the students' mania for carving upon stones. But it is certain that for a long time the young students kept up the tradition of the excursions

profession and " paying one another great honour and deference ". Cf. *Jacques Hillerin à Poitiers* by Abbé Auber, in the *Bulletin de la Société des Antiquaires de l'Ouest*, 1850.

[1] *Pantagruel*, ch. V.

[2] Its identification is all the more difficult because the eye of the Croutelles springs changes very rapidly, according to the observations of Dom de Monsabert, at present *curé* of this parish.

and pastimes which are described in *Pantagruel* as university rites[1].

In the company of the professors of the Law Faculty Rabelais used to meet officers of justice and magistrates: the lieutenant of the seneschal's court, the president and counsellors of the Court. With the advocates, the *procureurs* and their clerks, the recorders, notaries or tabellions, they constituted the "*monde palatin*", that is, the class of those who frequent the Palais de Justice (Law Courts), and who have an important place in Jean Bouchet's work.

The professional activity of these lawyers and practitioners was considerable, Poitiers being then, with Maine, the country of chicanery and lawsuits. "The peasants and rustics of Poitou", says Mercator[2], "are a riotous (quarrelsome) sort of people who love and look for lawsuits, clever and expert at making five be taken for four". Jean Bouchet who, as *procureur*, had no reason but to rejoice thereat, deplored it as a moralist:

> " Ils sont joueurs, jureurs et grans menteurs
> *Plaidars, noiseux*, voire grands detracteurs "[3].

Associated with magistrates, procurators, protonotaries and other representatives of the legal world, which Jean Bouchet shows us crowding into the great hall of the Palace before the mercers' stalls[4], Rabelais heard discussions upon jurisprudence, lawsuits, practice and procedure. He again found there the

---

[1] In a Latin poem composed to celebrate the arrival of the President, Achille de Harlay, and the Advocate, Barnabé Brisson, for the *Grands jours* (Extraordinary Assises) of 1580, Scévole de Sainte-Marthe represents the two of them being welcomed by all the places which they visited in their youth—Passelourdin, the Valley of the Clain, the Valley of Croutelles, the hill of St. Benoît:

> " Responsant colles, responsant florea circum
> Arva, sonansque nemus, præruptique invia rupes
> Lurdini et placidis ludit qui Clanus in undis,
> Quæque jacent rigua virides in valle Crotellæ
> Quique pii servat Benedicti nomine clivus,
> Nimirum et vobis olim loca nota verendæ
> Dum Themidis sacram huc pueri properatis ad ædem ".
>   Sc. de Sainte-Marthe, *Œuvres*, 1606, lib. I, p. 192.

[2] Edition of 1605, p. 165.
[3] (" They are gamblers, swearers, and great liars, *fond of lawsuits, quarrelsome*, and even great detractors ".)
Épitres morales et familières, To the tillers of the fields. A collection of verse in Poitevin dialect, published in 1572, *La Gente Poitevinerie*, which treats exclusively of peasant folk, is full of stories of lawsuits. Cf. the reprint by Morel-Fatio, 1877.
[4] *Épitres morales et familières*, Épître V.

topics to which he had already given ear both in his father's house and in the group of lawyers at Fontenay.

Besides, then, his initiation to the ancient literatures we must reckon among the fruits of his sojourn in Poitou his knowledge of law and his experience of legists and officers of justice. They will afford him, later, details or episodes for his books. Burlesque scenes, such as the mystification of the great clerk Thaumaste in *Pantagruel*[1], anecdotes of an entirely popular flavour, like the story of the smell of the leg of roast beef paid for by the sound of money[2], singular cases like that of Messer Nello de Gabrielis, who, having become deaf, followed a conversation by watching gestures and lip-movements[3], are found by research to be taken from books of law or jurisprudence[4].

Already, in *Pantagruel*, we find among the " gay fooleries " unexpected touches of legal erudition : such as, for example, the mention of a dozen laws which are considered especially difficult of intepretation[5]. They become more frequent in *Gargantua*. The story-teller there quotes the provisions of the *Digest* and of Justinian's *Novellæ* relative to the legitimacy of a child born eleven months after its father's death[6]. He will mix with the pleasantries of the *Bien Yvres* assembled under the willow-grove to " gulch up " Grandgrousier's " godebillios "[7], the phraseology of legal procedure—*compulsoire, reliefs d'appel, insinuations, formules de exhiber*. He will coin on this jargon of the Law Courts, puns which we can no longer understand without recourse to special lexicons.

Numerous indications show the Poitevin origin of this juridic lore. A true humanist's invective against the ineptitude of the glossarists, that is, the mediæval commentators of ancient law, is supported by the authority of one " named Du Douhet, the learnedest, the most expert and prudent . . ." of the Court of Paris[8]. Now, the Seigneur du Douhet, Briand

---

[1] Chs. XVIII–XX.   [2] *Third Book*, ch. XXXVII.   [3] *Ibid.*, ch. XIX.
[4] The first scene is based upon a gloss of Accursius upon the *Digest* (ch. X, *l. posteriori, de origine juris*) quoted by Budé in his *Annotationes ad Pandectas* ; the second is taken from a commentary by the Italian jurist, Giovanni Andrea, upon a text of the *Decretals* (I, 4, 10) ; the third from a gloss by the jurist Bartolus, *l. prima de verb. obligationibus*.
[5] Ch. XIII.   [6] Ch. II.
[7] Cf. *Gargantua*, ch. IV. " Godebillios (*gaudebillaux*) are the fat tripes of coiros (*coiraux*). Coiros are beeves fattened at the cratch in ox stalls, or in the fresh guimo meadows (*prez guimaux*). Guimo meadows are those, that for their fruitfulness may be mowed twice a year ".
[8] *Pantagruel*, chs. X–XIII.

Vallée, was in fact President of the Court of Saintes, at the time when Amaury Bouchard lived at Saint-Jean-d'Angély and received at his house Rabelais' companion, Friar Pierre Amy.

There is no part of his work more characteristic in this respect than the episode of Bridoye (Bridlegoose), which fills four chapters of the *Third Book*, published nearly twenty years after Rabelais had left Poitou[1]. " Our friend Bridlegoose ", as Pantagruel calls him, is a judge at " Fonsbeton "[2]. Much ingenuity has been wasted in the efforts to identify this locality. We need only look for it in the environs of Poitiers. Near the old Ligugé to Poitiers road, in the *Gros-bois* (Great Woods)[3], there is a spring named Fonbeton. The name of the culprit against whom Bridoye has pronounced a sentence which does not seem " very equitable "[4], the *élu Toucheronde*, has a Poitevin flavour about it : a *touche* in Poitou, means a wood or thicket[5]. Precisely on the border of a wood to the left of the road from Ligugé to Croutelles, is a hamlet called *Toucheronde*[6]. So far, we have not left the little *canton* in which Rabelais used to wander around Ligugé. But now the anecdote of Perrin Dendin, told by Bridoye[7], comes to evoke a dozen localities which are mostly outside these narrow limits, beyond " the capon's flight ".

" I remember, quoth Bridlegoose, that in the time when at Poictiers I was a student of law under *Brocadium Juris*, there was at Semarve one Peter Dendin, a very honest man, careful labourer of the ground, fine singer in a church desk, of good repute and credit, and older than the most aged of all your worships. . . . This honest man compounded, attoned, and agreed more differences, controversies, and variances at law, than had been determined, voided, and finished during his time in the whole palace of Poictiers, in the auditory of Montmorillon, and in the town-house of the old Partenay. This amicable disposition of his rendered him venerable, and of great estimation, sway, power, and authority throughout all the neighbouring places of Chauvigny, Nouaillé, Croutelles, Aisgne, Legugé, La Motte, Lusignan, Vivonne, Mezeaux, Estables, and other bordering and circumjacent towns,

---

[1] Chs. XXXIX–XLIII.
[2] Ch. XXIX.
[3] Its site is clearly marked on folio 38 of a plan of Ligugé Priory and its dependent fiefs drawn up early in the 18th century and kept in the Archives de la Vienne (D72, 25).
[4] Ch. XXXIX.
[5] Cf. *Fourth Book*, ch. XXXVI : " se liève Pantagruel pour descouvrir hors la *touche* de boys ". (" Pantagruel then arose from table, to visit and scour the *thicket* ".)
[6] Marked on folio 78 of the plan mentioned in note 3.   [7] Ch. XLI.

villages, and hamlets. All their debates were pacified by him ; he put an end to their brabling suits at law, and wrangling differences. By his advice and counsels were accords and reconcilements no less firmly made, than if the verdict of a sovereign judge had been inter- posed therein, although, in very deed, he was no judge at all, but a right honest man. . . .

There was not a hog killed within three parishes of him, whereof he had not some part of the haslet and puddings. He was almost every day invited either to a marriage-banquet, christening-feast, an uprising or women-churching treatment, a birthday's anniver- sary, solemnity, a merry frolic gossiping, or otherwise to some delicious entertainment in a tavern, to make some accord and agreement between persons at odds, and in debate with one another. Remark what I say ; for he never yet settled and compounded a difference betwixt any two at variance, but he straight made the parties agreed and pacified to drink together, as a sure and infallible token and symbol of a perfect and completely well-cemented reconciliation, a sign of a sound and sincere amity, and proper mark of a new joy and gladness to follow thereupon . . .

He had a son, whose name was Tenot Dendin, a lusty, young, sturdy, frisking roisterer, so help me God, who likewise, in imitation of his peace-making father, would have undertaken and meddled with the making up of variances and deciding of controversies between disagreeing and contentious party-pleaders. . . . And such was his confidence to have no worse success than his father, that he assumed unto himself the title of Lawstrife-settler. He was like- wise in these pacificatory negotiations so active and vigilant . . . that when he had smelt, heard, and fully understood . . . and found that there was anywhere in the country a debateable matter at law, he would incontinently thrust in his advice, and so forwardly in- trude his opinion in the business, that he made no bones of making offer, and taking upon him to decide it, how difficult soever it might happen to be, to the full contentment and satisfaction of both parties.

But so hugely great was his misfortune in this his undertaking, that he never composed any difference, how little soever you may imagine it might have been, but that, instead of reconciling the parties at odds, he did incense, irritate, and exasperate them to a higher point of dissension and enmity than ever they were at before. . . . This administered unto the tavern-keepers, wine-drawers and vintners of Semerve an occasion to say, that under him they had not in the space of a whole year so much reconciliation-wine, for so were they pleased to call the good wine of Legugé, as under his father they had done in one half hour's time. It happened a little while thereafter, that he made a most heavy regret thereof to his father. . . ."

Smarve, Perrin Dendin's country, is a little town half a league from Ligugé ; Mezeaulx, La Motte, Croutelles, line the road from Ligugé to Fontaine-le-Comte ; Aisgne, Vivonne, Lusignan, Nouaillé, Chauvigny adjoin it to the south and east. So many place-names of Poitevin localities and, in addition, so many precise details on the habits of the local peasantry seem to warrant the authenticity of this amusing anecdote. Frère Jean's only commentary is "that he was acquainted with Pierre Dendin at the time when he sojourned in the monastery of Fontaine-le-Comte, under the noble Abbot Ardillon "[1]. Frère Jean may well here speak for Rabelais.

But there is more : in Bridoye's address there are certain references to legal texts which, seemingly, are quoted only because they were familiar to the students of Poitiers. A gloss on the *Decretals*, on the heading *De regulis juris*, another on the tag : *Semper in obscuris quod minimum est sequimur*, had remained imprinted in Rabelais' memory because they supposed cases of which the scene had been the church or town of Poitiers[2]. Thus, it is really to Rabelais' stay in Poitou that we must attribute the sources of his legal erudition.

Likewise, his experience of legal circles is composed before all of the observations he made at the time of his adolescence both at Fontenay and at Poitiers. From that reason comes the moderation of the judgments he passed on them. At first sight, if we except Du Douhet[3], whom he mentions only with very great respect, and " the learned, wise, courteous, humane and just Tiraqueau "[4], his satirical shafts do not appear to have spared the " robins ". He has reproduced the grievances and the jeers of public opinion against the judicial authorities. He poked fun at the " gulpers of mists "[5], as the judges were called, because, being obliged to sit at seven o'clock, they swallowed the morning mists. He forbids legal practitioners the entry of the Abbey of Thélème, because they are " *masche-fains* ", that is to say, insatiable,—clerks, *basochiens*, officials, and scribes whom he calls " devourers of the people ". And Bridoye shows us all the ministers and agents of justice " the sergeants, catchpoles, pursuivants, messengers, summoners,

---

[1] Ch. XLIII.
[2] Ch. XXXIX. Cf. the *Sextum* (Sixth book of the *Decretals*). *De regulis juris*, rule 55, and the gloss : " *Ut ponamus quod papa hoc anno fecit mihi gratiam* in ecclesia pictaviensi . . . " and the gloss on rule 30 : " *Ponamus quod* in civitate pictaviensi *sunt duæ mensuræ* . . . ".
[3] *Pantagruel*, ch. X. We will meet Du Douhet again in ch. VI.
[4] *Prologue* to the *Fourth Book*.
[5] *Gargantua*, ch. LIV, and *Third Book, Prologue*.

apparitors, ushers, doorkeepers, pettifoggers, attornies, proctors, commissioners, justices of the peace, judge delegates, arbitrators, overseers, sequestrators, advocates, inquisitors, jurors, searchers, examiners, notaries, tabellions, scribes, scriveners, clerks, prenotaries, secondaries and expedanean judges " engaged in sucking forcibly and continually the purses of the pleading parties, as the bear licks her young, thus forming " to the suits already engendered, head and feet . . . which are the law pokes and bags "[1].

Pantagruel, at the end of the Bridoye episode, expresses himself likewise very severely about judges. Their hands, he says, " are full of blood and hearts of wry affections "[2]. To have recourse to their answers and judgments is worse than walking on snares. Cato, in the same way, in his day, " advised that every judiciary court should be paved with caltrops ".

But he immediately attenuates the severity of these judgments in throwing upon the judicial system itself the faults and defects commonly imputed to the judges. Pantagruel, indeed, shows that if there is injustice in the judicature it is the fault of the jurisconsult, Tribonian, who drew up its regulations in Justinian's day. Nothing good, he affirms, could come from this man, " a wicked, miscreant, barbarous, faithless, and perfidious knave, so pernicious, unjust, avaricious and perverse in his ways, that it was his ordinary custom to sell laws, edicts, declarations, constitutions and ordinances, as at an outcrop or putsale, to him who offered most for them ". Rabelais is here echoing an idea of his mentor Guillaume Budé, who had already stigmatised Tribonian's avidity[3]. Thus his lawyer's erudition suggests to him a reason in the historic order to explain this unjustice which popular satire summarily and brutally imputed to the judges themselves.

A fact about Bridoye which has not been sufficiently stressed, because he is confounded with Beaumarchais' Bridoison, is that he is not represented as a distasteful character. Pantagruel professes a great esteem for him. He interests himself in his son[4]. He hastens to plead with the President of the

---

[1] *Third Book*, ch. XLII.
[2] *Ibid.*, ch. XLIV.
[3] *Ibid.*
[4] *Ibid.*, ch. XXIX : " Do what you deem most expedient, quoth Pantagruel, and tell me if my recommendation can in anything be steadable for the promoval of the good of that youth. . . . I will use therein my best endeavours ".

Court of Parliament in favour of this judge, in whom he recognises a perfect candour, sufficient in itself to merit pardon of his lapse. If Bridoye is to be deprived of his position, let him be handed over to him and he will find in his kingdom " charges and employments enough wherewith to imbusy him ".

The fact that Rabelais wished for the reform of the faults of the judicial system—long drawn-out cases and the use of bribes—would not point to his being a rebellious spirit. As early as 1510, a Royal ordinance had stated that the greatest good which could be done to the King's subjects would be to curtail lawsuits. From Guillaume Budé to Michel de l'Hospital, there is not one jurisconsult or grand officer of justice who did not protest against what they termed " subversion of law " or " lengthening of suits ". In this chorus of protestations, Rabelais' voice is not distinguished by any particular harshness[1]. Marot is certainly much more violent than he in his satire of the " judges of Hell ". The friend of Tiraqueau, of Briand Vallée du Douhet, of Amaury Bouchard, of the good *procureur* Jean Bouchet is possessed of too much learning and experience not to temper his judgment of the " robins " with a moderation and nicety absent from popular satire. He sees in them more failings to amuse him than vices to stir up his indignation.

[1] With the exception of the " Furred Law-cats' " episode in *Book V* of which the authenticity is contested.

CHAPTER VI

SOJOURN AT THE UNIVERSITIES OF BORDEAUX, TOULOUSE, BOURGES, ORLEANS, PARIS (1528–1530)

DURING the first third of the 16th century it was not from the Universities that this knowledge of Greek and Latin literature, of which Rabelais had become enamoured, radiated. The centres of intellectual activity were elsewhere. The essential work of Humanists such as Erasmus and Budé was accomplished without their aid. However, since they alone had the privilege of giving that higher education in theology, law and medicine which Humanism aspired to renovate, and as some of their teachers were already won over to the ancient literatures, they exercised, in spite of their outworn methods, an attraction upon cultured minds[1]. They compelled their attention. How indeed could the Humanists afford to neglect them, since they alone delivered the diplomas which were the means of a livelihood for many? It is not, then, surprising that Rabelais, having visited or attended the Legal Faculty of Poitiers, should have had a desire to know some other universities of the kingdom.

Around 1527 he disappears from Poitou and, until the month of September, 1530, we lose sight of him. For what reasons did he decide to depart from these Abbeys of Poitou where life was so pleasant, and leave his friendly patron, Geoffroy d'Estissac? We do not know. But we may surmise that his presence and his services in the Bishop of Maillezais' household became less needed from the time the latter's nephew, young Louis d'Estissac, whose tutor Rabelais apparently was, got married (1527)[2].

---

[1] Many Humanists considered a knowledge of Greek, Latin and the *litteræ humanæ* to be the key to the medical and juridical sciences, but thought it, nevertheless, incumbent upon them to study these sciences in the only places where they were taught—the Universities. Christophe de Longueil says this in the letter quoted p. 65, n. 1.

[2] This conjecture is made by M. H. Clouzot, *La Brosse en Xaintonge*, R.É.R., V, 195.

If we have no authentic document to inform us as to the places in which he spent these three years, several sure indications lead us to conjecture that, before 1530, he visited the Universities of Bordeaux, Toulouse, Bourges, Orleans, and, finally, Paris, where he must have remained for a fairly long time ; for we find him, in 1532, very well versed in the topographical characteristics, the habits and customs of these towns, and in correspondence with residents in them. Now, he cannot have established these relationships or gained this knowledge between 1530 and 1532, since sure documentary evidence tells us that for these two years he lived at Montpellier and at Lyons.

It was, besides, natural, that he should wish to visit the Universities of Bordeaux or Toulouse. In the *cénacle* of Fontenay-le-Comte he had heard of the Bordeaux lawyers who corresponded with Amaury Bouchard and Tiraqueau. Besides, Toulouse boasted of its being the most renowned University in the kingdom, and it counted perhaps more followers of Humanism than any other provincial town with the exception of Lyons. At the very time when Rabelais was still in Geoffroy d'Estissac's service he may have had an opportunity of visiting these two University towns. The Bishop of Maillezais sometimes betook himself to Périgord, either to his Abbey of Cadouin, not far from Bergerac, where crowds of pilgrims went to venerate Christ's shroud, or to the Château of Cahuzac[1], in the neighbourhood, to look after the interests of his nephew and ward, Louis. Rabelais went with him.

In *Gargantua* he mentions Cahuzac[2] as a country difficult of entry, like Quimper-Corentin in La Fontaine's *Fables*. He quotes Cadouin in connection with famous relics[3]. Later on, in the *Fourth Book*, he alludes to the peculiar structure of the bridge of Bergerac[4] and describes an archery contest which

---

[1] Now Cauzac, near Les Tricheries, between Beauville and Saint-Robert in the canton of Castillonès, *arrondissement* of Villeneuve-sur-Lot, department of Lot-et-Garonne. Cf. Dr. de Santi, *Rabelais à Toulouse, Rev. XVIᵉ siècle*, 1921, p. 43.

[2] Ch. XII : " If you were to go from hence to Cahusac, whether had you rather ride on a gosling, or lead a sow in a leash ? ''

[3] *Gargantua*, ch. XXVII : " Some vowed a pilgrimage to St. James . . . Others sent up their vows to (St.) *Cadouin* ''.

[4] *Fourth Book*, ch. XXXIV : " For with his dreadful piles and darts nearly resembling the huge beams that support the bridges of Nantes, Saumur, *Bergerac* . . . ''. Bergerac is again mentioned, *ibid.*, ch. XL.

took place at Cahuzac between Louis d'Estissac and a neighbouring nobleman, the Vicomte de Lauzun[1].

It is, perhaps, on one of his journeys to Périgord that he
went as far as Bordeaux. He found the University to be poorly
attended : some years later, the *jurats* were to reduce by half
the number of professors owing to the scarcity of pupils. He
merely noted among the amusements the pastimes of the
"*guabarriers*" (porters) who played "*luettes*"[2], a Spanish
card game, on the Strand.

But among the members of the Parliament of Bordeaux, in
the capacity of counsellor, there was a magistrate for whom
Rabelais had the highest esteem, Briand Vallée du Douhet.
He was a native of Saintonge and had remained until 1527 at
the *siège royal* of Saintes, of which he became president. It is
there Rabelais had known him. He recounts later an anecdote
of the early days of their acquaintance which shows us this
grave personage endeavouring to verify an observation of
Pythagoras on the properties of odd and even numbers :

"Indeed, said Epistemon, I saw this way of syllabising tried at
Xaintes, at a general procession, in the presence of that good,
virtuous, learned, and just president, Brian Vallée, Lord of Douhait.
When there went by a man or woman that was either lame, blind
of one eye, or hump-backed, he had an account brought him of his
or her name ; and if the syllables of the name were of an odd
number, immediately, without seeing the persons, he declared them
to be deformed, blind or lame, or crooked of the right side ; and of
the left, if they were even in number ; and such indeed we ever
found them "[3].

Briand Vallée soon distinguished himself at Bordeaux by
his culture as a Humanist. The *literati*, whom he loved to

---

[1] *Ibid.*, ch. LII : "At *Cahusac*, said Gymnast, a match being made by the
lords of *Estissac* and Viscount *Lausun* to shoot at a mark, *Perotou* had taken
to pieces a set of decretals, and set one of the leaves for the white to shoot at :
now I sell, nay I give and bequeath for ever and aye, the mould of my doublet
to fifteen hundred hampers full of black devils, if ever any archer in the
country (though they are singular marksmen in Guienne) could hit the white.
Not the least bit of the holy scribble was contaminated or touched : nay,
and *Sansornin* the elder, who held stakes, swore to us, *figues dioures*, hard
figs, (his greatest oath), that he had openly, visibly, and manifestly seen the
bolt of *Carquelin* moving right to the round circle in the middle of the white ;
and that just on the point, when it was going to hit and enter, it had gone
aside above seven foot and four inches wide of it. . . . One of the Lord
d'Estissac's pages (named *Chamouillac*) at last found out the charm, pursued
Gymnast, and by his advice *Perotou* put in another white made up of some
papers of *Pouillac's* lawsuit, and then every one shot cleverly ".
[2] *Pantagruel*, ch. V.
[3] *Fourth Book*, ch. XXXVII.

gather around him, one of his biographers tells us, considered his house the home of the Muses.

Rabelais, then, expressed the general feeling of admiration which Briand Vallée's learning and wisdom inspired when, in 1532, he represented him, in an episode of *Pantagruel*, as the champion of the ideas of Renaissance jurisconsults against the traditions of mediæval jurisprudence[1].

The relationship between the two scholars was destined to be lasting[2]. It did not consist merely in an intercourse of learning : Briand Vallée, like Rabelais, was fond of a joke and his habits were none too strict. A Humanist, settled at Bordeaux, Antoine de Gouvea, accused him, in an epigram, of hiding in the depths of his cellar during thunderstorms ; in his cellar, he said, he does not believe there is a God. To which Vallée replied : " Antoine de Gouvea, son of a *marran* (converted Jew), does not believe there is a God, either in the cellar or in heaven ". The two adversaries, then, accused each other of being atheists. Rabelais intervened in an endeavour to appease by a joke the quarrel which might have ended ill for both of them. In six distichs, the only Latin verses of his composition that we have, he excused Du Douhet from going to hide, like a child in his mother's bosom, in the deepest part of his cellar : the thunderbolt, he said, strikes only high places, and Bacchus keeps away the thunderbolt[3].

Thus, Rabelais, at the very time he frequented the godly

---

[1] *Pantagruel*, ch. X : " Du Douhet, the learnedest of all, and more expert and prudent than any of the other " lawyers, proposes to deliver judgment not according to tradition, but according to evangelic and philosophic truth.

[2] Briand Vallée died in 1544. For a notice on him, together with some bibliographical notes, cf. Buche, *Lettres inédites de Boyssonné*, *Revue des langues romanes*, 1897, pp. 194–195.

[3] Cf. Marty-Laveaux, *op. cit.*, vol. IV, p. 396, for these epigrams by Antoine de Gouvea and Briand Vallée. We give here the Latin verses by Rabelais, published for the first time in the second edition of Burgaud des Marets, vol. II, p. 624, from an old MS. in the Bibliothèque Nationale :

> Patrum indignantum pueri ut sensere furorem
>   Accurrunt matrum protinus in gremium,
> Nimirum experti matrum dulcoris inesse
>   Plus gremiis, possit quam furor esse patrum ;
> Irato Jove, sic, cœlum ut mugire videbis,
>   Antiquæ matris subfugis in gremium :
> Antiquæ gremium matris vinaria cella est ;
>   Hac nihil attonitis tutius esse potest,
> Nempe Pharos sciunt atque Acroceraunia, turres
>   Ærias, quercus, tela trifulca Jovis
> Dolia non feriunt condita cellis,
>   Et procul a Bromio fulmen abesse solet.

Jean Bouchet and Abbot Ardillon's intimates, was in relationship with an atheist ? In truth, Briand Vallée's atheism may be disputed. How reconcile it with the creation of a certain course of theology which he founded in 1539 at the college of Guyenne, in Bordeaux ? This course was to be devoted to Saint Paul, but the foundation was annulled. The fact is significant, for Saint Paul was the Apostle dear to the Evangelicals, and, later, to the Reformers ; Vallée was, perhaps, merely one of the independent spirits who wished for the reform of the Church, and were indulgent towards all innovations in matters of religion.

Rabelais was to meet, besides, in the same district, a still bolder spirit, Julius Cæsar Scaliger. Brought from Italy by Antoine de la Rovère, Bishop of Agen, Scaliger had settled in that town in 1524, and practised medicine there until his death (1558).

He opened a school, drawing to him all the pedagogues, grammarians and doctors in the province. He had among his disciples Jean Schyron, who was soon afterwards to become one of the glories of the University of Montpellier[1]. It is extremely probable that Rabelais went to hear him.

In 1532, writing to Erasmus to inform him about Scaliger, he said of him : he is a man *who is well known to me*, a skilled physician, but, he added in Greek, the most downright atheist possible[2]. Scaliger was a more than doubtful Catholic ; he was proceeded against for Lutheranism by the Inquisitor of Toulouse and escaped the stake only because his case was placed in the hands of Briand Vallée. He denied the accusation of atheism, saying that, as an old student of the University of Padua, he was merely an Averroïst[3].

Rabelais thus attended some of his classes, but did not become his friend. It is even probable that he incurred the irascible Italian's anger, who later showered insulting epigrams upon him[4].

From Agen, he ascended the Garonne as far as Toulouse, admired the famous Mill of Bazacle, with its numerous

---

[1] Cf. Dr. de Santi, *Rabelais à Toulouse, Rev. XVIᵉ siècle*, 1921, pp. 41–62.
[2] *Vide infra*, ch. VIII.
[3] Busson, *Sources et développement du rationalisme dans la littérature française de la Renaissance* (1533–1601), Paris, Letouzey, 1922, p. 120.
[4] Cf. the articles by Dr. de Santi, *R.É.R.*, III, pp. 29–32, and *Rev. XVIᵉ siècle*, 1921, pp. 42 seq.

millstones[1], noticed the students' skill in dancing and playing with the two-handed sword[2]. It is there, perhaps, that he entered into relations with the most renowned Humanist of the province, Jean de Pins, and with his pupil and friend, Georges d'Armagnac, Bishop of Rodez, of whom he will say, in 1532, that he is long since his friend[3]. It may also have been at Toulouse that he met for the first time the Humanists Étienne Dolet and Jean de Boyssonné, whom he will meet again, later, at Lyons.

The towns of Bordeaux and Toulouse were, for various reasons, worth a visit from Rabelais ; but the scholar could not limit to them his tour of the French Universities. Paris was calling him. On the way, he halted at Bourges and at Orleans.

The University which Louis XI had founded in 1463 in his native town of Bourges was, from the outset of the 16th century, renowned for the study of law. The Italian jurist, Alciat, who came there as a professor, from 1529 to 1533, brought the celebrity of its Faculty of Laws to its apogee. He was the most brilliant representative of the Humanistic spirit in the teaching of law. His arrival at Bourges was a triumph. The students, some on foot, others on horseback, came to meet him and welcomed him in a preliminary harangue. Then, under the very walls of the town, he met a crowd of citizens and numerous horsemen who welcomed him. Licentiates, doctors, more than one hundred Abbots thronged around his chair and listened to him with such scrupulous attention that he was embarrassed by it[4]. That was in the spring of 1529. Rabelais had, perhaps, already passed through Bourges. He never speaks of Alciat[5]. But whereas he only characterises

---

[1] Mentioned in *Pantagruel*, ch. XXII.

[2] *Ibid.*, ch. V.

[3] In his letter to Erasmus, mentioned below, ch. VIII. Georges d'Armagnac was appointed Bishop of Rodez in 1529. He was in correspondence with Budé, who asked him to take the naturalist, Pierre Gilles, under his protection. Cf. Delaruelle, *Répertoire* . . . , pp. 229–230.—Jehan de Pins, Bishop of Rieux (*chef-lieu de canton* of the *arrondissement* of Muret, in the Haute-Garonne), had been Ambassador to Rome from 1520–1523. While there he translated Dion Cassius and bought Greek and Latin manuscripts for the Royal Library at Fontainebleau. For a sketch of the Renaissance at Toulouse, cf. Henri Graillot, *Nicolas Bachelier, imagier et maçon de Toulouse au XVIᵉ siècle*, Toulouse, 1914, 8vo, ch. I.

[4] From a letter written by him to Boniface Amerbach, at Bâle, quoted by M. P. E. Viard, *André Alciat*, 1492–1550 (Paris, 1926), p. 72, n. 4.

[5] It may be remarked that Alciat was on bad terms with Rabelais' first patron, Guillaume Budé, and was, as a general rule, not popular among French professors of Law.

the student-life in most of the other Universities by the games, pastimes and physical exercises which were practised in them, he shows us Pantagruel studying " a good long time, and profiting very much in the Faculty of the Laws " at Bourges, and the judgment that the Giant delivers, upon this occasion, on the *Pandects* and their mediæval commentators expresses exactly the opinion of Humanists upon these " goodly books " of law, dishonoured by a vile gloss[1].

Rabelais' stay at Bourges must have been of some duration to judge by the number and the precision of the details he gives us about this town. He mentions the great Bell called " the giant's bowl ", which was filled once yearly with wine for the poor[2]; the palace built by Jean, Duc de Berry; the great tower[3] built under Philippe Auguste, whose walls were, he says, *entaillées à la rustique* or " like points of diamonds "; the cross-bow of Chantelle, an old weapon kept in this tower[4]; the Tour-de-Beurre (Butter Tower) of Saint-Stephen's Cathedral which " melted before the sun[5] " and fell, the 31st December, 1506.

" Going from Bourges ", says Rabelais, " Pantagruel came to Orleans[6] ". It is the very itinerary his historian had followed. He had remarked on his entry into the city, the imposing

---

[1] " And he would sometimes say, that the books of the civil laws were like unto a wonderfully precious, royal, and triumphant robe of gold, edged with dirt; for in the world are no goodlier books to be seen, more ornate, nor more eloquent than the texts of the Pandects, but the bordering of them, that is to say, the gloss of Accursius, is so scurvy, vile, base, and unsavoury, that it is nothing but filthiness and villainy ". *Pantagruel*, ch. V.

[2] " And they served in this whitepot-meat to him (the infant Pantagruel) in a huge great bell, which is yet to be seen in the city of Bourges in Berry, near the palace, but his teeth were already so well grown, and so strengthened with vigour, that of the said bell he bit off a great morsel, as very plainly doth appear to this hour ". *Pantagruel*, ch. IV. On this bell cf. A. Lefranc, *Rev. XVIe siècle*, 1916, pp. 162–165.

[3] *Pantagruel*, ch. XV, and *Sciomachia*, vol. V, p. 307, in Marty-Laveaux' edition.

[4] " Therefore caused he to be made for him (the youthful Pantagruel), whilst he was yet little, a pretty cross-bow, wherewith to shoot at small birds, which now they call the great cross-bow at Chantelle, (which is at present in the Great Tower at Bourges) ". *Pantagruel*, ch. V.

[5] " And by the breaking of this stony armour there was made such a horrible rumble, as put me in mind of the butter-tower of St. Stephen's at Bourges, when it melted before the sun ". *Pantagruel*, ch. XXIX. M. Soyer, in his valuable *Topographie rabelaisienne (Berry)*, rightly points out (*R.E.R.*, VII, p. 72) that it was the predecessor of the Tour-de-Beurre (Butter-tower) which fell down in 1506. The " Butter Tower " was built from 1508–1525 and was so named because it was supposed to have been built with money given to obtain permission to eat butter in Lent. Rabelais plays upon the name : it is only a tower made of butter which could melt in the sun.

[6] *Pantagruel*, ch. V.

G

appearance of its walls[1], the gilded copper globe which sparkled at the top of the spire of Sainte-Croix Cathedral[2]. From the bridge which crossed the Loire, he had been enabled to see in the neighbouring islands of the Motte Saint-Antoine and the Motte des Poissonniers "store of swaggering scholars" engaged upon a sort of ball-game called *poussavant*[3]. The big and enormous bell of Saint-Aignan's Church, the chapel of Notre-Dame de Bonne-Nouvelle, where the students heard Mass, were still alive in his memory some years later[4]. At Orleans the favourite amusements of the student body were dancing and tennis ; the principal study, that of Civil Law. The University of Paris having no Faculty of Laws (but only courses in Canon Law), it is to the University of Orleans that the greater number of young Parisians who had to study law, came. Tennis, dancing and law—it is of these the youthful Pantagruel makes " the blazon and device " of the licentiates in the said University[5].

> So you have in your hand a racket,
> A tennis-ball in your cod-placket,
> A Pandect law in your cap's tippet,
> And that you have the skill to trip it
> In a low dance, you will be allowed
> The grant of the licentiate's hood.

The greatest figure in the School of Law was then Pierre de l'Estoile. In 1528-1529, he had among his pupils Calvin, his friend Pierre Daniel, Hellenist, another Hellenist[6], Gentien Hervet, and a friend of Pierre Daniel's, Claude Framberge. Did Rabelais become one of this group and did he meet Calvin there ? It is quite possible. One thing is certain, we find him twenty-five years later in correspondence with Pierre Daniel, become *bailli* of Saint-Laurent-des-Orgerils-lez-Orléans, and

---

[1] *Pantagruel*, ch. XV.
[2] " And of these brazen pills, or rather copper balls, you have one at Orleans, upon the steeple of Holy Cross Church". *Ibid.*, ch. XXXIII.
[3] *Ibid.*, ch. V.
[4] *Ibid.*, ch. V, *Gargantua*, ch. XXVII. Cf. Soyer, *Topographie rabelaisienne* (*Orléanais*), *R.É.R.*, VII, pp. 304–310.
[5] *Pantagruel*, ch. V.
[6] Greek had maintained a position of honour at Orleans since Aleander's stay there. About this period it was taught by two Germans, Melchior Volmar and Sterk, called Fortius of Ringelberg, who visited Lyons in 1530, and by a very young Frenchman, Louis, son of the professor, Pierre de l'Estoile. Cuissard, *Mémoire sur l'étude du grec à Orléans*, in the *Mémoires de la Société archéologique et historique de l'Orléanais*, t. XIX, (1883), p. 740.

with Framberge, then Canon of Sainte-Croix and Bishop's
" sealer "[1].

Leaving Orleans by the Paris gate, where he will place the
meeting of Pantagruel with the Limousin scholar, traversing
the " ample forest "[2] which sheltered the town on the north,
joyously following the main road, Rabelais reaches the capital.

In what circumstances did he come to Paris ? Was he still
a Benedictine ? Had he discarded the monk's habit to take
that of a secular priest ? If we accept literally the terms of
the petition he sent later to Pope Paul III, he seems to have left
his monastery of Maillezais without authorization from his
superior, and it is then he defrocked himself to go out into the
world[3]. On the other hand, M. Abel Lefranc has justly pointed
out the place given in Pantagruel's story at Paris to the Hôtel
de Saint-Denis, a vast building, situated in the *rue Saint-
André-des-Arcs*, at the corner of the *rue des Grands-Augustins*,
and which was the Benedictines' house of study[4]. It is there
the narrator lodges the giant Pantagruel[5]. Might it not be because he had himself stayed there on his arrival in Paris ?
He would have been in no need of recommendations in order
to find a welcome there : in 1528, the Abbey of Saint-Denis-en-
France,on which depended the Parisian house of Saint-Denis,had,
as Abbot, Aymar Gouffier, brother of the Admiral Bonnivet[6].

In any event, the house of Saint-Denis did not see Rabelais
for long. At Paris, he soon joined the ranks of the " *gyrovagic* "
monks, as they were then called. He mixed up with the
world, dressed in the habit of a secular priest, which entailed
the breaking of his vows as a religious and the incurring of
ecclesiastical censure, for the crime called *apostasia*. This

[1] H. Clouzot, *Les amitiés de Rabelais en Orléanais*, R.É.R., III, 156–175,
and Soyer, *Topographie rabelaisienne (Orléanais)*, R.É.R., VII, 311–321. *Vide
infra*, ch. XIII.

[2] In *Gargantua*, ch. XVI, he assigns an enormous area to it—thirty-five
leagues in length and about seventeen in width, at least before Gargantua's
mare had, with its tail, " overthrown all the wood . . . and thereby reduced
all the country to a plain champagne field ".

[3] " Absque licentia sui superioris a dicta ecclesia discedens, regulari
dimisso et presbyteri sæcularis habitu assumpto, per seculum diu vagatus ".
*Libellus supplex Franc. Rabelesii ad Paulum papam III, pro absolutione ab
apostasia obtinenda.* Marty-Laveaux, vol. III, p. 336. Cf. R.É.R., II, pp.
110–134.

[4] *Le logis de Pantagruel à Paris*, in the R.É.R., III, p. 48.

[5] *Pantagruel*, ch. XVIII. In *Gargantua*, ch. XXXIX, a brother Claude of
St. Denys is also mentioned.

[6] Cf. *Journal d'un bourgeois de Paris*, edited by Bourrilly (Paris, 1910),
p. 315

fault was common enough, and there was a lapsed monk whom Rome had once wished to make Cardinal : this was Erasmus, who had, likewise, thrown his Augustinian Canon's frock to the nettles to go out into the world. He had obtained from Julius II without difficulty the absolution of his *apostasy* and we shall see Pope Paul III showing the same indulgence for Rabelais' fault.[1]

The people with whom our unfrocked Benedictine mixed were the *gent scolaire* of the University. To prove this, it suffices to read in *Pantagruel* and *Gargantua* the numerous chapters given to the giants' sojourn at Paris : the conversation of the Limousin scholar on his way from the Academy of Lutetia, the catalogue of Saint-Victor's library, the meeting with Panurge, Pantagruel's argumentative prowess, the " qualities and conditions " of Panurge, how Panurge " put to a non-plus " a great scholar of England who wished to argue with Pantagruel, the taking away of the bells of Notre-Dame by Gargantua, the mission of Master Janotus de Bragmardo, how Gargantua was instructed by Ponocrates, and how he spent his time in rainy weather[2].

The streets, passages, by-ways and squares of the Hill of Sainte-Geneviève, astir with the motley throng of students, monks and professors, the *rue du Fouarre*, the colleges—Navarre, the Sorbonne, whose walls resound ceaselessly with the noise of argumentations—the theses or " conclusions " of candidates posted in the public places of the city, the scholars' jargon, their puns on the titles of the books in vogue, their meals at the inns of the Pomme de Pin, of the Castel, la Magdeleine, or la Mulle, their visits to ill-famed resorts of the Champgaillard, l'Abreuvoir-Maçon, the Cul-de-Sac, Bourbon, Huslieu, their clothes pawned while awaiting the money which their families send by sworn messengers, the practical jokes played on the watch or on the professors, the theologians gravely carrying hares' ears or foxes' tails attached to the back of their robes by some wag, the college Assembly troubled by the nauseating smell of a *tarte bourbonnaise*[3], the ceremonial of solemn occasions,

---

[1] This same Pope Paul III offers a Cardinal's hat to Erasmus in 1535.

[2] *Pantagruel*, ch. VI, VII, IX, X, XV, XVI, XVIII–XX ; *Gargantua*, ch. XVII–XXIV.

[3] " . . . A Borbonnesa tart, or filthy and slovenly compound, made of store of garlick, of assafœtida, of castoreum, of dogs' turds very warm, which he steeped, tempered and liquefied in the corrupt matter of pocky boils and pestiferous botches ". *Pantagruel*, ch. XXI.

the professors' insignia, the "orator" of the theologians wearing his *chaperon à queue* (tailed hood) pushing in front of him, like a drover of cattle, his "red-snouted beadle", the rivalry between Faculties, the students' walks and recreations in the Faubourg Saint-Marceau, their excursions into the adjoining country, to Gentilly, Boulogne, Montrouge, the Pont-Charenton, Vanves, Saint-Cloud—in fine, the whole of this "Latin country" which Rabelais calls up in these chapters with an abundance of accurate and precise detail met with in no other writer of the time[1].

For us moderns to whom the 16th century *Respublica Scholastica* is unknown, this picture, so life-like, seems at first rather confused. The reason is that the organisation of the University of Paris, after an existence of three centuries, had become complex[2].

The teaching establishments situated on the Hill of Sainte-Geneviève and the left bank of the Seine consisted at the time of some "pedagogies", or boarding-schools, monastic schools and colleges. The "pedagogies" had flourished at the University's origin in the 13th century ; in Rabelais' day, some professors took into their houses a small number of rich students. These establishments comprised only a small number of the total student-body. The monastic schools hold a more important position in the University. Each religious order has a *studium generale*, a sort of monastery-school, where the best students from the provincial monasteries come to study. Among these are : for the Order of Cîteaux, the college of Saint-Bernard, for the congregation of Cluny, the college of Cluny, for the Augustins, the Abbey of Sainte-Geneviève and the Abbey of Saint-Victor, for the Benedictines, the Hôtel Saint-Denis, for the Dominicans, the big convent in the rue Saint-Jacques (whence the Friars Preachers had got their popular name of Jacobins) which had been made famous

---

[1] He is quite at home in these surroundings. In the first edition of *Gargantua* he had placed the assembly of Parisian citizens, after the robbery of the bells of Notre-Dame, in the Sorbonne. Having decided, for the new edition of 1542, to strike out this name in every case where it occurred in the original text, he replaced it by *Nesle*. For the royal Hôtel de Nesle, on the site of the present Mint, had been from 1522 to 1527 the residence of a *bailli* created by François I to judge the University lawsuits. It was natural to make this seat of University jurisdiction the meeting-place of the people and of University.

[2] Cf. Renaudet's doctorate thesis *Préréforme et humanisme à Paris* (1499–1517), Paris, 1916.

by the teaching of Albert the Great and of Saint Thomas Aquinas.

Much more numerous were those colleges founded in the 13th and 14th centuries by churchmen and laymen, to house poor youths, who were thus spared the worries of material life for the duration of their studies. The most famous were the Collège d'Harcourt, the Collège de Bayeux, rue de la Harpe, the Collège de Laon or de Presles, rue du Clos-Bruneau, the Collège de Cornouailles, rue Galande, the Collège du Cardinal Lemoine, the Collège du Plessis, the Collège de Reims, the Collège de Tréguier, the Collège de la Marche, the Collège d'Autun, rue Saint-André-des-Arcs, the Collège de Marmoutier, the Collège des Écossais, the Collège des Lombards, the Collège de Sainte-Barbe, the Collège de Séez, the Collège de Coqueret, where Ronsard and Du Bellay will go, the Collège de Boncourt, dear to the Pléiade, the Collège de Montaigu, rue des Sept-Voies, near Saint-Étienne-des-Grez, and, finally, on the summit of the hill, near *la rue pavée d'Andouilles* ("the street paved with Chitterlings"[1]), Navarre, with its seventy scholars, and in the great rue Saint-Jacques, opposite the Collège du Plessis, the Collège de Sorbonne.

The University of Paris included four Faculties : Theology, Arts, Canon Law, and Medicine. The classes of the two latter were little frequented, whilst the Arts and Theological Faculties attracted a very great number of students. The monastic schools were open only to candidates for degrees in the Faculty of Theology, and, in the colleges, the "theologians" were, perhaps, more numerous than the "artians".

In both Faculties, oral exercises, namely, argumentations and discussions, were the ordinary test of study. An "artian" must have had two years at the University before submitting himself for the "determinance"; six months later, having carried out a solemn public discussion in the schools of his Nation, rue du Fouarre, and taken part for a month in a series of debates, he was entitled to receive the degree

---

[1] In the *Fourth Book*, ch. XLII, Rabelais connects the name of this street with an episode in Pantagruel's navigation : "They (the Chitterlings) were buried in heaps in a part of Paris, to this day called *La Rue pavée d'Andouilles*, the street paved with Chitterlings".

of *bachelier*[1] and present himself for his *licence* a year later.

All theologians, secular and regular, had to pass at the Sorbonne the final tests of their *licence*, which were three argumentations—the *great* and the *small ordinary* and the *sorbonique*. Three more solemn disputations, the *vespéries*, the *aulique* and the *résompte* were, in addition, demanded for the Doctor's degree.

The colleges of the Sorbonne and of Navarre, about 1530, grouped around their rostra the greater number of the theologians, all secular clerics being obliged to finish there their courses in theology. But there was another college with a reputation steadily increasing for a quarter of a century, namely Montaigu. Transformed by Standonck in 1483 into a sort of congregation comprising two hundred poor, and some rich, boarders, Montaigu was renowned for its authoritative teaching and the excessive severity of its regulations. The *capettes*, as its students were called, because their costume consisted in a closed cape, were subjected to a monastic régime : short sleep, hard beds, perpetual abstinence ; cooked fruits, vegetables, herrings and eggs as their entire food, and for the smallest faults a whipping in punishment. Erasmus, who spent four years there as a professor (1495–1499), had conceived a hatred for these walls reeking with theology. He had fallen sick from his diet of rotten eggs and his filthy cell[2]. Montaigu was known as a "lousy college"[3], to use an expression of Rabelais, whom the asceticism of its regulations revolted :

" The galley-slaves are far better used among the Moors and Tartars, the murderers in the criminal dungeons, yea, the very dogs in your house, than are the poor wretched students in the aforesaid college. And if I were King of Paris, the devil take me if I would not set it on fire, and burn both principal and regents, for suffering this inhumanity to be exercised before their eyes ".

But the Collège de Montaigu was " the most active of the Parisian schools "[4]. It possessed, at the beginning of the

---

[1] Bachelors were sometimes called upon to give lectures ; they were called *baccalaurei cursores*. Hence, the pun in ch. XVIII of the *Third Book* : " Je lui veulx constituer . . . quelque bonne rente, non *courante comme bacheliers* insensez, mais assise comme beaulx docteurs régents ".
[2] Cf. *Compendium Vitæ* (1524), and the *Ichtyophagia*.
[3] *Gargantua*, ch. XXXVII. On Montaigu College cf. Marcel Godet, *La congrégation de Montaigu* (Paris, 1912, 8vo), and his article *R.É.R.*, VII, pp. 285–305.   [4] Cf. Renaudet, *op. cit.*, p. 593.

century, the most formidable of the champions of terministic logic, John Mair, or Mayr[1], and his influence spread even to the Collège de Navarre, where another nominalist, Jacques Almain[2], was a professor. Two other Montaigu professors attracted attention by their zeal in hunting up every writing suspected of heterodoxy, Béda[3], and Tempête[4]. They left Montaigu, however, to go to the Sorbonne of which they represented the spirit for several years. For the Sorbonne was not solely a college destined for some students of theology. It had in residence associates (*socii*) who formed an institute of higher theological studies and supplied teachers. Every Saturday, they assembled in the chapel to argue and debate, and, as the house regulations were less austere than at Montaigu, the orator who behaved badly, for instance by sacrificing his regard for the truth to his desire for applause, was fined two casks of wine. Hence these expressions which have become proverbial with Rabelais : drink or " chopine " like a theologian[5], and also the facetious title of a book found by Pantagruel in the Library of Saint-Victor : *Badinatorium Sorbonniformium*[6].

The Sorbonne, in reality, did not trifle during the years which Rabelais spent in the capital. The theological Faculty of Paris had from the outset the mission of supervising all studies. The Popes, who, at the beginning of the 13th century, had created and protected the University of Paris, had intended it to be a centre of religious studies from which truth would shine forth upon the world[7]. It was, then, in its province to denounce every idea suspected of heresy. Since the infiltration of Lutheranism into France it devoted itself to this task, with such redoubtable ardour that its chief doctors, Pierre

---

[1] Rabelais attributes to him a treatise on the art of making *boudins*, a dish unknown to the " Capettes " : " *Majoris, de modo faciendi boudinos* ". *Pantagruel*, ch. VII.

[2] Rabelais jokingly makes him the inventor of a comb : " He combed his head with an Alman comb, which is the four fingers and the thumb ". *Gargantua*, ch. XXI.

[3] Béda was corpulent. Hence the facetious title of a book attributed to him by Rabelais—*De optimitate triparum*. *Pantagruel*, ch. VII.

[4] Tempête was " a mighty flogger of lads " according to Rabelais : " If pedants be damned for whipping poor little innocent wretches their scholars, he is, upon my honour, by this time fixed within Ixion's wheel, lashing the crop-eared, bob-tailed cur that gives it motion ". *Fourth Book*, ch. XXI.

[5] *Gargantua*, ch. XV and XVIII.

[6] *Pantagruel*, ch. VII.

[7] The mission of the University of Paris in this respect is ably set forth by Gilson, *Histoire de la philosophie du moyen âge*. 2 vol., Payot, 1920, vol. I, p. 132.

Cordonnier[1], Bédier, Nicolas Leclerc, Duchesne, Tempête, were on several occasions denounced to the King, as enemies of the public peace, too ready to imprison and burn good citizens, on the pretext of heresy.

The fact is that the Sorbonne, not satisfied with persecuting heresy, combated Humanism; not that Humanism was essentially hostile to the Catholic Faith, but because it limited the domain of philosophy by increasing that of *belles lettres*; it tended to weaken the Christian spirit by extolling the wisdom of the Ancients; and by practising the free examination of texts did it not risk striking a blow at the traditional interpretation of the Holy Scripture, and consequently overthrowing the Church? The Sorbonne, then, kept a distrustful eye upon Humanism, whose champion was then Erasmus.

It had forbidden young people to read his *Colloquia* because they ridiculed praying to the Virgin and the Saints, fasting and vows. It had condemned three short works of Erasmus, translated by Berquin[2]. It warned students to be on their guard against Greek: *Cave a græcis, ne fias hereticus*. But it could not stay the spread of Humanism, to the progress of which Rabelais, from 1528–1530, offers consoling testimony. Greek, which at first had been taught only in certain colleges (in 1529, at the Collège du Plessis) and some pedagogies, in Jacques Toussaint's and Nicole Bérault's houses, was now esteemed in ever-widening circles. The Italian, Giustiniani, the Germans, Gonthier d'Andernach and Melchior Volmar, had taught it to large numbers of students[3]. Precisely at the end of 1529 appeared Guillaume Budé's *Commentarii linguæ græcæ*, the greatest monument of the Hellenism of François I's time.

Did Rabelais meet at Paris this Guillaume Budé, who had been his patron when he was a monk at Fontenay-le-Comte? It is very unlikely. Budé was nearly sixty and lived a retired life. He had not given up encouraging Humanists' efforts, but his letters show him to us occupied about his health, domestic worries and the cares of his public offices. He had

---

[1] Cf. Renaudet, *op. cit.*, p. 594. The following title of a book in St. Victor's library is directed at Cordonnier: " *Sutoris adversus quendam, qui vocaverat eum fripponnatorem et quod fripponnatores non sunt damnati ab Ecclesia* ". *Pantagruel*, ch. VII.

[2] The *Symbole, Le Mariage chrétien, La Manière de trier*. Cf. Pineau, *Érasme, sa pensée religieuse*, Les Presses Universitaires de France, 1924, 1 vol. 8vo, p. 210.

[3] Cf. in the *Rev. XVIe siècle*, Delaruelle, *L'étude du grec à Paris de 1514 à 1530*, vol. IX, p. 51 ; *Le séjour à Paris d'Agostino Giustiniani* (1518–1522), vol. XII, p. 322, and *La carrière de Janus Lascaris depuis* 1494, vol. XIII, p. 95.

ceased, since 1525, following François I on his journeys. He was, nevertheless, obliged to go to Court every second day, when the King resided at Paris. He did not lose sight of a big project he had conceived fifteen years previously, and which was soon to be realised : the creation of the Royal Lectors' College.

Another Hellenist who had been connected some time with this project lived then at Paris : Janus Lascaris. Brought from Italy to France by Charles VIII and described in an account of the wages paid to the Italian workmen at Amboise, as a "doctor from Grecian lands", Lascaris, after many changes, had settled down at Paris, where he lived on a royal pension of 600 *livres*. It is possible that Rabelais there met him, a line in *Gargantua* seems to refer to him. The storyteller, having mentioned "the antique play tables", adds "as our good friend Lascaris playeth at it "[1].

The conclusion of the Cambrai peace and the return of the French royal princes, held as hostages in Spain for three years, had led to a quietening down of the persecution against heresy. The King directed himself, for a time, towards a policy of tolerance. It is at this period, the beginning of 1530, that the institution of the Royal Lectors, later the Collège de France, takes place—a modest creation, far below the hopes inspired in Humanists by François I's promises. Provision was made in the *Comptes de l'épargne* (Treasury accounts) to pay for public lessons which would be given by Danès and Toussaint in Greek, Vatable and Guidacerius in Hebrew, and Oronce Finé in Mathematics[2]. There were no letters patent granting statutes and privileges, no buildings assigned for the classes—the Lectors will have to obtain use of the free class-rooms in the Colleges of Cambrai and Tréguier. Even their pay will sometimes be overlooked. But the moral effect is considerable. Henceforth, there exists a teaching of the humanities (a chair of Latin will be created in 1534), free from the suspicious inspection of the Sorbonne. The ancient tongues are at last studied and taught for themselves, independently of the programmes and of the scope of the Arts and Theological Faculties. The advantage of intellectual superiority is transferred from the Sorbonne to

---

[1] *Gargantua*, ch. XXIV. It is quite possible that Rabelais and Lascaris may have met in Rome where they both were in 1534.
[2] Cf. Abel Lefranc, *Histoire du Collège de France* (1899), p. 109.

Humanism. Budé rejoices to see " good letters " cultivated, despite the war declared upon them by the factious, and to hear Greek resound in the schools and groups of cultivated persons[1]. Marot is soon to contrast with the " ignorant Sorbonne " the " trilingual and noble academy "[2]. Rabelais will put far back in the past, to the time when Gargantua lived, the Sorbonne's era of glory " which then was, but now is no more, the oracle of Leucetia[3]." A new era is beginning for *les bonnes lettres* : he salutes its arrival with enthusiasm[4] :

" Now it is, that the minds of men are qualified with all manner of discipline and the old sciences revived, which for many ages were extinct. Now it is, that the learned languages are to their pristine purity restored, viz., Greek, without which a man may be ashamed to account himself a scholar, Hebrew, Arabic, Chaldæan, and Latin. Printing likewise is now in use, so elegant and so correct, that better cannot be imagined, although it was found out but in my time by divine inspiration, as by a diabolical suggestion on the other side, was the invention of ordnance. All the world is full of knowing men, of most learned schoolmasters, and vast libraries ; and it appears to me as a truth, that neither in Plato's time, nor Cicero's, nor Papinian's, there was ever such conveniency for studying, as we see at this day there is. Nor must any adventure henceforth to come in public or present himself in company, that hath not been pretty well polished in the shop of Minerva. I see robbers, hangmen, freebooters, tapsters, ostlers, and such like, of the very rubbish of the people, more learned now than the doctors and preachers were in my time. What shall I say ? The very women and children have aspired to this praise and celestial manna of good learning."

[1] " Nunc vero exsibilata a pueris eorum temeritate et audacia, ob libros maxime græcos tabernæ et officinæ bibliopolarum visuntur et frequentantur. Ludi scholastici conventusque studiosorum, vocibus prœlegentium græcorum scripta personant ". *De philologia* (1530), ch. XXVI. He considers letters to have returned from exile : " literas vitæ restitutas postliminio ætatis nostræ videamus ". This metaphor, the return of " good Letters " from exile, was current before that of *Renaissance*, which has been finally adopted only since Voltaire's day.

[2]   " Autant comme eulx, sans cause qui soit bonne
          Me veult de mal l'ignorante Sorbonne :
          Bien ignorante elle est d'estre ennemye
          De la trilingue et noble académie
          Qu'as érigée ". *Épître au roy, du temps de son exil à Ferrare.*
     (" The ignorant Sorbonne, without just reason, is equally hostile to me :
          it is indeed ignorant being opposed to the trilingual and noble academy
          which thou hast established ".)

[3] *Gargantua*, ch. XVII.

[4] *Pantagruel*, ch. VIII. Letter from Gargantua to Pantagruel, studying in Paris. With the present day he contrasts the preceding age which " was darksome, obscured with clouds of ignorance, and savouring a little of the infelicity and calamity of the Goths, who had, wherever they set footing, destroyed all good literature ".

CHAPTER VII

On the 17th September, 1530, Rabelais affixed his signature on the matriculation register of the Faculty of Medicine of Montpellier, after having taken the prescribed oath to observe all the statutes and regulations of the said Faculty[1]. He took as patron (*pater*) in accordance with the custom a regenting doctor and his choice fell upon Jean Schyron, whom he had known at Agen with Julius Cæsar Scaliger[2]. Schyron had been for two years professor at Montpellier and was later to be Chancellor of the University.

Six weeks later, the 1st November, he was admitted a Bachelor of Medicine, the examination having been presided over by the same Jean Schyron[3].

This registration of Rabelais at the Faculty of Medicine of Montpellier marks a new direction in his life as a scholar. At the convent of the Puy-Saint-Martin, in Geoffroy d'Estissac's service, at Poitiers, and at Paris, he had studied Literature, Greek and Latin antiquity, and then Law : and now, at the age of thirty-six, seemingly devoid of all resources and

---

[1] The following is the text of this entry : Ego Franciscus Rabelæsus Chinonensis, diocesis Turonensis, huc adpuli studiorum medicinæ gratia. Delegique mihi in patrem egregium Dominum Joannem Scurronem, doctorem regentemque in hac alma universitate. Polliceor autem me omnia observaturum quæ in predicta medicinæ facultate statuuntur et observari solent ab iis qui nomen bona fide dedere, juramento, ut moris est præstito. Adscripsique nomen meum manu propria, die decima septima mensis septembris, anno domini millesimo quingentesimo trigesimo. Rabelæsus.

Cf. plate IIIb.

[2] *Vide supra*, ch. VI, p. 79. Rabelais refers to Schyron as Scurron : " The famous physician, Scurron, passing one day by this country, was telling us, that it (the Languedoc wind called *Cierce*) is so strong, that it will make nothing of overthrowing a loaded waggon ". *Fourth Book*, ch. XLIII.

[3] We learn of his admission to this degree from the following attestation (in Marty-Laveaux, *op. cit.*, vol. III, p. 308) :

Ego Franciscus Rabelæsus diocesis Turonensis, promotus fui ad gradum baccalaureatus, die prima mensis novembris, anno domini millesimo quingentesimo trigesimo, sub reverendo artium et medicinæ professore magistro Joanne Scurronio. Rabelæsus.

PLATE III

Ϝran⁵ Ɓabelϵſi καὶ τ̅ αὐτο̃ φίλϵϛν.

Ne quis alius impune, aut Venetiis aut uſquam lo-
corum hos Galeni libros imprimat, & Cle-
mentis VII. Pont. Max. & Sena-
tus Veneti decreto cau-
tum eſt.

Nunç vero ᵮranᶜᵘˢ /xærellus, me habet——

A. COPY OF GALEN WITH INSCRIPTION IN RABELAIS' HAND
(Sheffield Library)

B. FACSIMILE OF RABELAIS' INSCRIPTION AT THE UNIVERSITY OF MONTPELLIER

[face p. 92

without a situation, he decided upon providing himself with the necessary degrees to gain the means of existence from the exercise of the medical profession.

He had presumably been contemplating it for some time previously. The rapid progress he made from the early months of his stay at Montpellier proves that he was no novice at medical science. A legend shows him entering into discussions with his future professors on the very day of his arrival, and leaving them nonplussed. This much, at least, is certain, that when, two and three years later, he is writing *Pantagruel* and *Gargantua*, his memory teems with facts and theories of meteorology, optics, physics, botany and natural history. On all scientific questions his erudition is extensive and reliable. It thus seems likely that he had devoted himself to the medical sciences long before his registration at Montpellier.

Medicine was then only a department of the vast domain of " Philosophy " which Humanists were exploring : did it not include anatomy, physiology, physics, which they studied in Aristotle ? Natural history, which their study of Pliny and of Theophrastus revealed to them ? Consequently, few Humanists were entirely unacquainted with medical science. Guillaume Budé revises the Latin translation of Galen made by his friend the English doctor, Thomas Linacre. His own books of rough notes (*adversaria*) show us how he ransacks the works of Pliny, Celsus, Dioscorides, Paul of Ægina, in order to take notes on the names of plants, shrubs, colours and diseases.[1] Tiraqueau, in 1525, calls Rabelais' attention to a collection of medical letters published in Italy ; he himself is interested in the progress of medicine, which he praises in his *De legibus connubialibus*.

Other Humanists will go further in the study of the medical sciences ; such as Hubert Sussannée, who, having taught the humanities at Turin and Paris, took his Doctorate in medicine[2]; Jacques Dubois, who was physician and philologist[3] ; Jacques Peletier du Mans, grammarian and poet, who published a treatise on some passages from Galen.[4] Theoretic medicine came within the scope of the Humanists : with their knowledge of Latin and

---

[1] Cf. L. Delaruelle, *Répertoire analytique de la correspondance de Budé*, pp. 23, 64, and *Guillaume Budé*, p. 252.
[2] We return to Sussannée in ch. XIII.
[3] Cf., on Jacques Dubois, L. Thuasne, *Revue des bibliothèques*, vol. XV.
[4] Cf. *Jacques Peletier du Mans* by Abbé Clement Jugé (Paris, 1907).

Greek, they held the key to medical science contained in the technical treatises of the Ancients.

Thus, it is in the natural course of his humanistic studies that Rabelais arrived at the study of medicine, and perhaps even from his years as a monk at the time he was in touch with Tiraqueau. However, about the date of his beginning, he is decided definitely in 1530 on devoting himself especially to medicine and he comes to follow the teaching of the most renowned of French Medical Faculties, that of Montpellier.

Founded in the first quarter of the 13th century, the University of Montpellier had acquired a great reputation throughout Europe. Its Faculty of Law, which in Rabelais' day counted few students—" three scauld- and one bald-pated legist ", he tells us—was little spoken of ; but the prestige of its professors of the Medical Faculty was unsurpassed and students thronged around their chairs. The teaching consisted in reading and expounding Greek and Arabian books of medicine in a Latin translation. Botany was in great favour there. Practical exercises were done upon " dry anatomies ", that is, skeletons, and exceptionally by dissections of dead bodies, taken from the hospitals or gallows : the year 1530 saw two such dissections and the following year, three. Four regenting Doctors gave out this instruction from the Feast of Saint Luke (18th October) to Palm Sunday. This was called the " Great Ordinary " in contradistinction to the " Little Ordinary ", which went from Quasimodo Monday to Saint John's day. The lectures by professors were few in this second part of the scholastic year. The medical text-books were then expounded by the Bachelors who thus gave proof of their learning[1].

Rabelais, therefore, was a Bachelor fifteen days after the commencement of lectures, six weeks after his registration as a student, whereas apparently the period of study required from a candidate for this degree was two years[2]. Schyron, who knew the candidate, had, without a doubt, got him a dispensation in consideration of his previous studies. But to reach the Licence, that is to say, the Master's degree, the statutes prescribed six years' study : we shall see that Rabelais did not obtain the Doctor's degree until 1537.

[1] Cf. A. Germain's articles, collected in his work on *Les anciennes écoles de Montpellier* (Montpellier, 1881).

[2] This is the opinion of Dr. de Santi in his study of *Rabelais à Toulouse*, *Rev. XVIe siècle*, p. 51.

The new Bachelor did not take long to distinguish himself. For his probationary course during the " Little Ordinary " he selected works of Greek medicine : the *Aphorisms* of Hippocrates and Galen's *Ars parva*. Others before him had assuredly expounded these texts, but no one of them had been able, like him, to do so from the Greek text itself. The Latin version (Vulgate) had seemed to him very faulty by comparison with a Greek manuscript which he possessed and he undertook its improvement by additions and corrections from his own Greek manuscript. This commentary of the Greek medical writers and from the original text was an innovation, and the innovation, by reason, no doubt, of its very boldness, was appreciated, for the seats in the auditorium were crowded with people eager to hear the learned Bachelor[1]. Besides, for a long time there was no one capable of imitating him. The Faculty of Medicine was destined a second time to hear a commentary on a Greek text of Hippocrates, that of the *Prognostics*, in 1537 ; but the commentator will again be Rabelais.

These 1531 lectures on the Greek text of Hippocrates and Galen were more than a learned curiosity ; they were a manifestation in favour of the medical science of the Greeks which did not then reign undisputed at the University of Montpellier. Arabian medicine still counted stubborn partisans there ; until the end of the 15th century, Arabian medical writers, like Avicenna, had been expounded in preference to the Greeks. In Rabelais' day Avicenna still furnished the subject matter of one half of the lectures. But his star was already on the wane. The Humanists were discrediting the Arabians, accusing them of having altered and corrupted the precepts of their Greek masters. The prefaces of the medical treatises of the second quarter of the 16th century abound in recriminations against Avicenna and against the medicine of the Arabs, obscure, mutilated, bristling with errors[2]. We are not then surprised that Avicenna should have disappeared from the teaching of

---

[1] So Rabelais tells us in the preface to his edition of these *Aphorisms* published 1532. Cf. Marty-Laveaux, vol. III, p. 317.

[2] The text of these prefaces are given in Guillaume Cop (*Epistula Guill. Copi Basilensis in librum Galeni de affectorum locorum notione*, ed. of 1547, Lyons, G. Roville) ; in the *Clysteriorum campi . . . contra Arabum traditionem*, by Symphorien Champier, Bâle, 1552 ; in Martin Acakia's edition of Galen, Lyons, 1547 : " Itaque Galenum imitandum esse suadeo, non autem Arabum doctrinam obscuram, mutilam ac mancam erroribusque scatentem. Longe enim plus commodi vel ex hac Galeni ad Glauconem curandi ratione, quam ex universa Arabum doctrina te assecuturum confidenter adfirmo ".

the Faculty of Montpellier from 1557 onwards[1]. But the campaign against the Arabian tradition had been severe. Rabelais took part in it and a passage in *Gargantua* breathes his contempt for the " rabble of logger-headed physicians, muzzled in the brabbling shop of the Arabians[2]".

He believed, then, in the superiority of Greek scholars and physicians. He read them in the original, meditated upon them, commentated them. Amongst the volumes of his library which have reached us is a magnificent edition in five volumes of Galen's text, now at Sheffield Library[3]. He was so familiar with the treatises on ancient medicine that he could quote them, refer the readers of *Pantagruel* and *Gargantua* to them from memory with exact references. Let it not, however, be imagined that he accepted all their ideas without discussion. He had poked fun, for instance, upon occasion at this very Galen whom he quotes at least ten times during his narration of Pantagruel's and Gargantua's lives, and has given his verdict upon the puerile finalism of this " fine fellow " who declares in the ninth book of his treatise on the " Use and employment of our Members " (*De usu partium*) that the head was made for the eyes[4].

These are the main aspects of Rabelais' medical doctrine, as it appears from those of his publications which have followed his studies at Montpellier. He is before all a Humanist, that is, he sees no advancement possible for medical science except from a better knowledge of Greek and Latin treatises thereon. Dissections will indeed have place in his studies and in his career ; but, no more than the best of his confrères, will he assign to experimental work the rôle it will subsequently fill in the development of medicine. For him the most pressing need is to clear the text of the ancients' treatises of the glosses and erroneous interpretations by which the Arabians have corrupted it. That did not, however, mean swearing blindly on the word of the Greek Masters : their teachings could not be accepted when they were clearly in disagreement with reason or experience.

---

[1] Cf. A. Germain, *Les anciennes écoles de Montpellier*.
[2] *Gargantua*, ch. XXIII.
[3] Cf. the reproduction of the *ex-libris*, plate IIIa.
[4] *Third Book*, ch. VII. He likewise scoffed at the credulity of Democritus and Theophrastus who believed the mere touch of a certain herb would draw forth an iron wedge implanted in wood. *Fourth Book*, ch. LXII.

The university life of Montpellier did not consist entirely in study. It included, as in the other Universities of old France, numerous relaxations. The most important were the meals in common : dinner of welcome and of farewell, dinner on the Epiphany, dinner on the reception of every new Bachelor, etc. Rabelais will later remember these feasts when he mentions one of the wines of the country, Mirevaulx[1], among its attractions. The Epiphany feasting was accompanied by processions with banners, carnivals, dances and performances of morality plays and farces[2]. University types were represented on the stage. The medical men poked fun at the proud lawyers and the lawyers turned to ridicule the physicians who " smell of glisters like old devils " and feed on the urine or excrement of their patients :

" Stercus et urina medici sunt prandia prima "[3].

Rabelais has preserved for us the scenario of one of these farces, the " Moral comedy of him who had espoused and married a dumb wife . . ."

" The good honest man, her husband, was very earnestly urgent to have the fillet of her tongue untied, and would needs have her speak by any means. At his desire, some pains were taken on her, and partly by the industry of the physician, other part by the expertness of the surgeon, the encyliglotte which she had under her tongue being cut she spoke, and spoke again ; yea, within a few hours she spoke so loud, so much, so fiercely, and so long, that her poor husband returned to the same physician for a receipt to make her hold her peace. ' There are ', quoth the physician, ' many proper remedies in our art to make dumb women speak, but there are none that ever I could learn therein to make them silent. The only cure which I have found out is their husband's deafness '. The wretch became within few weeks thereafter, by virtue of some drugs, charms, or enchantments, which the physician had prescribed unto him, so deaf, that he could not have heard the thundering of nineteen hundred cannons at a salvo. His wife perceiving that indeed he was deaf as a door-nail, and that her scolding was but in vain, sith that he heard her not, she grew stark mad. Some time after, the doctor asked for his fee of the husband ; who answered, That truly he was deaf, and so was not able to understand what the tenour of his demand might be. Whereupon the leech bedusted him with a little, I know not what, sort of powder, which rendered him a fool immediately, so great was the stultificating

[1] *Pantagruel*, ch. V.
[2] Cf. A. Germain, *op. cit., passim.*
[3] *Pantagruel*, ch. V ; *Third Book*, ch. XXXIV.

H

virtue of that strange kind of pulverised dose. Then did this fool of a husband, and his mad wife, join together, and falling on the doctor and the surgeon, did so scratch, bethwack, and bang them, that they were left half dead upon the place, so furious were the blows which they received. I never in my lifetime laughed so much, as at the acting of that buffoonery (*Patelinage*) "[1].

It is, in fact, the farce of *Pathelin* which suggested a part of this scene : the husband pretending not to hear the doctor who claims his fee recalls Thibault l'Agnelet paying the advocate, Pathelin, with the answer he had himself taught him to give to the judge or cloth-merchant : *baa, baa*. As Rabelais makes very frequent allusions in his works to the farce of *Pathelin*, which he seems to have appreciated more than any of his contemporaries did, it has been surmised that this Montpellier *patelinage* may well have been of his own composition. That is extremely probable. We shall see that the rapidity with which he composed his first humorous work, *Pantagruel*, points to his having already dabbled in facetious literature. The comic anecdotes, caricatures, exaggerations, broad stories, were, as we shall see, the relaxation of the scholar. Why might he not as well amuse himself by writing the libretto of a farce, and borrowing from one of his favourite books *Pathelin* the theme of its *dénouement* ? In the same passage he names himself as having taken a part in the performance, and enumerates eight of his " ancient " friends who are supposed to have acted in the play as well. (Quite sufficient for four parts !) Some of them have remained obscure, their names being found only on the registers of the Faculty of Montpellier ; others were then, or later became, learned doctors ; such was Antoine Saporta, of a family of professors of medicine, who was himself Chancellor of the University and physician to the King and Queen of Navarre ; another Pierre Tolet, whom Tiraqueau considered to be one of the lights of contemporary medicine[2], and who had the merit of vulgarising this science by several works in French[3] ; another was Rondelet, Rondibilis as Maître François[4] calls him, who specialised in Natural History and particularly in the study of fish. " Hilaris erat et facetus " is said of him in an old biographical notice, and

---

[1] *Third Book*, ch. XXXIV.
[2] In his *De Nobilitate* (1540). Cf. *R.É.R.*, IV, p. 387.
[3] Cf. Brunot, *Histoire de la langue française des origines à* 1900, vol. II, *Le seizième siècle*, p. 39.   [4] *Third Book*, ch. XXXII seq.

these epithets could doubtless be applied to other study-companions of Rabelais. Has he not made gaiety one of the features of the good physician's make-up, whose conversation and appearance should tend to " rejoice the patient without offending God "[1]. It is, seemingly, at Montpellier that his medical studies and his relations with physicians revealed to him the therapeutic efficaciousness of joy and the beneficent properties of laughter.

This theme was largely disserted upon in the medical schools. Democritus and Hippocrates were consulted on the " moral cause of laughter "[2]. This sentence of Aristotle's was commented upon : " Alone of living beings, man is capable of laughter "[3]. Rabelais, among his masters and companions of the School of Medicine, was thus led to meditate upon laughter.

He was naturally inclined to gaiety. It is a trait which his friends at Fontenay-le-Comte and Poitiers passed over in silence in their praises of him, because for a Tiraqueau or a Jean Bouchet, in love with learning, nothing counted besides the encyclopædic learning for which the young monk, " a man of great Greek and Latin letters ", was remarkable. It is, however, certain that his cheerfulness, his good humour, his light-heartedness, had recommended him to his protector, Geoffroy d'Estissac. We shall see him displaying these same qualities in the letters which he sends him subsequently. The Franciscan tradition was not opposed to this gaiety.

---

[1] He gives a learned and copious exposition of this question in his *Epistle Dedicatory to the most Illustrious Prince, and most Reverend Lord, Odet, Cardinal de Chastillon*, prefixed to his *Fourth Book*.

[2] Cf. the *Traité du ris, contenant son essence, ses causes et ses mervelheus effais, curieusement recerchés, raisonnés et observés*, par M. Laur. Joubert, conselier et medecin ordinaire du Roy et du Roy de Navarre, premier docteur regeant, chancelier et juge de l'Université en médecine de Montpellier, and, especially, the treatise which follows it : *La cause morale du Ris, de l'excellent et très renommé Democrite, expliquée et temoignée par ce divin Hippocras en ses Épistres*. Paris, 1579.

These disquisitions upon laughter were common in the 16th century ; compare Ronsard's, on the same theme, in a poem to Belot, Conseiller et Master of Requests of the Royal Household :

Dieu, qui soubz l'homme a le monde soumis,
A l'homme seul, le seul rire a permis
Pour s'esgayer et non pas à la beste,
Qui n'a raison ny esprit en la teste.
Il faut du rire honnestement user
Pour vivre sain . . .

Œuvres, Ed. Laumonier (Lemerre), vol. V, 10.

[3] " Μόνον γελᾷ τῶν ζώων ἄνθρωπος," *De partibus animalium*, III, 10.

The Cordelier lived in joy, a joy which blossomed forth into somewhat coarse jests and jokes. The " Franciscan touch " has a tinge of " Gallic wit "[1]. As a student, on the Hill of Sainte-Geneviève, he had been able to amuse himself by practical jokes and witticisms ; nothing had hitherto gone contrary to Rabelais' tendency towards joyousness[2], and here he finds at the Faculty of Medicine the justification of this happy disposition in an oft-repeated phrase of Aristotle : that laughter is proper to Man.

In fact, this sentence occurs in the Greek philosopher's works merely as an incidental remark, giving forth a truth of common observation ; and he explains only the physiological process of the phenomenon of laughter. If Rabelais gives to Aristotle's words a general and philosophical import, if he later emphasises them by placing them as an epigraph at the beginning of his work[3] the reason is that they agree with his views upon nature and upon man which, on the whole, are optimistic.

Such tendencies could only be encouraged and confirmed by the general ideas traditionally current in the medical school. On two essential points indeed, the medical teaching of the Middle Ages and of the Renaissance is resolutely optimistic : it professes an almost unreserved admiration for the structure of the human body and holds nature to be well-disposed towards man.

A German *savant*, Wirchow, once declared that if the Creator had offered him an instrument of vision as imperfect as the eyes of Man, he would certainly have refused it as being an ill-constructed apparatus. The opinion of Doctors contemporary of Rabelais on the human body is diametrically contrary. They see in it only clever ingenuity. They praise its exact mechanism, and to express its harmonious organisation they

---

[1] Gilson in his *Rabelais Franciscain*, p. 19, proves this from some curious points of Franciscan habits.

[2] The confiscation of his Greek books at Fontenay-le-Comte would not seem to have had much effect upon him, as we have said. There is only one trace of bitterness against the Cordeliers in his work, the reference to the " ambush of the hob-goblins " laid for Pierre Amy, from which he escaped " safe and sound ". *Third Book*, chap. X.

[3] In the *Dixain* placed at the beginning of *Gargantua* in the second edition :
Mieulx est de ris que de larmes escripre,
Pour ce que rire est le propre de l'homme.
(Translated by Urquhart :
One inch of joy surmounts of grief a span ;
Because to laugh is proper to the man.)

have ready recourse to a Greek work which brings out this harmony: they called the body the *microcosm*, the little world, because it reproduces, on a smaller sale, the harmony of the great world or *macrocosm*. Their admiration for this "little universe", where all the organs work together for a common end, to sustain life, has been given lyrical expression by Rabelais through Panurge's mouth :

" The intention of the founder of this microcosm is, to have a soul therein to be entertained, which is lodged there, as a guest with its host, that it may live there for awhile. Life consisteth in blood, blood is the seat of the soul ; therefore the chiefest work of the microcosm is, to be making blood continually. At this forge are exercised all the members of the body ; none is exempted from labour, each operates apart, and doth its proper office. And such is their hierarchy, that perpetually one is the other's debtor. The stuff and matter convenient, which nature giveth to be turned into blood, is bread and wine. All kind of nourishing victuals is understood to be comprehended in those two, and from hence in the Gothish tongue is called companage. To find out this meat and drink, to prepare and boil it, the hands are put to work, the feet do walk and bear up the whole bulk of the corporal mass ; the eyes guide and conduct all.

The appetite in the orifice of the stomach, by means of a little sourish black humour, called melancholy, which is transmitted thereto from the milt, giveth warning to shut in the food. The tongue doth make the first essay, and tastes it ; the teeth to chaw it, and the stomach doth receive, digest, and chilify it. The mesaraic veins suck out of it what is good and fit, leaving behind the excrements, which are, through special conduits, for that purpose, voided by an expulsive faculty. Thereafter it is carried to the liver, where it being changed again, it by the virtue of that new transmutation becomes blood.

What joy, conjecture you, will then be found amongst those officers, when they see this rivulet of gold, which is their sole restorative ? No greater is the joy of alchymists, when, after long travail, toil, and expense, they see in their furnaces the transmutation.

Then is it that every member doth prepare itself, and strive anew to purify and to refine this treasure. The kidneys, through the emulgent veins, draw that aquosity from thence, which you call urine, and there send it away through the ureters to be slipped downwards ; where, in a lower receptacle and proper for it, to wit, the bladder, it is kept, and stayeth there until an opportunity to void it out in his due time. The spleen draweth from the blood its terrestrial part, viz. the grounds, lees, or thick substance settled in the bottom thereof, which you term melancholy. The bottle of the gall subtracts from thence all the superfluous choler ; whence it is brought to another shop or work-house to be yet better purified and fined, that is, the heart, which by its agitation of diastolic and systolic motions so neatly subtiliseth and inflames it, that in the right side ventricle it is brought to perfection, and through the veins is sent to all the members. Each parcel of the body draws it then unto itself, and after its own fashion is cherished and alimented by it. Feet, hands, thighs, arms, eyes, ears, back, breasts, yea, all ; and then it is, that who before were lenders, now become debtors. The heart doth in its left side ventricle so thinnify the blood, that it thereby obtains the name of spiritual ; which being sent through the arteries to all the members of the body, serveth to warm and winnow the other blood which runneth through the veins. The lights never cease with its lappets and bellows to cool and refresh it ; in acknowledgment of which good the heart, through the arterial vein, imparts unto it the choicest of its blood. At last it is made so fine and subtle within the *rete mirabile*, that thereafter those animal spirits are framed and composed of it ; by means whereof the imagination, discourse, judgment, resolution, deliberation, ratiocination, and memory have their rise, actings, and operation.

Cops body, I sink, I drown, I perish, I wander astray, and quite fly out of myself, when I enter into the consideration of the profound abyss of this world. . . . Yet is not this all. This little world . . . is so good and charitable, that no sooner is the above-specified alimentation finished, but that it forthwith projecteth . . . to eternize itself, and multiply in images like the pattern, that is children. To this end every member doth of the choicest and most precious of its nourishment, pare and cut off a portion, then instantly dispatcheth it downwards to that place, where nature hath prepared for it very fit vessels and receptacles, through which descending to the genitories by long ambages, circuits, and flexuosities, it receiveth a competent form, and rooms apt enough both in the man and woman for the future conservation and perpetuating of human kind "[1].

Thus our physicians of the Middle Ages and of the Renaissance believed that everything is arranged for the best in the organisation of the human body. We can discern only one reservation in their admiration : it concerns the physiology of women. Doctor Rondibilis, presented by Rabelais, formulates it as follows :

" When I say womankind, I speak of a sex so frail, so variable, so changeable, so fickle, inconstant, and imperfect, that, in my opinion, Nature, under favour nevertheless, of the prime honour and reverence which is due unto her, did in a manner mistake the road which she had traced formerly, and stray exceedingly from that excellence of providential judgment, by the which she had created

[1] *Third Book*, ch. IV.

and formed all other things, when she built, framed, and made up
the woman. And having thought upon it a hundred and five times,
I know not what else to determine therein, save only that in the
devising, hammering, forging, and composing of the woman, she hath
had a much tenderer regard, and by a great deal more respectful
heed to the delightful consortship, and social delectation of the man,
than to the perfection and accomplishment of the individual
womanishness or muliebrity ".[1]

It is probably from the Ancients that these ideas came.
Galen went far with these finalistic conceptions : is it not he
who said (and we have seen Rabelais making fun of this sentence) that the head was made for the eyes ? Did he not
admire Nature because she fixed the eyes in the head " as on
the top of a long pole, in the most eminent part of all the body[2],
to discover things from afar ? No otherwise than we see the
phares, or high towers, erected in the mouths of havens, that
navigators may the further off perceive with ease the lights of
the nightly fires and lanterns "[3]. Rabelais, doubtless, smiles
at this finalism, which recalls to our minds that of Bernardin
de Saint-Pierre in his *Harmonies de la nature* ; but the fault is
that of a system which was generally adopted around him,
and which we have no knowledge that he repudiated.

Nature was considered as maternal and protective for man.
The School of Salerno prescribed that one should not go against
it. We should even respect in a man the habits which have
become a second nature : *Condonandum est aliquid consuet-
udini ; Omnibus assuetam jubeo servare dietam*, are axioms of
the *Regimen Salernitanum*, taken from Hippocrates and expounded in the school[4]. Has not Nature put within our reach
everything which is useful for our health ? Why have recourse

---

[1] *Ibid.*, ch. XXXII.   [2] In his *De usu partium*, book IX.
[3] *Third Book*, ch. VII. Plato, following Anaxagoras, had brought these
teleological considerations into science. But Galen had built up a whole
physiological system from the axiom that Nature does nothing in vain.
Cf. Daremberg, *Histoire des sciences médicales*, pp. 212 sqq.
[4] Cf. the treatise *De cibi potusque ratione*, ex Leonhardo Fuchsio, appended
to Galen's works, published by Guillaume Roville, Lyons, 1547, p. 158.
" Consuetudines sunt acquisititiæ, seu alteræ naturæ. Etenim, ut scripsit
Hippocrates, quæ ex longo tempore consueta sunt, etsi deteriora sunt, in-
suetis minus molestare solent. Et iterum : condonandum aliquid consue-
tudini. Quod si quando ad insueta transire necessitas coget, tum id ne subito,
sed paulatim fiat. Repentinæ enim mutationes, inquit Hippocrates, vitandæ
et omne nimium, inquit idem, naturæ inimicum ; quod autem sensim fit,
tutum est ". Further commentaries on the same maxims of Hippocrates are
to be found in *Theses seu communes loci totius rei medicæ* . . . per Othonem
Brunfelsium, Strasbourg, 1532.

to remedies of foreign origin, brought from the Orient or from India ? writes Symphorien Champier, a confrère of Rabelais at Lyons, in a treatise on Botany. God and Nature place under the very hand of the sick in each country what is necessary for them[1]. Thus will Montaigne reason when he declares that the only therapeutic worthy of our confidence is natural agents, simples and thermal waters, and Molière himself will unsuspectingly follow the tradition of our old medical schools when he causes the following maxim to be enunciated before his *Malade Imaginaire* : that the best course for the patient to adopt is often to allow Nature to take its course unaided.

Thus, medical tradition can claim a share in what has been called Rabelais' naturalism for it also professed its belief in Nature and upheld that it must not be thwarted.

---

[1] Cf. *Campus Elysius Galliæ amœnitate refertus, quo sunt medicinæ compositæ herbæ et plantæ virentes ; in quo quidquid apud Indos, Arabos et Pœnos reperitur apud Gallos reperiri posse demonstratur : A Domino Symphoriano Campegio Equite aurato ac Lotharingorum archiatro compositus.* Lyons, 1533. We may mention another work of which the title likewise indicates the general spirit : *Hortus gallicus, pro Gallis in Gallia scriptus, verumtamen non minus Italis, Germanis et Hispanis quam Gallis necessarius. Symphoriano Campegio . . . authore, in quo Gallos in Gallia omnium ægritudinum remedia reperire docet, nec medicaminibus egere peregrinis, quum Deus et Natura de necessariis unicuique regioni provideat.* Lyons, 1532.

CHAPTER VIII

AT THE GREAT HOSPITAL OF THE PONT-DU-RHÔNE IN LYONS

In Spring of 1532 François Rabelais is in Lyons. The motives for which he had interrupted the course of his University studies at Montpellier and settled down in this town of Lyons which was to be, in his own words, the " seat of his studies "[1] for some years, can be easily surmised from the nature of the first work he undertook there. He was in need of resources. He could easily find them in a town where the booksellers and printers, who were very plentiful, had frequent recourse to scholars either to ask them for books to publish or to entrust them with the correction of their typographic proofs.

Lyons was then a commercial and intellectual centre of considerable activity. The free fairs instituted by Louis XI in 1462 drew to it four times yearly, at Epiphany, Quasimodo, August 2nd and All Saints, a crowd of traders from all the French provinces and from foreign countries—Flanders, Germany, the Swiss Cantons, Italy and Spain. Cloths, lace-work, haberdashery, headgear[2], musical instruments, arms, hardwear, pharmaceutical products, drysaltery, skins, tapestries poured in from every side to the quays on the right bank of the Saône, and into the Saint Paul and Saint Jean districts, the oldest part of the town, hemmed in between the river and the steep slopes of Fourvière hill[3].

All the moneys of every country being current at these fairs, Lyons had become the French exchange market. From

---

[1] " Lugdunum, ubi sedes est studiorum meorum. . . ." Letter to Jean du Bellay, September 1534. Cf. Marty-Laveaux, vol. III, p. 334.

[2] A work, composed in the latter half of the 16th century, Nicolay's *Description générale de la ville de Lyon* . . . (republished by the *Société de topographie historique de Lyon*, in 1881), informs us that the high-crowned hats of the Scotch mentioned by Rabelais (*Third Book*, ch. XXV, and *Fourth Book*, ch. XXX) were manufactured solely in Auvergne, and brought via Lyons to the countries of the Levant, Greece and Transylvania.

[3] Some of the houses built upon the hill-side had, according to *Gargantua*, ch. XII, their stables situated " at the very tops of the houses." Pictur-esquely-named passages gave access to them, the Ascent of *Tire-cul*, etc.

Geneva, Milan, Lucca, Florence, Genoa, bankers had come there to open up their exchange booths. Many had established themselves in the town and formed in it the nucleus of a foreign colony. A certain Thomas Gadagne had had built a sumptuous dwelling[1] and a family vault in the Church of the Célestins. Business, further increased by the frequent sojourns of the Court in the town during the Italian expeditions, soon found itself cramped in the quarter situate on the right bank of the Saône. On the far side of the sole bridge connecting it with the peninsula between the Saône and Rhône, merchants established themselves along the road which leads obliquely to the Rhône bridge. This was the *rue Mercière* (*Via Mercatoria*), of which many houses preserve still to-day, in their spiral stairways and mullioned windows, traces of the architecture of the time. It was continued by the rue Notre-Dame-de-Confort. Running into this street, at right angles, were the rues du Palais-Grillet, Ferrandière, and Thomassin.

There, more than in any other part of the town, the new printing industry had developed. There, in the imaginative words of a contemporary poet :

> En mille maisons, au dedans,
> Un grand million de dents noires,
> Un million de noires dents
> Travaille en foires et hors foires[2].

These black teeth are the typographic characters. To feed the increased working of this industry ink manufacturers, parchment makers, and letter founders multiplied in the neighbourhood. There also the booksellers kept their shops and put up for sale their new books at fair-times[3].

Some of them were of foreign origin, Italians like the Juntes, who installed themselves in the rue Thomassin in 1520, or Germans like Greiff of Wurtemberg, later known by the

---

[1] The Hotel de Gadagne, now the municipal museum. Rabelais mentions Gadagne as one of the richest people of his day : "They over and above must wish for gain, ay, and for the fine crowns, or *scudi di Guadaigne*". *Prologue* to the *Fourth Book*.

[2] (" Inside a thousand houses, a huge million of black teeth, a million of black teeth, work during and out of fair days ".)
Charles Fontaine, *Ode de l'antiquité et excellence de la ville de Lyon*, published in 1557.

[3] On the history of the City of Lyons cf. the fine work published under the direction of A. Kleinclausz : *Lyon, des origines à nos jours. La formation de la cité.* (Masson, 1925.)

name of Gryphius, or Sébastien Gryphe, who had established himself in 1523 in the same street and devoted himself to the publication of old texts and works of erudition[1].

These booksellers were in relationship with the lettered and learned men of the entire region. Not only did they supply their books but they received and forwarded their correspondence. One Michel Parmentier, bookseller At the sign of the *Écu de Bâle*, forwards for several years to Bâle, to the jurisconsult Boniface Amerbach, the letters which Professor Alciat sends him by messengers or merchants from Avignon, and later from Bourges, to Lyons, at the fair-times[2]. In the same way he sends on to Geoffroy d'Estissac the letters which Rabelais, resident in Rome, wrote to his first protector. A relationship of good services bound together savants and booksellers[3]. The erudite Étienne Dolet was for some time proof-corrector to Gryphius, and the physician, Michel Servet, filled the same function for the brothers Frellon, At the sign of the *Écu de Cologne*, in the *rue Mercière*.

Thus we can understand that Lyons, on which the Universities of Valence, of Avignon and of Montpellier depended for the production of printed books, should have attracted Rabelais after his first University successes. The booksellers of Lyons offered him a means of spreading his reputation abroad by publishing his works.

And, indeed, in the month of June, 1532, he published with Gryphius, " an accomplished printer ", his first learned work : Latin letters of a Ferrara doctor, Jean Manardi, on various medical subjects.

This Manardi, to whom leisure was assured by the liberality of a Mæcenas, Alfonso Trotto, had devoted himself especially

---

[1] On the world of the printers and booksellers cf. President Baudrier's *Bibliographie lyonnaise*. The printers, masters and associates, constituted a powerful corporation, respected by the authorities as it was one of the sources of the town's prosperity. Cf. Henri Hauser, *Étude critique sur la rebeine de Lyon*, (1529), in the *Revue historique* (1896, pp. 264–307).

[2] Cf. my article *A l'écu de Bâle*, Rev. *XVIe siècle*, 1926, p. 282.

[3] Witness the following verses of the Humanist Visagier, to Michel Parmentier :   " Devincis tibi cum bonos pœtas,
Rhetores pariter trahis disertos,
Præstans officium modo his, modo illis.
Eodem studio deos deasque
Omnes concilias. Tibi quid ultra
Jamque optem ? Nihil aut perennitatem ".

J. Vulteii Xenia . . . Lyons, 1537.

to the examination and commentary of manuscripts of Greek and Latin medical works. In 1525 he published his first collection of six letters on medicine. At Fontenay-le-Comte Tiraqueau, whose curiosity spread far beyond the domain of the legal sciences, had read these letters, admired them and recommended them to Rabelais, " as though they had been dictated by Pæon or Æsculapius ", the latter tells us[1]. So when a second volume of Manardi's, containing consultations and commentaries on Dioscorides and other ancient physicians or naturalists, appeared at Ferrara, Rabelais immediately recommended Sebastian Gryphius to publish an edition of it. He undertook to introduce Manardi to his French readers in a prefatory letter, his sole contribution to this edition. He dedicated it to Tiraqueau[2], in memory of their discussions upon Manardi's first collection and as a tribute to the legist who had composed a magnificent eulogy on medicine in his *De legibus connubialibus*. Humanism, besides, had provided lawyers and physicians with a similar system, as Rabelais points out in his prefatory letter. He enounces there in stately Ciceronian periods, ornamented with proverbs, popular sayings and familiar expressions, ideas dear to all Humanistic doctors.

In the first place he expresses surprise that the people continue to allow themselves to be gulled by the charlatanism of vain and grasping physicians[3]. Similar regrets are to be found, almost at the same time, from the pen of his colleagues, Symphorien Champier, Jean Canappe, Pierre Tolet.[4] Happily, he adds, the great are beginning to treat with respect doctors worthy of the name, that is, the scholars who have undertaken

---

[1] " Ejusque epistolas priores ita probabas ac si essent Pæone aut Æsculapio ipso dictante exceptæ." Ed. Marty-Laveaux, vol. III, p. 313.

[2] It is given in Marty-Laveaux, vol. III, p. 311 : *Franciscus Rabelæsus medicus Andreæ Tiraquello judici æquissimo apud Pictones.* S.P.D.

[3] " Nam quos plebs indocta aliquo in numero habuit hoc nomine, quod exoticam aliquam et insignem rerum peritiam præ se ferrent, eis si personam hanc καὶ λεοντῆν detraxeris, perfecerisque, ut cujus artis prætextu, luculenta eis rerum accessio facta est, eam vulgus meras præstigias, ineptissimasque ineptias esse agnoscat, quid aliud quam cornicum oculos confixisse videberis ? " Note the abundance of figures which adorn this style.

[4] Cf. S. Champier's *Mirouer des Apothicaires* (Lyons, 1531), ch. XI, and especially Pierre Tolet's *Chirurgie de Paulus Ægineta* (Lyons, Dolet, 1540) who, in his *Proème*, sympathises with the common people " deceived by a horde of charlatans (*lanterniers*) who come to France from several foreign countries, some of them professing the art of magic, others dressed in white, green, gray or red ".

to free the Greek and Latin texts from the glosses, interpolations and commentaries, amassed by the ignorant[1].

It is by discarding the mediæval glosses, which obscured the literal meaning of the *Pandects* and the *Code*, that contemporary skilled lawyers renovated the legal sciences : in performing a similar cleansing upon the medical works of the ancients, its lustre will equally be restored to medicine.

Rabelais gave at once a specimen of this method, entirely philological in principle, by publishing with Gryphius an edition of Hippocrates' *Aphorisms* : it was on sale at the August fair of 1532 (the dedicatory letter is dated July 15th)[2], doubtless simultaneously with Manardi's letters of which the dedicatory epistle is dated June 3rd.

He dedicated this work to Geoffroy d'Estissac. Already in the dedicatory epistle of Manardi's letters, he had charged Tiraqueau with his salutations to the Bishop of Maillezais, his very liberal protector, as he names him : " Mæcenatem meum benignissimum ". He renews his devoted assurances to his protector in this dedication written some weeks later : " All that my efforts can bring forth belongs by right to you ", he declares, " you have hitherto so far nurtured me by your kindness that wherever I turn my eyes nothing presents itself to my senses but the sky or the sea of your munificence "[3].

It is clear from his statements to Geoffroy d'Estissac that Rabelais had prepared this edition at Montpellier. At the request of Sebastian Gryphius, who projected the publication of a collection of medical works, he edits in pocket-size the Latin version of four books of Hippocrates ; the *Aphorisms*, the *Præsagia*, the *Ratio victus in morbis acutis*, and the *De Natura humana*, as well as Galen's *Ars medicinalis*, in the translation of the physicians Leonicenus, Cop and Brentius, which was the Vulgate of these works. On the opposite page of the version of the *Aphorisms* was the Greek text ; in the margins Greek notes and Latin glosses, some by Rabelais, others taken from various

---

[1] Vivès in his *De Causis corruptarum artium*, gives the names of these learned physicians : " Unde multi errores extiterunt Avicennæ, Rasis et aliorum Arabum . . . Quæ omnia Nicolaus Leonicenus, Hermolaus Barbarus, Thomas Linacer, Gulielmus Copus, Laurentius Laurentianus, Manardus, Ruellius patefecerunt, sive redarguendis falsis, sive asserendis veris ; quæ incipiunt jam esse passim nota ". Ch. V, *De Medicina*.

[2] Given by Marty-Laveaux, *op. cit.*, vol. III, pp. 317–319.

[3] " Tibi enim jure debetur quicquid efficere opera mea potest ; qui me sic tua benignitate usque fovisti, ut quocumque oculos circumferam, οὐδὲν ἢ οὐρανὸς ἠδὲ θάλασσα munificentiæ tuæ sensibus meis observetur ".

contemporary medical writers. In all, 187 notes for the 77 pages of the *Aphorisms*[1].

The interest of this publication is that it gives us an example of how the Humanist doctors conceived their task of advancing medical science. They aimed, at first, only at purging the ancient books of useless glosses or textual errors. Rabelais' commentary is purely philological. He limits himself to using for the amendment of a doubtful or obscure text the readings of a manuscript he considers better. Of experimental teaching there is no trace.

His philological method is, besides, extremely imperfect as was the textual criticism of his day[2]. Why should his manuscript be more trustworthy than the Vulgate ? Is it merely because it is better written ? What rules are followed in his choice of readings ? He does not tell us, nor can we surmise it. Several of his corrections are absolutely insignificant. He seems to have yielded often, not to the scruples of a philologist, but to the pleasure of confronting the hackneyed text with his own manuscript.

Such as it was, and notwithstanding all that has been said, this edition achieved a good measure of success[3]. Eleven years later, Gryphius reprinted it, reducing by two-thirds, it is true, the number of the marginal annotations.

These two learned publications, Manardi's *Medical Letters* and Hippocrates' *Aphorisms*, helped considerably to establish Rabelais' reputation as a doctor : *medici omnibus numeris absolutissimi*, said the title-page of the latter. They doubtless helped their author to his appointment, on November 1st, 1532, as physician to the Hôtel-Dieu[4].

---

[1] For further details cf. my study on *Les publications savantes de Rabelais*, in *R.É.R.*, vol. II, p. 67, and that of René Sturel, *Rabelais et Hippocrate*, *R.É.R.*, vol. VI, p. 97.

[2] There is a good synopsis of the history of textual criticism, by M. Félix Grat, in the *Bulletin de l'Association Guillaume Budé*, no. 13, October, 1926.

[3] Cf. my criticism (*Rev. XVIe siècle*, 1926, pp. 305–306) of the tradition, current in the 17th century, that Rabelais composed his Almanachs in order to compensate Gryphius for his loss on the sale of the *Aphorisms*.

[4] Information contained in the *Comptes de l'Hôtel-Dieu de Lyon* (Communal Archives, series EG.), a sheet of which Marty-Laveaux gives in reproduction, *op. cit.*, vol. III, pp. 324–325. It is an entry of moneys paid as salary to the physician, January 15th, 1532 (old style), for the months of November, December and January, namely, 10 *livres* (at the rate of 40 *livres* per annum). On the margin is the following note—" Physician's wages, a new physician in the place of M. Pierre Roland, who is named Françoys Rabellet ". His name is spelt *Rabellais* and *Rabellèse* in the same register for the years 1533 and 1534.

The " Grand Hostel Dieu de Notre Dame de Pitié du Pont-du-Rhône ", which gloried in its existence of almost a thousand years (legend attributed its existence to Childebert[1]), was an important establishment in the first third of the 16th century. Administered by " consuls-rectors ", who belonged to the bourgeoisie of Lyons, it increased its wealth yearly by legacies and donations[2].

Nothing is to-day remaining of the buildings which then housed it and which occupy a large extent of the plans of the period. But we possess a description of it[3], barely a few years later in date than Rabelais' stay there. In a large hall, divided into two parts by pillars and a lattice, were six rows of beds ; " with walnut bedsteads and tapestry hangings all clean, white and well-fitted out ", arranged so that all the patients could see the chapel situated at the end of the hall, where Mass was said daily[4]. On one side the men, on the other the women, who could see each other but not mix together. In the centre, a large fire-place where the patients go to warm themselves in cold weather ; the men on one side, the women on the other. In another building was a maternity ward for women in child-birth. Those suffering from contagious diseases were cared for in a special ward.

The care of the sick and attendance were carried out by a large staff : sixteen " reformed Magdalens ", all dressed in white, a purveyor, three male servants, five female servants, two nurses, a gardener, a porter, a resident apothecary, a barber-surgeon, a chaplain and a doctor.

The latter's duties consisted of a daily visit made at a fixed time of his own choice. He examined all the patients : there were from 150 to 220 of them sleeping, as was the custom, two or three in the same bed. He had also to inspect the staff, the " officers, male and female servants ". The barber-surgeon accompanied him on this round of inspection " to write down

[1] The hospital of royal foundation was in reality in the Saint-Paul quarter. Cf. Guigue, *Recherches sur Notre-Dame de Lyon, hôpital fondé au VIe siècle*, Lyons, 1876.

[2] Cf. Dagier, *Histoire chronologique de l'Hôpital général et grand Hôtel-Dieu de Lyon*, Lyons, 1830, 2 vols. 8vo, and Astier, *L'Hôtel-Dieu de Lyon*, 1912, 1 vol. 8vo.

[3] In *La police de l'aulmosne de Lyon*, Lyons, Seb. Gryphius, 1539, 1 vol. 4to.

[4] The same arrangement is still to be seen in the famous hospital of Beaune, founded in 1446 by the Chancellor Raulin.

his prescriptions concerning the art of surgery " and later to execute them under his supervision[1].

It is in these conditions that François Rabelais practised the art of medicine for the first time, and successfully, for statistics drawn up by a scholar of our time show that the death-rate decreased by 2 to 3 per cent during his stay[2]. His patients were poor—" with no clothes worth mentioning " is the description given on the form of entry of the greater part of the inmates. He himself was poorly paid, forty *livres* annually ; the same allowance was granted to the barber-surgeon. It was understood that the doctor of the Hôtel-Dieu " practised his art upon the poor more from charity than for the salary he received from the governors ". But he was looked up to as a person of some consideration.

We notice his circle of friends and correspondents enlarge and renew itself at this period. From his relations we can gather some information about his ideas and his tastes at this time.

He happened, for instance, to send, on the 30th November, 1532, a letter to Erasmus of which a part can be taken as a small profession of faith[3]. The occasion for this letter was one of those services which scholars of all times have done each other. Erasmus, towards the end of 1531, was thinking of publishing a Latin edition of Flavius Josephus' *Jewish Antiquities*. In order to get a manuscript of this Greek text he applied, but without avail, to the Toulouse Humanist, Jean de Pins, Bishop of Rieux. Another cultured prelate, Georges d'Armagnac, Bishop of Rodez, possessed a manuscript copy of Flavius Josephus. Rabelais was in touch with him. Besides, he knew of Erasmus' wish through a former secretary of his, Hilaire Bertoul (Bertulphus)[4] of Ghent, a good grammarian,

---

[1] *Forme du gouvernement œconomique du grand Hostel Dieu de Nostre Dame de Pitié du Pont du Rhône de la ville de Lyon* (Lyons, 1627), ch. XIX : Du devoir et office du médecin.

[2] Dr. Drivon, *L'Hôtel-Dieu au temps de Rabelais*, in *Lyon médical* (1904).

[3] This letter was published for the first time in Amsterdam, in 1702, in a collection called *Clarorum virorum epistolæ centum ineditae de vario generis eruditione . . . ex musæo Johannis Brant*. Text given in Marty-Laveaux, *op. cit.*, vol. III, pp. 322–323. The original is in Zurich (*Thesaurus Hottingærianus*), and described as a letter to Bernard de Salignac, whose name appears on an address ; it is really addressed to Erasmus. This has many times been pointed out, and recently so by L. Thuasne, *Revue des bibliothèques*, vol. XV, 1905, *La lettre de Rabelais à Erasme*.

[4] On Bertoul cf. Allen's note in his edition of the letters of Erasmus, vol. V, p. 13, and A. Roersch, *Revue générale de Bruxelles*, 1909, who supposes that

who, having taught at Toulouse, set up at Lyons early in 1532. Rabelais used his influence with Georges d'Armagnac and obtained the loan of his manuscript for Erasmus. This letter of November 30th was to announce that he was sending it on.

Erasmus was then at the height of his glory and we have no idea whether he paid any attention to this epistle from the Lyons doctor. It was worthy of moving him, so much is it overflowing with admiration and gratitude towards him. Rabelais declares that he would be the most ungrateful of men did he not proclaim that whatever he is, he is it through Erasmus. This protector of letters, this defender of the truth is his *spiritual father*[1].

No doubt, Erasmus' genius is so rich, his culture so varied, his learning so wide that there is hardly a single Humanist of his day who is not among his posterity. However, Rabelais' declaration is noteworthy. It is not a mere stylistic formula. It points out truly the origin of some of his general ideas which he inherits from Erasmus, from the *Praise of Folly* and the *Colloquies*. On both sides is the same absence of mysticism, the same imperious need to introduce reason into the practices of religion, the same hatred of scholasticism, the same horror of dogmatism. These two minds are certainly of the same family and the expressions of gratitude in Rabelais' letter can be taken literally.

Moreover, the concluding lines help us to a more accurate understanding of Rabelais' religious attitude. Having heard, from Bertoul, that Erasmus intends to answer the attacks of a lampoon, signed Scaliger, which Erasmus attributes to Aleander, one of his adversaries in the dispute about Ciceronianism, Rabelais informs his correspondent about this Scaliger. It is the name of an Italian doctor, exiled from Verona,

---

Rabelais got from him the few sentences of Dutch spoken by Panurge to Epistemon (*Pantagruel*, ch. IX). Bertoul figures in one of Erasmus' colloquies, in which there is a comparison of German inns with those of Lyons (*Diversoria*).

[1] " Patrem te dixi, matrem etiam dicerem, si per indulgentiam mihi id tuam liceret. Quod enim utero gerentibus usui venire quotidie experimur ut quos nunquam viderunt fœtus alant, ab aërisque ambientis incommodis tueantur, αὐτο τοῦτο σύγ' ἔπαθες, qui me tibi de facie ignotum, nomine etiam ignobilem, sic educasti, sic castissimis divinæ tuæ doctrinæ uberibus usque aluisti, ut quidquid sum et valeo, tibi id uni acceptum ni feram, hominum omnium qui sunt, aut aliis erunt in annis, ingratissimus sim. Salve itaque etiam atque etiam, Pater amantissime, Pater decusque Patriæ, litterarum adsertor ἀλεξίκακος veritatis propugnator invictissime ".

I

who lives at Agen. He is not without ability, but, adds Rabelais,—leaving Latin to take up Greek, as was usual with Humanists in their letters when they feared an indiscretion—but a more thoroughgoing atheist does not exist. As to his lampoon Erasmus need not worry about it, it is not for sale in the bookshops, no copies of it have yet reached Lyons ; in all probability Erasmus' friends in Paris have bought up the edition and destroyed it[1].

This epistle, which Rabelais signs with his title of doctor, shows him to be well informed of the literary disputes of his time. It shows us at the same time that at this date he has no tendency towards atheism since he casts as a reproach at Scaliger, who is in other respects worthy of esteem, the fact of his being an atheist.

In the list of Rabelais' new acquaintances there next comes a good religious, lettered, a servant of Dame Rhetoric, Antoine du Saix, of whom Rabelais wrote in *Gargantua*[2] that he was " a good friend of mine ". To see him dubbed in the same passage with the title of " master beggar (*commandeur jambonnier*) of the friars of Saint Anthony ", we take him at first for a fictitious character, but Antoine du Saix was, in fact, commander of the Hospitallers of Saint Anthony, at Bourgen-Bresse[3]. This order, originally from the Dauphiné, had important houses at Vienne, Lyons and Bourg. Its particular charitable function during the Middle Ages had been to care for the poor people attacked with the *mal des Ardents*, or Saint Anthony's fire. Among their privileges was originally that of allowing their pigs to wander at liberty in the streets of the towns to look for food, among the refuse-heaps. This custom had disappeared in Rabelais' day[4]. The Antonins,

---

[1] " Nam Scaliger ipse Veronensis est, ex illa Scaligerorum exsulum familia, exul et ipse. Nunc vero medicum agit apud Agennates, vir mihi bene notus, οὐ μὰ τὸν Δί' εὐδοκιμαθείς, ἔστι τοίνυν διάβολος ἐκεῖνος, ὡς συνελόντι φάναι, τὰ μὲν ἰατρικὰ οὐκ ἀνεπιστήμων, τ'ἄλλα δὲ πάντῃ πάντως ἄθεος, ὡς οὐκ ἄλλος πώποτ' οὐδείς. Ejus librum nondum videre contigit, nec huc tot jam mensibus delatum est exemplar ullum ; atque adeo suppressum puto ab iis, qui Lutetiæ bene tibi volunt. Vale καὶ εὐτυχῶν διατέλει. Lugduni, pridie Cal. Decemb. 1532.

Tuus quatenus suus
Franciscus Rabelæsus
Medicus.

[2] Ch. XVII.

[3] On Antoine du Saix cf. Joseph Texte : *De Antonio Saxano*, Paris, 1895, H. Guy, *Histoire de la poésie française au XVIe siècle*, vol. I, pp. 361–366, and the article which I contributed to *R.É.R.*, IX, pp. 221–248.

[4] Lyons was exempted from this tribute early in the 16th century in return for the payment every month of an *anée* of rye to the Antonins.

recognisable by the azure T marked on their habit or cloak[1] still went from house to house to collect offerings of bacon and ham, ringing a bell to give due notice of their arrival. Hence the name of *jambonniers* given to these collectors.

Du Saix in his writings ingenuously called himself by this nickname ; for he published several works, at the same time truculent and precious in style : a funeral oration upon Marguerite d'Autriche, the *Blason de Brou,* the *Esperon de discipline.* He professes therein a profound horror for the Lutheran heresy, urging, nevertheless, reforms in Church discipline. He is pitiless against religious of loose morals and criticises bitterly the luxury of the higher clergy. He is horrified at the ignorance which is too commonly found among monks, exhorts them to study, exalts the virtues of learning and recommends young people to become proficient in Latin and even in Greek. Like the Humanists, he despises scholasticism. Everything would be for the better in the formation of Christians if, instead of commenting Pierre Lombard, Duns Scotus, Occam or Bricot, " they adhered to the text of the Gospel ". In this respect— his ideas on scholasticism, his aspirations towards Church reform, his exhortations to cultivate profane literature[2]— Antoine du Saix came near to the Humanists and whatever intolerance he professed for heretical sects, we are not surprised that Rabelais should have declared familiarly that the Commander of Bourg was " a good friend of mine ". Antoine du Saix, in his invectives against the dissolute morals of the high clergy, followed the tradition of the " free " monks-preachers of preceding centuries. Lyons had preserved the souvenir

---

[1] The origin of this badge, called the azure *tau* or the "gallows", is obscure. It either represents St. Anthony's crutch in the desert, or it comes from the sign of salvation placed by the Angel of Ezechiel's vision (IX, 6) on the forehead of the elect : " Omnem autem, super quem videritis *thau* ne occidatis ". The bell, attached to the end of a stick, which St. Anthony in his effigies carries in his hand, is no doubt meant to recall that the Popes granted to the Antonins the right of ringing a bell when engaged in their collections in order to inform the faithful of their arrival. *Acta sanctorum,* vol. II, p. 522.

" St. Anthony's fire burn you ! " was a curse common in the Middle Ages ; it is frequently met with in Rabelais. The *fire* cured by St. Anthony was *ergotisme,* a sort of erysipelas. Mediæval artists represented it by flames placed under the Saint's feet.

[2] The title of his principal work is a whole programme in itself : *L'esperon de discipline pour inciter les humains aux bonnes lettres, stimuler à doctrine, animer à science, inviter à toutes bonnes œuvres vertueuses et morales, par conséquent pour les faire cohéritiers de Jésu-Christ, expressément les nobles et généreux. Lourdement forgé et expressément limé par noble homme fraire Antoine du Saix, commandeur de Sainct Antoine de Bourg-en-Bresse,* 1532.

of the most eloquent among them, the Franciscan Jean Bourgeois, who had founded at the end of the 15th century, in the quarter of Saint Paul, the convent of the Observance, and whom Rabelais mentions in his book[1].

He likewise recalls at the beginning of *Gargantua* the legend of another Friar Minor, famous in the 14th century for his attacks upon the Pontifical court of Avignon, Rocquetaillade. In the neighbourhood of the Great Hospital of the Rhône, in the cloister of the Franciscan Convent, the body of his father, a great benefactor of the Order, reposed in a stone tomb ; he himself was supposed to have been buried in the Franciscan convent of Villefranche-sur-Saône. A daring spirit, an " abstractor of quintessence", author of prognostications, and critic of abuses in the Church, this Franciscan had become a legendary personage whose memory was stirred up as the Reformation approached. Rabelais will find amusement in adding to his legend a humorous touch by crediting him with a miraculous birth[2].

The references which Rabelais, in his early work, makes to life at Lyons, are indicative of his wide range of interests. They are not centred solely upon its intellectual life. He noticed the beauty of " the pillars of Enay "[3], the four granite columns of Egyptian origin which support the central cupola of the church of Saint Martin of Ainay ; but he also observed the stables situated in the top of the houses in the Saint-Jean quarter[4], the cable used to bring salt from Tain to Lyons[5], the Saône " boatwomen "[6], and the " hawking pedlars and ballad-mongers " of Mt. Pilate[7], in Forez, who in Spring and Autumn, came to sell their harvest of turpentine wrapped in goatskins.

Meanwhile, he was working. In the Autumn of 1532, he brought out with Gryphius the third of his learned publications,

[1] *Third Book*, ch. VII, and *Fourth Book*, ch. VIII : " Panurge . . . preached and canted to them all the while like . . . another Friar John Burgess ".

[2] *Gargantua*, ch. VI : " Did not Rocquetaillade come out of his Mother's heel ? " I sketched some features of the Rocquetaillade legend in the *Rev. XVIe siècle*, 1924, pp. 232–237. Mlle Jeanne Odier has thrown an entirely new light upon the story of his life in her *Jean de Roquetaillade, moine franciscain du XVIe siècle. Sa Vie et ses œuvres*, Paris, 1925. (Position des thèses de l'École des Chartes. Promotion de 1925.)

[3] *Gargantua*, ch. XIV : " the pencase . . . was as big and as long as the great pillar of Enay ". Cf. *R.É.R.*, vol. VI, p. 385.

[4] *Ibid.*, ch. XII.   [5] *Pantagruel*, ch. IV.   [6] *Ibid.*, ch. XXX.

[7] *Gargantua*, ch. IX, *Pantagrueline Prognostication*, V.

the *Testament of Cuspidius*, which he dedicated to a friend in Poitou, Amaury Bouchard. The lieutenant-general of the Seneschal of Saintonge at the *siège royal* of Saint-Jean-d'Angély had become Royal Master of the Requests. On his way through Lyons he had seen with Rabelais the text of a Roman's will, Lucius Cuspidius, which seemed to him to offer new light upon the style of this sort of document in the days of the Republic. He had asked his friend to give him a copy of it. Rabelais had it printed at three thousand copies[1]; joined to another Roman legal document, a contract of sale, it formed a booklet of sixteen pages : *Ex reliquiis venerandæ antiquitatis, Lucii Cuspidii testamentum. Item contractus venditionis antiquis Romanorum temporibus initus*[2].

Rabelais stated in his dedicatory letter that many people pretended to have in their study the original manuscript of the will, but that nobody had been able to show it to him. It would have been extremely difficult to do so. This will was a forgery perpetrated at the end of the 15th century by an Italian Humanist, Pomponius Lætus, as the contract of sale had been by another Italian, Jovianus Pontanus. If other indications are lacking, the language of the contract revealed the recent origin of this document which was supposedly contemporaneous with the Roman republic. Neither Rabelais nor his correspondent, Amaury Bouchard, nor the learned jurists of the time suspected the genuineness of these documents, which had the honour of a second edition in 1549. The Italian Humanists' trick was not denounced until much later, in 1587, by a jurist who had become Archbishop of Tarragone, Antoine Augustin[3].

---

[1] Cf. the letter of dedication, Marty-Laveaux, *op. cit.*, vol. III, pp. 320-321.

[2] Cf. A. Heulhard, *Rabelais légiste*, Paris, 1887. The copies extant of this work are now very rare. There is one in the Bibliothèque Nationale, Paris, another in the Copley Christie Library, Manchester, a third in M. Édouard Herriot's library.

[3] The letter to Bouchard ends as follows : " Exspecto in dies novum libellum tuum de Architectura orbis, quem opportet ex sanctioribus Philosophiæ scriniis depromptum esse . . . ". What is this little book on the " Architecture of the World " which Rabelais wishes to see published ? M. Busson conjectures with probability that it is a manuscript of Bouchard's unpublished and now in the Bibliothèque Nationale. " *De l'excellence et immortalité de l'âme, extrait non seulement du Timée mais aussi de plusieurs aultres grecz et latins philosophes, tant de la pythagorique que platonique famille par maistre Amaury Bouchard, maistre des requestes ordinaires de l'hostel du roy*". It treats only of the immortality of the soul, but Rabelais may have thought that it contained the whole of the *Timaeus* and its system of cosmogony. Cf. Busson, *Les Sources et le développement du rationalisme dans la littérature française* (1533-1601), 1 vol. 8vo, Paris, 1922.

At the same time that Gryphius published the *Testament de Cuspidius*[1], another bookseller of Lyons, Claude Nourry, called Le Prince, was offering for sale *The horrible and frightful acts and prowesses of the very renowned Pantagruel, King of the Dipsodes, son of the great Giant Gargantua, composed newly by Master Alcofrybas Nasier.*

Alcofrybas Nasier was the anagram of *Françoys Rabelais*.

[1] This indication as to the date of the completion of *Pantagruel* is drawn from the last chapter. Rabelais there says "the registers of my brain are somewhat jumbled and disordered with the septembral juice". Cf. A. Lefranc, *Les dates de publication du Pantagruel, R.É.R.*, IX, pp. 151–159.

CHAPTER IX

PANTAGRUEL

IT is a far cry from Manardi's *Medical letters*, from the *Aphorisms* of Hipprocrates, and from the *Testament of Cuspidius* to *The frightful acts and prowesses of Pantagruel*.

Doubtless we can pick out in the dedicatory letters which serve as prefaces to these learned publications some humorous notes[1]; but the matter of the works themselves treats entirely of science and erudition. How did Rabelais come to write such a book?

We can suppose, without insulting him, that he sought first a pecuniary profit. The physician's salary at the Great Hospital of Lyons was so small! What consolation and satisfaction for Rabelais, after having known that "incomparable grief" which is called "lack of money"[2], to find a cure for it in the simple outpouring of his jovial and laughter-loving doctor's temperament. It is likely that in the course of his visits and sojourns at the Universities, Rabelais amused himself, like many other scholars of the time, by writing amusing trifles. The relaxations—*oysivetés*, as they were called—of many grave minds compose the bulk of the recreative literature of this period: they include the *Nouvelles récréations et joyeux devis* of the learned Bonaventure des Périers, the *Baliverneries* and the *Propos rustiques* of Noël du Fail, counsellor in the Parliament of Brittany, the smart, broad and sometimes ribald tales of the *Heptameron* of this Queen of Navarre, who was enamoured of Platonism and Christian mysticism. Like them, Rabelais may have sought relaxation from his Greek and Latin studies, at Paris or Montpellier, in trying his hand at comic compositions: parodies of counsels' speeches, caricature-sketches

---

[1] In the dedicatory letter to the *Aphorisms* numerous familiar terms of comparison occur. Rabelais says that the common people have the *flair of a rhinoceros*, and that anybody who would cure them of their erroneous ideas would accomplish a task as difficult as *blackening crows' eyes*.

[2] *Faulte d'argent, c'est douleur non pareille*, ("Lack of money is an incomparable grief"), is the refrain of a song, quoted in *Pantagruel*, ch. XVI.

of theologians, descriptions of university scenes in the "pindaric" jargon of the "Latin flayers", the invention of "villonesque" tricks which he lays to the account of students, sketches of farces, like the "moral comedy" of him who had married a dumb woman.

He was tempted one day to turn to account his comic *verve*, and perhaps some of his earlier compositions which he had kept in his pocket. At the time when he visited Sebastian Gryphius and listened eagerly to the conversations of *La Rue Notre-Dame-de-Confort* he heard of the remarkable success of a little work of facetious literature, a humble booklet in Gothic characters, published at Lyons without author's or bookseller's name, under the title of the *Great and inestimable Chronicles of the great and enormous giant Gargantua*. More copies of them were sold, he tells us, "in two months' time, than there will be bought of Bibles in nine years". He conceived the idea of a book "of the same stamp", that is to say of the same metal, in which, perhaps, he could insert or incorporate his still unpublished humorous compositions; and to exploit the success of the *Chronicles*, he resolved to announce that his book was a continuation of them. What he related was the life of Gargantua's son, the Giant Pantagruel. Moreover, he was to adopt the tone of these *Chronicles*[1]. What, then were they?

---

[1] In the *Prologue* to *Pantagruel* he takes pleasure in exalting their merits and recalling their success. "Most illustrious and thrice valorous champions, gentlemen, and others, who willingly apply your minds to the entertainment of pretty conceits, and honest harmless knacks of wit; you have not long ago seen, read, and understood the *Great and inestimable Chronicle of the huge and mighty giant Gargantua*, and, like upright faithfullists, have firmly believed all to be true that is contained in them, and have very often passed your time with them amongst honourable ladies and gentlewomen, telling them fair long stories, when you were out of all other talk, for which you are worthy of great praise and sempiternal memory.

And I do heartily wish that every man would lay aside his own business, meddle no more with his profession nor trade, and throw all affairs concerning himself behind his back, to attend this wholly, without distracting or troubling his mind with any thing else, until he have learned them without book; that if by chance the art of printing should cease, or in case that in time to come all books should perish, every man might truly teach them unto his children, and deliver them over to his successors and survivors from hand to hand, as a religious Cabala; for there is in it more profit, than a rabble of great pocky loggerheads are able to discern . . .

I have known great and mighty lords, and of those not a few who, going a deer-hunting, or a hawking after wild ducks, when the chase had not encountered with the blinks, that were cast in her way to retard her course, or that the hawk did but plain and smoothly fly without moving her wings, perceiving the prey, by force of flight, to have gained bounds of her, have been much chafed and vexed, as you understand well enough; but the comfort

They related the history of a family of giants, created by the enchantments of Merlin, the necromancer, for King Arthur's service[1]. From the bones of two male whales and the nail-clippings of Queen Genièvre, sprinkled with blood from Lancelot's wounds, Merlin brings miraculously to life the giants Grandgosier and Galemelle, of whom Gargantua will be born. He endows them with a gigantic mare and sends them to Arthur. Arrived at Mont Saint-Michel, Galemelle and Grandgosier die of a " continuous fever for the want of a purgative ". Merlin then brings Gargantua on a cloud, " to the seaside, near London " and presents him to King Arthur, who was at war with the Gos and Magos. With his club, a gift of Merlin, the giant crushes his suzerain's enemies : Dutchmen and Irishmen, Gos and Magos. He gathers prisoners in hundreds, squeezes them in the cleft of his sleeves, in the bottom of his hose, in his game bag, in his hollow tooth. His final prowesses are a single combat against a giant twelve fathoms high. In this way, he spends " two hundred years, three months and four days exactly ", then he is transported to the land of Faery by Morgane and Mélusine.

Where did the unknown author of the *Great Chronicles* gather the subject of his story ? We do not yet know. The Gargantuan legend seems to have been popular long before this publication ; we find in a register of accounts by the Bishop of Limoges' agent, in date of 1470, the name of *Gargantua* given as nickname to a guest of the Bishop's[2]. Merlin, King Arthur, Queen Genièvre, Lancelot, Morgane, Mélusine had for long furnished the subjects of the literature of the chivalric romances,

---

unto which they had refuge, and that they might not take cold, was to relate the inestimable deeds of the said Gargantua.

There are others in the world,—these are no flimflam stories, nor tales of a tub,—who, being much troubled with the toothache, after they had spent their goods upon physicians, without receiving at all any ease of their pain, have found no more ready remedy than to put the said *Chronicles* betwixt two pieces of linen cloth made somewhat hot, and so apply them to the place that smarteth, synapising them with a little powder of projection, otherwise called *d'oribus* ".

[1] Cf. Marty-Laveaux, *op. cit.*, vol. IV, pp. 25–56, for the text of the *Grandes Cronicques* of 1532 ; a reproduction in phototype of the original published by M. Seymour de Ricci, *R.É.R.*, VIII, pp. 57–92 ; and the refutation of their ascription to Rabelais in the *Introduction* to the critical edition of Rabelais' works, vol. I, pp. xxxviii *seq.*

[2] Nothing new has been said upon the origins (still very obscure) of the Gargantuan legend and its textual history since M. Abel Lefranc's synopsis of the question in 1912, in the *Introduction* to the critical edition of Rabelais, vol. I, pp. xxxviii–xlix.

placed within reach of the generality of readers by printing at the end of the 15th century.

Entirely popular were also the comic effects which brighten up the *Chronicles*. The author knew that he would provoke ingenuous laughter by the description of his hero's gigantic enormity, so he readily dwells upon the telling of how Gargantua lunched off two shipfuls of fresh herrings and three casks of salted mackerel; how he dined on three hundred cattle and two hundred sheep; how he carried off the bells of Notre-Dame de Paris to hang them on his mare's neck; how his peals of laughter were heard seven and a half leagues away; how, for his " hat with a cockade " he had to give the hat-maker exactly " two hundred hundredweight, two and a half pounds and one quart " of wool. For the narrator jokingly affects the most scrupulous exactness in the most impossible descriptions, as a guarantee of his veracity; and this specious exactitude is another feature of popular comedy.

Such is the work of which the success led Rabelais to write *Pantagruel*. He owes to it the general plan of his book, similar to that of the numerous heroic romances, of which printing then produced numerous retellings. Like these fabulous epics that the *Prologue* enumerates—*Robert the Devil, Fierabras, William without Fear* or *Huon of Bordeaux*—*Pantagruel* is in three parts: the miraculous birth of the hero, accompanied by a genealogy which brings him back across the centuries to the time of Abel's murder; then his childhood which tells us how the giant was brought up in the Universities of France and finally at Paris; finally, his " prowesses ", a journey on sea and a war against the inhabitants of Scythia or Dipsodie.

The hero of these adventures, Pantagruel, is a giant, who, like all the giants of earlier epics or romantic tales, Fierabras and Morgant, has strength and an appetite proportionate to his stature. But he stands apart from them by a peculiar characteristic: he has the gift of engendering thirst in all who approach him. This characteristic is not Rabelais' invention, any more than the name Pantagruel, which he gave to his hero. This name, without being popular, like that of Gargantua, was not unknown in France. *The Mystery of the Acts of the Apostles* of Simon Gréban, of which there had been numerous performances at the end of the 15th and beginning of the 16th century, had popularised it. Pantagruel was the name given therein to a little devil who reigned over one of the elements, water. He travelled maritime regions collecting salt and threw it during the night into drunkards' throats[1]. Subsequently, the same denomination had passed from the cause to the effect : Pantagruel in other texts of dramatic literature[2] signifies thirst, or an irritation of the throat which provokes thirst.

This devil, whose name was synonymous with thirst, must have been often spoken of in the summer of 1532. This year witnessed, the memoirs of the time tell us, an extraordinary drought, which began almost with Spring and lasted until All Saints, nearly six months[3].

How often, during this drought, must Rabelais have heard people saying that Pantagruel held them by the throat ? It is, doubtless, this circumstance which brought Rabelais to give this name of Pantagruel to Gargantua's son, whose fabulous life he was about to narrate. Equipped with this name, the giant was naturally endowed with the property of creating thirst which was proper to the little maritime devil of our mystery plays.

This singular power of Pantagruel's operates sometimes unknown to him, by his mere presence. The day he enters Orleans[4] when he is asked to hang a bell on the steeple of Saint-Aignan's, he first amuses himself ringing it through the streets, with the result that, at the noise of this bell-ringing, all the good wine of Orleans " turned instantly, waxed flat, and was spoiled " in the cellars, as happened, according to the popular belief, when it thundered. " Which nobody there did perceive till the night following ; for every man found himself so altered, and a-dry with drinking these flat wines, that they did nothing but spit, and that as white as Maltha cotton, saying : We have got the Pantagruel, and our very throats are salted ".

A little later[5] at Paris, the learned Thaumast, having to argue against Pantagruel, declares to the doorkeeper of the Hôtel de Cluny that he never experienced such a thirst : " I think that Pantagruel holds me by the throat ! " The students who are present at the disputation also experience an itching

[1] The discovery of the origin of this name is due to M. Abel Lefranc. Cf. *Introduction cit.*, pp. xiv–xv.

[2] The *Vie de Saint Louis par personnages* (end of the 15th century) and the *Sottie nouvelle à six personnages*, quoted by A. Lefranc, *ibid.*

[3] Cf. A. Lefranc, *ibid.*, ch. II, *La réalité dans " Pantagruel "*.

[4] *Pantagruel*, ch. VII.   [5] Cf. ch. XVIII–XIX.

in the throat when they hear Pantagruel's voice, powerful as the sound of a double cannon, calling them to silence. They " laid out their tongues a full half foot beyond their mouths, as if Pantagruel had salted all their throats ". It would seem, as Panurge puts it, that " the very shadow of Pantagruel engenders thirsty men, as the moon does catarrhs ".

Betimes, also, it is not merely metaphorically that Pantagruel catches people by the throat. Having met a Limousin scholar who answers his questions only by unintelligible phrases he thinks he is being tricked by him, and to revenge himself, in an angry impulse, he wrings his neck, but subsequently he yields to the poor fellow's appeals and releases his grasp. But the student, we are told, remained thirsty all his life as a result of it and died, some years later, " of the death Roland ", that is to say, of thirst[1].

Making his enemies thirsty is Pantagruel's best way of circumventing them. In the military expedition against King Anarchus he has recourse to a very curious stratagem to conquer his enemy[2]. By means of a released prisoner he announces to him a formidable attack and at the same time sends him a box full of very bitter drugs, euphorbium, grains of the black cameleon thistle, etc., assuring him that " if he were able to eat one ounce of that without drinking after it, he might then be able to resist him without fear ". Anarchus does not fail to taste the drugs. " But, as soon as he had swallowed down one spoonful of them, he was taken with such a heat in his throat, together with an ulceration in the flap of the top of the windpipe, that his tongue peeled with it, in such sort, that, for all they could do unto him, he found no ease at all, but by drinking only without cessation ; for as soon as ever he took the goblet from his head, his tongue was on fire, and therefore they did nothing but still pour in wine into his throat with a funnel ". Likewise did his captains, " bashaws ", and guards ; then the whole army began to tipple " so much and so long ; that they fell asleep like pigs, all out of order throughout the whole camp ". It is then that Pantagruel performs the action of the little devil of the mystery plays ; he takes up handfuls of the salt which he carries in a barrel attached to his belt and throws it upon the enemy soldiers, who " slept with an open gaping mouth ", with the result " that these poor wretches were by it made to

[1] Ch. VI.   [2] Ch. XXVIII.

cough like foxes, crying, Ha, Pantagruel, how thou addest greater heat to the firebrand that is in us."

In his duel with Loupgarou, Anarchus' captain of the Guards[1], Pantagruel has recourse again to his provision of salt. " He casts eighteen cags, and four bushels " of it into his enemy's mouth, throat, nose and eyes. The struggle continuing, Loupgarou flourishes his mace and his last words are a promise to free the earth of this scourge, Pantagruel : " Now, villain, will I not fail to chop thee as small as minced meat, and keep thee henceforth from ever making any more poor men athirst ".

Thus Rabelais utilised for numerous episodes, in an unforeseen way, the very name of Pantagruel, which he had chosen for his giant.

The effects which he could obtain from it were limited. A richer vein was to be found in the description of the size, the strength or the appetite of the personage. The author of the *Great Chronicles* had shown him how these comic effects can be exploited. In his turn, Master Alcofrybas amused himself by enlarging to a gigantic scale the physiological functions of his hero. Scarcely is he born than Pantagruel swallows up at every meal the milk of four thousand six hundred cows : for his soup he must have, not a mug, but a *timbre* (stone-trough) ; he devours half a cow which was suckling him. Hence he is tied into his cradle. One day that a bear came to lick his chaps, he broke loose his bonds and tore my lord the bear into little pieces[2]. Inventions of this kind were always assured of success with a popular audience : Rabelais could not fail to use them.

But the story-teller was bound to tire of these facile developments. He resolved to heighten these descriptions and imaginative tales by two sorts of popular humour, of which he found models in the *Great Chronicles*. It can be seen from our numerous quotations that they bring into fiction a meticulous exactitude. They give to a man the number of enemies fallen into Gargantua's mouth, and that of his prisoners. They are scrupulously exact in matters of weights and measures. " Note that it needed 400 ells of cloth to make a bandage for Gargantua's little toe, all but a half quarter exactly." Rabelais, likewise, gives the exact number of the troops engaged, of the enemies killed, of prisoners captured. He also is as

[1] Ch. XXIX.   [2] Ch. IV.

scrupulous as a clerk of the Courts about exactness in his figures. " You are to remark that in that year there was so great drought over all the country of Africa, that there past thirty and six months, three weeks, four days, thirteen hours, and a little more . . ."[1]. If he leaves some enumerations uncertain, it is following the example of the Bible : " besides women and little children " is a reservation, in Biblical style, which appears at the end of one of his fanciful enumerations[2].

A characteristic trait of popular legend is the practice of connecting with fabulous tales the origin of some historical or geographical peculiarities. This is another form of specious probability, which is all the more amusing as the fiction is plainly improbable. The *Great Chronicles* explained incidentally the lack of forests in Champagne and Beauce : Gargantua's mare as he passed had mowed them down with her tail. They pointed out the islets of Mont Saint-Michel and of Tombelaine as rocks brought there from the East by Grandgosier and Galemelle, Gargantua's father and mother. Of Pantagruel, also there remain many souvenirs in the French countryside, according to Maître Alcofrybas. Bourges preserves his " bell " ; it is what they call the " Giant's bowl ", which on festive days they filled with wine for the populace[3]. La Rochelle, Lyons and Angers keep the iron chains with which he was tied into his cradle[4] ; his cross-bow was to be seen at Chantelle castle[5], and Poitiers still prides itself upon the *Pierre Levée* which, with great ease, he set upon its four pillars, in the midst of a field so that the scholars might amuse themselves by climbing upon it and carving their names on it and " feasting [there] with store of gammons, pasties and flagons[6] ".

By this method of heightening his narrative some notes of geographical and historical reality are introduced into this fabulous story. Indeed, the third part of the book, the campaign against the Dipsodes, is the only one which is situated in an imaginary country, Utopia, which Rabelais places in eastern Asia, in the region of Cathay (China), at that time shrouded in illusive legends. The rest of the tale has France for its theatre. It is at Poitiers that the giant begins his studies, at Paris that he ends them, having, like many a scholar of the 16th century, gone the round of the Universities of France, visiting in turn

[1] Ch. II.   [2] Ch. XXXI.   [3] Ch. IV.
[4] *Ibid.*   [5] Ch. V.   [6] *Ibid.*

Bordeaux, Toulouse, Montpellier, Avignon, Valence, Angers, Bourges and Orleans, all of which towns Rabelais characterises by some feature of customs, studies or pastimes, taken from the University life to which he had been initiated.

His reading has afforded matter for his work as much as the details drawn from real life. He has himself mentioned the popular works which he must have read before undertaking to narrate in his turn the prowesses of his giant.

In this literature of the tales of Knights and Giants, there is a work which he mentions twice and which he has frequently used: it is the *Opus macaronicum* of the Italian monk Teofilo Folengo, called Merlin Coccai[1]. This poem, written in a mixture of Latin and of latinised Italian (whence its culinary name of *Macaronæa*), recounts the exploits of a hero, Baldus, backed up by three companions, each of whom represents a particular force or quality: Fracassus, the powerful, the giant who breaks everything, having as a club a bell clapper, Falchetto, the swift, and Cingar, the cunning. Like Merlin Coccai, Master Alcofrybas presents to us his hero aided, during his expedition against the Dipsodes, by four "officers", or "apostles": Eusthenes, the strong, Carpalim, the swift, Panurge, the cunning, and the learned Epistemon[2].

But the parts of these personages are not of equal importance. Eusthenes' strength is only once availed of[3]; of what avail could it be against that of Pantagruel, the Giant? Epistemon's skill is shown to us only when he manufactures "in the name of the nine Muses, nine antique wooden spits"[4]. Carpalim proves his fleetness of foot on only three occasions, to catch leverets[5], a roe-buck, and birds in full flight, to reach a fugitive horseman[6] and to go and set fire to the enemies' munitions[7].

Much more active and efficacious is Panurge's cunning. It is the complement of the Giant's strength in the campaign against the Dipsodes. There, Panurge has a completely useful and beneficent rôle. He is brave and, like Pantagruel's other "apostles", "ready to live and die"[8] with his master. He reassures his companions, instils confidence into them by the

---

[1] *Pantagruel*, ch. I: "Who begat Fracassus, of whom Merlin Coccaius has written", and, end of ch. VII: "*Merlinus Coccaius, de patria diabolorum*".
[2] The names are derived from Greek words: εὐσθενής, strong; καρπάλιμος, swift; πανοῦργος, knavish; ἐπιστήμων, learned.
[3] End of ch. XXVII.   [4] Ch. XXVI.   [5] *Ibid*.
[6] End of ch. XXV.   [7] Ch. XXVIII.   [8] Ch. XXVI.

augury of a stick broken upon two glasses which remain whole.[1]
He succeeds single-handed in discomfiting " very subtly " six
hundred enemy horsemen thanks to a trick[2] and by another
trick he causes the King of the Dipsodes' camp to be flooded
by the Giant[3]. Pantagruel has such admiration for his subtlety
that he does not hesitate to state in an inscription in verse that :

Slight is much more prevalent than might[4].

And when in his duel with Loupgarou he suddenly finds himself
disarmed, his " mast " having touched the Giant's enchanted
mace, he calls Panurge to the rescue[5]. Thus, in this war of
Dipsodie Panurge's cunning is an efficacious help to the Giant's
strength and Panurge is held up to our admiration as an
inventor of military stratagem.

We see him in an entirely different light in the episodes of
Pantagruel's stay at Paris. There he is just a scapegrace, a
worthy rival of Villon. His cuteness reveals itself by tricks
sometimes worthy of the hangman's rope. He has sixty-three
means of obtaining money " at his need, of which the most
honourable and most ordinary was in manner of thieving,
secret purloining, and filching ". He steals handkerchiefs
from " the pretty sempstress of the palace " ; he carries in his
pockets a whole burglar's outfit : " a picklock, a pelican, a
cramp-iron and some other iron tools, wherewith there was no
door nor coffer which he could not pick open ". Alcofrybas
describes him as " a wicked lewd rogue, a cozener, drinker,
roysterer, rover and a very dissolute and debauched fellow, if
there were any in Paris ". The most inoffensive manifestations
of his subtle wit are clownish tricks, the victims of which are
the sergeants of the watch, the poor masters of Arts, the theologians, the University doctors[6].

Thus is introduced into the " horrific " history of the Giant
an element which was the soul of our comic theatre in the Middle
Ages—mystification. An example of it—which in all likelihood
is taken from *Pathelin*—is the first meeting of Panurge and
Pantagruel. Panurge when questioned by the Giant as to his
name and situation answers him in German, then in Italian,

---

[1] Ch. XXVII.   [2] Ch. XXV.   [3] Ch. XXVIII.   [4] Ch. XXVII.
[5] " His mast broke off about three handfuls above his hand, whereat he
stood amazed like a bell-founder, and cried out, Ah, Panurge, where art
thou ? ". Ch. XXIX.
[6] Ch. XVI, *Of the qualities and conditions of Panurge, passim.*

in Basque, in Scotch, in Dutch, in Greek, in Latin, and finally in plain French[1]. In like manner, Pathelin jabbered in many tongues to the draper claiming the price of his cloth[2]. Other examples of this mystification are Panurge's thefts from the church collection-boxes[3], and the indignity to which he subjected a great Parisian lady who had rebutted him[4].

Where did Rabelais get the idea of these tricks ? The greater part of them are not of his own invention. They come from various sources and it is noteworthy that they are nearly all connected with University life, as though they represented some essays at comic composition put together by way of amusement at the period when Rabelais was visiting the Universities, and then hurriedly adapted to the Pantagruelian epic.

Take, for example, the episode of the discussion by signs which fills three chapters (XVIII-XX). A great scholar of England, Thaumast, having heard Pantagruel's knowledge extolled, came to debate with him. It is agreed that the discussions will take place in the Great Hall of the Collège de Navarre and that it will be conducted by " signs only, without speaking ", for the subjects on which Thaumast wants to be enlightened are " so arduous that words proceeding from the mouth of man will never be sufficient for unfolding them ". During the night, Pantagruel turns over all his treatises of philosophy, of the occult sciences and of divination. Panurge seeing his anxiety offers to debate in his place and gives assurances that he will satisfy the Englishman's curiosity. Pantagruel accepts, and Thaumast himself agrees to this substitution of pupil for master. Then begins a scene in dumb-show described in meticulous detail : to the grave gestures of Thaumast which refer only to philosophy and astrology (certain signs and certain numbers corresponded in some philosophical schools of antiquity to fixed ideas), Panurge answers by some grotesque gesticulations, beginning with a *pied-de-nez*[5] and ending by indecent buffooneries. Thaumast, who takes the whole proceedings seriously, declares himself satisfied : Panurge has cleared

[1] Ch. IX.   [2] *Maistre Pierre Pathelin*, verses 834-969.
[3] Ch. XVII.   [4] Ch. XXI.
[5] " Panurge suddenly lifted up in the air his right hand, and put the thumb thereof into the nostril of the same side, holding his four fingers straight out, and closed orderly in a parallel line to the point of his nose, shutting the left eye wholly, and making the other wink with a profound depression of the eyebrows and eyelids ". Ch. XIX.

K

up his doubts and has " discovered to him the very true well, fountain, and abyss of the encyclopædia of learning ". Thus the scholar is tricked by a clown !

On analysis, we can connect this scene with two themes, both of which Rabelais has borrowed from his reading. The scholar ridiculed by the clown is a scene frequently treated in mediæval satiric literature. The *Dialogues de Salomon et Marcoul*, quoted by Rabelais in *Gargantua*[1], contrast, for instance, the knowledge of Solomon, the wise man, with the vulgar common-sense of a person named Marcou, or Malcon. " He who ventures not has neither horse nor mule, says Solomon. He who ventures overmuch loses both horse and mule, answers Malcon ". The same theme is elaborated in two farces of the end of the 15th century, *le Gaudisseur et le Sot* and *le Gentilhomme et son page*[2].

As to the cross purposes arising from a discussion by signs, Rabelais knew a famous example of it, recorded in a gloss of Accursius, the jurist, the commentator of the *Digest* so adversely criticised by the Humanists of the Renaissance. Accursius describes how, one day, a certain wise man having come from Greece to Rome to see if the Romans were worthy of having laws, the Romans appointed a fool to argue with him. The Greek, for no obvious reason, probably through his ignorance of Latin, undertakes a discussion by signs. He raises one finger, signifying that there is only one God. The fool, thinking this finger was raised to put his eye out, raises two fingers and a thumb, to threaten his adversary with having both his eyes put out. The Greek takes these three fingers for a symbol of the Trinity. He then opens out his hand, signifying that all things are open to God. The fool takes this gesture as being a threat of a blow, and in response he waves his closed fist, which the Greek interprets as : God holds all things clasped in his hand. Thereupon he withdraws, judging the Romans on this test as being worthy to have laws.

Rabelais must often have laughed loudly with his friends at Fontenay-le-Comte, at this ridiculous anecdote set down in all seriousness by Accursius[3]. Budé quoted it precisely as a testimony to Accursius' ignorance in placing a discussion on

---

[1] *Gargantua*, end of ch. XXXIII, Picrochole's council.
[2] Quoted by Petit de Juleville, *Catalogue des farces et des soties*, p. 144.
[3] It is found in a gloss on the *Digest*, *l. posteriori, de origine juris*, which Rabelais mentions, *Pantagruel*, ch. X.

the Trinity at the period in which Rome came into contact with Greek civilisation. It is, then, in satiric literature and in a legal volume that Rabelais found each of the themes of this episode. He located it in the Great Hall of Navarre, and gave it as audience the entire student population of Sainte-Geneviève's Hill, a habit of whom he here mentions, that of interrupting by their applause the most arduous discussions. So that if Panurge's clownish dumb-show constitutes an entirely popular comic effect, its staging, on the other hand, is particularly interesting to students.

The same is true of many points in the recital of Pantagruel's stay in Paris. We may ask if Maître Alcofrybas in this part of his work has not forgotten that he intended his story for a popular audience, the humble readers of the Gargantuesque *Great Chronicles*. There are, in point of fact, five incidents which are fully intelligible for educated people only, while still mixed with plebeian jocularity.

In the first place, we have in Chapter VI Pantagruel's meeting with the " Limousin scholar who affected to speak in learned phrase ". Questioned by the Giant, this student answers in a " Pindarized " jargon, substituting for good old French words frenchified Latin words. According to the printer Geoffroy Tory[1], this is what was called in the Parisian schools *flaying Latin*. Pantagruel, annoyed at these obscure answers, seizes by the throat the vain-glorious scholar, who then hastens to implore God, Saint Martial, patron of Limoges, and the Giant himself, in the dialect of his country of turnips. " Now, said Pantagruel, thou speakest naturally ". The usual *dénouement* of farces when the mystifier is mystified! It is entirely popular in character, but who would pretend, if he did

---

[1] In his *Champfleury* (1529). The sentence which he quotes as a specimen of this jargon may have given Rabelais the idea for this chapter : " We transfretate the Sequane at the dilucul and crepuscul : we deambulate by the compites and quadrives of the urb ; we despumate the Latial verbocination ; and, like verisimilary amorabonds, we captat the benevolence of the omnijugal, omniform, and omnigenal fœminine sex ". Rabelais while ridiculing this jargon, was not himself free from the abuse of neologisms taken from Latin. But it must be remembered that a distinction was made between terms derived from Latin—those were considered praiseworthy which had no corresponding words in the vernacular, the others were left to mere pedants and " skimmers of Latin ". Thus, Fabri, of the school of the Grands Rhétoriqueurs, approves of this sentence : " *l'excellence* et *magnificence* des princes nous *induisent* à *contempler* leur *magnanimité* ", and condemns this one : " Si *ludez* (jouez) à la *pille* (balle, *esteuf*,) vous *amitterez* (perdrez) ", because *jouer*, *esteuf* and *perdre* are " good, current terms ".

not know Latin, to understand the scholar's speech whose
"genie is not apt nate to excoriate the cuticle of our
vernacular Gallic."

The first meeting of Panurge with Pantagruel[1] presents the
same difficulties for the reader who knows only the vernacular.
To the kind questions which Pantagruel puts him, the poor
wretch who is suffering "from a very urgent necessity to feed"
amuses himself by answering successively in German, Italian,
Basque, Dutch, Hebrew, Greek, Latin and various gibberishes,
before making use of his natural and maternal language which
he learned as a child in the Garden of France, Touraine.

The "repertory" of the fine books which Pantagruel found
in the Abbey of Saint Victor[2], in Paris, is again a scholar's
joke, funny only for cultured people versed in theological
and scholastic literature. There existed at that time a number
of works of spirituality and theology, whose titles afforded some
absurd metaphors such as *Biga salutis* (the *Perch of Salvation*)
or *Malogranatum vitiorum* (the *Pomegranate of Vice*). Rabelais
quotes them and then parodies them, inventing other books
with similar titles : the Clew-bottom of Theology, the Mustard-
pot of Penance, the Gamashes, *alias* the Boots of Patience, the
Cobbled Shoe of Humility, etc. He adds zest to the joke by
free double-meaning titles in macaronic Latin, satirical allusions to Reuchlin's quarrel with the Cologne theologians or the
quarrels of my lords of the Sorbonne with the Humanists.

A fourth episode, the speeches of two great lords and Pantagruel's judgment[3], can be traced in many passages to the
reform being then carried out in the juridical sciences under
the influence of Humanism[4]. The youthful Pantagruel has
become so celebrated by his public disputations with the regents
of the Faculty of Arts and the Sorbonne theologians that he is
called upon "to decide a controversy wonderfully obscure
and difficult" which has brought two great lords before the
Court of Parliament. After forty-six weeks of vain consultations, the magistrates decide to get Pantagruel's opinion. He
enquires whether the two parties to this lawsuit are still living
and, as he is answered in the affirmative, he considers that the
best course is to send for and question them. For what purpose
can be served by this rubbishy conglomeration of papers

[1] Ch. IX.   [2] Ch. VII.   [3] Chs. X–XIII.
[4] Cf. Preface to Manardi's *Medical Letters*.

and copies which is handed to him ? They are merely the opinions of mediæval jurisconsults, Accursius, Baldus, Bartolus, and " other old mastiffs ". Now, these legists were ignorant of everything which is necessary for an understanding of law— Greek, good Latin, Moral Philosophy, Ancient History. Dotards, chimney-sweepers, great tithe-calves, that is what these commentators of the Pandects were[1].

Consequently, Pantagruel proposes to have all these papers burned ; he then makes the two great lords appear in person before him. Each of them reels off an unintelligible speech which is merely a tissue of cock-and-bull-stories and wordy nonsense. Judgment is delivered in the same style. This scene itself is thus the most trivial buffoonery ; but, as we have seen, it is preceded by considerations in which are found all the grievances of the Humanist jurists, like Budé and Alciat, against the glossators upon the *Digest*, and their entire programme for the renovation of juridical studies by a knowledge of the humanities[2]. This invective is even the sole echo we have in French literature of the conflict between Humanism and mediæval tradition in the teaching of law. Although written in the vernacular, it is still too technical to have been likely to interest a popular audience.

The same can be said of a fifth episode, Gargantua's letter to his son Pantagruel, while a student at Paris[3]. It contains a whole educational programme, a veritable encyclopædia which the young student is to assimilate : " In brief, let me see thee an abyss and bottomless pit of knowledge ". It sketches a brilliant picture of the revival of good letters around 1532 and concludes with wise moral precepts : " Knowledge without conscience is but the ruin of the soul ". We are no longer engaged upon " fooleries " ; this entire chapter is wholly serious. Like the four preceding episodes it was intended for the lettered public, the masters and pupils of the Universities, rather than for the popular readers of the *Great Chronicles*. Thus, in the framework of the fictitious history of Pantagruel,

---

[1] Bonaventure des Périers calls them " non commentatores, sed tormentatores juris ".

[2] Cf. Alciat, end of preface to the *Prætermissa* (1518) : Cum enim in jure multa sint, *quæ sine cognitione studiorum humanitatis* percipi nequeunt " (quoted by Viard, *Alciat*, p. 229, note 1), and this declaration from *Pantagruel*, ch. X : " In respect of human learning (the *litteræ humaniores*), and the knowledge of antiquities and history . . . of all which the laws are so full, that *without it they cannot be understood* . . . ". [3] Ch. VIII.

Rabelais had placed some compositions which dated, doubtless, from his sojourn in the Universities. These episodes take up no less than one-sixth of the book.

He mixed with it also the tastes and ideas which are characteristic of Humanism under François I—enthusiasm for the restoration of good literature, disgust of scholasticism and of its agents,—the theologians,—contempt for the mediæval commentaries on the *Pandects*, the thirst for encyclopædic knowledge, and the praise of Greek, "without which a man may be ashamed to count himself a scholar."

We can go further ; he has entrusted to this humorous book his ideas upon religion. They are not to be looked for in certain satirical allusions to Alexander VI's debauches and to Julius II's ambition : his attacks upon Popes go no further in daring than those of Catholics whose orthodoxy is above suspicion, like Guillaume Budé or Jean Bouchet. Nor are they revealed to us by the familiar or jocular tone he adopts when speaking of Holy Writ, of the mysteries and ceremonies of Catholicism : such jokes were not then considered as sacrileges and it has been shown that other monks before him had committed even more serious ones without scandalising anyone. The healing of Epistemon, whose head had been cut off, contains touches which seem to us a parody on the Gospel miracles : they do not, however, imply a denial of these miracles. But Rabelais' religious thought has left its mark upon one passage of the epic of Dipsodie : in the vow Pantagruel takes at the moment when he is preparing to fight Loupgarou, King Anarchus' captain of the Guard. " Lord God ", cries the giant, " if it may please Thee at this time to assist me, as my whole trust and confidence is in Thee alone, I vow unto Thee, that in all countries whatsoever, wherein I shall have any power or authority, whether in this of Utopia, or elsewhere, I will cause thy Holy Gospel to be *purely, simply* and *entirely* preached so that the abuses of a rabble of hypocrites and *false prophets*, who, by *human constitutions* and *depraved inventions*, have impoisoned all the world, shall be quite exterminated from about me "[1].

That a Christian prince at the moment of attacking a barbarous enemy should make a vow to preach the Gospel in the states which victory will give to him, is in the tradition of the

[1] Ch. XXIX.

chivalric romances. But the very expressions which Pantagruel uses in this vow, however ordinary they may seem to us to-day, had then a very definite significance. *Human constitutions* and *depraved inventions* are the terms which were used in the pre-Reformers' groups, in the *entourage* of Marguerite de Navarre, Lefèvre d'Étaples, Briçonnet, to express all that which in the traditional Church did not seem to be of the pure essence of the Gospel, that is to say, the cult of the Virgin and of the Saints, veneration of relics, pilgrimages, indulgences, sometimes the Papacy and even confession. Those were the abuses of which the defenders against the attack of the pre-Reformers were the monks and theologians, " hypocrites " and " false prophets " as they were called in the same circles. " To preach the Gospel *purely* and *simply* "— these words which sum up their programme, were going to appear again in a famous speech, that written by Calvin and delivered by Cop, Rector of Paris University, on November 1st, 1533. It is known how the Sorbonne replied by calling for proceedings against the author of the harangue on grounds of heresy. Thus Rabelais at this date takes his place among those called " Evangelicals "[1], and, we shall see him, in *Gargantua*,

[1] I should here mention that M. Abel Lefranc (ch. III of his *Introduction* to the critical edition of *Pantagruel*) holds a completely different opinion. He considers that Rabelais' " hidden thought " is rationalistic—that he did not believe in the miracles of the Gospels and, from the outset of his literary career, that he " adhered to what the moderns call ' independent thought ' ".

M. Abel Lefranc's thesis is based : (1). Upon an interpretation of all the passages in *Pantagruel* which contain derisive references to or parodies on the *Holy Scripture ;*

(2). Upon the testimony of Calvin (who in his treatise on *Scandals* (1550) includes Rabelais among the materialists) and that of other Protestant writers like Henri Estienne ;

(3). Upon the testimony of orthodox Catholics ;

(4). Upon the testimony of neo-Latin poets like Visagier, who knew Rabelais between 1533 and 1540 ;

(5). Upon an interpretation of the IVth dialogue of Bonaventure des Périers' *Cymbalum mundi*, introducing two dogs, Hylactor and Pamphagus, the latter supposedly representing Rabelais. Confirmation of this identification is claimed from an epitaph composed by Joachim du Bellay, entitled *Pamphagi medici*.

I can only give here a *résumé* of his arguments and refer, for a detailed exposition, to his study quoted above. The following are the objections to his thesis :

(1). M. Gilson (*Rabelais franciscain*, p. 17) has pointed out that it is very difficult for a modern person to look upon Rabelais' irreverent expressions with regard to the Scriptures " in the same way that the average person amongst those for whom the author intended them must have looked upon them ". The standards of propriety of a former Cordelier and of the public he had in mind while writing escape us.—I had already pointed out this (in a study of *l'Écriture Sainte et la littérature scriptuaire dans l'œuvre de Rabelais,* attacking some of these *human constitutions, depraved inventions* and *abuses of false prophets* which Pantagruel swore to wipe out from his states.

Does this mean that Rabelais was deeply attached to the pre-Reformers' ideas ?   That he was ready to undergo any

R.É.R., VIII, pp. 257–330, and IX, pp. 423–436) from the fact that, in the expurgated edition published by Rabelais in 1542 with Juste, he had allowed jokes, which we would consider blasphemous, to remain and even added further ones.   M. Villey (in his review of the critical edition in the *Revue d'histoire littéraire de la France*, 1924, pp. 528–536), independently ot M. Gilson's work, makes the same reservations upon the bearing of Rabelais' irreverences and "lucianisms."   Besides, he objects, in the first place, that it would be strange did not the theologians who condemned *Pantagruel* discover this "hidden thought", and that the only danger they saw in it was its obscenity ; and, again, that rationalism is irreconcilable with the declarations contained in *Gargantua* in favour of the reading of Scripture and of the Evangelical preachers.

(2). The testimony of the Calvinists and of the orthodox Catholics must be taken cautiously, since Rabelais had attacked both.   Besides, it must be remembered that, between 1530 and 1550, the public, in whichever of the two camps they may be placed on religious matters, have become more chary of irreverence towards the text of the Scriptures.   Rabelais, free from these scruples, is suspect to both sides.

(3). The testimony of the Calvinists, says M. Villey, is valid only for the Rabelais they had known in Lyons, between 1536 and 1540, for Nicolas Bourbon de Vandœuvre, like Visagier, after reading *Pantagruel* and *Gargantua*, had not attacked these books ; or rather, should I add, Bourbon, who had reproached Rabelais with his obscenities in 1533, later made amends to him.

Besides is it certain that Visagier's epigrams are directed against Rabelais ? One of them seems aimed at a "Ciceronian", and Rabelais had taken no part in the *querelle du cicéronianisme*.

(4). The interpretation which M. Abel Lefranc places upon *Dialogue IV* of the *Cymbalum mundi* has been contested by M. Delaruelle (*Étude sur le problème du Cymbalum Mundi*, in the *Revue d'histoire littéraire de la France*, 1925, pp. 1–24).   The dialogue was written, according to M. Abel Lefranc, to urge Rabelais to enter the fray resolutely and give straightforward expression to his ideas upon Christianity and its mysteries.   M. Delaruelle points out that it is Hylactor (Des Périers) who, on the contrary, sets out to instruct Pamphagus, and that when the latter persists in his silence, his interlocutor allows their conversation to wander away from the point.

Another argument can be put forward against this interpretation of this dialogue.   The *Cymbalum Mundi* was written about 1537–1538, that is to say, subsequent to the *Affaire des placards* (October 18th, 1534) and to the inter- view of Aigues-Mortes, which marks the break between the Crown and the Reformation.   Is it likely that, at this date, Des Périers, who knew Rabelais' temperament, would have urged him, against all prudence, to set forth doctrines which attacked Catholicism ?

There is yet another objection which has not hitherto been stated : the composition of *Pantagruel* is contemporaneous with Rabelais' sending to Erasmus the famous letter of which I have already spoken, ch. VIII, pp. 112–114.   Having to give his correspondent information about Julius Cæsar Scaliger, what does he say about him ?   That he is an atheist—nobody more so.   If Rabelais, in 1532, had ceased to be a Christian and become a rationalist, would he have spoken thus of a colleague in irreligion ?

Lastly, if Rabelais were no longer a Christian in 1532, why would he have shown in *Gargantua* his sympathy for the Evangelicals which could only have had the effect of making him suspect to the theologians of the Sorbonne ?

sacrifice to secure their supremacy ? By no means. He might have said with Montesquieu : " I would very much like to be the confessor of truth, but not its martyr ". We may even be of the opinion that he spoke very lightly of Jean Caturce, or of Cahors, professor of law at Toulouse, who was burned alive in the month of June, 1532, for having expressed opinions savouring of Lutheranism : " Now God forbid that I should die this death ! " cries Pantagruel, when he learned that the scholars of Toulouse " did cause burn their regents alive, like red herrings ", " for I am by nature sufficiently dry already, without heating myself any further "[1]. Doubtless he thought, like Étienne Dolet, that it was senseless to endanger his life even in a good cause, by ridiculous and unbearable obstinacy[2].

On the whole, *Pantagruel* was a work sufficiently rich in plebeian jokes, farces, mystifications, puns, and cock-and-bull-stories to find favour with the same readers who had delighted in the *Great Chronicles*. Two editions of it were immediately sold : pirated editions soon appeared.

Maître Alcofrybas Nasier's name was associated with that of Pantagruel ; Rabelais took advantage of it to issue at the beginning of 1533 a *Pantagrueline prognostication* for the current year. Under this title of *Pronostications* or *prognostications* were offered for sale, along with almanacks, in book-selling centres, books of meteorological and political predictions. Parodies were written on them[3]. A Humanist from Antwerp who had taught Greek at Orleans and had settled down at Lyons in 1529, Joachim Sterk van Ringelberg, (in Latin Fortius Ringelbergius,) had just published with Sebastian Gryphius a sort of popular encyclopædia in Latin[4], which contained, in the chapter on Astrology, some jocose predictions. It was there announced that, during the coming year, the blind would see

[1] Ch. V.
[2] These expressions are used by Dolet in a letter to Guillaume Scève, 9th November, 1534, quoted by Richard Copley Christie, *Étienne Dolet, the martyr of the Renaissance* (1508–1546), 2nd edition, London, 1899, p. 207.
[3] The oldest one known is the *Prognosticon ex Etrusco sermone in latinum traductum ab anno Do. M. D. IX, usque in finem mundi*, added to the book of *Facetiæ* of the Humanist Babel, one of Melanchton's teachers.
[4] *De ratione studii* (1532). Cf. the following opinion of the Greek tongue contained therein, similar to Rabelais', *Pantagruel*, ch. VIII : " Lingua græca adeo necessaria est, ut vix quemquam dixerim eruditum qui eam ignoraverit ". Cf., on Joachim Sterk, Cuissard, *L'étude du grec à Orléans* in the *Mémoires de la Société archéologique et historique de l'Orléanais*, 1883. Cf. also Pietro Toldo, *Un imitateur ou un inspirateur de Rabelais*. *Revue d'histoire littéraire de la France*, 1900, p. 122.

but little or not at all, and the deaf would hear badly ; that old age would be incurable on account of preceding years ; that there would be wars between dogs and hares, between cats and mice, between wolves and sheep, and eggs and monks, etc.

Maître Alcofrybas, styling himself Pantagruel's cup-bearer, or architriclinus, treats the same humorous themes in his *Pantagrueline prognostication.* Having pointed out to his " benevolent reader " the necessity for verifying all news so as not to delude the poor world, he announces that the year will be dominated not by Saturn, nor Mars, nor Jupiter, but by God the Father ; that as a result of eclipses crabs " will go sideways and cordspinners backwards " ; that a horrible malady, an epidemic, will rage everywhere, namely " lack of money " ; that a great deal of goods of all kinds will be possessed by those who have plenty, etc. Among the humorous predictions we find an allusion to Pantagruel's kingdoms, the lands of Utopia and of Dipsodie, some jokes which appeared previously in Maître Alcofrybas' first work, and, finally, several quotations from St. Paul (*Romans* 2), the text preferred of the Evangelicals[1].

In the summer of this year, 1533, Lyons was *en fête.* On the occasion of the Dauphin's marriage with the Florentine Catherine de' Medici, King François I came to live there during the last weeks of May and the month of June.

To the usual festivities which periodically brightened up the hard-working city—planting of the printers' Maypole[2], election of the workmen's prince[3], carnival processions of the statue of Maschecroute (Gnaw-crush)[4], excursions to the Île-Barbe[5],—were added brilliant entertainments. Joyous animation reigned everywhere. The inns were full of horsemen of

[1] Rabelais also published, in the Spring of 1533, an Almanack in which, following a common usage, he took in advance the title of Doctor of Medicine. Cf. Marty-Laveaux, *op. cit.*, vol. III, p. 255.

[2] Known to us from a Latin poem by Dolet and a sonnet by Marot on a *mai* presented to the Governor, Pompone Trivulcio.

[3] On which we have a Latin poem by one Girinet. Cf. Ferdinand Buisson, *Sébastien Castellion*, vol. I, p. 35.

[4] Cf. *Fourth Book*, ch. LIX : " It was a monstrous, ridiculous, hideous figure, fit to fright little children : its eyes bigger than its belly, and its head larger than all the rest of its body ; well mouth-cloven, however, having a goodly pair of wide, broad jaws, lined with two rows of teeth, upper tier and under tier, which, by the magic of a small twine hid in the hollow part of the golden staff, were made to clash, clatter, and rattle dreadfully one against another ".

[5] Cf. Bonaventure des Périers, ode on the *Voyage de Lyon à Notre-Dame de l'Île-Barbe*, ed. Louis Lacour, vol. I, p. 54.

the King's suite[1], the streets thronged with a gay crowd. The Saône bridge was inadequate for the traffic between the two banks and it became fashionable to cross the river on barges covered with awnings, and rowed by boat-women, which gave a note of grace to this picturesque scene[2]. The noblest ladies of France and of Spain gathered in Court took part in the amusements and public festivals, which were presided over by the King and Queen, in prominent view on a raised platform.

The poet Jean Second, then at Lyons, gives a short description of these festivals in his diary. He names also the persons he met there : Hilaire Bertoul, his compatriot, and the painter Corneille de Lyon[3]. Another Humanist, the physician Hubert Sussannée, mentions among the friends he made during the Court's stay at Lyons, Rabelais, Barthélemy Aneau and Salmon Macrin[4]. These last two are also Humanists. Aneau (Annulus), a native of Bourges, had learned Greek under the direction of Melchior Volmar. He was then working upon a verse translation of Ovid's *Metamorphoses*, intended as a sequel to the translation undertaken and left unfinished by Marot. He taught rhetoric at the Collège de la Trinité of which he was to become principal in 1540[5].

Saumon Meigret, in Latin Salmonius Macrinus (whence Salmon Macrin), was almost a compatriot of Rabelais', being born at Loudun[6]. A pupil of Lefèvre d'Étaples and of Aleander, in relations with the Humanists Lazare de Baïf, Lascaris and Tagliacarne, tutor to the Royal children, he had taken a

---

[1] Cf. the *Itinera* of Johannes Secundus, pp. 43–44 of G. Prévot's translation, *Revue du Nord* (August–November, 1923).

[2] The Saône boatwomen also attracted Chateaubriand's attention : " The barks which cross this gentle river, covered with an awning and rowed by young women, form an amusing and agreeable sight for the eyes ". *Voyage en Italie* (1803). Rabelais mentions them, *Pantagruel*, ch. XXX : " When my lords the devils had a mind to recreate themselves upon the water, as in the like occasion are hired the boat[women] at Lyons . . . ".

[3] Cf. on Corneille de Lyon, Louis Dimier's great work, *Histoire de la peinture française au XVIe siècle* (Van Oest, 1926, 3 vols., 8vo).

[4] " Lugduni morari constitui ut aulæ nives atras et simulatione infuscatas larvas propius aliquando intuerer et Salmone Macrino, Francisco Rabelæso et Barthol. Anulo, Biturige, non vulgaribus amicis morigerarer, qui amicitiæ jure me illic, quamdiu hæsit aula regis, destinuerant ". Epistle prefixed to the *Alexandri quantitates emendatæ* (1538).

[5] On Barthélemy Aneau and the College of the Trinity at Lyons before 1540, cf. the articles published by L. Gerig in *La Revue de la Renaissance*, 1908–1911.

[6] Cf. V. L. Bourrilly, *Guillaume du Bellay*, p. 116.

foremost place among French neo-Latin poets by the publication of two collections of *Carmina* (1528 and 1530). In an *Ode* which appeared in 1537 he will express his admiration for Rabelais' learning, wit, and especially for his skill in medicine. He recalls with a pleased pride that he is almost from the same place as he, that the same air is breathed in their two countries, that the same serenity bathes their chestnut-planted fields and that an equal sweetness of character is found there[1].

[1] This ode runs as follows :—

Ad Franciscum Rablæsium Chinonien.
medicum peritissimum.

Idem Rablæsi pæne solum mihi est
Natale tecum : Juliodunicis
Nam Chino vicinus nucetis
Contigua regione floret ;

Aerque nostris civibus ac tuis
Hauritur idem, parque serenitas
Par ruris uligo beati,
Morum eadem quoque lenitudo.

Natalis agri concilians tibi
Vicinitas me, jungit amabili
Vinclo, sed impense tuarum
Vis sociat mage litterarum.

Chinonienses inter enim tuos
Unus, Rablæsi, es, cui Deus, et favens
Natura, doctrinam elegantem
Non neget, atque sales acutos ;

Unus lepores cui simul atticos
Et circularis dona peritiæ
Dilargiatur, florulentam et
Cognitionem utriusque linguæ.

Artem ut medendi præteream et tibi
Sudore multo parta mathemata
Quid luna, quid stellæ minentur,
Quid rapidi facies planetæ.

Tu non Galeno Pergamæo minor
Multus ab atris faucibus eximis
Lethi propinquantis, tuaque
Depositos opera focillas.

Quid quæque radix herbave conferat,
Ungues, tenes, et non secus ac tuos,
Famamque lucraris perennem,
Arte levans genus omne morbos.

Testes tuarum Parisii artium
Testisque Narbo Martius atque Atax
Et dite Lugdunum, penates
Sunt tibi ubi, placidæque sedes.

Salmonii Macrini Juliodunensis, cubicularii regii, Odarum libri sex ad Franciscum Regem Regum potentissimum, invictissimumque (Lyons, Sebastian Gryphius, 1537, 8vo.), folio 7 *verso,* the last ode of Book II.
This Ode, says V. L. Bourrilly, belongs to the year 1533 rather than 1537, " for it is noticeable that Macrin makes no reference to Rabelais' visits to Italy, a fact which in 1537 would be indeed extraordinary in a poet of habitu-

It is in the Summer of 1533 and on the occasion of the Court's stay at Lyons that Rabelais entered into relationship with Mellin de Saint-Gelais, the poet favoured of the courtiers. From being poetic secretary to various great ladies, Mellin, son or nephew of Octovien de Saint-Gelais, had become chaplain to the Dauphin, François, and the King was soon to appoint him Keeper of the Royal Library of Blois, transferred later to Fontainebleau[1]. He had the art of pleasing by his refined manners, his talent on the lute, his gallantry and his light poetry. He took care, besides, not to print his fugitive pieces and especially his compliments in rime, in order, perhaps, to be able to pass them off several times over as new ! But his verses were circulated secretly and doubtless it is in this way that Rabelais became acquainted with and published in *Gargantua*, with the approval of " Merlin the Prophet ", as he calls him, the two poems of the *Antidoted Fanfreluches*[2], and of the *Enigma in the form of Prophecy*[3], which describes in obscure terms a game of tennis.

Pantagruel was beginning to be talked about in Paris. In the month of August a production entitled *The Book of Merchants, extremely useful to all persons*, was given as the work of Pantapole " near neighbour of the lord Pantagruel "[4]. On September 25th a bourgeois of Paris, Jacques le Gros, in drawing up a list of books to read, mentions among a hundred titles of heroic romances and other amusing books, *Pantagruel*[5]. The 23rd October, the general assembly of the University of Paris having enquired from the Faculty of Theology why it had recently condemned the *Miroir de l'âme pécheresse* (*Mirror of the Sinful Soul*) by the Queen of Navarre, the theologian Le Clerc answered by giving the reasons for his latest censures :

---

ally scant inspiration, given to seizing eagerly upon any theme for treatment ". *Deux points obscurs dans la vie de Rabelais, R.É.R.*, vol. IV, p. 104, note 1.

If we accept this opinion, it would follow that in 1533 Rabelais had practised medicine at Paris and Narbonne, as stated in the final verse. But this verse may have been subsequently added at the time of its publication. The present second last verse seems a more fitting ending to the poem, promising, as it does, lasting fame to Rabelais :

> " Famamque lucraris perennem
> Arte levans genus omne morbos ".

[1] Cf. Molinier, *Mellin de Saint-Gelais*, Paris, 1910, and my article on *Rabelais et Mellin de Saint-Gelais, R.É.R.*, IX, 90.

[2] *Gargantua*, ch. II.   [3] *Ibid.*, ch. LVIII.

[4] Cf. *R.É.R.*, III, 327.

[5] Cf. A. Lefranc's article, *Les plus anciennes mentions du Pantagruel et du Gargantua, R.É.R.*, III, 217.

the *Miroir* had been condemned because, in defiance of a parliamentary decree it had not, although treating of matters of religion, been submitted to the Sorbonne for examination. As to *Pantagruel*, likewise condemned, it had been so on the same grounds as the *Forest d'amours* and other books of the same stamp, as being obscene[1].

[1] This fact is made known to us from *Le Registre des procès-verbaux de la Faculté de théologie de Paris pendant les anneés* 1505–1533, published by Léopold Delisle (cf. *R.É.R.*, VIII, pp. 290 seqq.) and from a letter of Calvin's to François Daniel, then at Orleans : " Ultimus verba fecit Clericus, parochus Sancti Andreæ in quem omnis culpa derivabatur, aliis a se amolientibus . . . Dixit . . . se pro damnatis libris habuisse obscænos illos Pantagruelem, Sylvam [amorum] et ejus monetæ ". Herminjard, *Correspondance des Réformateurs* (Geneva, Bâle and Lyons, 1878, 9 vols., 8vo), vol. III, p. 106.

CHAPTER X

FIRST JOURNEY TO ROME

AT the time when the Sorbonne was condemning *Pantagruel*, Rabelais had already provided himself with an ecclesiastical protector more influential than the distant Bishop of Maillezais: this was the Bishop of Paris, Jean du Bellay. This prelate had gained great prestige at Court by his cleverness in diplomacy. The King had entrusted him with difficult missions to England, of which the object was to win for François I, then at war with Charles V, the good graces of Henry VIII. In order to oblige the latter the Bishop of Paris had gone so far as asking the theologians of the Sorbonne to approve canonically the conduct of Henry VIII who, being desirous of marrying Anne Boleyn, had discovered excellent pretexts for repudiating his wife, Catherine of Aragon.

Jean du Bellay, then, was influential at Court, and the royal favour extended likewise to his brother Guillaume, Seigneur de Langey, who had acquired distinction on several missions to the Holy See and to the German Protestant princes with whom François I was seeking an alliance.

During the months of May and June, 1533, Jean du Bellay, being at Lyons during the King's visit, had been enabled to meet Rabelais, who had become a close friend of his *protégés*, Hubert Sussannée and Salmon Macrin. Some months later, on his return from a journey to London, he again passed through Lyons. He had been sent to Rome with the object of petitioning Pope Clement VII to withhold the sentence of excommunication announced against Henry VIII as a consequence of his divorce. The matter was an important one : the interdiction cast upon England following the excommunication would have seriously compromised France's commercial interests[1].

---

[1] Almost two years later, 15th Feb., 1536, Rabelais writes from Rome that " the Bull which was being prepared against the King of England to excommunicate him, and lay his Kingdom under a ban of interdiction and proscription, was not passed by the Consistory on account of certain articles *de commeatibus externorum et commerciis mutuis* ". *Lettres écrites d'Italie*, ed. Bourrilly, p. 3 (published by *La Société des études rabelaisiennes*, 1910).

Jean du Bellay suffered from sciatica. The pain was so intolerable that he could scarcely endure the journey in a litter[1]. He needed a physician, and thought of Rabelais whose reputation was already great[2], and whose good humour he had doubtless had the occasion of experiencing. He offered to take him to Rome, and the offer was accepted with enthusiasm. Rabelais was going to realise this dream which he had formed from the earliest days of his initiation to Humanism : travel through Italy and visit Rome, capital of the ancient world[3].

The 17th January, 1534 (new style), he received twenty-seven *livres tournois* of his salary as physician to the Grand Hôpital at Lyons, and the two travellers set forth. Presumably they followed the itinerary taken by all pilgrims, traders, couriers and diplomats. They crossed the Guiers at the Pont-de-Beauvoisin, ascended the Isère, and then the Arc valley, aided by the Savoy " mountain chestnuts "[4], these guides who " knew the mountain snowstorms as well as do sailors those of the sea "[5], then crossed the Alps by the Mont Cenis and descended to the Novalaise. By the early days of February, at latest the 8th, they were in Rome and staying with a prelate who was friendly to France, the Bishop of Faenza[6].

Jean du Bellay was concerting his efforts with those of the Royal Ambassador Ordinary to the Holy See, Charles Hémart d'Hénonville, Bishop of Mâcon, installed only a few months previously. Their diplomacy failed completely. However great was Jean du Bellay's eloquence on his admission to plead Henry VIII's cause before the Cardinals and the Pope—and Rabelais tells us that the subtlety of his ideas, the nimbleness of his dialectic, the dignity of his answers, the vivacity of his

---

[1] Letter from Jean du Bellay to the Sieur de Castillon, quoted by Bourrilly, *op. cit.*, p. 3.

[2] The *Chronologia omnium illustrium medicorum*, published at Frankfort in 1556, gives the year 1534 as the beginning of his reputation as a doctor. Cf. *R.É.R.*, III, 446.

[3] " Nam quod maxime mihi fuit optatum jam inde ex quo in litteris politioribus aliquem sensum habui, ut Italiam peragrare, Romamque orbis caput invisere possem, id tu mirifica quadam benignitate præstitisti ". From the dedicatory epistle to Jean du Bellay in the *Topographia antiquæ Romæ*.

[4] " The *chestnuts* (*marrons*) of the mountains of Savoy . . . ". *Pantagrueline Prognostication*, ch. VII.

[5] Martin du Bellay's *Mémoires*, quoted by H. Clouzot, *R.É.R.*, IV, 175.

[6] From a letter of Jean du Bellay to Montmorency, 15th March, 1534, quoted by V. L. Bourrilly, *Le cardinal Jean du Bellay en Italie, R.É.R.*, V, 275.

PLATE IV

PORTRAIT OF JEAN DU BELLAY
(Museum of Versailles, No. 3152)

[face p. 144

refutations, his ease of speech, the purity of his diction were admired—he won their applause, but gained nothing more. Sentence was pronounced against Henry VIII at the Consistory of March 23rd. Ten days later, Jean du Bellay, accompanied by his physician, left Rome.

This stay of barely two months had been put to good account by Rabelais. Attendance on the prelate did not take up his full day, and he employed his spare time in accordance with a programme which he had drawn up on leaving Lyons, in which his interests as a physician and as a Humanist both found place. He purposed to converse with the numerous scholars then in Rome on many problems which were causing him great trouble, he tells us; then, he wished to examine plants and drugs which he had been unable to obtain in France; and finally, having examined the sites and consulted the ancient texts he had brought with him, to draw up for himself a topography of ancient Rome[1].

His botanical expectations were not fulfilled. Italy did possess some botanical gardens in which Eastern plants were acclimatised, but they did not lie on the route which Rabelais followed[2]. He discovered only one plant which was unknown to him—a plane-tree, near Lake Nemi, probably in some prelate's or great lord's park[3]. For at this date the importation of this tree from Asia Minor, where it was admired by travellers, had scarcely begun, and that of Padua in Cardinal Bembo's garden, and that of Castello, in Cosimo de' Medici's, were mentioned as specimens. Some ten years later the gardens at Touvoie belonging to René du Bellay, Bishop of Le Mans, gloried in their turn in possessing the first plane-trees brought from Italy into France by Pierre Belon, the physician[4].

He met fewer scholars then he had expected. However, he entered into relationship with Nicolas Raince,—who, having been attached for eighteen years to the French Embassy, knew

---

[1] *Vide* dedicatory letter of the *Topographia antiquæ Romæ* to Jean du Bellay, Marty-Laveaux, *op. cit.*, vol. III, p. 333.
[2] There were botanic gardens at Castello, in Tuscany, in the Duke of Florence's gardens; at Chocachi, in Signor Rucellai's grounds, at Pisa and at Lucca. Cf. *L'Aventureuse existence de Pierre Belon du Mans*, by Dr. Paul Delaunay, Paris, É. Champion, 1926, pp. 79–80.
[3] " Plantas autem nullas, sed nec animantia ulla habet Italia, quæ non ante nobis et visa essent et nota. Unicam Platanum vidimus ad speculum Dianæ Aricinæ ". Dedicatory letter of *Topographia antiquæ Romæ*, Marty-Laveaux, *loc. cit.*
[4] Cf. Dr. Delaunay, *op. cit.*, pp. 91–92.

L

Rome perfectly,—with another secretary, Jean Sevin, with the Scriptor Apostolic, André Cave[1], with Master Jehan Lunel, Abbot of Saint-Sebastian-without-the-Walls[2]. He may have met Jean Lascaris who had left Paris for Rome three years previously.

The study of ancient Rome seems to have given Rabelais much more satisfaction. Of the edifices which the Popes were building to beautify their city he mentions only Saint Peter's basilica, " dilapidated and wanting a cover "[3], as work on it had been discontinued since Raphael's death (1520). On the other hand, if we take his word for it[4], all the monuments and streets of ancient Rome were soon familiar to him. We can picture him wandering on the site of the Forum, where cattle then grazed (it was named the *Campo Boario*), admiring the triple columns of the temple of the Dioscures, the only ones appearing above this land of ruins[5], studying the bas-reliefs of Septimus Severus' triumph, examining on Trajan's column the " form " of the ancient Roman toga[6], or, again, bending over the tombs, inscriptions and epitaphs along the Appian Way in order to " take an exact account of them "[7].

It is there, doubtless, he was initiated to the technique of ancient architecture. All the Humanists were very interested in it and they prepared the way for the coming of this classic style which, from François I's reign onwards, renewed at first the decoration of buildings and, then, the very art of architecture. But nobody, perhaps, has manifested more interest than Rabelais in this art which was new to France. In 1532, in *Pantagruel*[8], he mentions the two works which were the breviary of the architects of the day: *De re edificatoria* of Leone Battista Alberti, who showed how to use the study of ancient ruins for modern buildings, and the *De Architectura* of Vitruvius. After his visit to Rome we find many proofs of his knowledge of Græco-Roman architecture. He draws on the vocabulary special to this art. He is the first of our writers

---

[1] Cf. Bourrilly's *Introduction* to the *Lettres écrites d'Italie* . . . , pp. 5–6.
[2] Cf. Léon Dorez' article on Jehan Lunel, *Revue des bibliothèques*, 1905.
[3] *Fourth Book*, ch. XLV.
[4] Cf. dedicatory letter of *Topographia antiquæ Romæ:* " Quod erat postremum, id sic perfeci diligenter, ut nulli notam magis domum esse suam, quam Romam mihi Romæque viculos omneis putem ". Marty-Laveaux, *loc. cit.*
[5] Cf. Maurel, *L'Art de voyager en Italie* (Hachette, 1920), pp. 9–34.
[6] Cf. *Third Book*, ch. VII.   [7] *Fourth Book*, ch. XXV.
[8] Ch. VII.

to use certain architectural terms which subsequently became common. He employs some unusual terms, and takes care to explain them[1]. This architectural learning was one of the fruits of his stay in Rome[2].

Jean du Bellay also was interested in these archæological studies. The hunt for "antiques" was then fashionable in Rome. The Popes set the example by accumulating in the new galleries, connecting the Vatican with the Belvedere, marbles more or less mutilated, portions of pillars and bits of sculpture taken from the soil of Rome. The cardinals had excavations carried out in their *vignes* (as the country residences were then named) and a young French architect who was then studying these remains, Philibert Delorme, has recounted the treasures unearthed one day in Cardinal Gaddi's *vigne* : friezes, capitals and cornices " as well as innumerable scraps and fragments, very ancient, and more than admirable to the human eye "[3]. Jean du Bellay himself bought a fairly extensive *vigne* where he had some excavations carried out but without result.

A surer method of getting antiques was to apply to the

[1] Thus in ch. XLIX, *Fourth Book*, he writes : " Et pendoit en l'air ataché à deux grosses chaînes d'or au *zoophore* du portal ". (" It hung in the air, being fastened with two thick chains of gold to the *zoophore* of the porch ".) In the *Briéfve déclaration d'aucunes dictions plus obscures contenues en ce livre* he gives the following definition of *zoophore* : " Portant animaulx. C'est en un portal et autres lieux, ce que les architectes appellent frize : entre l'architrave et la coronice, onquel lieu l'on mettoit les mannequins, sculptures, escriptures et autres divises à plaisir ". (" Bearing animals. It is, in the porch or elsewhere, what architects call frieze, between the architrave and the cornice, in which place were put figures, sculptures, scrolls or other designs at will ".)
The architectural terms are especially numerous in the *Fifth Book* : in, for example, the description of the fountain of the Temple of Bacbuc—stylobates, arcelets, cymasults, doric undulations, architraves (ch. XLII).
Noël du Fail (*Contes et discours d'Eutrapel*, édition elzévirienne, vol. II, p. 297) describes the impression which these terms of a new art made upon our builders. He tells the story of Maître Pihourt, a mason of Rennes, summoned to a meeting of architects for the purpose of drawing up the plans of the château of Chateaubriant : " When he heard the great workmen of all France here summoned and assembled talking about nothing except frontispieces, pedestals, obelisks, columns, capitals, friezes, cornices, bases . . . he was quite dumbfounded, and ' paying them back in their own coin ', answered in a pseudo-technical jargon ' according to the equipolation of his heteroclites ' ". Cf. H. Clouzot's article with reference to this anecdote, *Rev. XVIe siècle*, vol. V, p. 18.
[2] There is a chapter on the technical vocabulary of architecture as found in *Pantagruel* and *Gargantua*, in Lazare Sainéan's *Langue de Rabelais* (Paris, 1922, 2 vols. 8vo). Cf. vol. I, pp. 51–64.
[3] Cf. H. Clouzot, *Philibert de l'Orme* (Paris, 1910), p. 32. It was no unnecessary precaution to collect and preserve these valuable remnants ; Philibert Delorme tells us that the limeburners of Rome used to make lime with all the bits of marble which they found.

agents and dealers in antiques, whose industry the collectors' mania had developed. A certain Valerio, secretary to Cardinal Ippolito de' Medici, undertook to supply the Bishop of Paris with ancient heads cleverly retouched or restored. The ambassador was commissioned to acquire them on behalf of the Grand Master, Anne de Montmorency, and of the Secretary of State, Jean Breton, sieur of Villandry. On March 15th, he announced to Montmorency the dispatch of a half-dozen heads, one of which, of Cæsar, was of a rare type. They were to be brought back by ships which had come with corn from France[1].

Meanwhile, Rabelais was engaged upon his topographical description of ancient Rome. He had adopted a very simple plan which consisted in dividing the territory to be described into four quarters, formed by two lines drawn, one from north to south, the other from east to west, and intersecting in the middle[2]. As an authority for this elementary geodetic method, our Humanist referred to Thales of Miletus.

Two of Jean du Bellay's household, both of them interested in antiquity, helped him at his work, Nicolas Leroy and Claude Chappuys. The first was a jurist in relations with the Orleans group of Calvin's friends[3]. The second, François I's librarian since the beginning of 1533, was confidential agent to the Bishop of Paris, and, moreover, a lover of belles lettres and a poet.[4] While they all three toiled, as Rabelais tells us[5], bringing together and putting into shape the material for this work, a Milanese, Bartolomeo Marliani, gave to the printing-presses of Rome a Topographia antiquæ Romæ.

Rabelais admits that he was pleased to be forestalled in his task by a work worthy of the consideration of the most learned. Marliani followed a different and much happier plan than this : he described Rome hill by hill, and left nothing to be desired by the most exacting curiosity. Rabelais considered himself free from the burden of finishing and issuing his own work : if he had groaned in the pangs of gestation, says he in medical style, at least the torments of delivery were spared him. He

---

[1] Cf. V. L. Bourrilly, Le cardinal Jean du Bellay en Italie, R.É.R., V. 236.

[2] " Ego ex Thaletis Milesii invento, sublato Sciothero urbem vicatim ducta ab orientis obeuntisque solis, tum Austri atque Aquilonis partibus orbita transversa partiebar, oculisque designabam ". Dedicatory letter of the Topographia antiquæ Romæ. Cf. Marty-Laveaux, op. cit., vol. III, p. 334.

[3] Cf. Heulhard, Rabelais, ses voyages en Italie . . . , p. 32, note 1.

[4] Cf. Claude Chappuys (?—1575), poète de la cour de François Iᵉʳ, by Louis P. Roche (Paris, Les Belles-Lettres, 1929, 1 vol. 8vo.).

[5] Marty-Laveaux, loc. cit.

simply published with Sebastian Gryphius, on his return to Lyons, an edition of this guide of Marliani's through ancient Rome.

The return journey was accomplished slowly and by easy stages. They halted doubtless at Florence. Duke Alexander de' Medici still observed strict neutrality as between the King of France and the Emperor, from which he was soon to change. The turn of events seemed favourable to Frenchmen for a long stay in the town. Our travellers, "studious, fond of visiting the learned, and seeing the antiquities of Italy", viewed "the situation and beauty of Florence, the structure of the Dome, the magnificence of the churches and palaces . . . the porphyries, the marbles, the ancient statues "[1]. They were admitted to the palace of " the richest banker in Christendom, after the Fuggers of Augsbourg "[2], Filippo Strozzi, who had a banking-house at Lyons. He had, the year preceding, accompanied to France his niece, Catherine de' Medici, who became by her marriage the wife of the Dauphin of France.

Among the curiosities of his dwelling figured a menagerie of strange animals, which was, and long remained, famous. One could see there porcupines, ostriches, and wild beasts : lions and another much rarer kind of animal, unknown in the West throughout the entire Middle Ages, of the size " of a very big mastiff, of the form of a cat, all striped in black and white "[3]. Scholars called them by the name which Pliny had given them, " Africans "[4], and they are since called tigers.

Had Rabelais had a previous occasion of seeing these wild beasts ? It is doubtful, although he declares that he did not see in Italy any animal which he did not already know. There was, true, a menagerie at Fontainebleau, but it is precisely in 1534 that it was enriched by the addition of lions and tigers sent to François I by Sultan Kheir-ed-Din Barbarossa[5]. He experienced, then, at this new sight a profound satisfaction of his curiosity. But the prosaic appetite of one of his companions,

---

[1] *Fourth Book*, ch. XI.

[2] So Rabelais styles him in his letter to Geoffroy d'Estissac from Rome, 30th Dec., 1535.

[3] Montaigne, in a Journal of his travels in Italy, thus describes tigers, of which he, for the first time, saw a specimen in the Duke of Ferrara's menagerie.

[4] *Fourth Book*, ch. XI.

[5] According to Loisel, *Histoire des Ménageries* (1912), vol. I, p. 201, cf. Sainéan, *L'Histoire naturelle dans l'œuvre de Rabelais, Revue du XVIe siècle*, 1915, p. 249.

a certain monk named Bernard Lardon, got no satisfaction therefrom :

" What can one see after all ? There are fine houses, indeed, and that is all . . . in all this same town I have not seen one poor lane of roasting cooks. . . . Now at Amiens, in four, nay five times less ground than we have trod in our contemplations, I could have shown you above fourteen streets of roasting cooks, most ancient, savoury and aromatic. I cannot imagine what kind of pleasure you can have taken in gazing on the lions and Africans, (so methinks you call their tigers,) near the belfry ; or in ogling the porcupines and ostriches in the Lord Philip Strozzi's palace. Faith and truth I had rather see a good fat goose at the spit. This porphyry, those marbles are fine ; I say nothing to the contrary ; but our cheese-cakes at Amiens are far better in my mind. These ancient statues are well made ; I am willing to believe it : but by St. Ferréol of Abbeville, we have young wenches in our country, which please me better a thousand times "[1].

Some critics have taken this sally, which Rabelais puts into the mouth of a monk with a culinary name, as a synopsis of his impressions of Italy. They have concluded therefrom that he was a stranger to æsthetic emotions. It is true that Rabelais does not name one Italian artist, but there is in his work ample indication of the attention he paid to works of art, tapestries, mosaics, beautiful architectural lines, and is there not a reminiscence of the famous Vatican *stanze* in the decoration he pictures for the gallery of the Abbey of Thélème[2] "all covered over and painted with the ancient prowesses, histories and descriptions of the world " ?

On the 18th of May Jean du Bellay arrived at Paris. Rabelais had already resumed his work at the Great Hospital of Lyons and, on the 1st of August, he was paid his salary for six and a half months, 25 *livres*, although he was not entitled to full salary, notes the clerk entrusted with the payment[3]. He had lost nothing by leaving his position to accompany the Bishop of Paris to Rome for three and a half months. A little later, in the dedicatory letter to Jean du Bellay which he put at the head of the Lyons edition of Marliani's *Topographia antiquæ*

---

[1] *Fourth Book*, ch. XI.
[2] *Gargantua*, end of ch. LIII. Cf. a contribution by Victor Waille to the Congress of Historical Sciences, held at Rome in 1903 (vol. VII of the Proceedings), on Rabelais' visits to Rome and the influence which the Italian Renaissance art may have had on him. *R.É.R.*, IV, 194.
[3] " It would seem that the [annual] wages of the physician are not more than XL *livres* ". Cf. Marty-Laveaux, *op. cit.*, vol. III, p. 325.

Romæ, he expressed all his gratitude to his benefactor, being happier, he declares, in having seen Jean du Bellay in Rome, than in having seen Rome itself.   He assured him of his gratefulness and showered praises upon him.   He had managed to obtain the favour of the prelate who was to remain his most faithful protector.

In the autumn of this same year, perhaps at the Lyons fairs of the month of August[1], Master Alcofrybas Nasier published *The very horrific life of the Great Gargantua, father of Pantagruel.*

---

[1] On the chronology of the early editions both of *Pantagruel* and *Gargantua*, cf. Abel Lefranc, *Étude sur le Gargantua*, ch. I, in his *Introduction* to vol. I of the critical edition.

CHAPTER XI

GARGANTUA

THE success of *Pantagruel* had encouraged Rabelais to write a new book of "*fooleries*". Without worrying about giving his *Pantagruel* the sequel referred to in the final chapter, forgetting the journeys, adventures and fabulous conquests, the descent to Hell and the visit to the regions of the moon which he had promised to publish " at Frankfort mart next coming "[1], he simply undertook the rehandling of the *Great Chronicles* which recounted the life of the giant Gargantua, whom he had made father to his Pantagruel. Thus the book which he wrote second became, in the chronological order of the stories, first in the series ; and *Pantagruel* will be henceforward the second book of his giants' epic.

This rehandling was really an original work. The groundwork of the popular booklet was filled in with a series of new episodes, treated with an art entirely foreign to the compiler of the *Great Chronicles*. The miraculous element ceased to be the author's main preoccupation. He did not, it is true, cease to astonish the reader by the Giant's abnormal proportions, but he felt the need of giving his fancies a basis in reality. Already certain traits of observation had made some pages of *Pantagruel* a true picture of contemporary life—those, for example, which describe the giant's sojourn in the Montagne Sainte-Geneviève. This tendency towards realism becomes constant in *Gargantua*. It is clear from the first part, which should traditionally have been devoted to the hero's miraculous birth. This birth is, indeed, extraordinary : having been " carried " for eleven months, the child makes its entry into the world by its mother's left ear ! But the circumstances which accompany this prodigy are of a less surprising nature. It takes place during a rustic carousal which Rabelais describes at length, as worthy of our attention.

[1] *Pantagruel*, ch. XXXIV.

152

The scene is laid in Chinonais, at La Devinière " in an afternoon on the third day of February "[1]. The inhabitants of neighbouring localities, Cinais, Seuilly, La Roche-Clermaud, Vaugaudry, Coudray-Montpensier, the Gué de Vède, and other places around, have been invited to eat the tripes of fattened beeves, " coiros fattened in guimo meadows " which Grandgousier had killed for salting. Since these tripes will not keep, the relations, friends and neighbours have, according to the rustic usage, been invited to feast thereon. The meal is followed by dancing on the grass of La Saulsaye, on the river's bank, then by a " reciner " or light meal. " Forthwith began flagons to go, gammons to trot, goblets to fly, great bowls to ting . . ." and Rabelais, who will describe in five lines Gargantua's fabulous birth, does not hesitate to devote a whole chapter to the conversational exchanges of these simple folk amid the tinkling of glasses and cups. They consist in encouragements to drinking or their opinions, in brief, on the dishes and the wine of the meal ; but, by a marvellous feat of realistic art, the storyteller has been able not only to convey the tone of these " bienyvres ", but also to convey to us the characters of the speakers : yokels, monks, soldiers, lawyers, goodwives[2].

The same taste for common reality is to be found in the story of the giant's childhood and youth. The episode of the taking away of the bells of Notre-Dame de Paris had given the author of the Great Chronicles an opportunity of showing us the giant's enormous appetite : he restores the bells on the condition that he be given for " dinner three hundred beeves and two hundred sheep ". Rabelais finds therein material for a description of Parisian University life[3]. The people, moved by the theft of the bells, assemble at the Sorbonne. There " after they had well ergoted pro and con, they concluded in Baralipton that they should send the oldest and most sufficient of the Faculty of Theology unto Gargantua "—a choice in conformity with hierarchic exigencies, the Faculty of Theology, sacratissima facultas, having precedence over the others, but which, nevertheless, stirs up latent jealousies among the Faculties : some urge that this mission would be more suitable for a Master of the Faculty of Arts, for an

[1] Gargantua, ch. IV.
[2] Ch. V. The textual commentary in the critical edition affords an interesting reconstitution of this scene.   [3] Chs. XVII–XX.

" orator " than a theologian. Notwithstanding these remonstrances Master Janotus is deputed towards Gargantua. Arrayed in " his most antic accoutrement liripipionated with a graduate's hood " the proud master " transported himself to the lodging of Gargantua, driving before him three red-muzzled beadles ", and dragging after him, for an escort, five or six " Artless Masters, all thoroughly bedraggled with the mire of the streets ".

The mere sight of this motley procession excites Gargantua and his followers to lively merriment. He decides to send the theologian to the buttery to drink ; and meanwhile, unknown to him, to return the stolen bells to the Mayor of the city, and then amuse himself by listening to the harangue, rendered unnecessary, of the fine orator. So Master Janotus harangues the giant in the style of the Faculty of Theology, parading his skill at handling syllogisms, quoting Scripture wrongly, speaking in bog-Latin, coughing, sneezing, spitting.

The harangue being delivered, Gargantua's friends are seized with so violent a fit of laughing that tears come to their eyes " by the vehement concussion of the substance of the brain ". Master Janotus, infected by their merriment, sets to laughing himself, foolishly, without knowing why. It remains for him, in his triumph, to experience the effects of his colleagues' jealousy. A lawsuit in which he is listed against them is the sequel of this episode. Many other traits of University customs are present in the picture of Gargantua's education by the theological regents which Rabelais draws partly from his own memories, enumerating the students' handbooks and usual games, and giving numerous sayings and jokes current in the Colleges. To his early education, which exaggerates to the point of caricature some features of the traditional education, the author opposes the programme of a new pedagogy, inspired by Humanism.

Then, the giant's education completed, begin, according to the ordinary plan of the chivalric romances, and in conformity with that of the *Great Chronicles*, his prowesses and feats of arms ; only, they are situated not in King Arthur's distant kingdom, nor in this fabulous region of Dipsodie where Pantagruel warred. They take place in the heart of Chinonais ; and on the instant, we see the giant's military exploits mingled with the life of the peasants of Rabelais' country,

so that the hero's warlike history is enriched with incidents
in which we get an image of country life at the time, and
even reminiscences of the local history of villages of the
province. The author's native district is brought before us,
its place-names, its scenery, its productions.

While Gargantua was terminating his studies in Paris, his
father Grandgousier lived peacably on his domain of Seuillé,
superintending the work in the fields, telling pleasant tales
to his wife and children, in the evening around the fire, " and,
waiting upon the broiling of some chestnuts " writing " upon
the hearth with a stick burnt at the one end, wherewith they
did stir up the fire "[1]. A vulgar incident, a quarrel between
villagers, came to disturb his peace. The *fouaciers* (cake-
bakers) of Lerné, a neighbouring small town, subjects of King
Picrochole, " third of that name ", while they were one day
bringing to town ten or twelve horseloads of their cakes, met
" in the broad highway " some shepherds of Seuillé, who were
watching two vines to prevent the starlings from stealing the
grapes. The shepherds asked the cake-makers " to give them
some for their money, as the price then ruled in the market ".
Instead of acceding to their request, the cake-makers over-
whelmed them with insults, " calling them brattling gabblers,
licorous gluttons, freckled bittors, mangy rascals, shite-a-bed
scoundrels, drunken roysters, sly knaves, drowsy loiterers, slap-
sauce fellows, slabberdegullion druggels, lubbardly louts, cozen-
ing foxes, ruffian rogues, paultry customers, sychophant-varlets,
drawlatch hoydons, flouting milksops, jeering companions,
staring clowns, forlorn snakes, ninny lobcocks, scurvy sneaks-
bies, fondling fops, base loons, saucy coxcombs, idle lusks,
scoffing braggards, noddy meacocks, blockish grutnols, doddipol
joltheads, jobbernol goosecaps, foolish loggerheads, flutch
calf-lollies, grouthead gnat-snappers, lob-dotterels, gaping
changelings, codshead loobies, woodcock slangams, ninnie-
hammer fly-catchers, noddiepeak simpletons, turdy-gut,
shitten shepherds, and other such like defamatory epithets "[2]
as angry boors apply to one another. A quarrel ensues, in
the course of which Marquet, Grand Banner-carrier of the
Confraternity of the cake-bakers, is wounded and the cakes
pilfered.

On their return to Lerné, the cake-bakers make haste to

[1] Ch. XXVIII.   [2] Ch. XXV.

complain to their King, " showing their panniers broken, their caps all crumpled, their coats torn ". On the instant Picrochole becomes furious and, without any enquiry, counsel or reflection, " commanded the ban and arrière ban to be sounded throughout his country ", and, the very same day, without declaring war, invades Grandgousier's country, whose subjects the shepherds of Seuillé were. His soldiers laid waste the country, carrying off cattle, " beating down the walnuts, plucking the grapes, tearing the hedges (vines), and shaking the fruit-trees "[1]. They did not meet with any resistance except in the close of the Abbey of Seuillé, which Friar Jean des Entommeures defended. Picrochole captures La Roche-Clermaud, and fortifies himself in it. It is there he receives the ambassador whom Grandgousier sends him in an endeavour to compose their quarrel[2]; there takes place the memorable council of war during which he plans to conquer the civilised world[3]; it is there that he will finally be seized and attacked by Gargantua[4], recalled from Paris, and by Friar Jean des Entommeures.

The whole Picrocholine war takes place around this castle which, in Rabelais' time, dominated the surrounding country, and whose vanished strength is proved even to-day by its imposing remains. All the military operations are explained by the topography of the region. All the place-names mentioned by the narrator are still to be found on maps of Chinonais. Thus, the geography of a region familiar to Rabelais is the first element of reality upon which his fiction is based.

Another, recently discovered, is local history. An old tradition identified the King of Lerné, Picrochole, with Gaucher de Sainte-Marthe, who was physician to the nuns of Fontevrault and Lord of Lerné. Documents from archives, explored by M. Abel Lefranc[5], have revealed that, shortly before the composition of *Gargantua*, this personage was in conflict with Rabelais' own father, who was his neighbour on several of his lands, notably La Devinière. An action at law had been taken by the community of boatmen and traders of the Loire and rivers " descending into it " against Gaucher de Saint-Marthe, who was hampering navigation on the river by the unusual practice of installing fisheries at Le Chapeau, above Saumur.

[1] Ch. XXVI.   [2] Ch. XXXI.   [3] Ch. XXXIII.   [4] Ch. XLVIII.
[5] Cf. the *Introduction* to *Gargantua* in the critical edition, pp. LX–LXX.

The plaintiffs' advocate was Maître Antoine Rabelais, and the townships which had entrusted him with their common cause were precisely those which Alcofrybas Nasier enumerates[1] as so many of Grandgousier's allies. Thus a neighbours' quarrel and a lawsuit in which the whole region around the rivers Loire and Vienne had taken part supplied the narrator with episodes, details and elements of reality which he transposed to the heroi-comical scale.

A still greater share of personal reminiscences was to be introduced into the story with the monk, Jean des Entommeures, the defender of the close of the Benedictine Abbey of Seuillé against Picrochole's army. Until Gargantua's arrival upon the scene of operations, it is he who organises resistance to the enemy. He then becomes the giant's lieutenant, rousing all his companions by his good-humour, his high spirits and his courage. "A right monk, if ever there was any, since the monking world monked a monkery", ignorant, dirty, coarse, gluttonous; but life overflows from all his acts as from all his words:

"What wine drink you at Paris? I give myself to the devil, if I did not once keep open house at Paris for all comers. . . . Do you know Friar Claud of the High Kilderkins? Oh the good fellow that he is! But I do not know what fly hath stung him of late, he is become so hard a student. For my part, I study not at all. In our abbey we never study for fear of the mumps, which disease in horses is called the mourning of the chine. Our late abbot was wont to say, that it is a monstrous thing to see a learned monk. By G——, master, my friend, *magis magnos clericos non sunt magis magnos sapientes.* . . . You never saw so many hares as there are this year. I could not any where come by a gosshawk, nor tassel of falcon. My Lord Bellonière promised me a lanner, but he wrote to me not long ago, that he was become pursy. The partridges will so multiply henceforth, that they will go near to eat up our ears. I take no delight in the stalking-horse; for I catch such cold, that I am like to founder myself at that sport. If I do not run, toil, travel, and trot about, I am not well at ease. True it is, that in leaping over the hedges and bushes, my frock leaves always some of its wool behind it. I have recovered a dainty greyhound; I give him to the devil, if he suffer a hare to escape him. A groom was leading him to my Lord Huntlittle, and I robbed him of him. Did I ill?

No, Friar John, (said Gymnast,) no, by all the devils there are, no!

So, (said the monk,) do I attest these same devils so long as they

---

[1] At the beginning of ch. XLVII.

last, or rather, virtue G——, what could that gouty limpard have done with so fine a dog ? By the body of G——, he is better pleased, when one presents him with a good yoke of oxen.

How now, (said Ponocrates,) you swear, Friar John. It is only (said the monk) but to grace and adorn my speech. They are colours of a Ciceronian rhetoric "[1].

Thus are mixed up in Friar John's sprightly conversation quotations from Scripture, familiar swear-words, monkish "apophthegms", allusions to people who were doubtless friends of Rabelais at the time he was a monk.

To reward this excellent servant, Gargantua grants him the foundation of an Abbey which is to be ruled "after his own mind and fancy", Thélème[2]. The description of this ideal abbey again presents to us numerous features taken from contemporary reality. The costume of the Thelemites is that of the gentlemen and "ladies of high degree" of the period of François I, described in accurate detail. As to the architecture of the edifice which is to shelter this new religion, it presents all the characteristics of the composite or Franco-Italian architecture of the early Renaissance. It has long been recognised and Rabelais himself points out[3] that he took as his model the Castle of Bonnivet, "Monsieur l'Admiral's" residence, which was one of the most beautiful in Poitou :

"The whole edifice was everywhere six stories high, reckoning the cellars under ground for one. The second was arched after the fashion of a basket-handle, the rest were sealed with pure wainscot, flourished with Flanders fret-work, in the form of the foot of a lamp, and covered above with fine slates, with an indorsement of lead, carrying the antique figures of little puppets, and animals of all sorts, notably well suited to one another, and gilt, together with the gutters, which jetting without the walls from betwixt the cross bars in a diagonal figure, painted with gold and azure, reached to the very ground, where they ended into great conduit-pipes, which carried away unto the river from under the house.

This same building was a hundred times more sumptuous and magnificent than ever was Bonnivet, Chambourg, or Chantilly ; for there were in it nine thousand three hundred and two and thirty chambers, every one whereof had a withdrawing room, a handsome closet, a wardrobe, an oratory, and neat passage, leading into a great and spacious hall. Between every tower, in the midst of the said body of building, there was a pair of winding, such as we now call lanthorn stairs, whereof the steps were part of porphyry,

---

[1] Ch. XXXIX.   [2] Chs. LII–LVII.
[3] In the early editions ; *vide supra*, ch. V, p. 63.

which is a dark red marble, spotted with white, part of Numidian stone, which is a kind of yellowishly-streaked marble upon various colours, and part of serpentine marble, with light spots on a dark green ground, each of those steps being two and twenty feet in length, and three fingers thick, and the just number of twelve betwixt every rest, or, as we now term it, landing place. In every resting place were two fair antique arches where the light came in : and by those they went into a cabinet, made even with, and of the breadth of the said winding, and the re-ascending above the roofs of the house, ended conically in a pavilion. By that vize or winding, they entered on every side into a great hall, and from the halls into the chambers "[1].

It is thus that, in his second work, Rabelais was showing his mastery : the fabulous story of the giant became for the most part, in his hands, a humorous tale or a picture of contemporary life, of which the principal interest was not to astonish by extravagant inventions, but to amuse by a faithful portrayal of life. Rabelais, besides, did not limit himself to describing the " states of life ", he denounced the abuses he met with in them ; he opposed his ideal to the reality which he esteemed degrading to man. We must not, it is true, take literally that declaration in the *Prologue* which announces an abstruse teaching, a " substantific marrow ", hidden in his book, " Pythagorical symbols, as well in what concerneth your Religion as matters of the public State and Life œconomical ". This declaration is made in a jesting tone : why should there not be found " dreadful mysteries " in my books, says he, " since the maxims of the Gospel have been discovered in Homer and in Ovid " ?—But if there is no esoteric doctrine in these " fooleries ", Rabelais has, at least, expressed his opinion, and in no roundabout manner, upon many serious questions.

With what eloquence, for example, he stigmatised war and the glory of conquest, these legacies of Gothic times ? Scourge accursed of the tiller of the soil and of the merchant, war yet kept its prestige in the eyes of kings, princes and nobles, of all who carried swords. The Humanists of the time—Erasmus, Thomas More, Guillaume Budé—considered it to be a survival of barbarism from which the monarchs of the new times should work to deliver their Kingdoms.

" The time is not now," says, in his turn, Grandgousier the pacific King in connection with Picrochole's warlike expedition, " the time

---

[1] *Gargantua*, ch. LIII.

is not now as formerly, to conquer the kingdoms of our neighbour princes, and to build up our own greatness upon the loss of our nearest Christian brother. This imitation of the ancient Herculeses, Alexanders, Hannibals, Scipios, Cæsars, and other such heroes, is quite contrary to the profession of the gospel of Christ, by which we are commanded to preserve, keep, rule, and govern every man his own country and lands, and not in a hostile manner to invade others; and that which heretofore the Barbarians and Saracens called prowess and valour, we now call robbing, thievery, and wickedness. It would have been more commendable in him to have contained himself within the bounds of his own territories, royally governing them, than to insult and domineer in mine, pillaging and plundering every where like a most unmerciful enemy; for, by ruling his own with discretion, he might have increased his greatness, but by robbing me, he cannot escape destruction. Go your ways in the name of God, prosecute good enterprises, show your king what is amiss, and never counsel him with regard unto your own particular profit, for the public loss will swallow up the private benefit. As for your ransom, I do freely remit it to you, and will that your arms and horse be restored to you; so should good neighbours do, and ancient friends, seeing this our difference is not properly war. As *Plato, lib.* 5, *de Repub.* would not have it called war but sedition, when the Greeks took up arms against one another, and that, therefore, when such combustions should arise amongst them, his advice was to behave themselves in the managing of them with all discretion and modesty "[1].

Thus the wisdom of the ancients and Christianity—the Bible and Plato—unite in furnishing arguments to Rabelais, spokesman for the Humanists in recommending to Renaissance monarchs a policy of peace.

But questions of politics were not the only ones to force themselves upon the attention of Humanists, any more than problems relating to " Life œconomical ". Religious reforms were increasingly exciting public opinion, and we have seen how, from the time of the publication of *Pantagruel*, Rabelais had taken up his position among the innovators who opposed the pure Gospel to "human institutions" and the "depraved inventions" of "False Prophets". The year 1533 had given these reformists great expectations: the Lenten Sermons preached at the Louvre by an "Evangelical ," Gérard Roussel, chaplain to the Queen of Navarre, had attracted a crowd of listeners. "We are undone," declared the theologian, Le Picard, "my pulpit is deserted. Only a few

[1] Ch. XLVI.

better for it, than to hear the life of Saint Margaret or some other *cafarderie*"[1].

Pilgrimages are another, and very " depraved human institution ". Do not some of them imply a belief in the power of the Saints to harm us ? Gargantua, having eaten six pilgrims hidden in his lettuce, and having cast them upon the ground with his toothpick, asks them where they were going. One of them, who had the characteristic name of Lasdaller (Sweer-to-go), answered him : " To Saint Sebastian, near Nantes to whom we were going to offer our vows against the plague " :

" Ah, poor men, (said Grandgousier,) do you think that the plague comes from St. Sebastian ?

Yes, truly, (answered Sweer-to-go,) our preachers tell us so indeed.

But is it so, (said Grandgousier,) do the false prophets teach you such abuses ? Do they thus blaspheme the Saints and holy men of God, as to make them like unto the devils, who do nothing but hurt unto mankind,—as Homer writeth, that the plague was sent into the camp of the Greeks by Apollo, and as the poets feign a great rabble of Vejoves[2] and mischievous gods. So did a certain Cafard or dissembling religionary preach at Sinay, that Saint Antony sent the fire into men's legs, that St. Eutropius made men hydropic, St. Gildas, fools, and that St. Genou made them goutish. But I punished him so exemplarily, though he called me heretic for it, that since that time no such hypocritical rogue durst set his foot within my territories. And truly I wonder that your king should suffer them in their sermons to publish such scandalous doctrine in his dominions ; for they deserve to be chastised with greater severity than those who, by magical art, or any other device, have brought the pestilence into a country. The pest killeth but the bodies, but such abominable impostors empoison our very souls."

And Grandgousier, in dismissing the pilgrims, points out why the practice of pilgrimages is to be forbidden : it cannot claim the authority of any text of the Gospels :

" Go your ways, poor men, in the name of God the Creator, to whom I pray to guide you perpetually, and henceforward be not so ready to undertake these idle and unprofitable journeys. Look to your families, labour every man in his vocation, instruct your children, and live as the good Apostle St. Paul directeth you : in doing whereof, God, his angels and sancts, will guard and protect you, and no evil or plague at any time shall befal you "[3].

Scholastic philosophy, monasticism, the cult of relics, belief in the Saints causing sickness, pilgrimages, popular

---

[1] Ch. VI.   [2] Hostile deities.   [3] Ch. XLV.

superstitions, these are so many abuses which Rabelais attacks in the name of the pure teaching of the Gospel. Clearly he sides with the party of Lefèvre d'Étaples, Briçonnet, the Queen of Navarre, these Evangelicals whose ideas, in this year 1534, seemed about to triumph. He mentions only with reverence the " good Evangelical preachers "[1], he pities the lot of those amongst them who are persecuted " for their faith "[2] and he puts in Grandgousier's mouth the form of salutation which they were fond of : " The peace of Jesus Christ, our Redeemer, be with thee "[3]; he quotes their favourite text " the good apostle St. Paul ". What is more, he reserves for them a place of honour in the Abbey of Thélème. The inscription placed upon the gate of this Abbey forbids entry to hypocrites and bigots, the *chats-fourrés* and *chicanous*, the envious and usurious. It declares only three classes of people worthy of being welcomed there : noble cavaliers, " ladies of high birth " and Evangelicals[4] :

> " Here enter you, pure, honest, faithful, true,
> Expounders of the Scriptures old and new.
> Whose glosses do not blind our reason, but
> Make it to see the clearer, and who shut
> Its passages from hatred, avarice,
> Pride, factions, covenants, and all sort of vice.
> Come, settle here a charitable faith,
> Which neighbourly affection nourisheth.
> And whose light chaseth all corrupters hence,
> Of the blest word, from the aforesaid sense.
> The Holy Sacred Word,
> May it always afford
> T' us all in common,
> Both man and woman,
> A spiritual shield and sword,
> The Holy Sacred Word."

It would be impossible to profess greater respect for the Gospels or more zeal for those who constituted themselves its champions against the " false prophets ". Can we conclude from that that Rabelais adhered fully to the Evangelicals' faith, or are these declarations merely pledges given to the

[1] Ch. XXIV.
[2] Ch. LVIII : " It is not now only, I perceive, that people called to the faith of the gospel, and convinced with the certainty of evangelical truths, are persecuted. But happy is that man that shall not be scandalized, but shall always continue to the end . . . ".
[3] Ch. XXIX.   [4] Ch. LIV.

religious party whose triumph, at this date, could be counted upon?

For us there is antagonism between the moral and religious ideal of the Evangelicals and that of Rabelais as it is reflected in his book. How could they unhesitatingly have crossed the threshold of this Abbey which had as its sole rule: *Do what thou wilt?* There is not a doubt that they would have approved of the founder's prescribing perpetual vows or the enslavement of human activities to the clock. They would, doubtless, have also found with satisfaction that, in place of the common chapel, the heart of ordinary monastic life, each apartment had its private oratory. But what would they have thought of this epicurean existence to which the community were invited? Clément Marot, given especially to refined pleasures[1], would perhaps have been contented with it. The author of the *Miroir de l'âme pécheresse*, the Queen of Navarre, real patron of the Evangelicals, would likely have despised it[2]. How otherwise could she feel than lost among these Thelemites, completely given to the joy of living, she who affirmed in one of her spiritual songs that the true Christian should love death as much as life? How could she have avoided seeing the amount of human pride —of *cuyder*, as she termed it—lurking in this fundamental principle of the rule of Thélème, that " men that are free, well-born, well-bred, and conversant in honest companies, have naturally an instinct and spur that prompteth them unto virtuous actions, and withdraws them from vice, which is called honour"? She, who in the conversations of her *Heptameron*, has twenty times denounced the subterfuges and

---

[1] In an *Épigramme à François Rabelais*, imitated from Martial, he has shown that the ideal existence for him was almost that imagined by the founder of the Abbey of Thélème :

> S'on nous laissoit nos jours en paix user,
> Du temps présent à plaisir disposer
> Et librement vivre comme il faut vivre,
> Palais et cours ne nous faudroit plus suivre,
> Plaids, ni procès, ni les riches maisons
> Avec leur gloire et enfumés blasons,
> Mais sous bel ombre, en chambre et galeries,
> Nous pourmenant, livres et railleries,
> Dames et bains seroient les passe-temps,
> Lieux et labeurs de nos esprits contents.

[2] " The point of intersection and of divergence of the two great currents [Humanism and Evangelism] which traversed the century are to be found in the person and in the works of Marguerite d'Angoulême ", M. H. Hauser, in his *Études sur la Réforme française* (Paris, 1909), p. 35.

falsehoods of this " honour ", would have declared this principle contrary to the idea which Christianity forms of man, a creature incapable of doing good without the help of grace. Would not she, who tended towards asceticism, have seen also that Rabelais' attacks upon the monks of his time reached, through the monastic institutions, the very principles of Christian life ?

For the Evangelism of the author of *Gargantua* was merely on the surface. It was the form which his Christianity had taken, under the persuasion of his reason, which tended to Deism. From his temperament, from his studies, from the influence of his masters,—and of Erasmus in particular,—from his reflexions, he had received a confidence in human nature incompatible with the principles of Christianity. We can constantly discern in his work this sentiment of human pride, in spite of such evangelical declarations as that of Grandgousier on " free will and sensual appetite, which cannot choose but be wicked, if by divine grace it be not continually guided "[1]. It is evident, for instance, in Gargantua's educational programme according to Humanistic theories[2], as much as in the Thélème episode. How lovingly has Rabelais described the wonderful effects of this new tutoring ! Hardly has the scholar, who had been rendered dull and stupid by his theologian regents, been entrusted to the pedagogue Ponocrates, than all his energies are aroused and developed. The programme of instruction which is given to him is encyclopædic, with the result that not one hour of the day remains free from it. Everything becomes an occasion for teaching him—meals, walks, recreations and even holidays. What does he not learn ? All languages and all sciences, the " liberal Arts " as well as the history of " ancient prowesses ". However, a wise hygiene, watched over by a prudent physician, regulates the hours of rising, of work, of dinner, the menu of his meals, the nature and duration of his exercises, the upkeep of the body and its functions : nutrition, respiration, evacuations, etc. For the body is exercised like the soul. Christian asceticism had despised it ; the Humanists, completely taken up with the struggle against ignorance, had exalted especially the work of the mind. Rabelais rehabilitates the body, all its organs and all its functions. He delights in swimming, rowing, climbing

[1] Ch. XXIX.   [2] Chs. XXIII–XXIV.

up the masts of ships, running out in the rigging, climbing
up trees and breaking branches :

" With two sharp well-steeled daggers, and two tried bodkins,
would he run up by the wall to the very top of a house like a rat ;
then suddenly come down from the top to the bottom with such an
even composition of members, that by the fall he would catch no
harm. . . . They tied a cable-rope to the top of a high tower, by one end
whereof hanging near the ground he wrought himself with his hands
to the very top ; then upon the same tract came down so sturdily
and firm that you could not on a plain meadow have run with more
assurance. They set up a great pole fixed upon two trees. There
would he hang by his hands, and with them alone, his feet touching
at nothing, would go back and fore along the aforesaid rope with so
great swiftness, that hardly could one overtake him with running ;
and then, to exercise his breast and lungs, he would shout like all
the devils in hell "[1].

Thus did Rabelais give himself the sight, pleasing above
all others to a doctor, of a healthy activity of the whole human
body.

His religious education is far from being the object of such
minute care in the Giant's new education. A reading from
Holy Scripture, with a commentary, a prayer morning and
night, grace after meals is about the extent of it. Under his
theologian regents, Gargantua mumbled numerous pater-
nosters and heard several masses daily : now we are shown him
going to hear the good Evangelical preachers, but only on rainy
days[2]. The impression left by the two episodes of Gargantua's
education and of Thélème, is that of a great trust in human
nature. To Rabelais as to Erasmus, whom he proclaimed as
his spiritual father, it does not appear fallen and incapable of
attaining to virtue. " I call nature ", said Erasmus, " a docility
and an inclination towards honesty "[3]. Man, he said, is born
for philosophy and virtue, as the bird for flying and the ox for
the plough. Similarly, Rabelais holds that constraint and
slavery alone pervert human nature, which, of itself, is urged
" to virtuous deeds ". Free man finds in the sentiment of
honour, innate in him, a rule of conduct.

[1] Ch. XXIII.
[2] Ch. XXIV. *Comment Gargantua employoit le temps quand l'air estoit
pluvieux.* " If it happened that the weather were . . . rainy . . . they
went also to hear the public lectures . . . and the sermons of Evangelical
preachers ".
[3] " Naturam appello docilitatem et propensionem, penitus insitam, ad res
honestas ". *De pueris statim ac liberaliter instituendis.* Cf. Pineau, *Érasme,
sa pensée religieuse* (Paris, 1924), p. 11, n. 1.

But this act of faith in human nature does not mean that our Humanists reject Christianity. They aspire to reconcile Evangelism and the spirit of the Renaissance. There is perhaps no more striking witness of this tendency, very general towards 1534, than *Gargantua*.

CHAPTER XII

SECOND JOURNEY TO ROME

SHORTLY after the publication of *Gargantua*, there occurred an event which was to give the theologians of the Sorbonne, for a time, sufficient prestige to obtain from the royal power measures of persecution against the Reformers and even against the Humanists[1]. During the night of the 17th and 18th October posters against the Mass—which was called sorcery— the Pope and cardinals, were posted in the public squares at Paris, Orleans, Rouen, Tours, Blois and even on the door of the King's apartment at Amboise. This act of insolence on the part of some zealots brought on an outburst of anger and let persecution loose. The King ordered a solemn procession of public reparation, which he followed himself with a torch in his hand, and that very evening six heretics were consigned to the flames. The repression was atrocious. In Paris, more than twenty Lutherans were burned, after having had their tongues pierced or their hands cut off. About two hundred of them were banished and their property confiscated. The Sorbonne was triumphant : it won from the King an edict forbidding all printing until further orders. Happily for the glory of the " Father of Letters," Guillaume Budé and Jean du Bellay[2] had this edict annulled before it was registered by Parliament, which would have given it force of law. The King contented himself with watching the booksellers more closely. The theologians and the Parliament had for some months every facility in tracking down whomever they suspected on grounds of religion.

The Humanists who had leanings towards Evangelism were frightened. Hitherto tortures and the stake had been only for ordinary folk : the *literati* seemed assured of the King's

[1] On the intellectual and religious situation in France in 1533–1534, *vide* V. L. Bourrilly and N. Weiss, *Jean du Bellay, les protestants et la Sorbonne* (1529–1535), in the *Bulletin de la Société de l'histoire du protest. français*, 1904, and *Introduction* to the critical edition, pp. xviii–xxii.

[2] According to Étienne Dolet, *Commentarii linguæ latinæ*, p. 266.

protection. One only amongst them had been burned in Paris, Louis de Berquin. Moreover, it was known that the King had once already saved him, and that, if the law had allowed no interval to elapse between the sentence and the expiation, at his execution in 1529, it was for fear the King might again intervene in his favour. But the *placards* against the Mass had been a direct affront to his Majesty, so he let the theologians gratify their rancours. No book had satirised, ridiculed and execrated them as copiously as *Gargantua*, so Rabelais did not ignore the fact that he had laid himself open to their anger. Was he going to await its effects ? Already, certain Humanists had displayed great eagerness to give assurances of their orthodoxy ; as, for instance, Jean Visagier who, after having attacked monks and theologians in his *Epigrams*, now congratulated the King on applying remedies to the ill of rising heresy and on burning in the sacred flames the heads of sects[1]. Rabelais simply disappeared for a time.

At the beginning of 1535 (new style) he is still at Lyons, where he gives to a printer an Almanack for the same year (beginning in March, according to the old style) in which he renews his declarations of the 1533 Almanack as to the vanity of prognostications. Alone, he says, those souls joined to Jesus Christ, " placed outside this gloomy prison of the earthly body ", know the future ; " to predict otherwise would be folly on my part and, on yours, simplicity in placing faith therein " ; and astrology is less than nothing. Plato and St. Matthew advise us rightly to put our trust from this searching after the future in the " government and unchangeable decree of the all-powerful God " : so we should merely supplicate and beseech Him " that His holy will be continually done both in heaven and on earth "[2].

The wisdom of the ancients and Christian teaching, Aristotle and St. Paul, Plato and St. Matthew, are gravely quoted one after another to turn men away from enquiring as to the future. The stars, as a matter of fact, foretell calamities for this year 1535, but if " Kings, princes and Christian communities give due reverence to God's divine word and govern themselves and their subjects according to it ", no happier year than it will be seen.

[1] *Epigrammata*, Lyons, 1537, p. 11.
[2] Given in Marty-Laveaux, *op. cit.*, vol. III, pp. 257–260.

Rabelais had, no doubt, little confidence in the wisdom of
" Kings and princes ", for he hastened to hide himself from the
possible effects of their whims. He left Lyons on the 13th
February, having received 13 *livres*[1] due to him on his salary
from August, 1534, to January, 1535. He had not notified
the hospital Rectors of his departure, but his colleagues were
soon aware of it, for on the following day three of them, Master
Charles des Marais, Pierre du Castel, and Jean Canape applied
to take his place. Nine days later, the Rectors deliberated as
to the qualifications of the candidates for the position left
vacant by Rabelais : it was then rumoured that he was at
Grenoble. Eventually, on March 5th, they appointed Pierre
du Castel, at an annual salary of 30 *livres*, in place of Rabelais,
who, says the record of their deliberations, " absented himself
from and abandoned the said hospital without notice or leavetaking ".

Where was he in the meantime ? Perhaps in Chinonais,
where he seems to have renewed his connection with Geoffroy
d'Estissac. Let us not forget that Rabelais was in an irregular
position with regard to the Church, being a lapsed monk, and
that it might be prudent for him in these times of persecution
to get near Monseigneur de Maillezais, Superior of the Benedictine convent which he had left to wander about the world.

He did not long stay there. In the spring of 1535, the
persecution had died down. The Pope had censured the cruelty
of the sufferings inflicted upon the heretics, and the King
directed Parliament not to proceed henceforward against the
Lutherans with full vigour. From Germany, numbers of
refugees returned to France. The proceedings against the
innovators in religious affairs were soon about to be discontinued. The relaxation took place all the more rapidly since
the King was desirous of reassuring his allies, the German
Protestant princes[2]. Thus was internal religious peace imposed
by the needs of external policy. The most active partisans of
these overtures for a reconciliation with the Lutheran princes
of Germany had always been the brothers Guillaume and
Jean du Bellay.

On May the 21st, the Bishop of Paris, who had, in the

---

[1] *Vide, ibid.*, p. 325.
[2] The steps taken to put an end to the persecution are detailed by Imbart
de la Tour in his fine work on *Les origines de la Réforme*, vol. III, *l'Évangélisme*
(1529–1538), pp. 559 *seqq*.

October preceding, urged the French cardinals to elect Cardinal Farnese to the Papacy, was nominated Cardinal by him, now Pope under the name of Paul III. He announced his intention of going to Rome to receive the hat. In reality, he was entrusted with a new diplomatic mission, concerning François I's policy in Germany. On June 8th, the Ambassador Ordinary to the Holy See, Hémard d'Hénonville, sent him word that he was expecting him. He showed his solicitude for the prelate in arranging apartments for him in his own house : " You will find the cellar cool "[1]. On July 15th, the Cardinal passed through Lyons. He there met Rabelais and a distinguished Humanist, Guillaume Pellicier, Bishop of Maguelonne, near Montpellier. The party set off immediately for Rome.

They halted at Ferrara, where resided a small Court which was half French. The Duchess was Renée, daughter of Louis XII, whose marriage in 1527, with Ercole d'Este, had been celebrated by Marot in an epithalamium. The happy future which the poet promised this daughter of France—gentle, pious, a patron of letters—had not been realised. She had taken some compatriots with her : Madame de Soubise and her daughter, Anne de Parthenay, married to M. de Pons ; besides, she very heartily extended hospitality to French people staying in or passing through Italy. The Duke was sometimes impatient or jealous on that account[2] ; and at the time when Jean du Bellay's party arrived at Ferrara there was question of sending back to France the Duchess's whole French household. The Cardinal interceded and obtained for Madame de Soubise permission to remain with her mistress until after her confinement.

What brought the Duke's irritation to its height was the facility with which the Duchess opened her house and her purse to those French people whom the religious persecution had obliged to take refuge in Italy. She had leanings towards Evangelism, and their condition of unfortunate proscripts recommended them to her. Rabelais may have met in her

---

[1] Cf. V. L. Bourrilly, *Le cardinal Jean du Bellay en Italie*, R.É.R., vol. V, p. 237.
[2] On the habits of the Court at Ferrara and the D'Este family, cf. M. H. Hauvette : *L'Arioste et la poésie chevaleresque à Ferrare au début du XVIe siècle*, Paris, Champion, 1927. Two good works on Renée of France are : Fontana's *Renata di Francia, duchessa di Ferrara* (Rome, 1889), and Emmanuel Rodocanachi's *Une protectrice de la Réforme en Italie et en France ; Renée de France, duchesse de Ferrare* (Paris, 1896).

entourage Jean du Bouchefort, chantor of the chapel royal, a friend of Marot, the Clerk of the Finances, Léon Jamet, sergeant of le Bois-Pouvreau in Poitou[1], and Clément Marot himself[2]. It is there, perhaps, were begun those friendly relations between them to which an epigram of Marot's bears witness[3].

From Ferrara Rabelais sent, on July 26th, a letter to Geoffroy d'Estissac, which is now lost. Four days later, he arrived in Rome and during the seven months he resided there, as if fulfilling an obligation of honour, he sent seven more letters to the Bishop of Maillezais. Of these eight letters five have been lost, but the last three (30th December, 1535, 28th January and 13th February, 1536) are preserved in copies which date from the beginning of the 17th century and by their publication, from one of these copies, by the brothers Sainte-Marthe in 1651.

Who would not expect to penetrate into Rabelais' intimacy by means of these letters ? Or, even, more simply, to come upon the graces or shrewdness of mind by which he possessed the art of pleasing the great ? They give us no such pleasure. Although he has penned the jokes of *Pantagruel* and *Gargantua*, Cardinal du Bellay's physician is, none the less, very reserved in his humour when he addresses his first protector. He does not permit himself to indulge in cynical sallies or buffooneries such as his legend attributes so freely to him. He does not go beyond underlining, with a malicious word or a sly smile, a comic situation. But the interest of these letters written from Rome consists neither in their spirit nor in their style. It is in the information they give us as to his occupations and impressions[4].

---

[1] Le Bois-Pouvreau lies two leagues to the west of Sanxay (Vienne), through which village Pantagruel passes on his way from Poitiers to Maillezais (*Pantagruel*, ch. V). Jamet is sometimes called " Seigneur du Bois-Pouvreau ". This title belonged to Geoffroy d'Estissac ; the Jamets, according to the records in the Archives, were " sergeants ", that is, stewards of this wood, as the Ronsards were " sergeants " of the forest of Gastine.

[2] On Marot at Ferrara, cf. Ph. A. Becker's *Clément Marot, sein Leben und seine Dichtung* (Munich, 1926), p. 103.

[3] *Vide supra*, p. 165, and Étienne Dolet, *Ad Franciscum Rabelæsum, de mutua inter se et Clementem Marotum amicitia*, in his *Carminum libri quatuor*, Lyons, 1538.

[4] These letters have been examined and their authenticity established by Jacques Boulenger : *Étude critique sur les lettres écrites d'Italie par François Rabelais*, R.É.R., I, pp. 97–121, and by Bourrilly in the introduction to his edition of Rabelais' *Letters, supra cit.*

We are told, in the first place, how these missives were directed towards Poitou. One of them was given to René du Bellay, sieur de La Turmelière, an elder brother of Joachim, the poet, who was returning from Naples where he had gone to buy some " coursers " for his master, the lord of Montreuil-Bonnin, near Poitiers[1]. But the usual method was different : it was the " big packet " sealed with wax, containing the official dispatches which Jean du Bellay and Hémart d'Hénonville sent to the King—the diplomatic post-bag[2]. Rabelais slipped into it the confidential letters, some of them in code, which he had written to the Bishop of Maillezais[3].

On the arrival of the royal courier at Lyons, the governor opened the packet, and his secretary, a friend of Rabelais', took the parcel addressed : " To Michel Parmentier, bookseller *At the Sign of the Escu de Bâle*[4] ". The latter was another of Rabelais' friends, who knew that this letter was to be sent to the Bishop of Maillezais. He sent it by messengers, taking care, so as to stimulate their zeal, to mark on it the fee they might claim on delivery of the packet to its recipient. As to Michel Parmentier's reward, it consisted in some kind words from Geoffroy d'Estissac, accompanied by a piece of old gold— a *royau*, *angelot* or *salut*—and trinkets and curios which Rabelais sent him from Rome for himself or his wife[5].

This means was, Rabelais tells us, safer than the bank messengers, which were often availed of, since the bankers had no scruples about pilfering and opening packages. And it had the advantage of costing nothing, at least as far as Lyons. Rabelais availed of this free post without stint. It was not merely private letters, curious, novelties, trinkets, or *mirelificques* which he sent to the wife of the bookseller Michel Parmentier, or to Geoffroy d'Estissac's niece by the diplomatic trunk ; he also filled it with packets of seeds intended for the Bishop's gardens, at L'Hermenault and Ligugé. For the botanist who had had the disappointment of finding in Italy, in 1534, only one new plant, a plane-tree, did not give up his searches and

---

[1] *Lettres écrites d'Italie* . . . , edited by Bourrilly, p. 65. The horses of Naples were well known in France, under the name of " coursers of the kingdom " or the " reign " (Italian *del regno*).

[2] *Ibid.*, pp. 35 and 45.

[3] *Ibid.*, pp. 34, 53, 66.

[4] Cf. my article *À l'Escu de Bâle*, in the *Rev. XVIᵉ siècle*, 1926.

[5] Bourrilly, *Lettres écrites d'Italie* . . . , p. 53.

this time he discovered ornamental and culinary plants. Acclimatising strange plants was a luxury which some great lords of the Renaissance were particularly given to ; thus, the Bishop of Le Mans, René du Bellay, adorned his gardens with jujube-trees, laburnums, locust-trees, and pistachio-trees. For the greater part, the plants whose seeds Rabelais sent to Geoffroy d'Estissac were more humble : Naples salads, like those the Pope grew in his private garden, chards, melons, pumpkins, Alexandrian pinks, *violes matronales*[1], and *Belveder*, a grass for keeping rooms cool in summer[2]. He sent along with them advice as to the sowing season, and on how to protect the young plants against frost, by " covering them . . . with rushes and light manure not quite rotten ", and did not fail to point out to his correspondent that the salads of Ligugé were more suited to his delicate stomach than those of Naples, " too hot and too hard ".

In addition to botany, the examination of the ruins of ancient Rome had been Rabelais' principal study eighteen months previously : he seems, on his second stay, to have paid more attention to contemporary Rome. His letters are a chronicle of Roman life, kept from day to day. The picture is living, heightened from time to time by a roguish jest. The mainspring of all the self-interest, intrigues, and cupidities which he contemplates is in the rivalry between François I and Charles V. King and Emperor are both striving to gain as an ally, or win over to their policy, the temporal power called the Holy See. The Papal city and court are divided into the French " party " and the Imperial " party ", and in the service of these two factions what a swarm of schemers of every kind ! Italy was, in the words of M. Bourrilly[3], a market of men : swordsmen, like the *condottieri*, penmen, scribes, diplomats, " artists in intrigue and virtuosos in treachery, compliant and haughty, greedy and starveling, scanning the horizon, scenting the wind, always ready to rush towards him who seemed about to bring fortune, power and glory to them ".

An unforeseen happening had suddenly thrown all these schemers into a flutter. The Emperor Charles V, having

---

[1] [A variety of violet. Cf. Sainéan, *Langue de Rabelais*, I, 148.] Dame's violet, or perhaps a kind of gillyflower. Cf. Dr. Delaunay, *l'Aventureuse existence de Pierre Belon*, pp. 88–89.

[2] *Lettres écrites d'Italie* . . . , pp. 68–69.

[3] *Le Cardinal Jean du Bellay en Italie*, R.É.R., vol. V, p. 265.

defeated Barbarossa before Tunis, on July 20th, and not wishing to follow up his successes by a crusade against Constantinople, had landed at Sicily and announced his intention of entering Naples and Rome. This meant that the political equilibrium in Italy between the King of France and the Emperor was broken, to the latter's advantage. Towns and princes turned towards the Emperor, and Rabelais noted all the embassies which passed through Rome to get to Sicily and capture the Imperial favour : one day, the Duke of Florence, Alexander de' Medici, then the Duke of Ferrara, then a courier from the Duke of Savoy, then deputies from Venice " four fine old grey-haired men ", and finally, envoys from Sienna. " I really believe ", concluded Rabelais, " that ambassadors will go towards the same Emperor from all the Italies ; and ", he added, " he knows how to play his part so as to draw money out of them ". For the Emperor had need of money[1], and the Pope was affected by the same " epidemial " malady. It was a question as to which of them would more cleverly " fleece "[2] certain Italian princes, such as, for example, the Duke of Ferrara. When Charles V proclaimed his intention of going to Rome to pay homage to the Pope, Paul III was in consternation at the calculation of how much this visit would cost him : he would have to supply three thousand mattresses for his escort to sleep upon[3], and buy up all the wine in the port : the Pope exacted levies from all his officers. Shortly afterwards, in order honourably to receive his Imperial visitor, he caused a triumphal road to be made, by knocking down numerous houses in order to widen the streets from the St. Sebastian Gate to the Palace of St. Angelo : this time the cost fell only upon the proprietors of the demolished houses.

The intrigues, covetousness and other ardent passions gave rise to bloody tragedies which Rabelais coldly notes down in his diary : Alexander de' Medici placing some of his agents in ambush to kill or poison Philippe Strozzi, whose property he covets[4] ; the assassination of a Portuguese ambassador[5] ; or, again, the rape and murder of a woman, a vendetta, a bastard's jealousy[6], etc. Rabelais has adapted himself to Roman standards. He is no longer revolted by these crimes. Subsequently, he will sum up his impressions of these Italian

[1] *Lettres écrites d'Italie* . . . , p. 74. [2] *Ibid.*, p. 43. [3] *Ibid.*, p. 38.
[4] *Ibid.*, p. 41. [5] *Ibid.*, p. 61. [6] *Ibid.*, p. 71.

morals in the following phrase : " At Rome a world of folks get an honest livelihood by poisoning, drubbing, lambasting, stabbing and murdering "[1].

Rabelais had had only a brief acquaintance with the Papal Court on the occasion of his first visit. But in 1535-1536 two matters bring him into contact with the offices and the higher functionaries of the Roman Curia. One of these was the resignation from his benefices by a certain Dom Philippe, doubtless a religious of Maillezais, in favour of his nephew. Geoffroy d'Estissac interested himself in the affair. He had unfortunately omitted to give Rabelais some essential information about the diocese from which the late Dom Philippe had originally come, his procurations, etc., and it is in vain that his correspondent got the clerks to look for the document containing his resignation in the Registers of the Law Courts for the years 1529–1531 : it cost him " two *Escus sol* "[2] without any result.

The second matter in which Rabelais was concerned was his own " apostasy ". He had laid aside the Benedictine habit without authorisation from his Superior ; he had moved around in the world in a secular priest's habit. He confessed his fault and asked absolution for it in a supplication which he sent to the Pope with Cardinal du Bellay's recommendation—an efficacious patronage. Immediately two highly placed personages took his request in hand, Cardinal Hieronimo Ghinucci, Judge of the Palace, a trusted servant of Paul III, and Cardinal Simonetta, Auditor of the Chamber[3]. What is more, the Pope himself deigned to point out the method of procedure necessary to obtain absolution. But on this point his administration knew more than he did. He proposed an expeditious procedure —having the bull registered by the Sommist[4] of the Apostolic Chamber (*camera apostolica*). That was neglecting his own tribunals which alone could render this act of absolution " irrefragable " everywhere. The supplication had to pass through one of these tribunals, as the cardinals recommended, the " Court of Contradicts " (*curia litterarum contradictarum*).

---

[1] *Fourth Book of Pantagruel*, ch. XII.
[2] Bourrilly, *op. cit.*, Letter I, p. 38, Letter III, pp. 66 and 67.
[3] *Ibid.*, Letter I, p. 35.
[4] This term, along with that of *abreviator* (scribe of the Curia), figures in the *blason* of Triboulet, *Third Book*, ch. XXXVIII. In ch. XIV of the same book, there is another souvenir of the Roman Curia : " *Fiatur*, says Panurge, *ad differentiam papæ* ", the Pope signifying approbation by the word *fiat*. Cf. *Lettres écrites d'Italie* . . . , p. 74.

N

Rabelais followed this procedure and, on January 17th, the
Pope granted him an indult which authorised him to return
to a Benedictine convent, at his choice, and to practise medicine
provided that, according to the customary formula, he used
neither the knife nor cautery and intended to make no profit
thereby[1]. By an act of graciousness the Sovereign Pontiff
dispensed Rabelais from the fee due in such a case, so that it
only remained for him to pay the " preferendary, procurator
and other such parchment-daubers ". " If my money runs
short ", he says to Geoffroy d'Estissac, " I will call upon your
alms "[2].

He did, indeed, find himself short of money, although he
managed his affairs as sparingly as was possible for him. So
he was constrained, a second time, to fall back upon " the
alms " (he himself repeats this term) of Monseigneur de Maillezais. The thirty *écus* which the latter had sent him had disappeared on " little scrawls of dispatches and hire of furniture
for his room and his upkeep in dress ". None of it has been
spent, he is careful to point out, in " wickedness ", nor on food,
for he drank and ate usually with Cardinal du Bellay or the
King's Ambassador Ordinary[3].

Rabelais, then, when he left Rome, had no personal grievance
against the tribunals and the chancellery of the Holy See.
He had paid the fee regularly due to the offices. He did not
find it excessive, since he considered that " the two *Escuz sol* "
which he had paid to the Clerks of the Registry, were very little[4],
" considering the great and troublesome task " they had had
in looking for documents relative to the late Dom Philippe's
resignation.

The granting of the Papal indult was to have, shortly afterwards, a sequel which, perhaps, the Pope had not foreseen.

Meanwhile, on February 29th, 1536, Jean du Bellay left
Rome hurriedly and in secret, before Charles V entered it.
Escorted by a few horsemen he arrived at Lyons. His intention
was, perhaps, to return to the Papal Court with fresh instructions. François I had decided otherwise. Then, safe-conducts
were given to the Cardinal's " family ", that is, his household,
which had stayed behind in Rome. So Rabelais set out on

---

[1] " Citra adustionem et incisionem, pietatis intuitu ac sine spe lucri vel
questus ". Cf. Marty-Laveaux, *op. cit.*, vol. III, pp. 348–351.
[2] Letter I, *op. cit.*, p. 36.   [3] *Ibid.*, p. 38.   [4] *Ibid.*, Letter III, p. 67.

April 11th, and at the beginning of May rejoined his protector in Lyons[1].

Some weeks later, the kingdom was in a great tumult. On June 2nd, the Imperial ambassador was dismissed, and war with Charles V began in the Pyrenees, in the Alps and in Picardy. The King repaired to Avignon to organise resistance to the Emperor who was invading Provence, while, under the direction of Montmorency, appointed Royal Lieutenant-General, Cardinal Jean du Bellay superintended the fortification of the Northern and Eastern frontiers and of the capital. Twenty thousand pioneers laboured to fortify Paris[2]. Rabelais was a witness of this fine military activity. He makes its image come to life again in the *Prologue* of the *Third Book of Pantagruel* :

" Some from the fields brought into the fortified places their moveables, cattle, corn, wine, fruit, victuals, and other necessary provision. Others did fortify and rampire their walls, set up little fortresses, bastions, squared ravelins, digged trenches, cleansed countermines, fenced themselves with gabions, contrived platforms, emptied casemates, barricaded the false brays, erected the cavalliers, repaired the contrescarpes, plaistered the courtines, lengthened ravelins, stopped parapets, mortaised barbacans, new-pointed the portcullices, fastened the herses, sarasinesks, and cataracts, placed their sentries, and doubled their patrol. Every one did watch and ward, and none was exempted from carrying the basket."

Formerly he had ridiculed the warlike spirit in Picrochole : he had discredited war, scourge of the people, ruin of the peasants. He now discovered a touching beauty in the sight of his compatriots, undertaking courageously and good-humouredly the trials and hardships of defensive warfare :

" Considering . . . every one is most diligently exercised and busied,—some in the fortifying of their own native country, for its defence,—others in the repulsing of their enemies by an offensive war ; and all this with a policy so excellent, and such admirable order, so manifestly profitable for the future, whereby France shall have its frontiers most magnifically enlarged, and the French assured of a long and well-grounded peace, that very little withholds me from the opinion of good Heraclitus, which affirmeth war, to be the father of all good things ; and therefore do I believe that

---

[1] These are the dates arrived at by M. Bourrilly in his edition of the *Lettres écrites d'Italie*.
[2] Cf. *Cronicque de François Ier* quoted by H. Lemonnier, vol. V, part 2, p. 91, of Lavisse's *Histoire de France*.

war is in Latin called *Bellum*, and not by antiphrasis, as some patchers of old rusty Latin would have us to think, because in war there is little beauty to be seen; but absolutely and simply, for that in war appeareth all that is good and graceful, and that by the wars is purged out all manner of wickedness and deformity. For proof whereof the wise and pacific Solomon could no better represent the unspeakable perfection of the divine wisdom, than by comparing it to the due disposure and ranking of an army in battle array, well provided and ordered."

At this date, he was at the Benedictine Monastery of St. Maur-les-Fossés, near Paris, of which Jean du Bellay was Abbot. That was the sequel to the proceedings which had ended up with Paul III's indult. This authorised him to enter a Benedictine monastery other than Maillezais. Obviously when Du Bellay sought this indult for him, he had the idea of keeping him a place in his Benedictine Abbey of Saint-Maur. The existence there must have been all the easier for his physician in that he would there escape from the monastic rule. For in 1533 documents tending towards the secularisation of this Abbey and its transformation into a collegiate church, with the Bishop of Paris as beneficiary, had been produced before the Roman Curia. Originally eight canonical prebends were provided for. A ninth was created, for Rabelais' benefit, at the time when the bull of secularisation was proclaimed, in August, 1536. Then occurred an incident which was bound to make Rabelais' dealings with the other canons very difficult : they, dissatisfied with seeing their prebend reduced by one-ninth in the interest of the new colleague which Jean du Bellay was imposing on them, sent a complaint to the Pope[1].

We have, as a matter of fact, a second supplication from Rabelais to Paul III[2], explaining the circumstances of his entry to Saint-Maur-les-Fossés, pointing out his scruples of conscience at taking advantage of a secularisation which had been decided before his admission to the Abbey as a monk, and requesting that he be confirmed in his canonry[3].

[1] On the secularisation of Saint-Maur, cf. M. Clouzot's articles in *R.É.R.*, vol. VII, pp. 259–269, and *Rev. XVIe siècle*, 1919, p. 280.
[2] The text of this *supplicatio* is given by Du Verdier, *Prosopographie des hommes illustres*, Lyons, 1604, in-folio, vol. III, p. 2453, and by Marty-Laveaux, *op. cit.*, vol. III, pp. 369-371.
[3] " Supplicat ut per indultum S. V. tutus sit tam in foro conscientiæ quam in foro contradictorio et aliis quibuslibet de præfatis, perinde ac si non receptus fuisset in dictum monasterium sancti Mauri quamprimum et antea

We do not know the Pope's answer. But Rabelais did not long stay at the collegiate of Saint-Maur. In discontinuing his residence there, he had no longer a right to a prebend. The principal advantage he drew from his short period in this deanship was to be canonically freed from his monastic vows[1]. He was about to resume his wandering life in the world in the habit of a secular priest.

quam obtenta fuit bulla erectionis ejusdem in decanatum et cum absolutione ".
Notice that Rabelais in this document is given the title of Doctor of Medicine although he had not yet received this degree, presumably because the scribe of the Curia who drew up his requests in legal form had attributed it to him on hearsay.

[1] There is a souvenir of Rabelais' stay at Saint-Maur in the *Third Book*, ch. III. Panurge there swears by " Saint Bab[o]lin, the good saint ". He is supposed to have been first abbot of Saint-Maur. His shrine was in the collegiate church. Cf. *R.É.R.*, vol. VII, p. 273.

CHAPTER XIII

TEN YEARS OF MEDICAL PRACTICE
1536–1546

EXCLUDED from the collegiate of Saint-Maur by his colleagues' jealousy, what was to become of Rabelais ? From what occupations could he derive the resources necessary for living ? He could neither stay with Cardinal du Bellay, who had returned to his customary residence in Paris, nor resume his post at the hospital in Lyons, where his place had been filled. His books had been successful ; there was published, in 1533, a new edition of *Pantagruel*, in Lyons, by Pierre de Sainte-Lucie, and one of *Gargantua*, by François Juste ; but literature in the 16th century did not create revenue. The publishers, or booksellers, received almost the entire profit, having, generally, only to give the author a gratuity when putting the books on sale.

In fine, medicine was the only resource within Rabelais' grasp, provided he found some occasion of practising his art. It will constitute his career for ten years. Until the publication of the *Third Book of Pantagruel* (1546) study and the practice of medicine will constitute the unity of his life, a wandering and sometimes disturbed life, but whose risks and uncertainties are due mainly to the unsettled disposition of Maître François, "lover of peregrinity", and to some imprudences of speech or of conduct.

His medical reputation was considerable. For contemporary scholars he is no longer merely " the man of great Greek and Latin letters " whom they admired at Fontenay-le-Comte : he has become one of the most famous physicians in the Kingdom ; this is the testimony borne to him, notably by one of the best Humanists of the time, Étienne Dolet, on a memorable occasion.

The adventurous career of this personage—grammarian, poet and printer—is well known. After a good course of study begun at Orleans and Paris, and then continued at Padua, under the direction of Simon de Villeneuve, he became enrolled at the University of Toulouse (1532). Elected *Imperator* of the " Nation of France " in 1534, he had pronounced such violent harangues against the Gascons and Aquitains, and then against the town of Toulouse itself, that the Parliament of this town had banished him. On the 1st of August, 1534, harassed in body and mind, he arrived at Lyons in company with his friend, Finet[1]. Rabelais was there at that time, having returned from his first visit to Rome. It was the time when that little Lyonnese confraternity of humanists, philologists and poets, which bears in their letters and in their works the title *sodalitium Lugdunense*[2], was being formed. Rabelais could there rub shoulders with Guillaume and Maurice Scève, the poets, Benoît Court, the author of a commentary upon the book of *Arrests d'amours* (*Edicts of the Court of Love*), a bibliophile and collector of antiques, Guillaume de Choul, collector of Greek manuscripts, Jérôme Fondule, who had associated in Italy with Christophe de Longueil and Simon de Villeneuve. Dolet belonged to this group. He was remarkable for his eagerness for work (he was to publish, in 1537, his *Commentarii linguæ latinæ*) and his vehemence in defence of Ciceronianism : Rabelais may have been hurt to hear him attack unreservedly his spiritual master, Erasmus, author of an anticiceronian dialogue, *The Scourge of Cicero* (*Ciceromastyx*)[3]. But Dolet had lived in Italy, he had known the intrepid thinkers of the Paduan school ; he was passionately fond of ancient literature : how could Rabelais but have felt himself attracted towards him ? A regrettable incident was destined to oblige Dolet to leave Lyons for a time. In the night of the 31st December, 1536, having been attacked in the street, he had the misfortune while defending himself, to kill his agressor, Guillaume Compaing, the painter. Before dawn, Dolet, fearing that he would

---

[1] On Étienne Dolet, cf. Richard Copley Christie, *Étienne Dolet, the Martyr of the Renaissance* (London, 1899), John Charles Dawson, *Toulouse in the Renaissance* (New York, Columbia University Press, 1923), and a study by Ph. A. Becker in his *Aus Frankreichs Frührenaissance Kritische Skizzen* (Munich, 1927).

[2] On this group cf. Visagier's dedication to Jean des Pins, Bishop of Rieux, of his fifth book of epigrams (Lyons, 1537), p. 187.

[3] " Sed fremant omnes licet, dicam haud dubie quod sentio. Sentio autem *Ciceromastigem* Dialogum a Desiderio Erasmo Roterodamo, aut sano, aut sicco numquam scriptum ". Étienne Dolet, dedicatory letter of the *Commentarii linguæ latinæ* (1536).

be unable to establish his innocence in Lyons, left that town for Paris. There, friends intervened with the King on his behalf. Pierre Duchatel, François I's reader, and the Queen of Navarre herself interceded in his favour. On the 19th of February the King granted him letters of pardon.

Immediately, some French scholars decided to celebrate this event by a banquet. Rabelais was present. He there met the most eminent Humanists of his generation. Besides Guillaume Budé were the Royal Lectors—the Hellenists Pierre Danès and Jacques Toussaint[1], the Latinist Nicole Bérault[2]. There were neo-Latin poets, Salmon Macrin, Nicolas Bourbon de Vandœuvre, Dampierre, Visagier, and, lastly, Marot. They talked about foreign scholars with whom they were in communication in their love for literature : Erasmus, Melanchton, Bembo, Sadolet, Vida, Sannazar.

Dolet devoted a Latin poem to the celebration of these agapes[3]. He enumerates the guests, giving each one individual praise. Rabelais is mentioned as the undisputed honour of Medicine : he could, it is said, recall the dead from Pluto's threshold and restore them to the light[4].

Six weeks later, April 3rd, Rabelais was at Montpellier where he paid his fees for the degree of Licentiate in Medicine[5]. On the 22nd of May, he was admitted to the Doctorate[6]. The admission to this last degree was merely a formality. The candidate, surrounded by professors dressed in their academic robes, and in the presence of a distinguished audience, exposed a thesis ; then he addressed his thanks to the Faculty. His sponsor (Rabelais' was one Antoine Griffi) introduced him and vouched for his learning. Firstly, the new Doctor received

---

[1] *Vide* on these Royal Lectors M. Abel Lefranc's *Histoire du Collège de France* (Paris, 1895).

[2] He was then in the service of the Cardinal de Châtillon, who was later to be one of Rabelais' patrons. Cf. Delaruelle, *Nicole Bérault*, biographical notes in the *Musée belge*, 1904.

[3] *Cœdis a se factæ et sui deinde exilii descriptio* in the *Doleti Carmina*, ed. 1538, p. 59.

[4]
    Franciscus Rabelæsus, honos et gloria certa
    Artis Pæoniæ, qui vel de limine Ditis
    Extinctos revocare potest et reddere luci.

[5] *Registres des matricules*, folio 384 verso.

[6] *Registre des Actes*, f. 33. Cf. Marty-Laveaux, *op. cit.*, vol. III, p. 372. Interesting details of the University ritual at the old Faculty of Medicine of Montpellier are to be found in Dr. Paul Delmas' studies on the *Séjours de Rabelais à Montpellier* (1922), and *Une soutenance de thèse médicale à Montpellier*.

his insignia : a gold ring, a gilt belt, a copy of Hippocrates, and a black cloth cap surmounted by a scarlet silk tassel.

We have seen that Rabelais had already added this title of Doctor of Medicine to his name in the Almanack he published at Lyons in 1533 and 1535 ; moreover, it had been given to him in the documents of the Papal chancellery in connection with his " apostasy ". This was an abuse which shocked nobody, the competence of the potential Doctor being beyond dispute[1].

The summer of the same year, 1537, saw him practising and even teaching at Lyons, and in what way ? By dissecting the corpse of a gallows-bird. What an honour for the wretch ! He might have been the prey of ravens or the plaything of the winds, and here, bending over him to gaze upon the wonderful arrangement of the human body, was an assembly of savants, listening eagerly to the lessons of the most learned of physicians. Such is the theme of a Latin poem in which Étienne Dolet commemorated this public demonstration of anatomy[2].

A dissection was then an event worthy of note. Not that they were unknown until then ; a few were carried out every year in the medical schools, at Montpellier, for example, as we have seen. Another of Dolet's epigrams, dedicated to Rabelais, describes for us another dissection-scene, but a less happy one, for the professor entrusted with the demonstration is so embarrassed that the audience wonders which is the more dumb, the corpse or the physician[3].

It is about the same time that, at the Collège de Tréguier, in Paris, Jacques Dubois, called Sylvius, expounding Galen " before a wonderful audience of scholars from all nations, used bring for the purpose of his demonstrations now the limb of an animal, now the thigh or arm of a hanged person ".[4] Noël du Fail, who was among the audience, in recounting this event emphasises its unusualness and finds amusement in describing the uneasiness of the spectators who were upset by the

---

[1] " Qui est in potentia actus, videtur esse in actu ", declares a legal dictum in this connection : " licentiatus in favorabilibus habetur pro doctore ". *Vide, R.É.R.*, vol. IV, pp. 270 and 396.

[2] *Cujusdam epitaphium qui exemplo edito strangulatus publico postea spectaculo sectus est, Fr. Rabelæso medico doctissimo, fabricam corporis interpretante*, in Dolet's *Carmina* (Lyons, 1538). Cf. Marty-Laveaux, *op. cit.*, III, pp. 377–378.

[3] *Doleti Galli Aurelii Carminum libri quatuor*, lib. 1, carm. LXVI : *Ad Franciscum Rabelæsum, De medico quodam indocto*.

[4] Noël du Fail, *Contes et discours d'Eutrapel*, XX (edit. Assezat, vol. II, p. 146).

nauseating smell of these bits of corpses. Dissections were, then, still of rare occurrence and Rabelais must certainly be considered as among the earliest popularisers of this method of medical teaching[1].

The new doctor's successes at Lyons were disturbed by an unexpected alarm. On August 10th, Rabelais, having been so imprudent as to give to an inhabitant of Rome over-detailed information on public affairs, was nearly imprisoned. A state of war existed. Cardinal de Tournon had been appointed, in October, 1536, Lieutenant-General for all the south-west provinces, in order to " oppose and resist the Emperor's enterprises "[2]. He was responsible, then, for the police regulations and carried them out diligently. He evidently held up letters addressed to foreign countries, and Rabelais' admitted of no doubt. It seems that his correspondent was " one of the worst ruffians " in Rome. To set an example and discourage all " writers of news " who were able neither to keep silence nor beware of watchful enemy ears, Cardinal de Tournon thought of imprisoning Rabelais. He would have done so had the latter not " acknowledged himself to the King and to the Queen of Navarre ". He contented himself with forbidding him to leave the town until the Chancellor, Du Bourg, to whom he sent the incriminating letter, should have decided his fate[3].

Some weeks later, Rabelais was at Montpellier, and, on September 27th, he took part in the solemn assembly of the Faculty of Medicine, at which was drawn up the programme of instruction for the *Great Ordinary*, from the feast of St. Luke (18th October) to the vigil of Palm Sunday. Admission to the Doctorate included, as a complement to the examination, the

---

[1] In the letter sent by Gargantua to his son, Pantagruel, while a student at Paris (*Pantagruel*, ch. VIII), dissections are recommended : " Then fail not most carefully to peruse the books of the Greek, Arabian, and Latin physicians, not despising the Talmudists and Cabalists ; and *by frequent anatomies* get thee the perfect knowledge of that other world, called the microcosm, which is man ".

Rabelais seems to have been a good surgeon. He is reputed to have invented an apparatus for healing fractures. *Vide*, Heulhard, *Rabelais chirurgien*.

[2] On his career as Lieutenant-General cf. J. Izaac, *Le Cardinal de Tournon, lieutenant-général du roi* (October, 1536–October, 1537) in *La Revue d'histoire de Lyon*, 1913.

[3] The text of this letter, without the date of the year, first published by Paulin Paris in the *Cabinet historique*, vol. IV (1858), pp. 548–551, has been reprinted by M. Bourrilly, who has shown that it should be assigned to 1537. *Deux points obscurs dans la vie de Rabelais*, R.É.R., IV, p. 105.

delivery of one term's course of lectures at the Faculty. Rabelais chose as the subject of his lectures the *Prognostics* of Hippocrates, and he expounded them from the Greek text, as he had already done for the *Aphorisms*[1].

His lectures were attended by a numerous audience, according to a letter from the Humanist Jean de Boyssonné to Maurice Scève, the Lyonnese poet[2]. He gave, besides, a public lecture in anatomy in the Great Hall of the Faculty[3]. And he practised medicine. Hubert Sussannée, the Humanist, got treatment[4] and advice from him on his way through Montpellier. Rabelais urged him to become a doctor. If he did not wish to practise medicine (he said familiarly, " to examine urines "), he could, at least, render service to the public, as the ancient physicians had done, by publications on diseases and their remedies[5].

Having completed the *Great Ordinary* course, on the vigil of Palm Sunday, Rabelais does not seem to have remained at Montpellier. In the middle of July, he was at Aigues-Mortes, during the interview between François I and Charles V. Some days later, the Seneschal of Provence's Lieutenant at the *siège* of Arles, Antoine Arlier, sent word to Étienne Dolet that Rabelais was on his way to Lyons, with the King[6].

That the author of *Pantagruel* and *Gargantua* should have been in the King's suite at such a time is an essential fact for the understanding of some characteristics of his subsequent work. The circumstances in which this interview between the King and the Emperor took place are well known. Pope Paul III, who wished to end heresy and restore the Catholic communion by means of a Council, had succeeded in first arranging a reconciliation between the Emperor and the King

---

[1] *Vide* Dr. de Santi, *Le cours de Rabelais à la Faculté de Montpellier* (18 octobre, 1537–1538), *R.É.R.*, III, p. 309, and Bourrilly, *Deux points obscurs dans la vie de Rabelais, R.É.R.*, IV, p. 113.

[2] This letter, unpublished, is in the Library of Toulouse. Cf. H. Jacoubet, *Quelques conjectures à propos de Boyssonné*, in Rev. *XVIe siècle*, 1924, p. 302, n. 1. On Boyssonné, cf. Jacoubet's thesis, *Les trois centuries de maistre Jehan de Boyssonné, docteur régent à Toulouse*, Paris, Toulouse, 1923 ; and *Les dix anneés d'amitié de Dolet et Boyssonné* (Toulouse, 1532—Lyon, 1542) in *la Revue du XVIe siècle*, 1925, pp. 290–321.

[3] According to the *Liber procuratoris* quoted by Gordon, *François Rabelais à Montpellier*, p. 37.

[4] As is clear from a poem in his *Ludi* (1538) : *Ad Rabelæsum, cum esset in monte Pessulano*, quoted by Marty-Laveaux, *op. cit.*, vol. III, p. 373.

[5] A *résumé* of this conversation is in Sussannée's *Alexandri quantitates emendatæ* (1539).

[6] In a letter, published by Émile Picot, in *R.É.R.*, vol. III, pp. 333–338 : *Rabelais à l'entrevue d'Aigues-Mortes (juillet,* 1538).

of France. This restoration of peace was, to his mind, the first step in his big project. On June 18th, 1538, he met the King at Nice, and on July 14th the latter examined at Aigues-Mortes, in agreement with Charles V, the remedies to be applied to the troubled state of public affairs. They promised each other friendship and mutual support, decided that they would persuade " those who had wandered to submit and agree in a friendly manner ", and undertook, if they refused, to use force[1].

Henceforward the policy of toleration towards the Reformers of France came to an end. A General Edict regulated the procedure to be followed in proceedings against heresy and all bailiffs and seneschals could examine into and judge cases concerning religion : they were entrusted with a mission which had until then been exclusively reserved to the sovereign courts[2].

This change of front in royal policy had its repercussion in the little confraternity of the *literati* of Lyons who formed Rabelais' circle of friends. The *sodalitium Lugdunense* had increased. Besides Étienne Dolet, who in his *Commentaries on the Latin tongue* mentioned Rabelais among the six most famous contemporary French physicians[3], and who exchanged verses with him on the occasion of receiving from him the recipe for preparing a sort of highly-spiced sauce, called *garum*[4], we find, about 1538, some new names. In the first place, Jean Visagier[5], in Latin, Vulteius. He had undertaken the defence of *Pantagruel* and *Gargantua* in an epigram published in 1536 : to somebody who pretended that the etymology of the name *Rabelæsus* was *rabie læsus* (afflicted with madness), he retorted that Rabelais' writing breathed not fury but gaiety :

Non spirant rabiem, sed tua scripta jocos[6].

---

[1] In a letter of Charles V to the Queen of Hungary, given in Imbart de la Tour, *Origines de la Réforme*, vol. III, *l'Évangélisme*, pp. 596–597.

[2] Imbart de la Tour, *ibid.*

[3] " Ex medicorum scholis ad certamen concurrunt Symphorianus Campegius, Jacobus Sylvius, Joannes Ruellius, Joannes Copus, *Franciscus Rabelæsus*, Carolus Paludanus ". Cf. *R.É.R.*, VIII, p. 373.

[4] The text of Rabelais' Latin poem, giving the recipe for *Garum* (a sort of anchovy paste), and Dolet's thanks for same, are given in Marty-Laveaux, *op. cit.*, III, pp. 376–377, from the edition of the *Carminum libri quatuor* (Lyons, 1538). Cf. with these verses of Rabelais, those quoted p. 78, n. 3.

[5] He is also called *Voulté* (*vide Rev. d'histoire littéraire de la France*, vol. I, p. 530), and his real name may have been *Faciot*.

[6] Visagier was supposed to have been aiming at Rabelais in a satirical epigram of his *Inscriptionum libri duo* (1538), against one *Rabella*, and in two pieces of his *Hendecasyllaborum libri quatuor* (1538), the first entitled *In*

Then, another neo-Latin poet who paid frequent visits to
Lyons, Nicolas Bourbon, from Vandœuvre in Champagne[1].
He had spent some years in England as tutor to Lord Hunsdon
and the Dudleys. Later he was entrusted with the education
of Jeanne d'Albret, Marguerite's daughter. Erasmus, in 1533,
ranked him amongst the best defenders of literature. It would
seem that his natural delicacy and his religious gravity had at
first inspired him with mistrust and repugnance for *Pantagruel*.
A poem in his book *Trifles*[2] reproached Rabelais with turning
students away from serious study and the love of Holy Scripture to debase them with obscure popular tales—lucrative
productions, but sullied with mud and filth. Five years later,
he judged Rabelais with more kindness since he requested him,
in an affectionate note, to remember him to their common
friends, Lateranne, Guillaume du Maine and Saint-Gelais[3].

Finally comes the poet who, perhaps, of all the poets of the
Lyons brotherhood, experiences the greatest admiration for
Rabelais, Gilbert Ducher, from Aigueperse in Auvergne, called
Vulton[4]. In a Latin epigram dedicated to Philosophy he paints

Luciani simium, the other *In quemdam irreligiosum Luciani sectatorem* (Cf.
A. Lefranc's *Introduction* to *Pantagruel*, pp. xliv and lvii, and A. F.
Chappell, *The enigma of Rabelais, an essay in interpretation* (Cambridge, 1924,
p. 21). The first of these pieces is rather harmless and there seems to be no
reason why Visagier should have disguised Rabelais' name as *Rabella*. The
other two are directed against someone who considered it impossible to use
the name *Christus* in Latin verses. This was an extreme example of the
purism of the Ciceronians ; Rabelais never professed his adherence to Ciceronianism. The person in question is more probably a disciple of Dolet's
whose identification remains to be discovered.

[1] Mr. A. Tilley devotes some pages of his *Studies in the French Renaissance*
to this neo-latin poet.

[2] *Nugæ*, Paris, Vascosan, 1533, 8vo.

[3] This note takes the place of the poem *In Rabellum* in the 1538 (Lyons)
edition of the *Nugarum libri octo*. It is called *Nicolai Bourbonii ad Rabelæsum
carmen*, and is as follows :—

> Jam raro Lateranus et Mainus,
> Occurunt mihi, Sangelaziusque :
> Nempe, urgentibus, aulicisque rebus
> (Ut sunt tempora) serio occupati :
> At tu, mi Rabelæse, quando abire
> Certum est, quo mea me vocat voluntas,
> Quo fatum potius vocat, traditque,
> Illis nomine dic meo salutem.

The three proper names mentioned are the following : *Sangelazius* is Saint-
Gelais ; *Lateranus* is Guillaume Lateranne, Abbot of Bon-Repos, François I's
almoner ; *Mainus* is Guillaume du Maine, tutor to Guillaume Budé's, and,
later, to François I's children, and finally Counsellor and Almoner of the
Duc d'Orléans.

[4] His two books of epigrams were published at Lyons, by Sebastian
Gryphius, in 1538.

her under the features of a Goddess rising up to the ethereal
regions of the stars and carrying with her her adepts, in the
first rank of whom Rabelais stands out as the only one whom
the poet mentions by name[1].

Various, indeed, no doubt, were the religious ideas of the
members of this group. From the perusal of their Latin poems,
—epigrams, trifles, amusements, hendecasyllables,—in which
the name of *Christus*, always printed in capitals, jostles with
the divinities of paganism, it is not easy to distinguish their
individual characteristics. In this rather monotonous *grisaille*
two features, in any event, are rather strongly marked and seem
common to all of them : the enthusiasm for ancient literature
and the aspiration towards a deep Christian life, freed from
the traditional forms. Humanists and Evangelicals—these
poets all are such in their verses. But it must be admitted
that their discussions sometimes betrayed other tendencies.
If we are to believe Sébastien Castellion, Calvin and Guillaume
Postel, there were even some complete freethinkers in this
group : the professor, Antoine de Gouvea, who had brought
back from the University of Padua the rationalistic ideas of
Pomponazzi, and who, as we have seen, was reputed to be an
atheist[2] ; Bonaventure des Périers, whose dialogues published
under the title of *Cymbalum mundi* (1537) alarmed the Sorbonne[3] ; Étienne Dolet, whom a secretary of Erasmus, Gilbert
Cousin, considered, in 1535, to be an atheist[4] ; and, finally,
Rabelais, of whom Calvin, in his *Treatise on Scandals* (1550),
will say that, along with Gouvea and Des Périers, " after having
at first relished the Gospel ", they afterwards thought that
" in so far as their souls were concerned, they differed in no wise
from dogs and swine "[5]. What facts or what words gave rise
to this opinion of Rabelais which Castellion, Calvin and Postel
accepted later ? What evidence supported it ? We do not

---

[1] This epigram, text and translation, has been published by M. Abel
Lefranc, *R.É.R.*, I, pp. 202–203. Cf. on Gilbert Ducher d'Aigueperse,
Ferdinand Buisson, *Sébastien Castellion, sa vie et son œuvre* (1515–1563),
(Paris, 1892), vol. I, p. 29.
[2] *Vide supra*, p. 78.
[3] M. Abel Lefranc's interpretation of these dialogues (*Introduction* to
Pantagruel, pp. lxi–lxv) is contested by M. Delaruelle, *Rev. d'hist. litt. de la
France*, 1925. *Vide supra*, p. 136, note.
[4] Cf. F. Buisson, *op. cit.*, I, pp. 45–47.
[5] Calvin, *Traité des Scandales*. In a sermon on *Deuteronomy*, ch. XIII
(1555), he has also attacked *Pantagruel*. Cf. Thuasne, *Études sur Rabelais*
(Paris, 1904), pp. 400–447. We shall later return to these attacks by Calvin.

know. In any event, we may take it as probable that a great
liberty of thought and of expression reigned among Rabelais'
friends, around 1537–1538, on questions of philosophy and
religion.

Everything changed when, after the interview of Aigues-
Mortes, our Humanists realised that the rupture between the
King and the Reformers was an accomplished fact. Then, they
were obliged to choose between the Catholic religion, whose
traditional forms the Sorbonne had succeeded in maintaining,
the reformed religion, whose dogmas and discipline Calvin had
lately formulated in his *Institutio Christianæ religionis*, or
libertinism. Very few Humanists went over to Calvinism.
The greater part of them had no desire to give up their peace-
able existence, or their benefices. Hiding, perhaps, their real
sentiments, they ceased to appeal for the advent of a Christianity reformed in its dogma or its discipline ; the rallying to
the side of orthodoxy which had begun following the *Affaire
des placards* had even increased. Our Lyons poets henceforth
refrained from attacking the religious Orders, the theologians,
popular devotions, Catholic tradition. Nicholas Bourbon de
Vandœuvre in publishing a new edition of his *Epigrammata*
substituted an *Ode to the Virgin Mary* for a poem *To the glory
of the very great and very good God*, which stigmatised the " em-
purpled she-wolf ", and " the hydra with the triple tiara ".
He changed the dedication of a piece he had written in 1533
to a *protégé* of the Queen of Navarre, Michel d'Arande, Bishop
of Saint-Paul-Trois-Châteaux, and now dedicated it to another
bishop of less doubtful orthodoxy, Jean Olivier. Étienne
Dolet himself threw a sop to the traditionalists by writing two
poems in honour of the Blessed Virgin, and by professing in his
Genethliacum (1538) his belief in God and in the immortality
of the soul[1]. Few, indeed, were they who dared resolutely to
depart from Catholicism.

Now it is at this juncture that we become aware of Rabelais'
admission, due, no doubt, to Cardinal du Bellay's patronage,
to the King's *entourage*. The writer who had made fun of
pilgrimages, devotion to the Saints, monasticism and the Jano-
tuses of the Sorbonne became a sort of official personage. He
was forced, henceforward, either to remain silent or to give

[1] Cf. in Hauser's *Études sur la Réforme*, the chapter on *Humanisme et
Réforme*.

up his usual subjects of raillery. We shall see that he also will throw sops to the orthodox party.

When Rabelais returned to Lyons, following the conference at Aigues-Mortes, he remained there ostensibly until the autumn of 1539. At the beginning of 1540, he is in Piedmont, with Cardinal Jean du Bellay's brother, Guillaume du Bellay, seigneur de Langey.

This personage, a soldier endowed with the talents of an administrator and a diplomat, had been appointed in 1537, after the conquest of Piedmont, Governor of Turin[1]. In reality, he performed the duties of Governor of the province in the absence of Montjehan, the Lieutenant-General, who lived there only on rare occasions. He had returned to France in December, 1538, having been replaced in this position by his brother, Martin du Bellay. On September 20th, 1539, he set out anew for Piedmont, with the task of assisting the new Lieutenant-General, Claude d'Annebault, in his government. It is then, probably, that he took with him the physician who had been in his brother's service, Doctor François Rabelais. Since Annebault returned to France after a few weeks, the responsibility of administration again fell entirely upon Langey.

It was heavy. The occupation of Piedmont was of capital importance for François I. The aim of his Italian policy continued to be the conquest of the Duchy of Milan[2]. He had indeed foregone it by the treaties of Madrid (1526) and of Cambrai (1529); but he did not cease to consider it a part of his patrimony, ready to assert the rights that Louis XII had claimed through his grandmother, Valentine de Visconti. In the event, then, of an expedition against the Milanese, Piedmont would have to be converted into a strong base. Hence, Langey's first care was to fortify Pignerol and Moncalieri, on the frontier of the Duchy of Milan. But it was advisable to make sure of the goodwill of the inhabitants. It was important to win hearts. Langey set about doing so. He

[1] On Rabelais' stay in Piedmont, cf. Arthur Heulhard, *Rabelais, ses voyages en Italie, son exil à Metz*, Paris, 1891, 8vo, and V. L. Bourrilly, *Guillaume du Bellay, seigneur de Langey*, Paris, 1905, 8vo.

[2] A sentence in the *New prologue* to the *Fourth Book* (1552) shows that Rabelais well understood the importance of the Duchy of Milan in François I's policy. Jupiter, about to restore to Couillatris (Wellhung) his lost hatchet, remarks that it is just as valuable to the woodcutter " as if it was worth the whole *duchy of Milan*. The truth is, the fellow's hatchet is as much to him as a kingdom to a King".

PLATE V

PORTRAIT OF GUILLAUME DU BELLAY
(Museum of Versailles, No. 3151)

[face p. 192

established for the good administration of justice a Parliament of Piedmont, whose president was François Errault, sieur de Chemans. Above all, he looked after the provisioning of the country, which had been tried by recent famines. Two years in succession he bought corn in Burgundy and Champagne, which he had transported by the Saône, the Rhône and the sea to Savone, and thence to Piedmont. He distributed it among the villages, giving for three *écus* a sack worth ten. He himself undertook the cost of transporting it, going heavily into debt in the King's service ; on his death, the better part of his estate paid the creditors who had advanced him the wherewithal to feed the Piedmontese. " The people ", wrote a historian, some time later, " found out full well the difference between a Governor, extortioner and pillager of his subjects, and a noble spirit, true father of the country "[1].

Rabelais, also, had occasion to admire the efforts of this great statesman, and it is Langey's policy he had in mind when, at the beginning of the *Third Book*[2], he opposed to the conduct of those Kings " devourers of their people ", that of Pantagruel, coloniser of Dipsodie.

" Remark therefore here, honest drinkers, that the manner of preserving and retaining countries newly conquered in obedience, is not (as hath been the erroneous opinion of some tyrannical spirits to their own detriment and dishonour,) to pillage, plunder, force, spoil, trouble, oppress, vex, disquiet, ruin, and destroy the people, ruling, governing, and keeping them in awe with rods of iron ; and, in a word, eating and devouring them, after the fashion that Homer calls an unjust and wicked king, Δημόβορον, that is to say, a devourer of his people. I will not bring you to this purpose the testimony of ancient writers. It shall suffice to put you in mind of what your fathers have seen thereof, and yourselves too, if you be not very babes. New-born, they must be given suck to, rocked in a cradle, and dandled. Trees newly planted must be supported, under-propped, strengthened, and defended against all tempests, mischiefs, injuries, and calamities. And one lately saved from a long and dangerous sickness, and new upon his recovery, must be forborn, spared, and cherished, in such sort that they may harbour in their own breasts this opinion, that there is not in the world a king or prince, who does not desire fewer enemies, and more friends. . . .

These are the philtres, allurements, Íynges, inveiglements, baits,

[1] Paradin, *Chroniques de Savoie*, quoted by Heulhard, *Rabelais, ses voyages en Italie, son exil à Metz*, p. 180.
[2] Ch. 1. Cf. Abel Lefranc, *Rabelais et les peuples conquis, Revue du XVIe siècle*, 1914, pp. 285–287.

and enticements of love, by the means whereof that may be peaceably retained, which was happily acquired. Nor can a conqueror reign more happily, whether he be a monarch, emperor, king, prince, or philosopher, than by making his justice to second his valour. His valour shows itself in victory and conquest ; his justice will appear in the good will and affection of the people, when he maketh laws, publisheth ordinances, establisheth religion, and doth what is right to every one, as the noble poet Virgil writes of Octavian Augustus.   . . . Victorque volentes
Per populos dat jura."

Rabelais' duties in Langey's service are known to us from some letters which the Bishop of Montpellier, Guillaume Pellicier, then ambassador at Venice[1], sent to him. Langey was fond of literature. While a student in Paris, at the age of eighteen, he had composed a Latin poem in hexameter verse, the *Peregrinatio humana*, copied on Guillaume de Digulleville's *Pèlerinage de la vie humaine*. He had crossed the Alps to complete his studies in Italy : he had been in contact with the Ciceronian, Longueil, at Padua, and, at Pavia, with Simon de Villeneuve, pupil of Pomponazzi and Dolet's professor. He delighted in the company of learned and cultured persons. From Venice, Paul Manucius sent him, through the medium of Pellicier, copies of Cicero just issued from his presses[2] : he was careful to stamp the binding with Langey's arms. It was Rabelais who furnished Pellicier with information as to these arms, and it is he who was notified of the dispatch of the books. So he was entrusted with the care of Langey's private library. Pellicier also used to ask him for roots of rare plants : some *nardus celtica* and some *anthora* " with their earth in some little boxes, so as to make them, if possible, *alumnæ* and citizens in our garden of this city [of Venice], and with that, some other such for medicinal purposes, as you informed me you would do. . . ." Thus, the science of the botanist who had formerly embellished the gardens of L'Hermenault and of Ligugé, was now availed of by the Ambassador of France to the Serene Republic for the adornment of a Venetian garden.

The same letters show us that Pellicier kept Rabelais informed of the progress of his search for Greek books for the

[1] On Pellicier cf. Jean Zeller, *La diplomatie française vers le milieu du XVI⁰ siècle, d'après la correspondance de Guillaume Pellicier* (1539–1542), Paris, 1880, 8vo, and *Correspondance de Guillaume Pellicier*, published by Tausserat-Radel, Paris, 1899, 8vo.

[2] *Épîtres familières, Épître à Atticus.*

Royal library of Fontainebleau. Pierre Duchatel, Bishop of Tulle, François I's librarian, had commissioned him to buy Greek works in Venice, a great market for ancient books, or at least to have copies of some of them made. Pellicier had found some of Galen's works and four "collators" were employed in copying them. He hoped the Governor of Piedmont would send him some resources, for the outlay involved in having this copy made "amounted to almost as much as the ordinary outlay". Pellicier, besides, gratified Langey with many minor attentions. He used to send him small gifts, such as a "pot of green ginger", and did not disdain to pass a joke with his physician and secretary. The first in date of these letters has for its object a medical consultation of a rather peculiar nature. The wife of Philippus Saccus, President of Milan, had just given birth to a daughter, five and a half months after the husband and wife "had come together for the first time". The President, who did nothing inconsiderately, had noted with precision the *terminus a quo* : "25th October, 1539, at four hours of the night before the full moon". And the accouchement had taken place the 13th April, 1540. Hence, he asked the Doctors' colleges of Venice and Bologna whether the child was legitimate and if it were "vital".

On the first point, the doctrine generally admitted was that "the child born after seven months" was legitimate. To know if it were viable, there was, seemingly, nothing to do but wait. But it would be showing ignorance of Humanist doctors' habits to suppose that they would simply refer to experience before first consulting the ancients. So they looked up the works of Hippocrates, Pliny and Avicenna. Unhappily, the passage of Hippocrates which would have been decisive, "in the book of the Semester", was altered in the manuscripts. Thus did medicine depend upon textual criticism, and that is what authorised Rabelais to declare, in the preface to his edition of the *Aphorisms*, that there was no more urgent task for scholars than to restore the true text of the medical works of the Greeks and Romans[2]. In the end, the doctors of Bologna had given

---

[1] These letters of Pellicier are given in Marty-Laveaux, *op. cit.*, vol. III, pp. 382–386.

[2] "In quibus vocula unica, vel addita, vel expuncta, quin et apiculus inversus, aut præpostere adscriptus, multa hominum milia haud raro neci dedit". Dedicatory letter of the *Aphorisms* of Hippocrates, cf. Marty-Laveaux, *op. cit.*, III, p. 317.

their opinion that the Hebrews, Arabians and Chaldæans, who counted their months by moons, would have found seven moons in the said child's " time " and would have declared it to be legitimate. Pellicier asked Rabelais for his opinion. We have not got the latter's answer. Doubtless, in order to reassure Saccus, who had some claim on the gratitude of all the King's servants, he opined with the same facility as those Panta-gruelists, mentioned in *Gargantua*, who " declared it to be not only possible, but also maintained the lawful birth and legitima-tion of the infant born of a woman in the eleventh month after the decease of her husband "[1].

Honoured with Langey's confidence, welcomed by all among the Governor's associates, occupied with botany, medicine or the ancient literatures, Rabelais seems to have been happy at Turin. However, an accident, similar to that which had nearly caused him to be imprisoned at Lyons, in 1537, by Cardinal de Tournon, happened to him. For having written in a letter information or opinions which it would have been preferable not to mention explicitly, or even to keep to himself, he was subjected to annoyance for some time[2]. The recipient of the letter was one Barnabé de Voré, sieur de la Fosse (in Latin, Fossanus). Langey had employed him upon diplomatic missions in Germany, between 1532 and 1538. In 1540, he was at Rome. But he had abandoned the Du Bellays' policy, which was one of complete tolerance towards the Protestant princes, and gone over to the party of Poyet, the Chancellor, and of Cardinal de Tournon, who desired no tenderness for Reformers, internal or external. Rabelais, who did not suspect this change of attitude, had written to him quite freely, perhaps in order to explain to him Langey's views on the political situation. De la Fosse showed around his letter, which was even brought to the Court of France. One of Jean du Bellay's secretaries, Claude Cottereau, informed Jean de Boyssonné, who was then at Chambéry, of it ; he notified a familiar of Langey's, Guil-laume Bigot, of it by letter, and it is this letter which informs us as to the incident. Rabelais was blamed, he tells us, for not choosing his correspondents more carefully, or for writing to them about such important questions, and De la Fosse

[1] Ch. III.
[2] I follow here the conclusions of M. Bourrilly who has studied this matter in his *Deux points obscurs de la vie de Rabelais*, *R.É.R.*, IV, p. 103.

was reproached with showing a friend's letter around so carelessly.

A second letter of Boyssonné's to Bigot lets us know that Rabelais had incurred some trouble as a result of these indiscretions. He did not know what line of action to adopt. Where was he at the time ? In Chambéry or Lyons ? We do not know. We can follow his movements only by Pellicier's or Boyssonné's letters, and many facts certainly still escape us about this period of his existence[1].

There is, for example, one episode to which it is impossible to assign a date, or an accurate place—the death of a natural son which he had at Lyons, and which died at the age of two years. Here is the information which can be gathered from some Latin verses of Boyssonné, the only contemporary to mention this child of Rabelais'. He was called Théodule (in Greek, Servant of God), and Boyssonné makes this name the theme of several of his poems : if the child has left this world, it is because he was in a hurry to go and live in Christ ; if he died young, it is a proof that he is beloved of God ; he prays that all be, like him, servants of God. Beside this Christian inspiration, some notes give witness to the pagan culture of the Humanist who is author of these verses. And, incidentally, it is without the slightest embarrassment that he takes as his subject, for poems which were not meant to remain unpublished, a priest's natural child. He even shows us Roman prelates (*romanos pontifices*) petting this little being whose fatherland is Lyons and whose father is Rabelais : two very big things in the universe[2]. What prelates had bent over young Théodule's cradle ? Boyssonné's allusion is vague ; but there were then, in France, as well as in Rome, numerous high dignitaries of the Church who had personal reasons for not being scandalised because a priest violated his vow of chastity[3].

In the month of March, 1541, Rabelais was again at Turin. He was arranging the dispatch of some plants to Guillaume Pellicier, who, for his part, sent him some marjoram and

---

[1] Cf. *R.É.R.*, IV, pp. 48 and 125.

[2] " Lugdunum patria, at pater est Rabelæsus : utrumque
Qui nescit, nescit maxima in orbe duo.

[3] On this episode cf. Heulhard, *op. cit.*, Boyssonné's poems are among the MSS. of Toulouse Library, *Fonds du clergé*, no. 31, folios 31, 85 and 177. They are given in Marty-Laveaux, *op. cit.*, vol. IV, pp. 394–395.

amomum. Shortly afterwards, Langey lost his wife, who was buried in Turin Cathedral. Boyssonné composed a Latin elegy to the dead lady and requested Rabelais to convey it to Langey.

Meanwhile, the murder by Imperial agents of the King's envoys to Venice, Fregose and Rincon, threatened to start anew the war between François I and Charles V. In the beginning of November, 1541, Langey returned to France to acquaint the King of the state of Italian affairs. Rabelais accompanied him. He halted at Lyons to give his publisher, François Juste, instructions for the publication of a new edition of *Gargantua* and *Pantagruel*. He made many corrections in the original text, dictated by his concern for peace.

In order to have no more quarrels with the Sorbonne he everywhere replaced the words *theologians, sorbonagres, sorbonicoles* by the term *sophist*. Since the Humanists called the scholastic philosophy of the theologians, sophistry, these corrections could mislead nobody. They merely indicated that the author wished to spare the theologians' pride by ceasing to ridicule them openly.

As to the witticisms on the text of the Scripture, all were maintained without any attenuation. Rabelais even added new ones, putting, for instance, in the mouth of the *Bien-Yvres*, conversing at La Saulsaye, the word of Christ on the Cross : *Sitio*[1]. These were not considered likely to shock the theologians. Only some over-impertinent resemblances between the " fooleries " in *Gargantua* and the word of the Gospel were suppressed.

These precautions were vain—for some months later *Pantagruel* and *Gargantua* were included by the theologians of the Sorbonne in the list of works which they censured, at the Parliament's request. They at least showed some concern for prudence in Rabelais. What, then, must have been his indignation when he heard that Étienne Dolet had surreptitiously published a new edition of the original, unexpurgated text of *Pantagruel* and *Gargantua* ! It amounted to a betrayal. Dolet, whose character was becoming more and more violent, had made enemies of nearly all the members of the Lyonnese fraternity. Visagier and Nicolas Bourbon had broken with him. Marot,

---

[1] *Gargantua*, ch. V. Cf. my study on *l'Écriture Sainte et la littérature scripturaire dans l'œuvre de Rabelais, R.É.R.*, VIII, pp. 257–330, and IX, pp. 423–436.

hurt, perhaps, at finding him so distant from him in his scorn of religious sentiment, was preparing to erase his name from the new edition of his works and even to attack him openly. Dolet complained of " the calumnies of men ", and his isolation forms a poignant spectacle[1]. When he goes to the stake in 1546, he will not find one voice amongst his former friends to give him proof of their sympathy[2].

The pirated edition of *Pantagruel* and *Gargantua* published by Étienne Dolet drew a protest from Rabelais. For it is he, without any doubt, who inspired, if he did not compose, the *Notice to the Reader* which the publisher, Pierre de Tours, François Juste's successor, printed at the head of a new edition of *Gargantua* and *Pantagruel*, published this same year, 1542. Dolet is there called a plagiarist, accused of having plagiarised the professors and grammarians Villanovanus, Nizolius, Calepin and Robert Estienne, denounced for having fraudulently claimed an exemption from royal privileges, and ridiculed in his pretensions as a perfect Ciceronian.

The last sheets of Dolet's pirated edition contain a little work : *The wonderful navigations of Pantagruel's disciple, called Panurge*, which had already been published three times since 1538. It is the work of an imitator of Rabelais and was often reprinted at the end of his own works. We shall see later that Rabelais will take from it the subject-matter for some episodes of the *Fourth Book* ; but, by not printing it in the François Juste collective edition in 1542, he showed sufficiently that he did not recognise it for his own[3].

---

[1] We have already seen (*v. supra*, p. 183, n. 3) the insults which Dolet publicly gave to Erasmus who, in his eyes, was wrong in not considering Cicero as the sole model of Latinity for his contemporaries. He speaks in the following manner of these scholars whose views upon orthography did not coincide with his own : " I will say what I have to say about them [accents] briefly and plainly, without any show of learning or any jumble of Greek and Latin. I call jumble the excessive use of terms from these languages, made by *haughty fools*, and not by resolute men, full of sound judgment ". *La manière de bien traduire d'une langue en aultre . . . Des accents*, Lyons, É. Dolet, 1540. (The opening phrases of his treatise on Accents.)

[2] The youthful Théodore de Bèze was the only Humanist to give him the honour of a poem, in Latin. Cf. Richard Copley Christie, *Étienne Dolet, the Martyr of the Renaissance*, 1508–1546 (London, 1898, 2nd ed., p. 476).

[3] The absence of geographical names is, in my opinion, a proof that Rabelais is not the author of this work. How could he, who bore in mind the map of the world recently discovered by navigators, have described an odyssey without putting into it numerous geographical proper names ? Only one occurs in the *Disciple—Greater India*,—the wonderful land which cast its spell over the imagination of even the most ignorant persons. Cf. the *Introduction* to my edition of the *Fourth Book* (É. Champion, 1909), p. 35, n. 3.

At the same time as Juste republished *Pantagruel* and *Gargantua*, Sebastian Gryphius published the *Stratagems, that is to say, prowesses and ruses of war of the pious and most famous Chevalier de Langey at the beginning of the third Cæsarean war*, translated from the Latin of François Rabelais by Claude Massuau. This last-named was a familiar of Langey's at Turin. We know his book only by its title, which is given in the *Bibliothèque françoise* of La Croix du Maine and Du Verdier. We have no indication as to the scope of this work or its character. The Latin original was possibly only a fairly general discourse, an essay in historiography in the style of Paulus Jovius. For us, it is merely a further testimony of Rabelais' admiration for the Governor of Piedmont.

While Langey repaired to the Court, where he received the collar of the Order of St. Michel, Rabelais stayed with friends ; on the 1st March, 1542, he was at Saint-Ayl, between Meung and Orleans, staying with the captain of Turin Castle, Étienne Lorens, who also had accompanied Langey to France. He resided then in his seigniorial château of Saint-Ayl, situated near the Loire, on a slope planted with famous vineyards. At its foot, some trees sheltered a spring, near which, according to tradition, Rabelais used to come to work. The church contained relics of St. Sylvanus, the little Zaccheus of the Gospel[1], whom the *Prologue* of the *Fourth Book* recommends as an example to those tempted to observe no moderation in their desires. Some Orleans Humanists gathered together at Étienne Lorens' house. They were mostly legists : François Daniel, Calvin's companion and friend, licentiate of laws, advocate, *bailli* of Saint-Laurent-les-Orgerils-lez-Orléans ; Claude Framberge, " sealer " of the Archbishopric, the ecclesiastical officer entrusted with the levying of the charges accruing from the episcopal seal ; Jean Pailleron, Assessor of the *aides* in the *élection* of Orleans ; and, finally, Antoine Hullot, licentiate of laws, advocate of the powerful community " of the traders frequenting the River Loire and the rivers descending thereinto ", seigneur of La Cour-Compain, in the parish of Chécy. Claude Massuau, the translator of the *Stratagems*, was himself lord of Belle-Croix, in the parish of Saint-Ayl, and related to the Framberges.

The existence of this little group is known to us by a humorous

[1] St. Luke, ch. XIX.

letter which Rabelais sent, " the first day of March ", to Hullot, " in Christendom, at Orleans ". Of all Maître François' missives it is the only one which recalls the style of his " fooleries ", the only one which truly has a " pantagruelic " flavour[1]. The " Bailiffs' bailiff's bailiff ", as Hullot was familiarly called, is invited to come and rest at Saint-Ayl from the " sprees " and festivities in which he has taken part in Paris. It is Lent. The food will be none the less exquisite for being meatless. From the neighbouring Loire will be dragged " by their hair . . . certain species of carp-like fish ", hairy-jawed barbels or young barbels. The cellar will supply good wines, well lightened (*dépouillés*) preserved " like a *sang-réal*[2], or a second or even fifth (*quint*) essence ". Thus, in this hermitage, they will observe the will of " this great, good, Pitiful God, who never created Lent, but did indeed create Salads, Herrings, Hake, Carp, Pike, Dace, Graylings, Bleaks, *Rippes*, etc., as well as good wines . . ."

This short note begins with a quotation from the farce of *Pathelin*[3] and contains a Latin pun of the sort which was current among the lawyers[4] : there is a postscript requesting a copy of Plato which " Monsieur le Scelleur ", Claude Framberge, had once already lent Rabelais.

At the beginning of May, Langey returned to Turin. Soon the frontiers of Piedmont were assailed by the Imperial forces. The Governor, suffering from gout and with a tumour on his

---

[1] It is contained in P. de l'Estoile's *Registre Journal*, with the following note : " Thursday, 22nd (of January, 1609) M. du Puy gave me the following letter of Rabelais', amusing, but authentic, and copied from the original". The best text of this document is that published by M. Jacques Soyer (who has verified all the proper names upon original documents in archives) in *R.É.R.*, VII, 306, *Topographie rabelaisienne (Berry et Orléanais)*.

[2] [Rabelais has taken this term *Sang gréal* or *sangréal* from the Arthurian Romances. It is from the *Saint Graal* (Holy Grail), and had come to signify not the vase which had held the Blood of Christ, but the healing balm itself which the vessel contained. Rabelais frequently uses it in the general sense of something rare and wonderful. Cf. *Fourth Book*, ch. XLII : " Mustard was their *sangreal*, and celestial balsam, of which, laying but a little in the wounds of the fallen Chitterlings, in a very short time the wounded were healed, and the dead restored to life ". Cf. M. Plattard's note on this passage in his edition of the *Fourth Book* (Paris, 1929, Fernand Roches), p. 303 ; and Lazare Sainéan, *La langue de Rabelais* (Paris, E. de Boccard, 1922), vol. I, p. 334.]

[3]
        He, Pater Reverendissime
        Quomodo bruslis, quæ nova !
        Parisius non sunt ova !
  Cf. *Pathelin*, v. 960–961.

[4] " Item les bons vins, singulièrement celui *de veteri jure* enucleando . . ." The pun is on *jus* which means both *law* and *drink*.

foot, made a final inspection of the defences. Then, unable to move, with only the use " of his brain and of his tongue ", he prepared for death. The 13th November, he made his will, distributing his books, his horses, his gilt harnesses. " To the sieur de Rabelais, the said sieur testator orders . . . fifty *livres tournois* yearly[1] until such time as his heirs shall have provided for him, or cause him to be provided for, in the Church to the sum of three hundred *livres tournois* annually . . ." He ordered his funeral to take place in Turin and his body to be interred in the Cathedral, where his wife's remains already reposed. But, soon afterwards, he expressed a desire to see France again. Carried in a litter, he crossed the Alps at the end of December. The 10th of January, he expired at Saint-Symphorien-en-Laye, at the foot of the Tarare mountain, four leagues from Roanne.

Rabelais, who accompanied him, has recalled in his book his last moments. From his account, it would seem that the heavens had warned the earth[2] of the coming departure of this " so illustrious, generous and heroic soul " by " prodigies, monsters and other foreboding signs, that thwart the order of Nature ". He mentions none of these prodigies ; but anyone who has read the *Memoirs* or *Chronicles* of the time knows with what facility the people of the sixteenth century interpreted as prodigies certain natural phenomena : earthquakes, floods, comets, storms, etc. Rabelais, then, is here following ideas which were commonly accepted around him.

" I remember it, (said Epistemon,) and my heart still trembles within me, when I think on the many dreadful prodigies that we saw five or six days before he died. For the Lords D'Assier[3], Chemant, one-eyed Mailly[4], St. Ayl, Villeneufve le Guyart[5], Master Gabriel, physician of Savillan[6], Rabelais, Cohuau, Massuau,

---

[1] Given in Heulhard, *op. cit.*

[2] *Fourth Book*, ch. XXVII.

[3] Captain François Galliot de Genouillac, seigneur d'Assier, only son of the Grand Écuyer, and Grand Master of the French Artillery. Langey had him sent to Piedmont with his company in April, 1542. Cf. Bourrilly, *Guillaume du Bellay*, p. 348.

[4] Mailly-le-Borgne was an artillery officer.

[5] Charles d'Aunay, seigneur de Villeneuve-la-Guyart, had married Louise du Bellay, Langey's sister.

[6] Gabriel Taphenon, a doctor of Savigliano, in Piedmont, belonged to Langey's household, and was left fifty *écus soleil* by the latter's will. Cf. Heulhard, *op. cit.*, p. 167.

Majorici[1], Bullou[2], Cercu[3], alias Bourgmaistre, Francis Proust, Ferron, Charles Girard[4], Francis Bourré, and many other friends and servants to the deceased, all dismayed, gazed on each other without uttering one word ; yet not without foreseeing that France would in a short time be deprived of a knight so accomplished, and necessary for its glory and protection, and that heaven claimed him again as its due."

Langey on his death-bed kept his lucidity of mind. It seemed as if he had the faculty of foretelling the future, as if his soul, says Rabelais, already participating in the Life Divine had received from it the gift of prophecy. " The last three or four hours of his life he did employ in the serious utterance of a very pithy discourse, whilst with a clear judgment, and spirit void of all trouble, he did foretell several important things, whereof a great deal is come to pass, and the rest we wait for. Howbeit, his prophecies did at that time seem unto us somewhat strange, absurd, and unlikely ; because there did not then appear any sign of efficacy enough to engage our faith to the belief of what he did prognosticate "[5].

The hero being dead, his body was embalmed by Rabelais and by Maître Gabriel Taphenon, a physician of Savigliano, then placed in a coffin and brought to Le Mans, along the valley of the Allier and that of the Loire. Langey's household was in disorder : the deceased's papers were ransacked and the manuscript of his Memoirs stolen by a German servant. Rabelais, according to what Martin du Bellay wrote to his brother, the Cardinal, had never thought of looking after these Memoirs " which he thought were stored away in the mule-trunks which were not opened "[6]. The funeral procession had stopped at Saint-Ayl, at Étienne Lorens' house, while waiting for Jean du Bellay to choose the burial-place. He was undecided between Paris, Le Mans or Vendôme. Finally, he decided that his brother should be buried in the Cathedral of Le Mans. The ceremonies took place on the 9th March : they were celebrated

---

[1] One Antoine de Mairicy is mentioned in Langey's will with a legacy of 200 livres tournois.

[2] Langey left to the Signeur de Bullou in his will a " gilt harness ", a " courser " and a " big horse ".

[3] Jean de Cercus is left a " further gift in addition to that which he received on his marriage ".

[4] According to Langey's will Charles Girard was a churchman. Nothing is known about Cohuau, Proust, Ferron, or Bourré.

[5] Third Book, ch. XXI.

[6] Cf. Bourrilly, Guillaume du Bellay . . . , p. 366.

with extraordinary pomp. Among the four gentlemen who held the corners of the funeral pall was the Seigneur de la Possonnière, Louis de Ronsard : his son, Pierre, aged nineteen, was a witness of the solemn honours paid to the remains of a great servant of the King. The poets celebrated Langey's memory in Latin and in French. Marot, then at Geneva or in Savoy, composed his epitaph and evoked, in one of his latest poems[1] :

> L'esprit du preux Guillaume du Bellay
> Tant travaillé des guerres piedmontoises.

In the Cathedral of Le Mans, his brothers caused a mausoleum to be erected to him ; the architectural portion of it has been ruined, but the sculptures remain and they rank among the finest of the period[2].

The memory of the " learned and valiant " Seigneur de Langey was to remain living in Rabelais' mind. We find in his work numerous reminiscences of the time he had spent in Piedmont in his service : now, a description of plants common in the region[3], the agarie mushroom and the larch-tree ; or, the mention of the four bastions of Turin[4] ; or again, perhaps, some reminiscences of the works of fortification which he may have seen while accompanying the Governor on his rounds of inspection[5]. But from the tone in which he speaks of Langey, we feel that, throughout this third sojourn in Italy, nothing had left a deeper impression on him than the sight of the activity of this great soul, truly universal, endowed for thought as well as for action, and who commanded admiration by his learning, his quiet earnestness and his strength.

What happened to Rabelais after Langey's burial ? We lose trace of him for two years. From the allusions which he makes in the *Third Book* to certain places—the Hyères Islands[6] and Poitou[7]—we can assume further peregrinations. He had to find means of livelihood. He never received the income left to him in Langey's will, for in this estate the debit far exceeded

---

[1] *Complaincte de Monsieur le Général Guillaume Preud'homme.*

[2] M. Bourrilly, *op. cit.*, pp. 372–375, attributes them to a sculptor of Le Mans, Noël Huet.

[3] *Third Book*, ch. LII.   [4] *Fourth Book*, ch. LXV.

[5] *Third Book*, Prologue ; *Fourth Book*, ch. LXII.

[6] Cf. Title of the *Third Book* (1546) : . . . " Composé par M. François Rabelais . . . *calloier des isles Hyères* ".

[7] *Vide supra*, p. 70, a long list of obscure Poitevin place-names quoted in the *Fourth Book*, ch. XLI.

the credit side. In addition, he lost his first patron, Geoffroy d'Estissac, who died the 30th of May, 1543. He may still have received at the hands of his nephew, Louis d'Estissac, the same kind welcome that he had formerly known at L'Hermenault and the Priory of Ligugé. It is possible that he again became a guest at Cahuzac or in Louis d'Estissac's properties in Poitou.

Some days after the Bishop of Maillezais' death, one of Langey's familiars, François Errault, sieur de Chemant, President of the Parliament of Turin, was appointed Chancellor of France, and Boyssonné urged his friend Rabelais to rejoice at the event[1]. It may be due to the patronage of this high magistrate that Rabelais was named Master of the King's Requests. The *Discours de la Court*[2], a poem composed in 1543 by Claude Chappuys, his companion during his first stay in Rome, names as *Masters of the Requests*, Maïnus, Saint-Gelais, Salignac, Danesius, Salmon Macrin,

> Et Rabelais à nul qu'à soy semblable
> Par son sçavoir partout recommandable.

He is placed among the scholars. There were other *Maîtres des requêtes* chosen among the poets, as Héroët, Macault, La Borderie, Salel. Their title was honorary. The active *Maîtres des requêtes* resided at Paris and served by quarters. The others, if they so desired, followed the Court, their only prerogative being to belong to the King's *entourage*. This facility of approach to the King is enough to explain how Rabelais managed to obtain, the 19th September, 1545, a privilege for the printing of the " sequence . . . of the Heroic deeds and sayings of Pantagruel ". " Desiring ", says the royal document, " that good letters be promoted throughout our Kingdom for the utility and erudition of our subjects ", privilege, leave and licence is granted for ten years to " our beloved and faithful Maître Françoys Rabelais, Doctor of Medicine of our University of Montpellier "[3]. Such complimentary terms are sufficient proof that Rabelais was then well

---

[1] " In hac autem Chamani fortunæ accessione spero eum quoque commodorum tuorum curam aliquam habiturum, qui eum semper coluisti et observasti diligentissime hominisque ingenium et conditionem singularem semper es admiratus ". Toulouse Library, MSS., *Fonds du clergé*, no. 17, pp. 180–181. Cf. Marty-Laveaux, *op. cit.*, vol. IV, p. 400.

[2] Cf. Heulhard, *op. cit.*, pp. 155 *seq.*

[3] In Marty-Laveaux, *op. cit.*, vol. III, p. 387.

in favour. But the title of *Maître des requêtes*, given to writers, was accompanied neither by pension nor salary ; and we do not know what were Rabelais' means of existence at the time. " Lack of money " was doubtless the principal motive which urged the Doctor of Medicine to publish a sequel to his first two books of gay " fooleries ".

Where, meantime, did he reside between the years 1543 and 1546 ? Presumably in the West of France. A sojourn in Poitou seems to us probable. As witnesses of it we have numerous mentions in the *Third Book* of people and places of this province—here[1], the favour of being remembered is granted to the Abbot of Fontaine-le-Comte, Antoine Ardillon, whose name he had previously brought into *Pantagruel* when he republished it in 1542 with François Juste[2] ; there, eleven place-names, some of them obscure, quoted in the anecdote of Perrin Dandin[3], or the name of a humble spring, the Fons-Beton, and of a grove, the Touche-Ronde, in the neighbourhood of Ligugé, given, one to an imaginary jurisdiction, the other to an imaginary culprit in the Bridoye episode. The legal world of Poitiers, the toponymy of the region, the rustic habits of the Poitevin countryside, are evoked with ease and accuracy in this episode. Rabelais, when he composes it, has clearly freshened up, in the very places where his youth was passed, memories which remained dear to him. It is in Poitou or in nearby Chinonais, his native country, that he wrote the *Third Book*, which appeared at the beginning of 1546 (n.s.).

---

[1] Ch. XLIII. *Vide supra*, p. 72.
[2] Ch. V. This reads in the early editions : " They passed by Legugé, then by Lusignan " ; and in the 1542 edition : " They passed by Legugé, *visiting the noble Abbot Ardillon*, then by Lusignan, etc. ".
[3] Ch. XLI. *Vide supra*, p. 70 *seq.*

CHAPTER XIV

THE THIRD BOOK OF PANTAGRUEL

THE recent condemnation of the two first books by the Sorbonne (1543), made even after Juste's edition of *Gargantua* had presented an expurgated text, should have urged Rabelais to greater prudence in his new work. And he does, in fact, refrain in his *Third Book* from the ridiculing of Scholasticism and the sharp satires of the theologians which are characteristic of *Gargantua*. The book does contain a theologian, Father Hippothadeus, but he has none of the absurdities of Janotus. He is treated with respect by all present, and Pantagruel stoutly objects to a sally of Panurge, who said by way of amusement in his presence that all theologians are heretics. " Their whole and sole employment ", protests Pantagruel, " is by their deeds, their words and writings, to extirpate errors and heresies (far from being tainted with them) and to plant deeply in the hearts of men the true and lively Catholic faith "[1]. Rabelais, then, far from attacking the theologians, bore witness to their orthodoxy. What an excellent reference our Masters, the gentlemen of the Sorbonne, had there !

It would have been more difficult for him to refrain completely from poking fun at the monks. Friar John had his place among the characters of the story. Consequently, his presence recalled to Rabelais' mind all his memories of the days of monkhood : the " metaphors extracted out of the claustral kettle "[2], and the " matter of breviary " quoted in a wrong sense or out of its context, and a hundred more tricks of humour. There is, for example, the sprightly story, taken from Erasmus[3], which leads Pantagruel to declare that " all the monks, friars, and nuns fear less to transgress the commandments of God than their provincial statutes ". The witticism was not an unfair one, any more than the comparison of the mendicant orders with a swarm of insatiable beasts—black, white, ash-coloured,

---

[1] Ch. XXIX.   [2] Ch. XV.   [3] Ch. XIX.

207

and tawny—which is to be found in Raminagrobis' words on his death-bed[1]. It by no means scandalises good Friar John, for it was quite common. Besides, if François I's changed attitude towards the Reformers had put an end to the attacks of independent thinkers against the Sorbonne, we have no reason for believing that it led them to respect the monks. Does not the Queen of Navarre declare in the *Heptameron* that she knows not one story calculated to reflect the slightest credit on the Friars Minor[2]? And, in fact, there is in the *Third Book* an eloquent invective against the monks who meddle with businesses " contrary by the whole Diameter " to their "states ", by favouring and blessing marriages contracted unknown to the parents or without their consent[3]. But Rabelais risked nothing in castigating these unworthy monks, these " Pastophorian mole-catching priests " who, in return for ready money, legalised by their presence unions contracted against the wish or without the consent of fathers and mothers. This was an abuse which French jurists had, long since, denounced and of which they advocated the reform, until a Royal edict of 1556 declared those children who contracted marriage *sine parentum consensu*[4] disinherited of their parents' goods. Rabelais, in stigmatising and consigning to an ignominious death the monks who abetted these marriages was, therefore, serving a cause dear to the hearts of French legists. He became a sort of official publicist in putting into Gargantua's mouth this advice : " Dearly beloved son, have care that such law be not received in this kingdom ".

While taking care, then, to safeguard himself from the theologians, without denying himself this endless source of humour,—the monks—Rabelais, the *Prologue* tells us, had undertaken to tell Pantagrueline stories in order to amuse his companions engaged in the defence of their country. In reality, Pantagruel yielded the principal place to Panurge. The narrator was tired, probably, of repeating the description of the stature, strength and appetite of his giant.

Already in *Gargantua* the " giant " theme was frequently neglected. In the *Third Book* there is no longer any question of " horrible and frightful prowesses ". The title more modestly announces some " heroic deeds and sayings of Pantagruel ".

[1] Chs. XXI–XXIII.   [2] *Nouvelle* XXXI.   [3] Ch. XLVIII.
[4] Cf. Isambert, *Recueil des lois*, vol. XIII, p. 469, and my historical and juridical study on this question apropos of *L'invective de Pantagruel contre les mariages contractés sans l'aveu des parents*, in *Rev. XVIe siècle*, 1927, p. 381.

But we would look in vain even for heroic exploits. The giant takes part in no war. His prodigious strength, become useless, is passed over in silence. The story-teller forgets to call our attention to the enormity of his giants. We are surprised to see old Gargantua entering a dining-room without bending to pass through the doorway, and sitting down modestly at the head of the common table, on an ordinary chair[1]. The interest of the narrative is elsewhere—it is concentrated on Panurge.

The first eight chapters continue the history of Dipsodie from the point at which Pantagruel left it, namely, after the defeat of Anarchus, sovereign of the Amaurotes. They show us how Panurge, in reward for his war-services, receives the " Lairdship of Salmiguondin " and spends in fourteen days " the certain and uncertain revenues of his Lairdship for three whole years ". He is reduced to going into debt, and, as Pantagruel remonstrates to him that he was wrong in wasting his money and borrowing, he answers by a double apology of his wastefulness and of his debts. Never yet had Rabelais displayed such exuberance of speech nor so much subtlety of argument :

" Everybody cries up thrift, thrift, and good husbandry. But many speak of Robin Hood that never shot in his bow, and talk of that virtue of mesnagery, who know not what belongs to it. It is by me that they must be advised. From me, therefore, take this advertisement and information, that what is imputed to me for a vice hath been done in imitation of the University and Parliament of Paris, places in which is to be found the true spring and source of the lively Idea of Pantheology, and all manner of justice. Let him be counted an heretic that doubteth thereof, and doth not firmly believe it. Yet they in one day eat up their bishop, or the revenue of the bishopric (is it not all one ?) for a whole year ; yea, some-times for two. This is done on the day he makes his entry, and is installed. Nor is there any place for an excuse ; for he cannot avoid it, unless he would be hooted at and stoned for his parsimony.

It hath been also esteemed an act flowing from the habit of the four cardinal virtues. Of Prudence in borrowing money before hand ; for none knows what may fall out. Who is able to tell if the world shall last yet three years ? But although it should continue longer, is there any man so foolish, as to have the confidence to promise himself three years ?

What fool so confident to say
That he shall live one other day ?

[1] Ch. XXXV.

P

Of Commutative Justice, in buying dear (I say upon trust) and selling goods cheap, (that is, for ready money). What says Cato in his *Book of Husbandry* to this purpose ? The father of a family, says he, must be a perpetual seller ; by which means it is impossible but that at last he shall become rich, if he have of vendible ware enough still ready for sale. Of Distributive Justice it doth partake, in giving entertainment to good (remark good) and gentle fellows, whom fortune had shipwrecked, like Ulysses, upon the rock of a hungry stomach with provision of sustenance : and likewise to good and young wenches (remark, good and young). For, according to the sentence of Hippocrates, Youth is impatient of hunger, chiefly if it be vigorous, lively, frolic, brisk, stirring, and bouncing. Which wanton lasses willingly and heartily devote themselves to the pleasure of honest men ; and are in so far both Platonic and Ciceronian, that they do acknowledge their being born into this world not to be for themselves alone, but that in their proper persons their country may claim one share and their friends another.

The virtue of Fortitude appears therein, by the cutting down and overthrowing of the great trees, like a second Milo making havoc of the dark forest, which did serve only to furnish dens, caves, and shelter to wolves, wild boars and foxes, and afford receptacles, withdrawing corners, and refuges to robbers, thieves, and murderers, lurking holes and skulking places for cut-throat assassinators, secret obscure shops for coiners of false money, and safe retreats for heretics ; laying woods even and level with the plain champagne fields and pleasant heathy ground, at the sound of the hautboys and bag-pipes playing reeks with the high and stately timber, and preparing seats and benches for the eve of the dreadful day of judgment.

I gave thereby proof of my Temperance in eating my corn whilst it was but grass, like an Hermit feeding upon sallets and roots, that, so affranchising myself from the yoke of sensual appetites to the utter disclaiming of their sovereignty, I might the better reserve somewhat in store, for the relief of the lame, blind, cripple, maimed, needy, poor, and wanting wretches. In taking this course I save the expense of the weed-grubbers, who gain money,—of the reapers in harvest-time, who drink lustily, and without water,—of gleaners, who will expect their cakes and bannocks,—of threshers, who leave no garlic, scallions, leeks, nor onions in our gardens, by the authority of Thestilis in Virgil,—and of the millers, who are generally thieves— and of the bakers, who are little better. Is this small saving or frugality ? Besides the mischief and damage of the field-mice, the decay of barns, and the destruction usually made by weasels and other vermin. Of corn in the blade you may make good green sauce, of a light concoction and easy digestion, which recreates the brain, and exhilarates the animal spirits, rejoiceth the sight, openeth the appetite, delighteth the taste, comforteth the heart, tickleth the tongue, cheereth the countenance, striking a fresh and lively colour, strengthening the muscles, tempers the blood, disburdens the midriff, refresheth the liver, disobstructs the spleen, easeth the kidneys, suppleth the reins, quickens the joints of the back, etc."[1].

If the extraordinarily brilliant dialectician's talent of this dazzling paradox can be said to go back to any tradition it must be that of those parodies upon legal pleadings and argumentation which the *Bazochiens* practised at Shrovetide. But during all the centuries that feats of dialectics flourished in our country never had the facetious literature of the Universities or the Law Courts created anything either in Latin or in French to approach this masterpiece.

The *châtelain* of Salmiguondin's debts were, thus, only a pretext for allowing Rabelais to parade in these paradoxes the mental training he had formerly received in the battles of scholastic philosophy. Flat, indeed, is the sentence in which Pantagruel answers this brilliant apologia. Borrowings, he gravely declares, are to be approved of only in two cases—when the work has not gained the reward it deserved, and where there has befallen an " unexpected loss of goods "[2]. Decidedly, Panurge's fancy was more suited to the narrator's humour than the Giant's wisdom.

When Panurge's debts have been paid by his suzerain, the new *châtelain* declares that he is thinking of marrying and, henceforward, almost the entire book will be taken up by this one question : will Panurge get married ?

How did Rabelais come to make this subject the principal theme of the *Third Book* ? The programme which he sketched in 1532 for a continuation of *Pantagruel*[3] indicates clearly that he contemplated conjugal infelicity for Panurge, as a theme for jokes which would, presumably, act as an interlude to the Giant's fabulous exploits. But the *Third Book* by no means shows us Panurge " married and made a cuckold within a month after his wedding ". It is merely a question of whether he will get married. To ascertain the fate which marriage holds in store for him many forms of divination are resorted to, grave persons are consulted. It affords the writer an occasion of discussing fortune-telling and, especially, of discoursing upon marriage. He expounds his general ideas upon women, and that was, around 1545, a subject especially appropriate for arousing interest in his readers.

[1] Ch. II.   [2] Ch. V.   [3] In his farewell to the reader, ch. XXXIV.

Rabelais, as we have seen, was not one of those bookworm scholars who are ignorant of the world. On the contrary, he was interested in and had a keen sense for topical affairs. Already, in 1532, he had exploited the popular taste for tales of giants' prowesses in composing his *Pantagruel*. The principal part of the *Third Book* is born of a desire to exploit another literary fashion. Towards 1545, the favourite subject of conversation and discussion among fashionable and literary people was the comparison between man and woman. To which of the two sexes should be assigned the advantage over the other ? Should women be held as equal or inferior to men ? The question was an old one which periodically occupied poets, romancers and moralists for the past hundreds of years. Already in the 14th century one of the two authors of the *Roman de la Rose*, Guillaume de Lorris, chivalrously extolled women, whilst his successor, Jean de Meung, declared them all without exception to be destined one day or another to infamy. At Fontenay-le-Comte this dispute had brought André Tiraqueau and Amaury Bouchard to loggerheads, and Friar François Rabelais may have had the opportunity of listening to them arguing, the one for, the other against, women[1]. In 1542, a Platonic poet of the Queen of Navarre's following, Antoine Héroët, had published in honour of women a poem entitled the *Parfaicte Amye*. It immediately achieved a marked success at Court and among the pre-Pléiade Petrarchian poets. The upholders of the superiority of the masculine sex answered it. La Borderie contrasted with the " perfect mistress " a type of woman much more common in the world, the frivolous and inconstant woman, *l'Amye de Court*. Fontaine, the poet, answered with the *Contre-Amye de Court*, and the renewed controversy brought forth numerous poems and dissertations. Rabelais considered that a book of clever or humorous discussions about marriage would benefit from this movement of interest in all that concerned the nature of woman[2].

He knew also, through having composed almanacks and prognostications, how eager men are to know the future and what a hidden attraction the different methods of divination exercise

---

[1] *Vide supra*, ch. II, pp. 25 *seqq.*

[2] The reflection of contemporary events and ideas in the *Third Book* is one of the new views on Rabelais advanced by M. Abel Lefranc. Cf. *Le Tiers Livre et la Querelle des femmes*, *R.É.R.*, II.

upon their minds. He therefore added to the consultation, properly so-called, an " exploration " by divination of Panurge's marital fate. By this means, he reintroduced into his story the miraculous element which he had banished from it, when, through lassitude and disgust, presumably, he had given up the invention of " terrible prowesses " and of a fabulous epic. And, especially, he was choosing thereby a subject which lent itself readily to his taste for displaying his erudition, and for introducing long expositions and for cultivating the pursuit of the exceptional cases.

Of this taste which Rabelais possessed in common with every scholar of his day—great compilers and skilful rummagers —there are already some indications in the first two books. *Gargantua*, for instance, offers[1], in connection with the symbolical meaning of the colours " white and blue ", a long discussion based on a " logical rule " of Aristotle's confirmed by the authority or the example of the Thracians, of the " Cretes ", of Lorenzo Valla, of the *Gospel*, of the *Liber Thobiæ*, the *Apocalypse*, the town of Alba, Rome, Pericles,—" Duke of Athens ",—Alexander of Aphrodisius, Proclus, Xenophon, Galen, Avicenna, and some other authors. Obtaining evidence of this nature in the writings of the Ancients, bringing it together, and grouping it was a pastime dear to our scholars. A whole literature of vulgarisation has resulted from it, that of the " diverse lessons " or " readings ", now forgotten[2]. Rabelais had given a good part of his spare time to compilations of this nature and the result of these leisure occupations is to be found in the *Third Book*.

We are not astonished at this display of erudition when Panurge is concerned with " explaining " the future by the *Sortes Virgilianæ*, that is to say, by interpreting Virgil opened at hazard. This was a method of divination renewed from the Ancients, and favoured by Humanists only, and the citing of famous examples—Alexander Severus, Hadrian, Claudius, Gordian, etc.—are in no wise out of place.

But whatever be the means of divination to which Pantagruel has recourse, be it popular or learned, the writer's method is always the same—a long dissertation justifies the method of

[1] Ch. X.
[2] Consult on this point Pierre Villey's *Sources et évolution des Essais de Montaigne* (Paris, 1910), vol. I. He was the first to point out the importance of these works of the scholars in 16th century literature.

divination adopted and a discussion, no less learned, advises upon the interpretation of the reply which Panurge obtains. If, for instance, he consults a soothsayer of the village of Panzoust—a vulgar fortune-teller—Rabelais quotes in favour of the choice of this personage Alexander the Great, and Roman Juno, and Aurinia, and Velleda, and Pythagoras, and Socrates and Empedocles. Then, the Sibyl's verses, variously interpreted by Pantagruel and Panurge, call forth corroboration by Demo-critus, Dioscorides, Catullus, Propertius, Tibullus, Porphyrus, " quick Philosopher, Eusthatius on the Iliad of Homer, and by many others ".

But Panurge's obstinacy is very great : the Virgilian Lotteries which have foretold him that he would be deceived, beaten and robbed have not deterred him from his project of marriage. He betakes himself to other means of divination : dreams, the Sibyl of Panzoust, Nazdecabre, the mute, Ramin-agrobis, the poet, Herr Trippa, the magician, each giving rise to learned disquisitions and debates.

Finally, Panurge decides to seek advice from a theologian, a doctor, a philosopher, and a lawyer. Pantagruel assembles them at a feast (with the exception of Bridoye, who has been summoned to appear before the Court of Parliament). Each one of them is questioned in turn and it is here takes place the consultation proper about women. Hippothadeus gives Pan-urge every assurance of happiness, provided that he marries a replica of the strong woman described by Solomon ; and Rondibilis, the doctor, leaves him no illusions about the fragility of woman. As to Trouillogan, the philosopher, he belongs to the Pyrrhonists and " ephectics " who reserve their opinions on all questions.

Disappointed at the wise men's answers, Panurge has recourse to Triboulet, the clown, wisdom being sometimes expounded from the mouths of fools : but this consultation is no more favourable than the others. Pantagruel and Panurge then decide to go to Cathay to consult the oracle of the Holy Bottle. The book ends with the preparations for the departure of Pantagruel's fleet.

The learning displayed by Rabelais in this consultation on marriage is composed of Latin, and even Greek, aphorisms, anecdotes and apophthegms. Its sources are the orators, poets and historians and, above all, the compilators. He owes more

to Gellius, Athenæus and Macrobius than to Plato or Virgil.
On the whole, it corresponds with the general culture of a
Humanist of his day. But Rabelais was, in addition, a legist
and a physician. From his knowledge of juridical and natural
sciences, he got the matter for two long digressions : Bridoye's
defence, and the praise of Pantagruelion.

The very day on which Bridoye, a judge at Fonsbeton[1],
was invited by Pantagruel to come to advise Panurge on the
question of his marriage, a Sheriff of the Parliament of Myrel-
ingue[2] had just come to summon him to appear in person before
this sovereign Court in order to defend a judgment which he
had given against the *élu* (subsidy-assessor) Toucheronde[3]
and against which the latter had appealed. He answers the
summons and Pantagruel is present at the hearing, which is
private. The Court asks Bridoye to account for the contested
judgment, which does not seem entirely fair. " For all his
reasons and excuses ", he simply says that he has become old,
that his sight has become feeble, and, hence, he may not have
clearly seen the points of the dice and may have taken a four
for a five, for instance, more especially since, in this affair,
he had used his smallest dice.

But what have dice to do with it ? asked the President,
dumbfounded. What dice do you mean ?—The dice of judgments, replies Bridoye, *alea judiciorum* ; and he quotes an
abundance of legal texts in which this expression occurs.
In the literal sense *alea*, it is true, means a *die*. In legal phraseology this metaphor meant the hazard of judgment[4]. Bridoye
interprets it literally, and the four thousand irreproachable
judgments which he has delivered during his forty years'
practice of his profession, have all been arrived at by a throw
of dice, *alea judiciorum*.

What, then, is your manner of procedure ? asks the President. " I conform myself ", answers Bridoye, " to the custom
of the judicatory, unto which our law commandeth us to have

---

[1] *Vide supra*, ch. V, p. 70.

[2] This name is fictitious. The term " centumviral " applied by Rabelais
to this Court (*Third Book*, ch. XXXIX) shows that he had in mind the
Parliament of Paris, frequently referred to in the Latin texts of the time as
centumviralis curia.

[3] *Vide supra*, ch. V, p. 70.

[4] Cf. the following expressions employed by Rabelais, *Third Book*, ch. V—
" L'amour que votre grâce me porte est hors le *dez d'estimation* " ; and ch.
XXIX : " les perfections d'un chacun sont hors tous *dez de jugement* ".

regard ". After having studied conscientiously all the documents of the case, I take the Defendant's bags (the *dossiers* were, at that time, put not in covers or files but in linen bags with labels on them) ; I place the said bags at the top of the table in my study and " liver chance " to the Defendant, that is to say, I throw the dice for him, the word *chance*, from the Latin *cadentia*, meaning precisely the fall of the dice. " That being done, I thereafter lay down upon the other end of the table the bags and sachels of the Plaintiff . . . then do I likewise and semblably throw the dice for him, and forthwith liver him his chance." I then give judgment in favour of him whom the chance of the dice has favoured.

But, objects the President, why not have recourse to the dice when the parties come before you for the first time ? What purpose do the documents and briefs contained in the bags serve ?—They serve me, answers Bridoye, in three ways, " exquisite, requisite and authentic ". Firstly for the form, which is so important in law that often " the formalities destroy the materialities and substances ". Secondly, they furnish me with an " honest and healthful " exercise. For, indeed, nothing is more salubrious or " more aromatizing, in this palatine world, than to empty bags, turn over papers, quote rolls, fill panniers and take inspection of causes ". Thirdly, this procedure allows time to mature the suit. Do not doctors wait until a boil is ripe before piercing it ? Nature itself teaches us to gather fruits when they are ripe, to marry our daughters when they are mature, to do nothing " but in a full maturity ". Perrin Dendin settled all the Poitevin villagers' disputes because he was content to wait until the dispute was ripe and the parties tired of pleading. It is therefore necessary to postpone judgment until the suits have reached maturity and are perfect in all their members.

Yes, but how do you proceed in criminal cases, asks the President, when the guilty party is caught in the very act ?— The formalities are still necessary, answers Bridoye ; but one written document, whatever it be, is sufficient to give birth to others. Hence, I request the Plaintiff to begin by taking a sleep, for instance, and to bring me an authentic document juridically witnessing that he has slept. It is inconceivable that this first document would not give rise to a crowd of others.

When they have multiplied in sufficient numbers to fill numerous bags, I again take up my dice.

The cause has been heard, and the President orders Bridoye to withdraw from the Court. His whole reasoning is based on plays upon words proper to the Latin language, the only one which was used in the teaching of the legal sciences. Bridoye depends upon his dice to pronounce his judgments because he interprets literally the expression *alea judiciorum*. Every detail of his subsequent procedure is justified by a pun of the same kind. He places the " bags " of the Plaintiff and of the Defendant opposite each other on his table, because an axiom states that clarity is born of opposition : *opposita juxta se posita magis elucescunt*. If he employs dice when the rights of the contending parties are obscure, it is in virtue of one of the rules of law (*Regulæ juris*) taught in the Schools—

Semper in obscuris quod minimum est sequimur.

And again, by playing on metaphors common in judicial language—the *body* or the *members of a process*—Bridoye likens the lawsuit to an organic being, which, at first shapeless like a young bear before the she-bear has licked it, is gradually brought to " perfection in all his members " : these are the " writings " and the " bags ".

Bridoye's reasoning is, then, constructed upon a series of puns which would scarcely have been understandable to any body except the " Palatine world " and the legists, who would be aware of the real meaning of the technical terms and sayings which Rabelais uses in a wrong sense. The same processes and the same comic effects recur in the details of the quotations of legal authorities. They are abundant in these four chapters, each one accompanied with repelling accuracy of detail, by title, paragraph, chapter and verse. Quoted in a wrong meaning, they become puns which were probably current among the audiences of the Faculty of Laws or the Courts. Such, is for example, the " peculiar (*peculiaris*) permission of the usher ", which becomes a " pecuniary permission ", for " *pecuniæ obediunt omnia*, as Baldus says in *l. singularia ff. Si certum pet. etc.*" Or again, the etymology of the word *muscarii* given by Bridoye, in connection with certain magistrates whom he surprised one day in their chamber of justice playing at muss (*mouche*, fly), that is, hitting with their caps the person appointed to be the *mouche*. These people who play muss, these *muscarii*, are excusable, he says, in virtue of the law de *excus-andis artificibus*. This law does, in fact, speak of *muscarii ;* only this word, which comes from *muscum* and not *musca*, designates the perfumiers who manufacture musk, and the *excusatio* granted to them by this law is an exemption from taxes limited to a few categories of artisans. These puns on *muscarii* and *excusandis* escape anyone who is not conversant with the text of the Code where these two words occur. Jokes of this kind were intended only for lawyers.

Similarly the chapters devoted to *Pantagruelion*[1] are a learned enigma, intended for naturalists and physicians. Pantagruel's vessels, about to depart to the Land of the Holy Bottle, are plentifully loaded with the herb called *Pantagruelion*. The narrator describes this herb minutely to us, its "little root somewhat hard and rough and roundish, terminating in an obtuse point, white, with few filaments "; its round stalk, "cane-like . . . full of long threads, straight, easy to be broken, jagged, snipped, nicked and notched a little after the manner of pillars and columns slightly furrowed . . . its branches ; its leaves, slit round about like unto a sickle and as betony ; its seed spherical, rhomboid. . . ." The reader familiar with botany will already have found the solution to the enigma : Pantagruelion is the name which Rabelais gives to hemp. But this erudite description is not intended for specialists only, like the long digression in which the writer enumerates six plants which take their name from their finder ; ten others which have kept the name of their place of origin ; two which have been named by antiphrasis ; ten which are called after their properties, four, for their admirable qualities ; seven, in memory of fabulous metamorphoses ; sixteen, through their resemblance to something ; and six on account of their shape. There was then a public who found pleasure in reading this catalogue.

This purely technical learning is rare. However learned may be the contents of the *Third Book*, they usually are neither dry nor tedious. Rabelais' learning is that of a scholar who has kept in touch with life. As in the preceding books, he mixed with his talk a host of points taken from his observation of contemporary manners. In the first place, we have his personal memories—here, a mention of Pierre Amy consulting

[1] Chs. XLIX–LI.

the " Virgilian Lotteries " before leaving the convent of the
Puy-Saint-Martin[1]; there, a recollection of the " learned
Villanovanus[2] ", the scholarly professor who had been Étienne
Dolet's teacher. The organic confusion of a fasting man recalls
to Rabelais the disorder of the fairs of Fontenay or Niort[3].
Ramínagrobis, the poet, has some features of Jean Lemaire
de Belges and of the Rhétoriqueur, Crétin. Rondibilis resembles
Rondelet, Rabelais' fellow-student in Montpellier, and Hippothadeus may be Jacques Lefèvre d'Étaples[4]. The scene has
suddenly been changed from Utopia to Touraine, and it is
indeed a village sorceress, a fortune-teller, who is described
in the " Sibyl of Panzoust " as being " in a pitiful bad plight
and condition . . . ill apparelled, worse nourished, toothless,
blear-eyed, crookshouldered, snotty . . . and drooping . . .
making ready a porridge of wrinkled green coleworts with a
swerd of yellow bacon, mixed with a twice-before-cooked sort
of waterish, unsavoury broth "[5]. Her accoutrements and household utensils are genuinely those of the district. Bridoye is a
living figure of a contemporary magistrate, a perfect representative of the " Palatine world " which Rabelias knew so well.
As for Triboulet, he is represented as coming by water from
Blois, which was, in fact, the native town of this jester, and of
the six phrases which he utters, one—" Buzançay hornpipe "—
is reminiscent of a village in Sologne. So that reality, and
usually humble reality, is mingled with learning to brighten it.

And did not the subject chosen by Rabelais lend itself to
jokes ? In giving his opinion of the *querelle des femmes*, he had
an opportunity of playing with a subject which for centuries
had furnished material for our tales, *fabliaux* and farces. The
malice of woman,

> " Ces éternels péchés dont pouffaient nos aïeux "[6],

it is that which excites his caustic *verve* and calls up in his
memory sayings, witticisms and jokes all referring to the
misfortunes of marriage. This was pre-eminently the *thème*

---

[1] Ch. X.   [2] Ch. XIII.   [3] *Ibid.*
[4] Conjecture of M. Abel Lefranc.
[5] Ch. XVII. Panzoult is a *commune* in the canton of l'Île-Bouchard, in the
Indre-et-Loire. There can still be seen a dwelling hollowed out in the
rock, which is supposed to have been the grotto of Rabelais' " Sibyl ".
However, the sorceress's " straw-thatched cottage " is not described as a
grotto.
[6] Alfred de Musset, *Sur La Paresse*, v. 40.

gaulois and Rabelais had no difficulty in finding comic anecdotes to illustrate his disquisitions. Hence, he made no endeavour to invent them. Hardly four or five of them are his own ; the rest are taken from the common stock-in-trade. But with what essentially personal artistry they are told ! Take, for example, this anecdote intended to show that women ordinarily long for things prohibited :

" I have heard it related, and it hath been told me for a verity, that Pope John XXII, passing on a day through the Abbey of Fontevrault, was in all humility required and besought by the Abbess, and other discreet mothers of the said convent, to grant them an indulgence, by means whereof they might confess themselves to one another, alleging, That religious women were subject to some petty secret slips and imperfections ; which would be a foul and burning shame for them to discover and to reveal to men, how sacerdotal soever their function were : but that they would freelier, more familiarly, and with greater cheerfulness, open to each other their offences, faults, and escapes, under the seal of confession. There is not anything, (answered the Pope,) fitting for you to impetrate of me, which I would not most willingly condescend unto : but I find one inconvenience. You know, confession should be kept secret, and women are not able to do so.—Exceeding well, (quoth they) most Holy Father, and much more closely than the best of men.

The said Pope on the very same day gave them in keeping a pretty box, wherein he purposely caused a little Linnet to be put, willing them very gently and courteously to lock it up in some sure and hidden place, and promising them, by the faith of a Pope, that he should yield to their request, if they would keep secret what was enclosed within that deposited box : enjoining them withal, not to presume one way nor other, directly or indirectly, to go about the opening thereof, under pain of the highest ecclesiastical censure, eternal excommunication.

The prohibition was no sooner made, but that they did all of them boil with a most ardent desire to know and see what kind of thing it was that was within it. They thought it long already, that the Pope was not gone, to the end they might jointly, with the more leisure and ease, apply themselves to the box-opening curiosity. The Holy Father, after he had given them his benediction, retired and withdrew himself to the pontifical lodgings of his own palace. But he was hardly gone three steps from without the gates of their cloister, when the good ladies throngingly, and as in a huddled crowd, pressing hard on the backs of one another, ran thrusting and shoving who should be first at the setting open of the forbidden box, and descrying of the *Quod latitat* within. On the very next day thereafter, the Pope made them another visit, of a full design, purpose, and intention, as they imagined, to dispatch the grant of their sought and wished-for indulgence. But before he would enter into any chat or communing with them, he commanded the casket to be brought unto him. It was done so accordingly ; but, by your leave, the bird was no more there. Then was it, that the Pope did represent to their maternities, how hard a matter and difficult it was for them to keep secrets revealed to them in confession, unmanifested to the ears of others, seeing for the space of four-and-twenty hours they were not able to lay up in secret a box, which he had highly recommended to their discretion, charge, and custody "[1].

A feeling of life and the choice of expressive details characterise these tales. These qualities which we have already noted in the previous book, here reach their point of perfection.

They are to be found in the portrayal of the characters. They are more numerous in this book than in *Gargantua* and *Pantagruel*. The *Third Book* first brings together those who were met with in each of the two preceding books—the giants, Gargantua and Pantagruel, their followers and particularly Friar John and Panurge. In addition new figures appear. They retain without doubt real individual characteristics which correspond to originals known to Rabelais, but they strike us mainly by their appearance of general truth. These are, Judge Bridoye, the theologian Hippothadeus, and Doctor Rondibilis.

Hippothadeus is the unctuous, placid and scrupulous theologian who methodically confesses Panurge and easily finds in Christian morality the answers to questions which perplex his questioner. The only difficulty would be to put his precepts into practice, since they presuppose that virtue in which Panurge is most lacking—Patience.

Rondibilis is a doctor after Rabelais' own heart. He derives his knowledge from good sources, the Ancients. But he is fond of expounding it at length and has no intention of adapting it to Panurge's individual case. The Faculty of Medicine, he declares, knows, in conformity with " the resolution of the ancient Platonics ", five means of restraining the carnal concupiscence from which Panurge complains that he is suffering, the fifth being marriage. And, although his client can have no possible interest in any but the last, he must nevertheless listen to the exposition of the four other cures which are wine taken immoderately, certain drugs and plants, assiduous labour and fervent study[2].

[1] Ch. XXXIV.   [2] Ch. XXXI.

Then the learned physician descends from the empyrean of speculative considerations to the ground of material interests : Panurge " approaching somewhat nearer to him clapped into his hand, without the speaking of so much as one word, four rose nobles. Rondibilis did shut his fist upon them right kindly ; yet, as if it had displeased him to make acceptance of such golden presents, he in a start, as if he had been wroth said : He, he, he, he, he, there was no need of anything, I thank you nevertheless. From wicked folks I take nothing, and from honest people I refuse nothing. I shall be always, sir, at your command. Provided that I pay you well, quoth Panurge. That, quoth Rondibilis, is understood "[1].

Panurge in the *Third Book* is perceptibly different from the " apostle " who, in the campaign of Dipsodie, helped the giant's strength[2] with his cunning, his " slight ". His character is rather that which Rabelais had attributed to him when he presented him to us as the Giant's companion on the Hill of Sainte-Geneviève. He was then represented as flying from blows " whereof he was naturally fearful "[3]. This cowardice is developed to a remarkable degree in the *châtelain* of Salmi-guondin. He is repeatedly terror-stricken—when visiting the Sybil of Panzoust, in presence of Nazdecabre, and in Ramin-agrobis' room, which he sees already overrun with devils because the good poet has spoken ill of monks. Terror is his most ordinary behaviour at the shadow of the slightest danger.

Moreover, this superficial brilliance in argument, with which Rabelais had endowed him even in *Pantagruel*, supplies him with numerous sophisms to flatter his desires or illusions. Neither the advice, nor the predictions, nor the experience of others can bring him to face realities. Whatever may be the answers which his questions meet with (and they all advise him against getting married) the ingenuity of his mind always puts upon them some interpretation favourable to his desires. On that account, the portrayal of this personage takes on a general character. Panurge represents not only cunning or cowardice. He illustrates a tendency common to all mankind —facility in allowing oneself to be blinded by self-love, desire or passion. Which of us can boast, when the heart is pre-occupied by some violent desire, of being impervious to the

---

[1] Ch. XXXIV.   [2] *Vide supra*, pp. 127–128.
[3] *Pantagruel*, end of ch. XXI.

sophisms that our reasoning advances, or to the illusions of our imagination ? Of what weight are the advice or experience of others in crises where the individual seeks self-realisation by following the inner laws of his own being ?

" Nous n'écoutons d'instincts que ceux qui sont les nôtres,
Et ne croyons le mal que quand il est venu "[1].

Rabelais, like the great comic artist he was, has drawn the most comic effects from the influence of these pre-occupations upon the general temperament of his personage. With what eagerness does Panurge invite Father Hippothadeus to his wedding immediately the theologian advises him to marry in order to escape from his concupiscence. " Grammercy, my good father. In truth I am resolved now to marry, and without fail I shall do it quickly. I invite you to my wedding. By the body of a hen, we shall make good cheer, and be as merry as crickets. You shall wear the bridegroom's colours, and, if we eat a goose, my wife shall not roast it for me. I will intreat you to lead up the first dance of the bride's maids, if it may please you to do me so much favour and honour ".

But since Hippothadeus cannot guarantee Panurge that his marriage will be a happy one, according as he enumerates the conditions upon which conjugal bliss depends, the latter's enthusiasm gradually fades away, and gives place to smothered impatience, so that the conversation comes to an end with impatient words : " My honest father, I believe it will be your best not to come to my wedding. The clutter and dingle-dangle noise of marriage guests will but disturb you and break the serious fancies of your brain. You love repose with solitude and silence ; I really believe you will not come. And then you dance but indifferently, and would be out of countenance at the first entry. I will send you some good things to your chamber, together with the bride's favour, and there you may drink our health, if it may stand with your good liking "[2].

In contrast to Panurge's blindness and impatience are Pantagruel's calm and reflection. He is the wise man according to Rabelais. It is from him, no doubt, we are to expect the result of the consultation on marriage. Rondelet gives us Rabelais' opinion of women when, having regard to her

---

[1] La Fontaine, *L'Hirondelle et ses petits.*   [2] Ch. XXX.

inconstancy and imperfection, he sees in her an error of Nature. The reasons of this fragility and inconstancy being of the physiological order, there is no room for hoping that woman will ever improve[1]. Does it not follow that marriage should be avoided and that Panurge's hesitancies are even to be approved of ? Such is not Pantagruel's opinion :

" We see ", he says, " some so happy in the fortune of this nuptial encounter, that their family shineth, as it were, with the radiant effulgency of an idea, model, or representation of the joys of paradise ; and perceive others, again, to be so unluckily matched in the conjugal yoke, that those very basest of devils, which tempt the hermits that inhabit the Deserts of Thebais and Montserrat, are not more miserable than they "[2]. What, then, is to be done ? When once one goes about it, give it a fair chance, like the lansquenets, who, at the moment of charging, " bow their heads, kiss the ground and recommend the success of the residue to the disposure of Almighty God ".

This solution is a common-sense one, and in no way original. Pantagruel usually stops at these average ideas. The hero which he was in the 1532 book has become a philosopher ; but his philosophy is hardly anything besides the reflection of a fine healthy state of body and mind. It consists, before all else, in maintaining perfect serenity in the face of events and granting the maximum of indulgence to human follies. He remonstrates with the extravagant *châtelain* of Salmiguondin who has squandered his fortune—then he pays his debts[3]. Panurge having adopted an unusual style of dress, he protests that we should not run contrary to others on questions which are in themselves indifferent[4]. Herr Trippa's astrology and

---

[1] Cf. the passage quoted p. 102 : " When I say womankind, I speak of a sex so frail, etc."   [2] Ch. X.

[3] " Pantagruel, being advertised of this his lavishness, was in good sooth no way offended at the matter, angry nor sorry. . . . He only drew Panurge aside, and then, making to him a sweet remonstrance and mild admonition, very gently represented before him in strong arguments, That, if he should continue in such an unthrifty course of living, and not become a better mesnagier, it would prove altogether impossible for him, or at least hugely difficult at any time to make him rich ". *Third Book*, ch. II. " Howsoever let us leave this discourse, and from henceforward do not hang upon creditors, nor tie yourself to them. I make account for the time past to rid you freely of them, and from their bondage to deliver you ". *Ibid.*, ch. V.

[4] " Every one overflowingly aboundeth in his own sense and fancy ; yea, in things of a foreign consideration, altogether extrinsical and indifferent, which in and of themselves are neither commendable nor bad, because they proceed not from the interior of the thoughts and heart, which is the shop of all good and evil ". Ch. VII.

many other forms of divination seem to him mere foolishness ;
but he has some respect for the vaticination of the dying. It
is clear that, in the wisdom of the Ancients, it is the Stoic
formula *Nil mirari*, which best corresponds to that serenity
which is the capital virtue Rabelais has endowed him with :
" He took all things in good part, and interpreted every action
to the best sense. He never vexed nor disquieted himself with
the least pretence of dislike to anything, because he knew that
he must have most grossly abandoned the divine mansion of
reason, if he had permitted his mind to be never so little
grieved, afflicted, or altered at any occasion whatsoever. For
all the goods that the heaven covereth, and that the earth
containeth, in all their dimensions of height, depth, breadth
and length, are not of so much worth, as that we should for
them disturb or disorder our affections, trouble or perplex
our senses or spirits "[1].

[1] Ch. II. Cf. with this, the definition of *Pantagruelism* given in the *New
Prologue* to the *Fourth Book* : " *C'est certaine gayeté d'esprit conficte en mespris
des choses fortuites*". (" It is a certain Jollity of Mind, pickled in the scorn of
Fortune ".)

CHAPTER XV

IN order to ensure for the *Third Book of Pantagruel* a quiet fate Rabelais had taken numerous precautions : he had asked for, and obtained, from the King a " privilege " to print it ; he had, in a dedicatory poem of ten verses, placed his work under the protection of the Queen of Navarre ; he had refrained from any epigrams against the theologians of the Sorbonne ; he had joined his protest to those of the royal jurists who wished to forbid marriage *sine parentum consensu*. It was in vain : the *Third Book* was condemned by the Sorbonne, just as the first two had been.

What were the reasons for this ecclesiastical censure ? We know them only from the defence which Rabelais wrote of his case, some years later, in an epistle to Cardinal de Châtillon placed as a dedication to the *Fourth Book*. They reproached his work with being " stuffed with various heresies " although they could not anywhere " show one single instance "[1]. A printer's error which had substituted the word *ass* (*âne*) for *soul* (*âme*) in the phrase : " His *soul* goeth infallibly to thirty thousand panniers full of devils "[2], is said to have been instanced as an indication of the author's irreligion. And Rabelais scores a victory by quoting such an example of his enemies' bias to discover " sparks of heresy " in his text. He adds that King François I, who had caused these books to be " carefully and distinctly read to him by the most learned and faithful anagnost (reader) in this kingdom, . . . abhorred a certain envious, ignorant, hypocritical informer (*quelque mangeur de serpens*) who grounded a mortal heresy on an *n* put instead of an *m* by the carelessness of the printers ".

In other times, this laughable misprint would have been judged inoffensive. It had already occurred in the *Cent*

---

[1] Marty-Laveaux, *op. cit.*, vol. II, p. 250.
[2] *Third Book*, ch. XXII.

Nouvelles nouvelles[1] without shocking anybody. But this happened during a phase of reaction against Lutherans and freethinkers. The year 1546 beheld the execution of Étienne Dolet, burned in the Place Maubert for having, amongst other things, attributed to Plato the statement that man is annihilated after death. The *Third Book* did not, it is true, attack the theologians nor expound heretical ideas. But it breathed a quiet indifference with regard to religious questions to which theologians attached the highest importance. Whoever on his death-bed disdained the aids of religion was suspected of heresy. Now, that is exactly the case with the poet Raminagrobis, on the point of death, who feels himself already reposing in the bosom of God, having chased from his room the mendicant friars in white, black, brown and speckled habits[2]. Panurge is seized with terror at the idea of the evils that this iniquity may bring upon the house into which he has come : he imagines that the dying man's room is already full of devils. But Friar Jean des Entommeures is not in the least scandalised : he is amused at Panurge's cowardice. And, no doubt, to Rabelais' mind, this scene was only a humorous theme. The theologians thought otherwise.

By the 28th March, 1546, Rabelais, who was disturbed by the Sorbonne's condemnation of his book, had crossed the frontier to Metz[3]. He hastened to write thence to Jean Sturm, rector of the *gymnasium* of Strasbourg, one of the Du Bellays' best diplomatic agents in Germany. He thought, perhaps, of going to Sturm to Saverne or Strasbourg; and the latter assured Cardinal du Bellay that he would come to his aid as soon as he arrived. But Rabelais was to remain at Metz.

It is difficult to know what kept him there. He was, perhaps, afraid of feeling too much out of his element in Alsace, where the language spoken was German. In Metz, a free town of the Empire, French was the spoken language. Its intellectual life was not, indeed, very intense. Metz had produced barely one Humanist, in the first quarter of the 16th century, the

---

[1] *Nouvelle* LXXIX.   [2] *Third Book*, ch. XXI.
[3] This date is known to us from a letter of John Sturm's to Cardinal du Bellay, on March 28th of a year not given. M. A. Lefranc has shown that it must be assigned to 1546 (*R.É.R.*, III, 6) because of a reference in it to Charles V's entry into Spires. This is what Sturm says in it with reference to Rabelais : " Tempora etiam Rabelæsum ejecerunt e Gallia φεῦ τῶν χρόνων. Non dum ad nos venit [Sturm is at Saverne]. Metis consistit ut audio, inde enim nos salutavit. Adero ipsi quibuscumque rebus potero cum ad nos venerit."

jurist Claude Chansonnette, and he had left it to teach in Bâle and Fribourg-en-Brisgau.[1] Protestantism counted many adherents there[2] and a wide tolerance of ideas seems to have reigned, for, before Rabelais, a physician of François I, of German origin, John Gonthier d'Andernach, had sought refuge there in 1537.[3]

One circumstance may have decided Rabelais upon taking up his residence at Metz—the fact that his friend Étienne Lorens, seigneur of Saint-Ayl, had a house there, where he used to stay during his frequent journeys in Alsace, as *liaison*-agent between Jean du Bellay and François I's German allies. The house which Rabelais occupied in the Jewish quarter, in the *Ju-rue*, was still to be seen at the beginning of the eighteenth century, according to Le Duchat[4]. Was it Étienne Lorens' house ?

The municipal Register of Accounts testifies that he quickly entered the service of the municipality—but in what capacity is not specified. It has been conjectured that he was Physician to the town, but there are no real grounds for the supposition. Before him, many doctors, including John Gonthier d'Andernach, had been employed as councillors, orators or secretaries to the Municipality, with the task of representing the magistrature elsewhere or dealing with disputed matters. Rabelais' salary was, in fact, that corresponding to the post of councillor and not that of doctor[5]. It came to one hundred and twenty *livres* annually, about two thousand four hundred gold francs (£96). This was much more than Rabelais used to receive fourteen years previously at Lyons, as physician to the Great Hospital of the Rhône. It was insufficient for his needs. Hence, we need not be surprised at the terms of a letter which he sent, on February 6th, 1547, to Jean du Bellay.

It is a further appeal for assistance. He complains of the

---

[1] It is he who had plagiarised Tiraqueau's *De legibus connubialibus*. *Vide supra*, p. 26.

[2] On the political and religious situation at Metz before 1552, cf. Gaston Zeller's excellent work, *La réunion de Metz à la France* (1552-1648). Part I, *L'occupation*. (Publications de la Faculté des Lettres de l'Université de Strasbourg, fascicule 35), 1926.

[3] He had there prepared the second edition of his treatise on *L'Anatomie du corps humain*, which was published at Lyons in 1541. In 1542, he went to Strasbourg.

[4] In his edition of Rabelais, vol. IV, p. 311, note 7.

[5] This has been pointed out by M. Gaston Zeller in an article on *Le séjour de Rabelais à Metz, Rev. XVIe siècle*, 1927, fasc. 1.

" necessity and anxiety " to which he is reduced and begs for an *alms*. " In truth, Monseigneur, if you have not pity on me, I do not know what I am to do, unless in extreme despair, I enter the service of somebody here, with obvious damage and loss to my studies. It is impossible to live more frugally than I do, and however little you may give me of the great goods with which God has endowed you, I shall pull through by poor living and honest conduct as I have hitherto done, for the honour of the house from which I issued on my departure from France "[1].

The Seigneur de Saint-Ayl, upon whom Rabelais counted to explain more fully his misery to Cardinal du Bellay, merely forwarded his letter without even joining to it a word of recommendation. He preferred to draw the Cardinal's attention to one of his agents in Alsace, whose poverty, doubtless, seemed to him more real than that of the Metz town-councillor.

On 24th June, Rabelais was still at Metz, and received thirty *livres* for the quarter from Easter to the Feast of Saint John. The remainder of the Register of Accounts being missing, it is not known how much longer he remained in the town's employment. It is probable that he left in the first quarter of 1548 (n.s.). François I's death (March, 1547) had brought about a change in Jean du Bellay's position. He had been ordered by Henri II, along with all the French cardinals, to go to Rome to live. He was entrusted with the office of " Protector of the affairs of France " in Italy, with full authority over the other cardinals. He was suffering from sciatica and pains in his loins. He needed a doctor ; every cardinal had one in his household. So he sent for Rabelais. The latter, therefore, left Metz, where he had been about two years.

His subsequent writings contain some traces of this stay : a Lorrain saying—*Deu, Colas faillon*, of which he gives the

[1] This letter, given in full by Marty-Laveaux (*op. cit.*, vol. III, p. 390), is in the Library of the Medical Faculty of Montpellier (H. 24, fol.) and is one of a collection belonging originally to Jean Bouhier, Conseiller in the Parliament of Dijon. It was first published by Libri in the *Journal des Savants*, 1842, p. 44.

On Rabelais' stay in Metz, cf. Heulhard, *op. cit.* ; A. Lefranc, *Les dates du séjour de Rabelais à Metz*, R.É.R., III, pp. 1–11 ; Romier, *Notes critiques et documents sur le dernier voyage de Rabelais en Italie*, R.É.R., X, pp. 113–142 ; H. Clouzot, *Le véritable nom du seigneur de Saint-Ayl*, R.E.R., III, pp. 351–366, and *Nouveaux documents sur Saint-Ayl*, R.É.R., VI, pp. 190–195 ; my Introduction to the " partial edition " of the *Fourth Book* (1548), Paris, 1909 ; and the article by Gaston Zeller, *supra cit.*, p. 228, note 5.

translation, " De par Saint Nicolas, compaignon "[1] (By St. Nicholas, my friend) ; an allusion to the *Graulli*, or dragon of Saint Clement, a statue of a monster which was carried in procession in the streets of Metz on the feast of Saint Mark and on Rogation-days, " well mouth-cloven, having a goodly pair of wide, broad jaws, lined with two rows of teeth, upper tier and under tier, which, by the magic of a small twine hid in the hollow part of the golden staff, were made to clash, clatter and rattle dreadfully one against another "[2].

For Rabelais had utilised the free time which his duties allowed him, to begin the composition of a fourth book of his *Pantagruel*. While passing through Lyons, on his way to Italy, being in urgent need of money, he hurriedly gave his manuscript to the bookseller Pierre de Tours, François Juste's successor, who published the work[3], dated 1548, simultaneously with an Almanack[4] for the same year, 1548.

This edition, which is usually referred to as the partial edition of the *Fourth Book*, represents only about one-third of the complete book. It ends abruptly, with an unfinished sentence, in the middle of an episode, which is the eleventh chapter of this text and the twenty-fifth in the complete edition. The large proportion of additions and corrections made by Rabelais in the definitive text proves that this early version was composed hastily and that he himself considered it imperfect. Why then did he publish it ? Firstly, in order to obtain some money before going to Italy, and also, perhaps, to proclaim his innocence and reply to his calumniators. For his prologue enlarges upon this idea which he had already expressed : that his writings are merely " fooleries " designed to cheer " the sick, gouty and hapless ", they are " comical pastimes neither offending God, nor the King, nor anyone else ". In truth, with the exception of one invective in the *Prologue* against the

---

[1] *Fourth Book*, ch. VI, and *Brièfve declaration d'aucunes dictions plus obscures contenues au quatriesme livre*.

[2] *Fourth Book*, ch. LIX.

[3] Possibly at the beginning of 1548. It was believed, following Heulhard, that a reference to *Henricus* (coins stamped with the effigy of Henri II), in ch. III, *Fourth Book*, showed that the date of the printing of this book must be placed later than January 31st, 1548, the date on which these coins were issued. M. Romier has shown (*art. cit.*, p. 229, note 1, pp. 128–129) that from the outset of Henri II's reign, double gold *écus* were struck at the Paris Mint and called *Henris*.

[4] We know of this Almanack only from a reference to it in La Croix du Maine and Du Verdier. Cf. C.P.P. Plan, *Bibliographie rabelaisienne*, p. 231.

" *caphards, cagots, Matagotz, Botineurs, Papelards, Burgotz, Patespelues, Porteurs de Rogatons, Chattemites* ", and against all calumniators of his writings, not expressly specified, there occurs neither an attack nor a satirical shaft directed against the Sorbonne or the monks. A single witticism on the decrees of the " Mateologians ", which he apologises for not being conversant with, and a reference to a Pythagorean thesis on the mortality of the soul[1] (followed immediately, be it remarked, by the words " nevertheless, the contrary is the truth ") represent the total daring of his pen. Moreover, as an extra precaution, they are erased from the complete edition. Hence, he was able to set out for Italy with a feeling of security for his work, which could not be criticised except by calumniators. As far as his person was concerned, it was beyond the reach of these enemies since it crossed the frontier.

The " continuation of the Pantagrueline story " which, according to the declaration of the *Prologue*, the author consents to " grant " to the prayers of his readers, is the odyssey of Pantagruel, in search of this Holy Bottle, the Oracle of which is to put an end to Panurge's perplexities concerning his marriage. It is the story of a voyage, its landings, encounters, storms and descriptions of foreign countries. Voyages of this kind were traditional, since Homer, in all epics and in these prose epics which the adventure tales were. Rabelais had already included one in his first work—the Giant's circumnavigation while going from Honfleur to Dipsodie, that is Scythia (the country of Thirst, *sitis*), by the usual route of the Portuguese navigators who followed the African and, then, the Indian coasts. The " conclusion " of this book included among the adventures of Pantagruel, which were still to be described, a voyage on the Atlantic to the Cannibal and Perlas Islands, in the southern Lesser Antilles. An imitator had, as we have seen, composed the *Navigations of Panurge*, in which we might look in vain for a mention of some of those new countries which Portuguese, Spanish, or French navigators had just discovered.

This was a notable blunder, which a writer acquainted with the interests of the cultivated public would not have committed. Rabelais was not unaware that the discovery of Canada by Jacques Cartier and Jean Alphonse le Saintongeois

[1] Ch. X.

(1534) had created a great feeling of interest in maritime affairs, navigation, explorations and the discovery of the great seafaring routes. He knew that, in particular, the great aim and constant efforts of our navigators had been directed towards the discovery of a passage by North-Western America leading to the fabled Cathay, Northern China. It was while looking for this north-western passage that Cartier had discovered Canada. Rabelais, then, decided to assign the same itinerary to Pantagruel's fleet, setting forth to the country of the Holy Bottle, for the advice of the pilot-in-chief was,

" Seeing that the Oracle of the Holy Bottle lay near Cathay, in the Upper India, . . . not to steer the course which the Portuguese use, while sailing through the torrid Zone and Cape Bona Speranza, at the south point of Africa, beyond the equinoctial line, and losing sight of the Northern Pole, their guide, they make a prodigious long voyage ; but rather to keep as near the parallel of the said India as possible, and to tack to the westward of the said Pole, so that, winding under the North, they might find themselves in the latitude of the port of Olone, without coming nearer it for fear of being shut up in the frozen sea ; whereas, following this canonical turn by the said parallel, they must have that on the right to the eastward, which at their departure was on their left. This proved a much shorter cut "[1].

Having once indicated this itinerary, the author takes full liberty in joining to a number of real data, obtained from the study of maps, or the perusal of the narrative of Cartier or other navigators, a host of imaginary elements, creations of his own imagination or fabulous traditions. His narrative recalls the 16th century maps or planispheres on which are to be seen beyond the coast-lines, drawn in conformity with the explorers' descriptions and filled with place-names still in use to-day, a hinterland inhabited by fabulous beings, such as unicorns, or pigmies in battle against cranes.

Three episodes stand out particularly in this first edition of the *Fourth Book*—the meeting with Dindenault, the storm and the call at the Island of Procuration.

It is from Folengo's *Macaronea* that Rabelais borrowed the idea for the first two. He treats them with a realistic touch which marks them with a stamp of originality. In Folengo the whole interest of the episode lies in the unexpectedness of Cingar's trick. Some Ticinese peasants, who had engaged for

[1] Ch. I.

their own use the ship moored in the harbour, find the hero
Baldus and his escort on board. They protest against this
intrusion by armed men, a dangerous company for honest
peasants. Baldus wants to punish this insolence. Cingar—
the Panurge of this burlesque *épopée*—cannot endure seeing
a gentleman draw his sword upon this rabble; it remains
for him to punish, by a trick of his own, the peasants' insolence.
Scarcely has the ship arrived in the open sea when, addressing
one of the peasants, he expresses a wish to buy a sheep. The
Ticinese, delighted at this unexpected good fortune, gives him
one without haggling over the price. Cingar pays him in false
coin, and, suddenly, throws the animal overboard, with the
result that all the sheep in the ship rush after it one by one.
Folengo then revels in a lengthy description of the sea covered
with these wool-bearers and of Neptune swallowing up their
flesh.

Rabelais changes the interest of the scene. Panurge is not
concerned with a nondescript shepherd taken from amongst
a crowd of peasants. He has before him a " somebody ",
whom the author describes in truculent terms : Dindenault,
of Taillebourg, in Saintonge, on the borders of Gascony,
boastful, proud and vainglorious. His first words are a joke
which is insulting to Panurge, who replies with an insult.
The quarrel is hushed up and a reconciliation arranged ; the
two enemies are even prevailed upon " to drink in course to
one another ". But Panurge plans his revenge. It is simply
a question of getting the drover to sell him one of his sheep.
The bargaining scene is the one which Rabelais has described
most fully. Panurge answers Dindenault's insolent boasting
in praise of his goods with the most imperturbable patience.

" This done, Panurge earnestly entreated him to sell him one of
his sheep. But the other answered him, Is it come to that, friend
and neighbour ? Would you put tricks upon travellers ? Alas,
how finely you love to play upon poor folk ! Nay, you seem a rare
chapman, that is the truth of it. Oh what a mighty sheep merchant
you are ! In good faith, you look liker one of the diving trade, than
a buyer of sheep. Adzookers, what a blessing it would be to have
one's purse, well lined with chink, near your worship at a tripe-
house, when it begins to thaw ! Humph, humph, did not we know
you well, you might serve one a slippery trick ! Pray do but see,
good people, what a mighty conjuror the fellow would be reckoned.—
Patience, (said Panurge,) but waving that, be so kind as to sell me

one of your sheep. Come, how much ?—What do you mean, master of mine ? (answered the other). They are long-woolled sheep : from these did Jason take his golden fleece. The order of the house of Burgundy was drawn from them. Zwoons, man, they are oriental sheep, topping sheep, fatted sheep, sheep of quality.—Be it so, (said Panurge,) but sell me one of them, I beseech you, and that for a cause, paying you ready money upon the nail, in good and lawful occidental current cash. Wilt say how much.—Hark ye, friend of mine, (answered the other,) with the fleece of these, your fine Rouen cloth is to be made ; your Leominster superfine wool is mine arse to it ; mere flock in comparison. Of their skins the best cordovan will be made, which shall be sold for Turkey and Montelimart, or for Spanish leather at least. Of the guts shall be made fiddle and harp strings, that will sell as dear as if they came from Munican. What do you think of it, hah ?—If you please, sell me one of them, (said Panurge,) and I will be yours for ever. Look, here is ready cash. What's the price ? This he said exhibiting his purse stuffed with new Henricuses. Neighbour, my friend, (answered the merchant,) they are meat for none but Kings and Princes ; their flesh is so delicate, so savoury, and so dainty, that one would swear it melted in the mouth. I bring them out of a country where the very hogs, (God be with us,) live on nothing but Myrobalans. The sows are fed only with orange-flowers "[1].

And Dindenault continues his harangue, enriched it is true with all Rabelais' humour, but also with jokes, familiar touches, and thrusts, which remind us of the fair-greens of Touraine or Poitou, impossible in its extraordinary fluency, and yet painting a true picture of a type of cattle-dealer.

The storm, which takes up the first third of the 12th of the *Macaronea*, furnished Rabelais with the contrast between the hero, Baldus' activity, and the inertia and cowardice of Cingar. He likewise draws a contrast between the behaviour of the affrighted Panurge and that of the energetic Friar Jean des Entommeures. Folengo, in addition, had drawn colourful effects from the confusion reigning on the ship during the tempest—the confusion of shouts and commands, the creaking of pulleys, the whistling of the wind in the rigging. But his description was vague. With Rabelais it becomes admirably clear, even technical :

" Wilt thou come, ho devil ? (said Friar John). Midshipman, my friend ; O the rare lieutenant !—Here, Gymnast, here on the poop. Boy, younker, see hoyh. Mind the pumps, or the devil choke thee. Hast thou hurt thyself ? Zoons, here fasten it to one of these blocks. On this side, in the devil's name, hay—so my boy. Ah ! Friar John

[1] Ch. III.

(said Panurge,) good ghostly father, dear friend, do not let us swear, you sin. . . . By the virtue (said Friar John) of the blood, the flesh, the belly, the head, if I hear thee again howling, thou cuckoldy cur, I will maul thee worse than any sea wolf. Ods fish, why do we not take him by the lugs and throw him overboard to the bottom of the sea ? Here, sailor, ho honest fellow. Thus, thus, my friend, hold fast above. In truth, here is a sad lightning and thundering ; I think that all the devils are got loose ; it is holiday with them ; or else Madame Proserpine is in child's labour ; all the devils dance a morrice "[1].

The abundance of nautical terms is one of the striking features of this description—names of the sails and of the rigging, commands, names of the various parts of the ship, sailors' swearwords and slang. Rabelais has drawn upon this jargon to give precision and colour to his narrative ; then, gradually, as often happens with him, he has, so to speak, become drunk with the sound of these new words ; he has collected them together, piled and heaped them up for the pleasure of deriving an artistic joy from the very richness of this strange vocabulary.

The landing on Procuration Island, abode of the Catchpoles (*Chicanoux*) is the first of these satirical allegories which Rabelais will make the main subject of the *Fourth Book* in the definitive edition. The process, well known since Aristophanes, consists in picking out of society a class of individuals who have, as features in common, the same habits, the same vices, the same defects, the same professional taint. Rabelais isolates from the world and relegates to the Île de Procuration (Pettifogging Island) all those sergeants and other judicial officers who were popularly referred to under the name of Catchpoles. Among those acts which characterise this class of individuals, he chooses those which most easily lend themselves to farcical treatment. It may happen that the " catchpoles " when giving notice of their " exploits "—legal writs and summonses—are liable to be beaten by the people on whom they serve them. Rabelais makes this the essential part of their profession. The Catchpoles earn their living by being thrashed ; " blows are their true harvest ". Friar John, to whom this strange manner of living is explained, tests the nature of the Catchpoles, by punching one of them " on his red snout " :

" He had no sooner picked him out from the rest, but I perceived they all muttered and grumbled ; it was through envy, and I heard

[1] Ch. IX.

a tall young Catchpole, a notable scholar, a pretty fellow at his pen, and (according to public report) much cried up for his honesty at Doctors-Commons, making his complaint and muttering, because this same crimson phiz carried away all the practice ; and that if there were but a score and a half of bastinadoes to be got [in all the territory] he would certainly run away with eight [and a half] and twenty of them. Friar John so unmercifully thrashed, thumped and belaboured him, back and belly, sides, legs, and arms, head, feet, and so forth, with the home and frequently repeated application of one of the best members of a faggot, that I took him to be a dead man : then he gave him the twenty ducats ; which made the dog get on his legs, pleased like a little king or two. The rest were saying to Friar John, Sir, Sir, brother devil, if it please you to do us the favour to beat some of us for less money, we are all at your devilship's command, we are all at your command, they said likewise to Panurge, to Gymnaste and others ; but none of them heeded them "[1].

Thus, in this earlier version of the *Fourth Book*, Rabelais, leaving aside the discussions and dissertations which filled the *Third Book*, has returned to the narrations—the *narrés*, as he himself calls them. It can even be said that he does not overdo the parade of learning which characterised the preceding book. Some, however, do occur ; for example, in the chapter[2] where we are told the strange death of Bringuenarilles, the swallower of windmills. This personage, who is here mentioned for the first time by Rabelais, is taken from the work entitled the *Merveilleuses Navigations de Panurge*, where he is described as swallowing a windmill " with the miller and his dog "[3]. Rabelais conceives the idea of making him die a most fantastic death. " He choked himself with eating a huge lump of fresh butter at the mouth of a hot oven, by the advice of physicians ". And Rabelais in this connection takes occasion to quote for us seven strange deaths, of which five are narrated by ancient authors, and to introduce in this development a parenthesis, of equally learned origin, upon Alexander the Great's meeting with the " Gymnosophists of India ".

Such are the features of this partial edition of the *Fourth Book* which Rabelais may have begun before coming to Metz and of which he will not publish the continuation until 1552.

At Rome, then, where he was in the summer of 1548[4],

---

[1] Ch. VI.   [2] Ch. VII.   [3] Ch. VIII. *Vide supra*, p. 199.

[4] We have a receipt of June 18th given by Rabelais for the sum of 32 *écus* paid to him by Arnauld Combraglia, of Paris, under his own signature or in

his time was divided between his duties as physician to the Cardinal, whose health was precarious, and learned conversations with some Humanists. He met there the Bishop of Rodez, Georges d'Armagnac, he of whom he had been able to state as far back as 1532, in his letter to Erasmus, that he had long since been his friend. This prelate, who had been ambassador at Venice from 1536 to 1539, was then ambassador at Rome. Paul III had made him Cardinal in 1544. He had with him amongst his followers a Humanist devoted to the study of architecture, Guillaume Philandrier[1]. Rabelais mentions him as a " great friend " in a note of the *Briéfve declaration* . . . appended to the 1552 edition of his *Fourth Book*, concerning the word *Æoliopyle*, a scientific term. " It is ", he says, " a closed bronze instrument, in which is a little opening, and if you put water into it and place it near the fire, you will see air come forth steadily from it. . . . See ", he adds, "what our great friend and lord, M. Philander, has written thereon, in his work on the first book of Vitruvius "[2]. Indeed, another Humanist then living in Venice, Pierre de Paschal, having occasion to write to Philandrier, in September, 1548, does not fail to send through him his greetings to Rabelais.[3] Rome sheltered, in addition, a young French poet, Louis des Masures, who had left France for some reason still unknown. He will later on take pleasure in recalling the time when he listened to Rabelais,

> Qui de Gargantua recite
> Le sens, la force et l'exercite[4].

Another of Rabelais' writings dates from his third stay in Rome—a description of the festivities which took place on the occasion of the birth of Louis, Duke of Orleans, second son of Henri II and of Catherine de' Medici. The prince was

---

Cardinal du Bellay's name. There is a fac-simile of this document in Heulhard, *op. cit.*, pp. 271–273. M. Romier has discussed it (*art. cit.*, pp.121–123). It is a letter of exchange drawn by a Paris bank on a bank in Rome, in payment of some debt or other.

[1] Born 1505, at Châtillon-sur-Seine, where his house, with its façade decorated in Renaissance style, is still to be seen. He was in touch with Guillaume Budé (Delaruelle, *Guillaume Budé*, p. 273), and entered the service of Georges d'Armagnac about 1533. He published in 1544 his *Annotationes in Vitruvium*.

[2] Marty-Laveaux, *op. cit.*, vol. III, p. 203.

[3] Pierre de Nolhac, *Un humaniste ami de Ronsard, Pierre de Paschal, Revue d'hist. litt. de la France*, 1918, pp. 44–45.

[4] Louis des Masures, *Œuvres poétiques*, 1557, quoted by Heulhard, p. 209. (" Narrating the intelligence, strength, and skill of Gargantua ".)

born on 3rd February, 1549, in the Castle of Saint-Germain. The news, by some unknown prodigy, was immediately known in Rome and confirmed a week later by bank couriers. An envoy of the King arrived on March 1st to bring official tidings of it to the Pope and French Cardinals. There were banquets and fireworks on three successive evenings. The Cardinal du Bellay decided as a sign of rejoicing to stage the spectacle of sham naval battles (*naumachia*) and land battles (*sciomachia*). The Naumachy took place on the Tiber, on 10th March, but was spoiled by a flood in the river. On the other hand, the Sciomachy " on land " took place very successfully, March 14th, on the Piazza SS. Apostoli, the finest in Rome after the Piazza d'Agone, in front of the palace where Cardinal du Bellay resided.

Rabelais was present at this festival and he sent a description of it, intended for the French Court, to the Cardinal de Guise, at Paris. He described in detail the different episodes of the *fête* : the arrival of the crowds who quickly filled not only the palaces, houses, stands, galleries and platforms, but even the roofs of the neighbouring houses and churches ; then, as a prelude, a bull-fight, in which two bulls were killed by gladiators and another by three big Corsican dogs[1] ; the comic interludes by Moret, chief jester of Italy ; the arrival of the combatants on foot and horseback to the music of fifes and drums ; the march past of the soldiery, dressed in the livery of their leader, Orazio Farnese, himself resplendent in a uniform stitched with gold and embroidered with crescents, emblems of Diane de Poitiers. For the favourite had not been forgotten in this celebration in honour of a son of the Queen. There shortly appeared, accompanying Diana, a band of young women dressed like nymphs " wearing on their foreheads a silver crescent ", and with their hair falling down loosely on their shoulders. One of her handmaidens having withdrawn to tie the string of her shoe, soldiers issued forth from a Castle of brick and wood, erected in the middle of the square, and suddenly bore her off. Then Diana went to Orazio Farnese to implore his aid, and the war began between his men-at-arms and the Castle garrison. The clash of horsemen, cannonades, volleys of carbines, single combats, the attack on the Castle

---

[1] We know from Joachim du Bellay's *Regrets* that the greater part of these amusements, more especially bull-fights, were then fashionable in Rome.

after it had been mined and a breach made in it, the assault and all the usual episodes of a siege were cleverly staged, with the help of the Holy Father's " bombardiers ", of Italian firework-makers and a French " salpeterer ". The battlefield, shrouded in a cloud of pungent smoke, was strewn with broken lances. Two warriors lay there. Two clowns rushed forward, one to hear their confessions, the other to relieve them of the money in their pockets : then, the spectators discovered that they were only " men of hay ".

A gargantuan feast followed this tourney : " thirty pun-cheons of wine " were drunk at it, " and one hundred and fifty dozen loaves of fine bread lasted no time, not to mention the other ordinary bread ". One thousand five hundred " oven delicacies ", pasties, tarts and cream-tarts were served. The grace having been recited to music, a singer chanted a Latin ode, composed by Cardinal du Bellay in honour of the new-born child, and his mother, a daughter of Tuscany. It had been intended to stage a comedy, but the one already given by Cardinal d'Armagnac had failed to excite interest, so it was deemed preferable to bring out some masks and dancers. Then the ball commenced and lasted till morning. On the two succeeding evenings there were once more fireworks and bonfires. Thus the birth of a son to the French King was destined, thanks to Cardinal du Bellay's munificence, to leave glad and lasting memories in the minds of the people of Rome.

While he was thus taking care of his master's, the King's, interests his prestige at Court was being undermined by intrigue. In July, Henri II deprived him of his functions as Plenipotentiary of France, at the Roman Court, and sent him a colleague in the person of Ippolito d'Este, Cardinal of Ferrara. Du Bellay could not get on with him and asked for his recall. He left Rome, on September 22nd, accompanied by Rabelais. The latter had already prepared his protector's apologia. He turned again to his narrative of the festivities of March 14th, and wrote it afresh, adapting it to the French public's taste[1], and emphasising particularly his praise of the brothers Du Bellay : a reference to the Castle of St. Angelo was a pretext

---

[1] Given in full by Marty-Laveaux, *op. cit.*, vol. III, pp. 391–413. Note that Rabelais cast the young Prince's horoscope " destined for such great things in chivalry and heroic deeds, as his horoscope shows, provided he escapes a somewhat sad aspect in the western angle of the seventh house ". Louis d'Orléans died while still an infant.

for recalling " the late Guillaume du Bellay, seigneur of Langey, of eternal memory ", and he took every occasion of sounding the Cardinal's praises[1]. On his way through Lyons, he gave his manuscript to Sebastian Gryphius who published it some time later under the following title : *The Sciomachia and festivities given in Rome at the Palace of Monseigneur the most reverend Cardinal du Bellay, for the happy birth of Monseigneur of Orleans. All of which is taken from letters written to Monseigneur the most reverend Cardinal de Guise, by M. François Rabelais, doctor of medicine.*

His protector had already set out again for Rome. Pope Paul III had died on November 10th, and the King had immediately ordered Cardinal du Bellay to take part in the Conclave. The prelate embarked at Marseilles towards the end of November, accompanied by Cardinals de Guise, Châtillon and Vendôme. The Conclave ended on 7th February, 1550, with the election of Julius III as Pope ; but Jean du Bellay returned to France only in the autumn[2].

Rabelais, in the meantime, had not resumed the composition of his *Fourth Book*. His courage had been for a time daunted by the attacks and calumnies of " certain Cannibals " ; as he explained later, " I had resolved not to write one jot more ". The most violent attack which had yet been made on his book and his morals had appeared during the year 1549. It consisted of a few pages, carefully put in inverted commas so as to arrest the reader's attention, of a book of piety entitled *Theotimus*, from the name of one of the characters in it[3]. The author, Gabriel de Puits-Herbault, in Latin *Putherbeus*—a religious of Fontevrault, doctor of the Faculty of Paris—denounced in three dialogues the danger of bad reading. In this category he placed our entire romantic literature—Ogier the Dane and Arthur of Brittany, Lancelot of the Lake and the Epistles of Helisenne de Crenne. He repeated Gerson's attacks upon the *Roman de la Rose*, discovered poison in the greater part of those works recently translated from the Italian, in Marot's *Adolescence Clémentine*, in the *chansons* of the prevailing fashion,

---

[1] Romier, *art. cit.*, pp. 134–138.

[2] According to Romier, *Le dernier voyage de Rabelais en Italie, R.É.R.*, X, 116.

[3] The full title is *Theotimus sive de tollendis et expungendis malis libris iis præcipue, quos vix incolumi fide ac pietate plerique legere queunt, libri tres* (Paris, Jean Roigny, 1549, 8vo). The preface is dated Hautes-Bruyères, 1st March, 1547 (old style).

and in all the manifestations of art and literature which breathed the spirit of the Renaissance. But his indignation or wrath is nowhere equal to that which " Pantagruelism " provokes in his theological mind, eager to defend " *nos maîtres* " of the Sorbonne[1]. Why he is not sent to Geneva, along with the theological dissenters, the clown who invented this clownish word, if indeed he still be of this world, for he left France at the outset of the new reign to follow the cardinals to Rome ! He is as impious as he is dangerous by his books. Nothing is wanting to his perversity : he knows neither fear of God nor respect of man. He spends his days in drunkenness, in gluttony, in living in Greek fashion, in sniffing the odour of kitchens, in vomiting forth poison in his writings, so that it is to be marvelled at how a prince of the Church can admit him to his intimacy. In the opinion of all who are in touch with him, Rabelais is even more unworthy in his acts than in his writings. That piety which he had abandoned is daily revenged by the host of vices which he is heaping up within himself !

This diatribe, which was all the more noticeable from the fact that the printer's trick of putting it between inverted commas emphasised it to the reader's attention, did not pass unnoticed. Charles de Sainte-Marthe, the Platonic poet, in a work which he published a year later, congratulated at length the monk of Fontevrault for having denounced the Atheists and Epicureans, whom he himself was preparing to combat[2]. The Sorbonne theologians, who so far had attracted no recruits to their aid (with the exception of Sagon) in their struggle against Humanism and the Renaissance spirit, found at last somebody to second their endeavours—Puits-Herbault showered praises upon them, likening these ramparts of the Catholic faith to so many Atlases[3].

Rabelais, as can be readily understood, was not unmoved by these attacks. He had complained, in his *Third Book* and in the *Prologue* to the partial edition of his *Fourth Book*, of the devilish calumniators who vilified his works ; but without

---

[1] Pp. 180–183. In side-notes : *Rabelæsus Genevæ haud impune impure scriberet. Rabelæsus quid hominis sit.*

[2] Cf. his *In psalmum nonagesimum pia admodum et christiana meditatio ;* and M. Abel Lefranc's article showing that these attacks of Puits–Herbault and Charles de Sainte-Marthe are, besides, an echo of the old quarrel between the Rabelais and Sainte-Marthe families ; *R.É.R.,* IV, *Rabelais, les Sainte-Marthe et l'enraigé Putherbe.* [3] P. 237.

R

expressly naming any of them. He reserved for Puits-Herbault the shame of representing, along with Calvin, in an episode of the *Fourth Book*, the *cafards*, *chattemites*—" church vermin " —and other hypocrites, the spawn of Antiphysis, the antinatural monster[1].

For he finally resumed the " continuation of the Pantagruelian mythologies ". One of the most influential personages in the new reign, Odet de Coligny, Cardinal de Châtillon, encouraged him to do so. He assured Rabelais that François I had had *Gargantua* and *Pantagruel* read to him without finding any passage suspicious. King Henri II had done likewise, and had even promised the Cardinal that he would grant for the printing of the remainder of the work " his royal privilege, and particular protection for (the author), against (his) slandering adversaries[2] ".

And, in fact, on August 6th, 1550, a " privilege . . . in the King's name, the Cardinal de Chastillon being present " was granted to Rabelais to reprint those of his works which had been " depraved and disguised ", " to bring to light and [offer for] sale the continuation of Pantagruel's heroic deeds and sayings "[3]. Shortly afterwards, in a second interview, Odet de Coligny confirmed these good tidings to Rabelais, and he again discussed them with him during a visit which he paid to Saint-Maur, whither Jean du Bellay had betaken himself, " for the recovery of his health after a long and lingering malady ", in the spring of 1551.

[1] " Depuys elle engendra les Matagotz, Cagotz, et Papelars, les maniacles Pistoletz, les Demoniacles Calvins imposteurs de Genève; *les enraigez Putherbes*, Briffaulx, Caphars, Chattemites, Canibales, et aultres monstres difformes et contrefaictz en despit de Nature ". Le Motteux' version of this passage is : " Since that, she begot the hypocritical tribes of eaves-dropping dissemblers, superstitious pope-mongers, and priest-ridden bigots, the frantic Pistolets, the demoniacal Calvins, imposters of Geneva, the scrapers of benefices, apparitors with the devil in them, and other grinders and squeezers of livings, herb-stinking hermits, gulligutted dunces of the cowl, church vermin, false zealots, devourers of the substance of men, and many more other deformed and ill-favoured monsters, made in spite of nature ". *Fourth Book*, end of ch. XXXII.
[2] This information, given in the *Author's Epistle Dedicatory* to Cardinal de Châtillon at the beginning of the *Fourth Book*, has been examined by Romier, *art. cit.*, *R.É.R.*, X, pp. 138–140.
[3] This " privilege " is given in full by Marty-Laveaux, *op. cit.*, vol. II, pp. 3–4. One proof that this " privilege " was by no means unnecessary and that Rabelais' misgivings as to the fate of his book were not unfounded, is that an inquisitor of the ecclesiastical province of Toulouse had included " the book of Pantagruel and Panurge " in an Index of prohibited books and songs (*Bulletin de la Société de l'histoire du protestantisme français*, I, pp. 15–24).

Being thus reassured by Cardinal de Châtillon, whose " honourable encouragement " had in the end " inspired him with spirit, and with invention, freed from all intimidation "[1], and confident that his protector will prove to him " a second Gallic Hercules " against his detractors, Rabelais " drew his pen " and in the year 1551 finished his *Fourth Book*.

Cardinal Jean du Bellay had resigned the bishopric of Paris in favour of his cousin, Eustache du Bellay[2], but he had reserved to himself the right of nomination to the livings. The 18th January, 1551, his vicar-general, Jean Ursin, appointed Rabelais to the cure of Saint-Martin-de-Meudon[3]. At the same time Cardinal du Bellay, Bishop of Le Mans, granted him that of Saint-Christophe-de-Jambet, in the Sarthe. Thus was realised the Seigneur de Langey's wish, who had asked in his will that his physician be provided with ecclesiastical benefices giving a total income of at least 300 *livres*.

Rabelais, no doubt, drew this income, but it is nearly certain that he did not personally do duty as *curé* ; the registers mention only his *vicaire*, Pierre Richard[4]. So the parish of Meudon was never the residence of the " *joyeux curé* " to whom it owes its fame. He lived, seemingly, at Saint-Maur-les-Fossés, " that paradise of salubrity, serenity, conveniency, and all desirable country pleasures "[5], where Du Bellay, who perhaps had spent the winter at Le Mans, was completing his convalescence. The Cardinal was embellishing his dwelling. He was unable, through want of money, to execute the grandiose plans which Philibert Delorme had submitted to him in 1536. The house had only one block of buildings instead of three. But, having thus reduced it, the decorative work was proceeded with. In the garden, for instance, in October, 1550, Delorme was engaged in superintending the construction of an arched balcony, on rustic pillars, with a rest-arbour, a spacious walk fifty-eight metres long by five wide. It is there that Rabelais probably renewed acquaintance with the learned disciple of Vitruvius, to whom he later refers, perhaps in memory

[1] *Epistle Dedicatory to the Cardinal de Chastillon*, end.
[2] The 15th March, 1550.
[3] The document directing this appointment is given in Marty-Laveaux, *op. cit.*, vol. IV, p. 417. Cf. a study of it by H. Clouzot, *Conjectures sur Medamothi, R.É.R.*, IX, 459.
[4] Lebœuf, *Histoire du diocèse de Paris*, vol. III, p. 230.
[5] *Epistle Dedicatory to Cardinal de Chastillon*, in Marty-Laveaux, *op. cit.*, vol. II, p. 251. Cf. H. Clouzot, in *R.É.R.*, vol. VII, pp. 259–284.

shafts of satire of Protestant pamphleteers or those of Joachim du Bellay's *Regrets*. In the *Fourth Book* he satirises the Roman Curia for the first time, concentrating all his attacks upon a single abuse—the temporal ambition of the Holy See. This attack will form a complete episode, that of Papimanie[1].

---

[1] M. Léon Daudet, who, as is well known, is a great admirer of *Pantagruel* and *Gargantua*, advances, in a recent essay (*Les horreurs de la guerre*, Paris, 1928), the theory that Rabelais was a manner of semi-official publicist for the furtherance of the Royal policy. This theory appears to me to be true only for the chapter, in the *Third Book*, against marriages contracted without the consent of the parents, and for the Gallican satire upon the Papacy sketched in *Pantagruel* (ch. XXX) and extensively developed in the *Fourth Book*, in the chapters on the Decretals.

Being thus reassured by Cardinal de Châtillon, whose " honourable encouragement " had in the end " inspired him with spirit, and with invention, freed from all intimidation "[1], and confident that his protector will prove to him " a second Gallic Hercules " against his detractors, Rabelais " drew his pen " and in the year 1551 finished his *Fourth Book*.

Cardinal Jean du Bellay had resigned the bishopric of Paris in favour of his cousin, Eustache du Bellay[2], but he had reserved to himself the right of nomination to the livings. The 18th January, 1551, his vicar-general, Jean Ursin, appointed Rabelais to the cure of Saint-Martin-de-Meudon[3]. At the same time Cardinal du Bellay, Bishop of Le Mans, granted him that of Saint-Christophe-de-Jambet, in the Sarthe. Thus was realised the Seigneur de Langey's wish, who had asked in his will that his physician be provided with ecclesiastical benefices giving a total income of at least 300 *livres*.

Rabelais, no doubt, drew this income, but it is nearly certain that he did not personally do duty as *curé* ; the registers mention only his *vicaire*, Pierre Richard[4]. So the parish of Meudon was never the residence of the " *joyeux curé* " to whom it owes its fame. He lived, seemingly, at Saint-Maur-les-Fossés, " that paradise of salubrity, serenity, conveniency, and all desirable country pleasures "[5], where Du Bellay, who perhaps had spent the winter at Le Mans, was completing his convalescence. The Cardinal was embellishing his dwelling. He was unable, through want of money, to execute the grandiose plans which Philibert Delorme had submitted to him in 1536. The house had only one block of buildings instead of three. But, having thus reduced it, the decorative work was proceeded with. In the garden, for instance, in October, 1550, Delorme was engaged in superintending the construction of an arched balcony, on rustic pillars, with a rest-arbour, a spacious walk fifty-eight metres long by five wide. It is there that Rabelais probably renewed acquaintance with the learned disciple of Vitruvius, to whom he later refers, perhaps in memory

[1] *Epistle Dedicatory to the Cardinal de Chastillon*, end.
[2] The 15th March, 1550.
[3] The document directing this appointment is given in Marty-Laveaux, *op. cit.*, vol. IV, p. 417. Cf. a study of it by H. Clouzot, *Conjectures sur Medamothi*, *R.É.R.*, IX, 459.
[4] Lebœuf, *Histoire du diocèse de Paris*, vol. III, p. 230.
[5] *Epistle Dedicatory to Cardinal de Chastillon*, in Marty-Laveaux, *op. cit.*, vol. II, p. 251. Cf. H. Clouzot, in *R.É.R.*, vol. VII, pp. 259–284.

of former meetings in Rome, with an Italian title—" *Messere* Philibert de l'Orme, King Megistus's principal architect "[1].

In order to thank the King and interest him in his fortunes, Rabelais thought wise of giving an earnest of his good-will. Precisely in this year 1551, a chance of serving or of flattering the King presented itself. Henri II was in conflict with the Holy See. The bad feeling had begun in 1547. Henri II had hardly ascended the throne when he issued from Fontainebleau an edict remedying various abuses of the Roman Curia in the appointment to ecclesiastical livings and establishing a check upon Notaries Apostolic and bankers in correspondence with the Holy See. It was the edict of the " little dates " which Ronsard welcomes in one of his odes as a big reform of happy augury for the new reign.[2] Julius III's policy had irritated the French King. Elected in 1550 through the efforts of the French Cardinals, this Pope had gone over to the Emperor, Charles V. He aimed at wresting the Duchy of Parma from Octave Farnese, whom Henri II supported. He even proclaimed the deposition of this prince, when he learned that he was united by a treaty to the King of France. Henry II thereupon dismissed the Legate from his Court, and the so-called " War of Parma " began.

Never since the time when Julius II was arming Italy against Louis XII, had relations been so strained between the French King and the Pope. Those acquainted with the intentions of the two parties thought that France was on the verge of a

---

[1] *Fourth Book*, ch. LXI. Cf. H. Clouzot, *Rev. XVIe siècle*, 1921, pp. 243-244.
[2] *Au Roy Henri II*, in Book V of his *Odes :*

> " Ton œil vigilant, qui contemple
> Tes vassaux en divers costez,
> A contemplé de Dieu le temple
> Que nos banquiers par fauz exemple
> Combloient de larrons eshontez ;
> Et doctes en chiquaneries
> N'enduroient en un seul quartier
> Qu'un bénéfice fust entier
> Troublé de mille tromperies.
>
> " Mais or' bulles et signatures
> Et dattes levez par avant,
> Mandats, faux titres, escritures
> Depravez par leurs impostures
> Seront certains doresnavant ;
> Si bien que le moine et le prestre
> Possédans en paix leurs maisons
> Feront pour toy leurs oraisons
> Et pour les loix que tu fais naistre ".

schism. The old leaven of Gallicanism was fermenting everywhere. The Sorbonne declared that the King owed the Pope
no allegiance in political affairs[1]. The jurist, Charles Dumoulin,
published a commentary of the edict of the *petites dates*, which
was full of recriminations against the policy of the Holy See[2].
He recalled to memory Philippe le Bel's legist, Pierre de Cugnières, who had been the first to oppose the usurping claims of
Rome[3], and reviewed all the episodes of the Royal resistance
to the encroachments of the Papacy. He pointed to the Kingdom drained of its resources by Papal extortions, and calculated
at one million *livres* the total sum of money which went yearly
to Rome ; he enumerated the fourteen methods employed in
this enormous extortion.

A Gallican campaign was, therefore, begun in France against
the Roman Curia. Rabelais took part in it. Hitherto he had
been satisfied with ridiculing Julius II, Louis XII's enemy,
in his early work, and with good-humouredly poking fun at a
few other Popes. There was nothing edifying in the two Pon-
tiffs he had seen at Rome, Clement VII and Paul III ; they
were too taken up with family interests. Rabelais merely
says of them that he was none the better off for having seen
them[4]. He knew also that the Cardinals' morals were not
above reproach but he had never spoken of them in his book,
and we might look in vain for anything to compare with the

---

[1] On this episode cf. Romier, *La crise gallicane de* 1553, in the *Revue
historique*, 1911 and 1912.

[2] The title of Ch. Dumoulin's work gives the spirit of it : *Commentarius
ad Editum Henrici Secundi regis Galliarum contra parvas datas et abusus curiæ
Romanæ et in antiqua edicta et senatusconsulta Franciæ contra annatarum et id
genus abusus, multas novas decisiones juris et praxis continens.*

[3] Pierre de Cugnières, or Du Coignet, had been turned to ridicule by his
adversaries for having attempted to " clip the nails of ecclesiastical power
and jurisdiction ". (Du Fail, *Eutrapel*, III.) They had called after him a
grotesque head, sculptured on the right side of the choir of Notre-Dame de
Paris, on which the wicks of candles were pressed in order to extinguish them.
Had the Gallican crisis of 1551 reawakened the memory of this person ? We
note that Noël du Fail speaks of him some years later, that Joachim du Bellay
composed a *Satyre de maistre Pierre du Cuignet* on the *Pétromachie de l'Université de Paris*, and that Rabelais alludes to him in the *Prologue* to the *Fourth
Book* (1551) : " Vous les associerez à maistre Pierre de Cuignet, par vous jadis
par mesmes causes pétrifié . . . en office de estaindre avecques le nez, comme
au jeu de Fouquet les chandelles, torches, cierges, bougies et flambeaux
allumez ". [" You may associate them with master Peter du Coignet, whom
you formerly petrified for the same cause . . . to perform the office of
extinguishers, and with their noses to put out the lighted candles, torches,
tapers, and flambeaux ".]

[4] *Fourth Book*, ch. XLVIII : " Ay, ay, answered Panurge, yea, verily,
gentlemen, I have seen three of them, whose sight has not much bettered me ".

shafts of satire of Protestant pamphleteers or those of Joachim du Bellay's *Regrets*.   In the *Fourth Book* he satirises the Roman Curia for the first time, concentrating all his attacks upon a single abuse—the temporal ambition of the Holy See.   This attack will form a complete episode, that of Papimanie[1].

---

[1] M. Léon Daudet, who, as is well known, is a great admirer of *Pantagruel* and *Gargantua*, advances, in a recent essay (*Les horreurs de la guerre*, Paris, 1928), the theory that Rabelais was a manner of semi-official publicist for the furtherance of the Royal policy.   This theory appears to me to be true only for the chapter, in the *Third Book*, against marriages contracted without the consent of the parents, and for the Gallican satire upon the Papacy sketched in *Pantagruel* (ch. XXX) and extensively developed in the *Fourth Book*, in the chapters on the Decretals.

CHAPTER XVI

THE FOURTH BOOK OF 1552

THE complete edition has two prefaces—an *Epistle dedicatory to the most illustrious Prince and most reverend Lord Odet, Cardinal de Chastillon*, and the author's *Prologue aux lecteurs bénévoles*. In the Epistle, Rabelais cleverly recalls the fact that the Cardinal had sponsored his book in obtaining for him a permit to print it, and presents his justification against the calumnies directed against his preceding book : his sole object in writing this continuation of the " Pantagruelian fables " is to cheer up and soothe " the absent who labour under affliction " just as he does " to the present that stand in need of his art and advice ". He had enunciated the same idea in his first work and repeated it recently in the prologue to the partial edition of the *Fourth Book*. The tone of the new prologue is a different one. Freed from the constraint of setting forth his personal apologia, Rabelais is entirely concerned only with the pleasure of conversing familiarly with his readers. He compliments them on their recent harvests, invites them to drink, tells them how his own health is, and, amid innumerable puns, tags, approximations and other plebeian jokes, enlarges upon this theme—that we should wish for good health and nothing more ! For moderate desires are the only ones which are satisfied, as can be seen from " little dapper Zaccheus ", spoken of by St. Luke, and the anecdote of the wood-cutter who had lost his axe.

Among this commonplace chatter we find some allusions to the happenings of the day, which are outside the province of a mere popular story-teller. Some are concerned with politics, and show that Rabelais is well acquainted with the events of internal and external history. He is *au fait* with the progress of the distant wars between the Tartars and Muscovites, the disputes between the Sultans of Persia and of Turkey, the recapture of Tripoli by the Knights of St. John of *nobilitati deroget,* he drew up a list of the most famous physicians, ancient and modern. The names of the principal physicians of the 16th century are given therein—Fernel, Dubois, Pierre Tolet of Lyons, Manardi of Ferrara. But one might look in vain for the name of a French doctor who had published at Lyons, in 1532, and dedicated to Tiraqueau, the second collection of Manardi's *Medical Letters* ; who, in the same year, had published Hippocrates' *Aphorisms,* subsequently to having expounded them in his lectures at Montpellier ; and who had gained for himself a reputation as a clever anatomist and skilled practitioner, witnessed to by Dolet, Macrin, Boyssonné and Sussannée. From this catalogue of the leading medical men of his time, Tiraqueau has omitted Rabelais.

Was the latter hurt by this indifference on the part of the jurisconsult who had encouraged his beginnings in " Philology " ? In any event, he endeavoured to conciliate him by this allusion to one of his recent publications—a study on the legal tag *le Mort saisit le Vif.*

We have seen that the partial edition of the *Fourth Book* published in 1548, had been hurriedly put together. Returning to the opening chapters of his story, the author set himself to improve upon the original version. As he had already done with new editions of his previous works, he added learned references and popular jokes. He also made corrections which show us what was his conception of stylistic improvements[1]. He multiplied, for instance, the reduplication of terms affected by the Humanists in imitation of Cicero's prose. He substituted popular words for some learned terms, changed the order of the words,—usually to give to the sentence an archaic flavour, for the older graces of style and vocabulary were suited to the character of *bonhomie* which he was desirous of imparting to his narrations. Finally, he added two new episodes to his tale —the landing at the polar region of Medamothi (in Greek, *No-where*) and the farcical story of the *Chicanous'* (Catchpoles') drubbing by Basché.

The plan adopted by Rabelais for Pantagruel's wanderings left full play to his imagination. After the learned disquisitions of the *Third Book,* he now returned to the romance of adventures. The miraculous element was an essential feature of

[1] For a detailed study of these alterations, cf. the *Introduction* to my edition (1909) of the text of 1548, pp. 8–23.

CHAPTER XVI

THE FOURTH BOOK OF 1552

THE complete edition has two prefaces—an *Epistle dedicatory to the most illustrious Prince and most reverend Lord Odet, Cardinal de Chastillon,* and the author's *Prologue aux lecteurs bénévoles.* In the Epistle, Rabelais cleverly recalls the fact that the Cardinal had sponsored his book in obtaining for him a permit to print it, and presents his justification against the calumnies directed against his preceding book : his sole object in writing this continuation of the " Pantagruelian fables " is to cheer up and soothe " the absent who labour under affliction " just as he does " to the present that stand in need of his art and advice ". He had enunciated the same idea in his first work and repeated it recently in the prologue to the partial edition of the *Fourth Book.* The tone of the new prologue is a different one. Freed from the constraint of setting forth his personal apologia, Rabelais is entirely concerned only with the pleasure of conversing familiarly with his readers. He compliments them on their recent harvests, invites them to drink, tells them how his own health is, and, amid innumerable puns, tags, approximations and other plebeian jokes, enlarges upon this theme—that we should wish for good health and nothing more ! For moderate desires are the only ones which are satisfied, as can be seen from " little dapper Zaccheus ", spoken of by St. Luke, and the anecdote of the wood-cutter who had lost his axe.

Among this commonplace chatter we find some allusions to the happenings of the day, which are outside the province of a mere popular story-teller. Some are concerned with politics, and show that Rabelais is well acquainted with the events of internal and external history. He is *au fait* with the progress of the distant wars between the Tartars and Muscovites, the disputes between the Sultans of Persia and of Turkey, the recapture of Tripoli by the Knights of St. John of

247

nobilitati deroget, he drew up a list of the most famous physicians, ancient and modern. The names of the principal physicians of the 16th century are given therein—Fernel, Dubois, Pierre Tolet of Lyons, Manardi of Ferrara. But one might look in vain for the name of a French doctor who had published at Lyons, in 1532, and dedicated to Tiraqueau, the second collection of Manardi's *Medical Letters* ; who, in the same year, had published Hippocrates' *Aphorisms*, subsequently to having expounded them in his lectures at Montpellier ; and who had gained for himself a reputation as a clever anatomist and skilled practitioner, witnessed to by Dolet, Macrin, Boyssonné and Sussannée. From this catalogue of the leading medical men of his time, Tiraqueau has omitted Rabelais.

Was the latter hurt by this indifference on the part of the jurisconsult who had encouraged his beginnings in " Philology " ? In any event, he endeavoured to conciliate him by this allusion to one of his recent publications—a study on the legal tag *le Mort saisit le Vif*.

We have seen that the partial edition of the *Fourth Book* published in 1548, had been hurriedly put together. Returning to the opening chapters of his story, the author set himself to improve upon the original version. As he had already done with new editions of his previous works, he added learned references and popular jokes. He also made corrections which show us what was his conception of stylistic improvements[1]. He multiplied, for instance, the reduplication of terms affected by the Humanists in imitation of Cicero's prose. He substituted popular words for some learned terms, changed the order of the words,—usually to give to the sentence an archaic flavour, for the older graces of style and vocabulary were suited to the character of *bonhomie* which he was desirous of imparting to his narrations. Finally, he added two new episodes to his tale —the landing at the polar region of Medamothi (in Greek, *Nowhere*) and the farcical story of the *Chicanous'* (Catchpoles') drubbing by Basché.

The plan adopted by Rabelais for Pantagruel's wanderings left full play to his imagination. After the learned disquisitions of the *Third Book*, he now returned to the romance of adventures. The miraculous element was an essential feature of

---

[1] For a detailed study of these alterations, cf. the *Introduction* to my edition (1909) of the text of 1548, pp. 8–23.

this *genre*. The themes used in *Pantagruel* and *Gargantua* could find place once more in his story. As a matter of fact, Rabelais probably considered that he had come to the end of the resources with which the description of the Giant supplied him. Only once does he call attention to Pantagruel's enormity —when he makes him shed tears " as big as ostrich's eggs "[1]. There is only one instance of the Giant's prodigious strength and skill—when his ship is about to be attacked by a " physeter " (sperm whale), Pantagruel slays the monster with beams[2], which he throws at him from afar, like darts, striking him on the chine, the tail, and the sides " so that the body of the physeter seemed the hulk of a galleon with three masts, joined by a competent dimension of its beams, as if they had been the ribs and chain-wales of the keel ".

Other forms of the marvellous have appealed to his imagination. On the way to Cathay, he tells us of an island whose inhabitants live upon wind only. There is no allegory ; the wind in question is not the conventional synonym of glory. *Ruach*, the name of the island, means " air " in Hebrew. The poor live by means of fans, and the great lords feast themselves by getting beneath the sails of windmills[3].

Not far from his wonderful island, another island, surrounded in mystery, is reached. It is inhabited by old men, the Macreons, and covered with a forest, deserted to all appearance, but which is, in reality, " the dwelling-place of the demons and heroes ". It is there they take refuge after their death, which is always heralded by omens and accompanied by meteorological phenomena—comets, earthquakes, storms at sea, etc. The enumeration of these superstitions, which were still alive in the 16th century, affords Rabelais an occasion of describing in terms of emotion Guillaume du Bellay's death at Tarare and of narrating, from Plutarch, " a very sad story of the death of a Hero, the great Pan ". He follows very closely in his translation the words of the Greek writer, but adroitly emphasises the strange character of the anecdote by some pathetic details. He marks out each incident, gradually adding to the interest of the story, and increases the impression of mystery at which Plutarch had aimed :

" Epitherses, the father of Æmilian the rhetorician, sailing from Greece to Italy, in a ship freighted with divers goods and passengers,

[1] Ch. XXVIII.   [2] Ch. XXXIV.   [3] Ch. XLIII.

members of this monster's body and some trivial object ;
amusing, at first, by the unexpectedness of certain comparisons,
it soon becomes tiresome through its lengthiness and dull
monotony[1].

Laughable stories are introduced, as in the *Third Book*,
to relieve the narrations and discourses of the characters.
They seem to pour in from all the provinces of France.   One
chapter gives an account of six singular happenings which took
place, respectively, at the house of Professor Irland in Poitiers,
in the Convent of the monks at St. Olary at Montpellier, in an
apothecary's shop at Le Mans, in a tailor's workshop in Paris,
at an archery-ground at Cahuzac in Périgord, not to mention
a wedding feast and a domestic scene to which no place is
assigned[2].   It is possible that Rabelais may have invented some
of these anecdotes, but how many of them seem associated with
his own personal recollections, and how numerous are the
places in the Kingdom which had left in the savant's memory,
continually urged on by wanderlust, picturesque and amusing
souvenirs !

We first find the recollections of Chinonais and Touraine in
some piquant jokes—the Seigneur de Basché's revenge for the
annoyance caused him by the fat Prior of St. Louant[3] ;   the
Seigneur de Guyercharois' answer to his host who introduced
to him his pages disguised as girls[4] ;   the rascals of Seuilly
hospital exploiting the pity of the public by displaying their
wounds to them[5].   Poitou contributes references to the red
Poitevins[6] ;   Mélusine, the fairy, and her castles of " Lusignan,
Parthenay, Vovent-Mervent and Pouzauges "[7] ;   the legend
of Villon retired " in his old age " to Saint-Maixent, where he
produces Passion plays[8].   Then comes " Brittany, with its
paspié and country dances ", the *trioris fredonnisés*[9] ;   its
islands, which are the haunts of pirates[10] ;   Saintonge and the
President of the Tribunal of Saintes, Briand Vallée, Seigneur du
Douhet, who tested, on the occasion of a general procession, an
admirable invention of Pythagoras[11] ;   Guyenne, where there
was a famous hermit to be seen at Lormont, between Blaye and
Bordeaux[12] ;   Languedoc, and its wind, called Cierce, which,

[1] Chs. XXX–XXXII.
[2] Ch. LII.   *A continuation of the miracles caused by the Decretals.*
[3] Chs. XII–XV.   [4] Ch. X.   [5] Ch. L.   [6] Ch. IX.
[7] Ch. XXXVIII.   [8] Ch. XIII.   [9] Ch. XXXVIII.
[10] Ch. LXVI.   [11] Ch. XXXVII.   [12] Ch. LXIV.

according to "the famous physician Scurron", overturns
waggons laden with the wines of Mirevaulx, Canteperdrix,
Frontignan[1] ; Dauphiné, with its mountain " like a toadstool ",
which, " as any can remember ", had only yet been once
climbed, by " Doyac, who had charge of King Charles the
Eighth's train of artillery "[2] ; Savoy, with Chambéry, whose
inns are frequented by French and Italian travellers[3] ; Lyons,
its delicacies, and the monstrous effigy of Maschecroute which
was carried in procession on carnival-days[4] ; Metz, with its
Dragon of St. Clement or Graoulli[5] ; Paris, and its " Street
paved with Chitterlings "[6]. From his travels in Italy we get
the anecdote of the ventriloquist Jacobe Rhodigine of Ferrara[7] ;
the vengeance wreaked upon the Milanese by Emperor Barbarossa for an affront offered to him[8] ; the curious epitaph,
found on the Via Flaminia[9], of a man who died from a cat's
bite ; the strange cure for constipation used by Messer Pantolfe
de la Cassina, of Sienna[10] ; an expression used by the courtesans
of Rome[11] ; phrases[12] and words[13] in Italian.

These personal souvenirs abound even in the commentary
which Rabelais added to his work under the title of *Brièfve
déclaration d'aucunes dictions plus obscures*[14]. It is there he
mentions the obelisk which can be seen at Rome " near the
temple of St. Peter ", and the Bishop of Caramith, who was
Rabelais' tutor in Arabic at Rome, and who stated that the
noise of the Nile waterfalls could be heard as far distant as
three days' journeying, " which is as far as from Paris to Tours";
and, lastly, " our great friend and lord Monsieur Philandrier ",
who explained the instrument described by Vitruvius under
the name of Æolipyle.

Some of these references to contemporary happenings and
events are, besides, intended as flattery for the King. It was
pleasing to the national pride to recall the exploits of the Lords
of Termes and Desse, who recaptured from the English, in

---

[1] Ch. XLIII.   [2] Ch. LVII.   [3] Ch. LXVII.   [4] Ch. LIX.
[5] Ch. LIX.   [6] Ch. XLII.   [7] Ch. LVIII.
[8] Ch. XLV.   [9] Ch. XVII.   [10] Ch. LXVII.
[11] Ch. IX : " La grande manche (*mancia*, " tip ", payment) que demandent
les courtisanes romaines ".
[12] Ch. XLV : *Ecco lo fico*, and the three Italian phrases used by Messere
Pantolfe de la Cassina in ch. LXVII. The translation of these phrases is given
in the *Brièfve déclaration*.
[13] *Boye* for *bourreau* (executioner) in ch. XLV.
[14] Marty-Laveaux, *op. cit.*, III, pp. 194 *seqq.*

nothing less than that supreme God, who rules in heaven, replied they, we mean the God on earth . . . the Pope "[1]. And the Papimanians hasten, with transports of joy, to congratulate these lucky travellers who have had the honour of seeing the Pope. A collection is made to give them a banquet. Then Homenas, Bishop of Papimany, brings them to the temple where they are permitted to kiss a stick, which has touched a badly executed image of the Pope, kept under thirty-two key-holes, and fourteen padlocks. On feast-days, the Bishop of Papimany tells them, the mere sight of this image exposed to the people, grants them " full remission of all the sins which they remember they have committed, as also a third part, and eighteen quarantaines of the sins which they have forgot."

Meanwhile, all these exhibitions of idolatry of the Holy Father are continually interspersed with references to the *Decretals*. Soon Bishop Homenas talks to his guests of nothing else except these *Decretals*, and Rabelais names his chapters *How Homenas, Bishop of Papimany, showed us the Uranopet Decretals* (ch. XLIX), *Table-talk in praise of the Decretals* (ch. LI), *A continuation of the miracles caused by the Decretals* (ch. LII), *How by the virtue of the Decretals, gold is subtilely drawn out of France to Rome* (ch. LIII).

What, then, are these *Decretals*, so dear to the Papimanians ? They are a collection of documents of canonical jurisprudence. Up to the 13th century, ecclesiastical law was based upon the Canons and Decrees of the Councils collected by a monk of Bologna, Gratian, in a work called the *Decretum*. In 1234, Pope Gregory IX ordered his chaplain, a Dominican, Raymond of Pennafort, to make a compilation of all the regulations and constitutions of preceding Popes, in five books, called *Decretals*. These *Decretals* were sent to the Universities of Bologna and Paris, and were thenceforward to have the force of law for the interpretation of the Decrees and the Canons. They were followed by a sixth book, the *Sextum*, drawn up under Boniface VIII, in 1278, the *Clementinæ*, sent by Pope Clement V to the Universities of Paris and Orleans in 1313, and, finally, in the beginning of the 15th century, this *corpus* of jurisprudence was completed by the addition of two new series of Decretals, the *Extravagantes* of Pope John XXII and

[1] Ch. XLVIII.

PLATE VI

B. RAYMOND OF PENNAFORT RECEIVING THE
DECRETALS FROM POPE GREGORY IX
Library of Tours, ms. 587, 14th century)

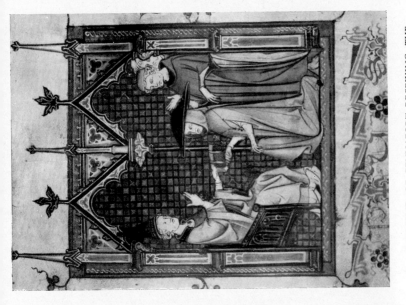

A. A " PHYSETER "
(From Descelliers' planisphere)

[*face p.* 258

the *Extravagantes communes*, thus called because they were, so to speak, outside (*extra*) the official collection.

The publication of the *Decretals* had coincided with an extension of the Holy See's temporal power. In the Middle Ages, emperors, kings and princes encroached upon the Pope's rights in the spiritual sphere. In return, the Popes aimed at the acquisition of power in secular affairs. According as they endeavoured to extend their jurisdiction—by intervening, for example, in the nominations to ecclesiastical benefices, or by bringing before their own tribunal cases relative to the dissolution of marriages,—they legalised their claims by a system of jurisprudence entered into the *Decretals*. French lawyers, then, were right in considering these letters as the legal instrument of the Pope's temporal policy. They were in their eyes " a new law ", differing from the " old law " contained in Gratian's *Decretum*, where there is no mention, says a canonist[1], " of reserve of benefices, nor prevention, nor devolution ", nor first fruits, nor abeyances, nor, in a word, of any of these means by which the Papacy was aiming at the right of nomination to ecclesiastical benefices or of reserving to itself part of their revenues.

We can, then, see the significance of this hymn to the *Decretals* which Rabelais puts in the mouth of Homenas, Bishop of Papimany. His naïve praises have the effect of a satire upon the temporal power of the Popes.

" But what, (on your conscience) was it, do you think, that established, confirmed, and authorised those fine religious orders, with whom you see the Christian world every where adorned, graced, and illustrated, as the firmament is with its glorious stars ? *The Holy Decretals.* What was it that founded, under-propped, and fixed, and now maintains, nourishes, and feeds the devout monks, and friars in convents, monasteries, and abbeys ; so that did they not daily and nightly pray without ceasing, the world would be in evident danger of returning to its primitive chaos ? *The Sacred Decretals.* What makes and daily increases the famous and celebrated patrimony of St. Peter in plenty of all temporal, corporeal, and spiritual blessings ? *The Holy Decretals.* What made the Holy Apostolic See and Pope of Rome, in all times, and at this present, so dreadful in the universe, that all Kings, Emperors, Potentates, and Lords, willing, nilling, must depend upon him, hold of him, be

[1] Durand de Maillane, *Dictionnaire de droit canonique et de pratique bénéficiale*, Lyons, 1770.

crowned, confirmed, and authorised by him, come thither to strike
sail, buckle, and fall down before his holy slipper . . . *The Mighty
Decretals of God.*"

An ironical defence of these *Decretals*, which all the upholders
of the King's jurisdiction and of the Gallican Church denounced
as the instrument of the Roman Curia's usurpations, such is
the singular form which the satire of the Pope's temporal
power takes in Rabelais.   There occurs in it some minor
elements, such as the reference to the indignation caused in
France at the sight of Pope Julius II " while the Christian
commonwealth was in peace, . . . most furiously and cruelly
making war " on Louis XII, or jests upon " the mirific slipper "
which all the potentates of the world come to kiss, but the main
theme of this description of the customs of Papimany is the
ironical praise of the *Decretals*.   As well as the learning of the
canonist, we see his souvenirs of the University appearing
again.   Rabelais mentions eight " dreadful " chapters of the
Decretals which had the " aurifluous " energy to draw yearly
to Rome from France four hundred thousand ducats (and they
are precisely those chapters treated of in Dumoulin, the jurisconsult's book).   He recalls to mind Robert Irland, professor
of Canon Law at Poitiers, and explains how the book in the
arms of the University represents the *Decretals*.

Immune from attack by virtue of his position as the defender
of Gallicanism, Rabelais attacks both the fanaticism of the
Pope's adherents (Homenas condemns the new heretics who
despise the *Decretals*[1] to all sorts of tortures) and the temporal
ambitions of the Papacy.   To Panurge, who refers to Julius II
making war " most furiously and cruelly ", Homenas replies :
" It is not only lawful for him to do so, but it is enjoined him
by the sacred *Decretals* ; and if any dare transgress one single

---

[1] " Yet these devilish Heretics refuse to learn and know it.   Burn them,
tear them, nip them with hot pinchers, drown them, hang them, spit them at
the bunghole, pelt them, paut them, bruise them, beat them, cripple them,
dismember them, cut them, gut them, bowel them, paunch them, thrash them,
slash them, gash them, chop them, slice them, slit them, carve them, saw
them, bethwack them, pare them, hack them, hew them, mince them, flea
them, boil them, broil them, roast them, toast them, bake them, fry them,
crucify them, crush them, squeeze them, grind them, batter them, burst them,
quarter them, unlimb them, behump them, bethump them, belump them,
belabour them, pepper them, spitchcock them, and carbonade them on grid-
irons, these wicked Heretics !   Decretalifuges, Decretalicides, worse than
homicides, worse than patricides, Decretalictiones of the Devil of Hell ".   Ch.
LIII.

iota against their commands, whether they be emperors, kings, dukes, princes, or commonwealths, he is immediately to pursue them with fire and sword, strip them of all their goods, take their kingdoms from them, proscribe them, anathematise them, and destroy not only their bodies, those of their children, relations, and others, but damn also their souls to the very bottom of the most hot and burning cauldron in hell "[1]. It is against such claims as these that both the lawyers who upheld the Royal claims, and even the theologians of the Sorbonne protested, at the time when the War of Parma threatened to place Henri II in armed conflict with the Pope.

Rabelais could thus count upon his attacks on the *Papimanes* and the *Decretals* to gain the King's favour. Had he not, moreover, taken to task another category of people disliked by King Henri II, the Calvinists ? He had joined them, in the same reprobation, with his bitterest enemy, Gabriel de Puits-Herbault. Shrovetide's peculiar anatomy had recalled to Pantagruel's memory the apologue of Physis and Antiphysis as told by the Italian Humanist, Cœlius Calcagninus. " Physis (that is to say, Nature) at her first burthen begat Beauty and Harmony, without carnal copulation, being of herself very fruitful and prolific. Antiphysis, who ever was the antagonist of Nature, immediately, out of a malicious spite against her for her beautiful and honourable productions, in opposition begot Amodunt and Dissonance, by copulation with Tellumon ". Of the tribe of Antiphysis are " the hypocritical tribes of eaves-dropping dissemblers, superstitious pope-mongers and priest-ridden bigots, the frantic Pistolets, *the demoniacal Calvins, impostors of Geneva,* [*the raging Putherbes,*] the scrapers of benefices, apparitors with the devil in them, and other grinders and squeezers of livings, herb-stinking hermits, gulligutted dunces of the cowl, church vermin, false zealots, devourers of the substance of men, and many more other deformed and ill-favoured monsters, made in spite of Nature "[2].

Thus, at the same time that he expressed in the form of an apologue his admiration for Nature, the mother of beauty and harmony, Rabelais replied both to the attacks of Catholic bigots, like Puits-Herbault, and of Calvin. The Reformer had just declared in his treatise *De Scandalis* (1550) that Rabelais

---

[1] Ch. L.   [2] Ch. XXXII.

was one of these learned men who, having tasted the Gospel,
had lapsed into irreligion and materialism[1].

What really was Rabelais' religion at this date ? Like the
majority of Humanists who had taken part in the pre-Reformation movement, he had remained in the Catholic Church after
François I's definite break with the instigators of the French
Reformation. His position in a Cardinal's service, his official
title of Master of the Requests, the care of his material interests
were not the sole, nor, perhaps, the principal motives for his
decision. Evangelism satisfied fully his need of complete liberty
of religious thought. Did it not consist for him, as for the
Humanists in general, in the exercise of his critical faculty, the
study of the texts of the Ancients, the free examination of
traditional beliefs and practices? But from the time that Calvin
published his *Institution of the Christian Religion*[2], Evangelism,
properly speaking, no longer existed : there existed a detached
sect of the Catholic Church, with its religious teaching and its
cult, which little by little was progressing on the road to that
organisation, by which it finally developed into the French
Reformed Church. Since its dogmas, as formulated by Calvin,
were no less rigid than those of the theologians of the Sorbonne,
since its morality was strict, since it even proved to be very
sensitive upon the question of the respect due to Holy Scripture,
the word of God, Rabelais had very good reason to feel more
at ease in the traditional Church.

At the same time, he reserved the right of absolute liberty
of judgment upon the latter. There are a thousand indications

---

[1] " Agrippam, Villanovanum, Doletum et similes volgo notum est tanquam
Cyclopas quospiam evangelium semper fastuose sprevisse. Tandem eo pro-
lapsi sunt amentiæ et furoris, ut non modo in filium Dei exsecrabiles blasphe-
mias evomerent, sed quantum ad animæ vitam attinet, nihil a canibus et
porcis putarent se differre. Alii ut *Rabelaysus,* Deperius et Goveanus, gustato
evangelio, eadem cæcitate sunt percussi. Cur istud ? nisi quia sacrum illud
vitæ æternæ pignus sacrilega ludendi aut ridendi audacia ante profanarant?"
De Scandalis, vol. VIII, p. 45, of the *Opera Calvini,* ed. Baum, Cunitz and
Reuss. Five years later Calvin again attacked Rabelais and the Cardinals
who were his patrons : " Here is a boor who mocks the Holy Scriptures :
like this devil called Pantagruel and all this filth and scurviness. . . . They
are mad dogs who disgorge their ribaldry against the majesty of God and
wished to pervert all sacred things. . . . But, what! they are abetted by
Cardinals ; they are favoured by them and uphold them ; and we can even
see the names of their reverences emblazoned in these five works !" (Alluding
to the *Epistle dedicatory to Mgr. Odet de Chastillon* at the beginning of the
Fourth Book), *Third Sermon on Deuteronomy,* 16th Oct., 1555, *Opera Calvini,*
Baum, Cunitz and Reuss, vol. XXVII, p. 261.

[2] The first edition in Latin appeared in 1536 ; the first French edition in
1541. The latter has been republished, under the direction of Abel Lefranc,
by Henri Chatelain and Pannier, Paris, (Champion, 1911, 2 vols. 8vo).

of this, savouring of "libertinism". True, he says, that if he
found "one single spark of heresy" in his book, he himself
"would, like the Phœnix, gather dry wood, kindle a fire, and
burn himself in the midst of it"[1]. But, without wishing to
"calumniate" him, like "certain cannibals, misanthropes,
and perpetual eavesdroppers", we can pick out in the *Fourth
Book* of 1552 more than one sign of his mental independence.
How could the theologians but have frowned upon reading
(ch. XLVI) "that the devil of Pope-Figland and his little devils
despair of breakfasting upon the souls of students since of late
years they have joined the Holy Bible to their studies", in
spite of "the hypocrites of the tribe of Levi" who tried "taking
from the enlightened book-mongers their St. Paul, either by
threats, revilings, force, violence, fire or faggot"? Rabelais
knew well the Sorbonne's principles upon the question of the
translation of the Scriptures into French. For fear, it said, of
seeing a repetition of the heresies of the Vaudois and the
Albigensians it refused to allow the sacred text to fall into the
hands of simple and ignorant people in a vernacular translation.
Marot's translation of the Psalms of David, which had been
tolerated at first, had finally come under this general ban ;
and it is precisely one of Marot's Psalms, *Quand Israel hors
d'Ægypte sortit* . . . that the Pantagruelian navigators and
the Thalassians sing when Pantagruel's fleet is setting out[2].
Finally, if, in the episode of the *Decretals*, the raillery is aimed
directly at the idolatry of the Papacy only, does it not follow
that religion, in the form of one of its oldest traditions—respect
for the Pope, Vicar of Jesus Christ—is hit by some of the shafts
aimed at superstition ? In the same way, the author of *Tartufe*
at a later date, by ridiculing a religious hypocrite, wounds
sincerely pious souls. And was it not awakening sympathy
for the "new heretics" to represent the ridiculous Homenas
clamouring for tortures and sufferings in punishment of their
irreverence and their "quibbles"?

What place did religious questions hold in Rabelais' everyday thought ? It is not easy to conjecture from this book of
"gay fooleries". His readiness in the treatment of subjects
calculated to glorify the mind of man and exalt "human
pride", is, however, to be remarked. We have already found it
in *Gargantua*. In the *Third Book*, we have it in the description

[1] *Epistle dedicatory to Mgr. Odet*, Marty-Laveaux, *op. cit.*, vol. II, p. 250.
[2] Ch. I.

given expression to his admiration for Tiraqueau's learning and goodness.   But these tributes, dispersed in his humorous works, seem to have left unmoved the jurisconsult, now established on the path of honours.   Immediately upon his appointment as *Conseiller à la Grand Chambre*, in 1541, which he obtained directly by special favour without passing through the *Chambre des enquêtes*, he had acquired great prestige in the Parliament. A year later, he was the judge-advocate who drew up the decree of condemnation against the first French edition of Calvin's *Institution of the Christian Religion*[1], and, thenceforward, he had never shown any indulgence towards those who were indocile towards the Theologians.   It is not, then, surprising that he did not oppose the edict forbidding the sale of the *Fourth Book*, which had been banned by the Sorbonne.   Six months previously, when promulgating the Edict of Châteaubriant, which placed the whole business of printing and bookselling under the supervision of the Sorbonne, the Parliament had blamed certain " officers of justice " for their negligence in taking action in respect of books which were suspect.   Tiraqueau gave them the example of that zeal which he expected from them.   He showed them the futility of counting upon his friendship as against the sentences of the Sorbonne.

What became of Rabelais after this condemnation of his book ?   The Humanist Denys Lambin, who was at Lyons at the end of 1552, there heard that he had been imprisoned. Having made enquiries at Paris in December, he wrote to Henri Estienne that he knew nothing definite about the fate of the author of *Pantagruel*[2].

These mentions of Rabelais in Lambin's correspondence are, along with his resignation of the two livings of St. Martin-de-Meudon and St. Christophe-de-Jambet, on the 9th of January, 1553 (new style)[3], the latest documents which refer to Rabelais in his lifetime.   Subsequently, we find no references to him except as to one already deceased.   When and how did he die ?   We do not know.   One thing only is certain—

[1] Cf. *Bulletin de la Société de l'histoire du protestantisme français*, 1893, p. 550.
[2] Henri Potez, *Trois mentions de Rabelais à la fin de l'année* 1552, *R.É.R.*, I, 57.
[3] *Vide* Marty-Laveaux, *op. cit.*, vol. III, p. 418, for the text of these two resignations, taken from the Archives of the Secretariat of the Archbishopric of Paris, and first published by Rathery, in 1857, in his *Life* of Rabelais, prefixed to his edition of the works.

of this, savouring of " libertinism ". True, he says, that if he found " one single spark of heresy " in his book, he himself " would, like the Phœnix, gather dry wood, kindle a fire, and burn himself in the midst of it "[1]. But, without wishing to " calumniate " him, like " certain cannibals, misanthropes, and perpetual eavesdroppers ", we can pick out in the *Fourth Book* of 1552 more than one sign of his mental independence. How could the theologians but have frowned upon reading (ch. XLVI) " that the devil of Pope-Figland and his little devils despair of breakfasting upon the souls of students since of late years they have joined the Holy Bible to their studies ", in spite of " the hypocrites of the tribe of Levi " who tried " taking from the enlightened book-mongers their St. Paul, either by threats, revilings, force, violence, fire or faggot " ? Rabelais knew well the Sorbonne's principles upon the question of the translation of the Scriptures into French. For fear, it said, of seeing a repetition of the heresies of the Vaudois and the Albigensians it refused to allow the sacred text to fall into the hands of simple and ignorant people in a vernacular translation. Marot's translation of the Psalms of David, which had been tolerated at first, had finally come under this general ban ; and it is precisely one of Marot's Psalms, *Quand Israel hors d'Ægypte sortit* . . . that the Pantagruelian navigators and the Thalassians sing when Pantagruel's fleet is setting out[2]. Finally, if, in the episode of the *Decretals*, the raillery is aimed directly at the idolatry of the Papacy only, does it not follow that religion, in the form of one of its oldest traditions—respect for the Pope, Vicar of Jesus Christ—is hit by some of the shafts aimed at superstition ? In the same way, the author of *Tartufe* at a later date, by ridiculing a religious hypocrite, wounds sincerely pious souls. And was it not awakening sympathy for the " new heretics " to represent the ridiculous Homenas clamouring for tortures and sufferings in punishment of their irreverence and their " quibbles " ?

What place did religious questions hold in Rabelais' everyday thought ? It is not easy to conjecture from this book of " gay fooleries ". His readiness in the treatment of subjects calculated to glorify the mind of man and exalt " human pride ", is, however, to be remarked. We have already found it in *Gargantua*. In the *Third Book*, we have it in the description

[1] *Epistle dedicatory to Mgr. Odet*, Marty-Laveaux, *op. cit.*, vol. II, p. 250.
[2] Ch. I.

of Pantagruelion, which gives him an occasion of showing the
fertility of invention in the human mind, as exemplified in
the use of hemp fibre.   He dilates freely upon all its uses[1]
—cloth, garments, ropes, tents, mill-sails, paper, nets, etc.—
and, in his vision of future progress, he forsees aerial travel,
destined one day to succeed and supplant maritime travel, and
using, like it, Pantegruelion[2].   In the *Fourth Book*, the episode
of Messer Gaster leads him to pass in review all the human inventions which have for their object the production and the
preservation of corn[3].   It is Gaster, the belly, who is the
" noble Master of Arts ".   At his command the very heavens
tremble, and all the earth shakes ".   " Every one is busied, and
labours to serve him ".   Without exaggerating the range of this
sketch of " historical materialism " (for Rabelais, this theory
is merely a paradox which he works out with an extraordinary
richness of expression) the pleasure which our author takes in
linking the productive effort of the mind to an elemental necessity
of our physical nature, cannot be passed over unnoticed :

" From the beginning he invented the smith's art, and husbandry
to manure the ground, that it might yield him corn.

He invented arms, and the art of war, to defend corn.   Physic
and Astronomy, with other parts of Mathematics, which might be
useful to keep corn a great number of years in safety . . . he
invented water, wind, and handmills. . . . He contrived means to
convey it out of one country into another. . . . He invented carts
and waggons, to draw him along with greater ease. . . . He devised
boats, gallies, and ships (to the astonishment of the Elements) to
waft him over to barbarous, unknown, and far distant nations,
thence to bring, or thither to carry corn."

Even the invention of artillery, which Rabelais elsewhere
terms " diabolical "[4], here wrests from him a cry of admiration.

Such is the industriousness of the human mind : for " Physis
(that is to say, Nature) is of herself very fruitful and prolific "[5].

[1] Ch. LI.
[2] Jean Jaurès, an enthusiastic reader of Rabelais, has frequently alluded
in his speeches to the importance of this eulogy on the uses of hemp, as a
symbol of man's industry.   *Vide R.É.R.*, III, 239, and X, 171.   [3] Ch. LXI.
[4] *Pantagruel*, ch. VIII : " as, by a *diabolical suggestion*, on the other side,
was the invention of ordnance ".
[5] *Fourth Book*, ch. XXXII, Apologue of Physis and Antiphysis.   This
apologue is taken from a fable of Cœlius Calcagninus, entitled *Gigantes*.   The
Italian's version, as its title indicates, was written with a moral aim : *Argu-
mentum, vitia præter naturam genita, bonitate principum expugnari, virtutesque
allici*.   Rabelais' indebtedness to it hardly goes beyond the description of the
monstrosities born of Antiphysis, who are symbolical of all the individuals
who go against Nature.

CHAPTER XVII

LAST YEARS AND DEATH. THE FIFTH BOOK OF
PANTAGRUEL

THE *Fourth Book* appeared in February, 1552 (new style), its printing having been completed on January 28th, the date also of the *Epistle dedicatory to Mgr. Odet de Chastillon.* It was too late for the Gallican satire upon Papimany to assure the complete immunity of the entire work. Already the Pope and the King of France had taken the first steps which were to lead to their reconciliation. The Duke of Ferrara, Ercole d'Este, had brought Julius III to apologise to Henri II and the latter had agreed to receive another Nuncio. The Connétable de Montmorency, weary of the dispute, sent the Cardinal de Tournon to Rome, in January, to re-establish peace between the Holy See and France. It was signed on April the 29th[1].

Attacks upon the Roman Curia were no longer in season : the King's party discountenanced them. The Parliament of Paris condemned Charles Dumoulin's book, of which the Connétable de Montmorency had said that it would do more for the King than an army of thirty thousand men. The author was even condemned as a heretic and obliged to flee, for a time, to Switzerland. On the 1st of March, the Council of Parliament signed a decree forbidding booksellers, " in view of its censure by the Faculty of Theology ", to expose for sale " the fourth book of *Pantagruel* under pain of bodily chastisement "[2].

Among the twelve judges present on the Council that day were Michel de l'Hospital, the future Chancellor of France, and André Tiraqueau whose wisdom and equity Rabelais had praised in the prologue. Since those far-off days when the two scholars had conversed upon Law and Literature under the laurel-grove in Fontenay-le-Comte, Rabelais had many times

---

[1] Cf. L. Romier, *La crise gallicane de* 1551. *Revue historique*, 1912, p. 23.
[2] The text of this decree is given in Marty-Laveaux, *op. cit.*, vol. III, pp. 420–421.

given expression to his admiration for Tiraqueau's learning and goodness. But these tributes, dispersed in his humorous works, seem to have left unmoved the jurisconsult, now established on the path of honours. Immediately upon his appointment as *Conseiller à la Grand Chambre*, in 1541, which he obtained directly by special favour without passing through the *Chambre des enquêtes*, he had acquired great prestige in the Parliament. A year later, he was the judge-advocate who drew up the decree of condemnation against the first French edition of Calvin's *Institution of the Christian Religion*[1], and, thenceforward, he had never shown any indulgence towards those who were indocile towards the Theologians. It is not, then, surprising that he did not oppose the edict forbidding the sale of the *Fourth Book*, which had been banned by the Sorbonne. Six months previously, when promulgating the Edict of Châteaubriant, which placed the whole business of printing and bookselling under the supervision of the Sorbonne, the Parliament had blamed certain " officers of justice " for their negligence in taking action in respect of books which were suspect. Tiraqueau gave them the example of that zeal which he expected from them. He showed them the futility of counting upon his friendship as against the sentences of the Sorbonne.

What became of Rabelais after this condemnation of his book ? The Humanist Denys Lambin, who was at Lyons at the end of 1552, there heard that he had been imprisoned. Having made enquiries at Paris in December, he wrote to Henri Estienne that he knew nothing definite about the fate of the author of *Pantagruel*[2].

These mentions of Rabelais in Lambin's correspondence are, along with his resignation of the two livings of St. Martin-de-Meudon and St. Christophe-de-Jambet, on the 9th of January, 1553 (new style)[3], the latest documents which refer to Rabelais in his lifetime. Subsequently, we find no references to him except as to one already deceased. When and how did he die ? We do not know. One thing only is certain—

---

[1] Cf. *Bulletin de la Société de l'histoire du protestantisme français*, 1893, p. 550.

[2] Henri Potez, *Trois mentions de Rabelais à la fin de l'année* 1552, R.É.R., I, 57.

[3] *Vide* Marty-Laveaux, *op. cit.*, vol. III, p. 418, for the text of these two resignations, taken from the Archives of the Secretariat of the Archbishopric of Paris, and first published by Rathery, in 1857, in his *Life* of Rabelais, prefixed to his edition of the works.

that his death took place before the 1st of May, 1554. Upon
this date were published, at Poitiers, the *Premières Poésies
de Jacques Tahureau* of Le Mans, which contain an epitaph on
Rabelais :

> Ce docte nez Rabelays, qui picquoyt
> Les plus piquans, dort soubz la lame icy,
> Et de ceux même en mourant se moquoyt
> Qui de sa mort prenoyent quelque soucy.

As has been pointed out[1], this epitaph gives us not only the
approximate date of Rabelais' death, which we can deduct
from the date on which it was published, but also some indication as to his attitude in the face of death—some jesting words
to those who were sorrowing over his death, keeping, to the
end, the serenity of the Pantagruelist, by going to " look for
the great Perhaps " with a joke on his lips, to reassure his
friends[2].

In November of the same year, 1554, Ronsard published,
at Paris, his *Bocage*, which contains, amongst its sixty-seven
pieces, eight epitaphs, the first being Rabelais'. During the
second half of 1553, he had published various works—a reprinting of the *Odes*, the *Livret de Folastries*, a new impression
of the *Amours*, a second edition of the fifth book of his *Odes*—
in which he could have placed his epitaph on Rabelais. If
we do not find it in the second edition of the fifth book of the
Odes, which contains an elegy on the death of Antoine Chas-
teigner, deceased in 1553, and an epitaph on Jean Martin, the
reason probably is that Rabelais was still alive when this work
appeared (August, 1553)[3].

Rabelais, then, died presumably in the latter half of 1553
or at the beginning of 1554. The traditional date, 9th of
April, 1553, is not met with for the first time until 1710, and
then in a literary text—the preface to the *Lettres écrites pendant*

---

[1] Abel Lefranc, *Remarques sur la date et sur quelques circonstances de la
mort de Rabelais*, R.É.R., I, 59–65.

[2] This serene and gay attitude in the face of death may have given rise
to the legend which, at an early date, represented Rabelais as dying with jokes,
or even buffooneries, on his lips. His last words are said to have been, " Drop
the curtain, the farce is over ". This was a common metaphor of Catholic
preachers : " Vita presens est *une farce* ", says the Franciscan Michel Menot,
" sed in morte . . . ecce quod opportet deponere indumenta corporis nostri
. . . corpus enim vadit à pourriture et l'âme s'en va à l'aventure ". Cf.
Rev. XVIe siècle, 1924, p. 326.

[3] Cf. H. Vaganay, *La mort de Rabelais et Ronsard*, R.E.R., I, 143, and
Laumonier, *L'épitaphe de Rabelais par Ronsard*, R.É.R., I, 205.

the name of the printer, was published ; and, in 1559, a third edition, again giving neither the name of the publisher nor the town where it was published[1]. Clearly, the success of Rabelais' work was being freely exploited, in spite of both the Royal privilege of 1551, which had asserted the author's proprietary rights, and of the decree of Parliament which forbade the sale of the *Fourth Book*.

Then appeared, in 1562, the continuation of Pantagruel's odyssey, under the following title : *L'Isle Sonante Par M. Françoys Rabelays, qui n'a point encores esté imprimée ne mise en lumière : en laquelle est continuée le navigation faicte par Pantagruel, Panurge et autres ses officiers*[2].

The work contains sixteen chapters and three main episodes —the arrival at Ringing Island, *l'Île sonnante* (eight chapters), the arrival at Wicket Island, *l'Île du Guichet*, inhabited by the Furred Law-cats, *Chats fourrés* (five chapters), and the visit to the Island of the Apedefts, or Ignoramuses (one chapter). These three episodes are conceived upon the same plan : all three are satirical allegories, similar to the description of the islands of the Papimanians and the Catchpoles in the *Fourth Book*.

The island, to which the pilot gives the name *Triphes*[3], is resounding with the noise of bellringing, which the travellers hear while still a long distance off at sea. It is inhabited by birds, kept in magnificent cages. These birds are, moreover, like men—indeed, they differ from them only by their plumage ; " some of them were all over white as swans, others as black as crows, many as grey as owls, others black and white like magpies, some all red like red-birds, and others purple and white like some pigeons ". The males are called Clerg-hawks, Monk-hawks, Abbot-hawks, Bish-hawks, Cardin-hawks, and one Pope-hawk " who is a species by himself ". The females are the Clerg-kites, Nun-kites, Priest-kites, Abbess-kites, Bis-kites, Cardin-kites and Pope-kites. They are not indigenous but come from foreign parts, especially from Isle Bossart, where abound the " crooked, crippled, blinding, limping, ill-favoured and deformed, an unprofitable load to all the earth ", or from

---

[1] Cf. P. P. Plan, *Les éditions de Rabelais de 1532 à 1571* (Paris, 1906), pp. 188, 194.

[2] This text has been reprinted for the first time, with an introduction by Abel Lefranc and Jacques Boulenger in *R.É.R.*, 1905.

[3] From the Greek τρυφή, delicacy, luxury.

the country called Breadless-day (*Jour-sans-pain*). They are recruited, besides, from amongst the " frantic inamoradoes, who, when crossed in their wild desires, grow stark, staring mad, and choose this life suggested to them by their despair ", or even those " who have done some rogue's trick or other heinous villany ".

They never work. Why should they ? For from all the rest of the world " a plenty and overflowing of all dainty bits and good things " is sent to them, except from certain northern regions, which, however, will rue it, affirms the sacristan Ædituus, who guides the travellers.

When Pantagruel asks to see the Pope-hawk, he is shown him in his cage, attended by two little " Cardin-hawks and six lusty Bish-hawks ". Panurge describes him as a " filthy whoopcat ". Keep quiet, says Ædituus, if he heard you blaspheme, " thunderbolts, lightnings, storms, bulls and the devil and all " would issue forth from the basin at his feet. A Bish-hawk who, deaf to the singing of a beautiful Abbess-kite, is sleeping soundly, stimulates anew Panurge's mischievous humour. He is about to throw a stone at the bird's mitre to awaken it, but Ædituus stops him. " Hold, hold, honest friend ! strike, wound, poison, kill, and murder all the kings and princes in the world, by treachery or how thou wilt, and as soon as thou wouldest, unnestle the angels from their cock-loft ; Pope-hawk will pardon thee all this : but never be so mad as to meddle with these sacred birds, as much as thou lovest the profit, welfare, and life not only of thyself, and thy friends and relations alive or dead, but also of those that may be born hereafter to the thousandth generation ; for so long thou wouldest entail misery upon them ".

This transparent allegory, the allusions to Papal excommunication, to the heresies and schisms of the northern European countries, to the lax morals of the Court of Rome, to the medley of colours formed by the habits of the numerous religious orders who flocked to Rome, were especially interesting for a certain category of French readers in 1562—the Protestants. This year was filled with the first Civil War. Michel de l'Hospital had in vain published, in January, an edict granting, under certain reserves, liberty of worship to the adherents of the Reformed Church ; the Parliament refused to register it. Then, on March 1st, the skirmish of Vassy had given the signal for the massacres and caused the first armed rising of the Huguenot leaders. It was in this atmosphere of conflict, amid the hatreds and reprisals set loose by the atrocities of men like Baron des Adrets and Monluc, that this satirical picture of the Roman Curia appeared. What a pleasure for the Huguenots to read these pages ridiculing the Pope ! How they must have enjoyed the scathing irony of this sentence of a hermit of Ringing Island : " Whoever does not fast at Quarter Tense is a rank heretic, and wants nothing but fire and faggot ! "

The second episode, that of the Furred Law-cats, seemed equally apposite as an expression of their rancour against the Parliament, these justiciaries

> Aux meurtriers si bénins, des bénins les meurtriers
> Tesmoins du faux tesmoing, les pleiges des faussaires[1].

The Furred Law-cats inhabit the " Wicket " where Pantagruel's companions disembark, after they had passed " Procuration " and " Condemnation " :

" The Furred Law-cats are most terrible and dreadful monsters, that devour little children, and trample over marble stones. . . . The hair of their hides does not lie outwards ; and every mother's son of them for his device wears a gaping pouch. . . . They have claws so very strong, long, and sharp, that nothing can get from them what is once fast between their clutches. . . . They hang all, quarter all, behead all, murder all, imprison all, waste all, and ruin all, without the least notice of right or wrong ; for among them vice is called virtue ; wickedness, piety ; treason, loyalty ; robbery, justice. Plunder is their motto, and when acted by them, is approved by all men, except the heretics "[2].

Their Archduke, Grippeminault, a kind of monster whose hands are full of gore, whose snout is like a hawk's bill, whose fangs or tusks are like those of an overgrown brindled wild boar, cannot say a sentence without punctuating it with the words, Or ça (Well, come now). He propounds to them a riddle which Panurge solves satisfactorily. But the travellers are not allowed to go out again by the wicket until the same Panurge throws down on the floor among them " a large leathern purse stuffed with gold crowns ". At the sound of the gold " the Furred Law-cats . . . all began to bestir their claws, like a parcel of fiddlers running a division : and then

---

[1] A. d'Aubigné, *Tragiques, La chambre dorée.*   [2] Ch. XI.

fell to it, squimble, squamble, catch that catch can. They all said aloud, These are the fees, these are the gloves ; now, this is somewhat like a tansy. Oh ! it was a pretty trial, a sweet trial, a dainty trial ".

Scarcely have Pantagruel's companions escaped from the dangers of the " Wicket " than they land on the Island of the Apedefts[1], " with long claws and crooked paws ". Their sole working utensils are parchment, ink-horns and pens. Amid gibbets, gallows and racks, they live on the juice which a large wine-press squeezes out of various bunches of grapes : the *extraordinaire*[2], tithes, loans, gifts, gratuities, escheats, forfeitures, demesne, privy purse, post-offices, lordships of manors, etc. They are called Apedefts (Ignoramuses) because " they neither are, nor ought to be clerks, and all must be ignorant as to what they transact here ; nor is there any other reason given, but The court hath said it ; The court will have it so ; The court has decreed it "[3].

These terms, and the names given to the various parts of the wine-press—the spindle is called *receipt*, the trough *costs and damages*, the hole for the vice-pin *state*, etc.—clearly show this episode to an be allegorical description of the *Chambre des comptes*. It points to an accurate knowledge of the working of this *Chambre*, its offices, grades and particular phraseology. It is much more technical than the allegory of the Furred Lawcats, of which it immediately reminds us.

This latter is quite general. We find in it none of these distinctive characteristics which are frequent, for example, in the Bridoye episode. We are especially astonished to find that Grippeminault and his agents make no use of legal citations, then common in the talk of legists.

We are no less surprised at the total omission of certain details which Rabelais formerly employed in the portrayal of his favourite characters. Pantagruel does not say one word which savours of " pantagruelism ", that philosophic phlegm with which the author endowed him in his preceding books. Friar Jean has forgotten his usual swearwords. He even swears, like the Bishop of Papimany, by the *Decretals*—" By the sacred memory of the *Extravagantes* ! "—and not once does the

---

[1] From the Greek ἀπαίδευτοι, ignorant people.
[2] [*L'extraordinaire des guerres*, an extra tax levied in time of war.]
[3] Ch. XVI.

T

to the tree on which all Zoïluses and calumniators are told to go and hang themselves[1], etc.

All the chapters of *Ringing Island*, with the exception of the chapter on the Apedefts, are then given, with some variations and an appreciably more correct topography. Then, the story of the navigation is continued, the episodes being more varied than in *Ringing Island*. The travellers then visit the Isle of Forth (*Outre*), whose inhabitants are all bloated and puffed like leather bottles (*outres*), and die by bursting with a loud report[2]. On a ship which they encounter they meet with Hans Cotiral, an alchemist, who is reminiscent of Herr Trippa in the *Third Book*[3]. They disembark at the Kingdom of Quintessence.[4] This is the country of philosophical abstractions. Aristotle is there revered as " the peerless pattern of all Philosophy ", and godfather to *Entelechia* (perfection), although many scholars and learned men of the other world call her *Endelechia* (continuity). As attendants she has a troop of people with Greek and Hebrew names. She cures the sick with a song and expresses herself in the Pindaric jargon of the Limousin scholar. Her officers, the abstractors, spend their time in accomplishing some of the feats which the wisdom of nations holds to be impossible, such as making Ethiopian blackamoors white or milking he-goats. At meals, the Quintessence eats nothing but ambrosia, and drinks nothing but nectar.

Supper being over, " a ball in the manner of a tournament " begins. It is a game of chess in which the pieces are composed of pages and nymphs dressed, some in gold, the rest in silver. They move to music, with many salutations on the part of the gold side to the silver side, and great applause at each advantage which either party gains over the other.

The travellers next reach the Island of Odes where " the ways walk "[5] and the Island of Sandals (*Île des Esclos*) inhabited by the Semiquaver Friars (*Frères Fredons*) who speak only in monosyllables[6]. Their talk leads Epistemon to descant

---

[1] These borrowings from the preceding books in the *Fifth Book* have been examined by Marty-Laveaux, *op. cit.*, IV, pp. 314–316.

[2] Ch. XVII.

[3] Herr Trippa is supposed to represent Cornelius Agrippa of Nettesheim, author of *De incertitudine et vanitate scientiarum* and of *De occulta philosophia*, whom Rabelais had perhaps met at Grenoble, in 1535. Cf. A. Lefranc, *Rabelais et Cornelius Agrippa, Mélanges Picot*, 1913.

[4] Chs. XVII–XXIV.   [5] Ch. XXVI.   [6] Chs. XXVII–XXVIII.

on the institution of Lent, which had already been attacked
in the *Fourth Book*, in the description of Shrovetide, " father
and foster-father to Physicians "[1]. Pantagruel proves here,
by examples and on the authority of the " vicar of Jambet ",
that is of Rabelais, that " far from macerating and bringing
down our pampered flesh, weaking and subduing its lusts and
assuaging the venereal rage " it " forwards the propagation
of mankind ".

A call at the Land of Satin[2], where the plants, animals
and men are all made of " damask and flowered velvet ", that
is to say of tapestry, furnishes a fine description of strange
wild beasts—elephants, rhinoceroses, unicorns, hydras,
phœnixes, etc. " A diminutive, monstrous misshapen old
fellow called Hearsay ", lives there. He it is who inspires a
host of historians and geographers, from Herodotus and Pliny
to Jacques Cartier, with so many wonderful descriptions of
Pigmies, Cannibals and Ægipans. From him also the natives
of Perche and Maine learn their profession of witnesses, for
which they are famous right down to the date of Racine's
Plaideurs.

" Having been scurvily entertained " in the Land of Satin,
the travellers arrive at Lantern-land[3], whose inhabitants live
on lanterns, that is to say, on chimæras. There they meet
with all the famous lanterns, that of La Rochelle and that of
Pierre Amy, Bartolus " the lantern of law "[4] and " greater
light of the apothecaries "[5].

Under the guidance of a lantern offered by the Queen of
Lantern-land, the Pantagruelists at last arrive at the Island
of the Holy Bottle[6]. After some propitiatory ceremonies, they
are admitted to the temple where it is kept. The doors of the
edifice, its floor of mosaic, representing the exploits of Bacchus,
and its wonderful lamp form the matter of a detailed description, based on Greek writers like Lucian and on the *Songe
de Polyphile* by the Italian Colonna[7]. In the centre is situated

---

[1] *Fourth Book*, ch. XXIX.   [2] Chs. XXIX–XXXI.
[3] Chs. XXXII–XXXIII.
[4] He was called in the Law schools, *lucerna juris*.
[5] The title of a famous treatise on pharmacy.   [6] Ch. XXXIV.
[7] Rabelais drew upon this work, which appeared at Venice in 1499 (republished by Paul Manucius in 1545, translated into French by Jean Martin,
and published, in 1546, by Jacques Kerver), for some parts of his description
of Thélème. He mentions it in *Gargantua*, ch. IX, under the title *Songe
d'amours*.

a fountain of admirable workmanship, of symbolical precious
stones, of which the water " by imagination, tastes like any
wine that the drinker fancies to drink ". Finally, Panurge is
brought to listen to the Bottle, hidden in the middle of the
temple. " Then was heard the word : *Trinch* ", that is, drink !
Bacbuc then expounds the oracle " In wine is truth "—wine
has " in its power to fill the soul with all truth, learning and
philosophy ".

Let Panurge, then, drink wine, and be the " expounder "
of his undertaking !—That is precisely, remarks Pantagruel,
what I told you " when you first spoke to me about it ".
Thus, the entire journey has been useless for Panurge ! The
" true Priestess " merely repeats the advice given him by
Pantagruel when first they spoke about marriage—" Are not
you assured within yourself of what you have a mind to ?
The chief and main point of the whole matter lieth there. All
the rest is merely casual, and totally dependeth upon the fatal
disposition of the heavens "[1].

Meanwhile the travellers enter into Bacchic transports.
Panurge, Friar Jean and Pantagruel, seized by " poetic fury "
improvise doggerel poems (*rithmailleries*), the platitude of
which is equalled only by their coarseness. The style becomes
more dignified in their leavetaking of Bacbuc ; a " pontifical
gravity " characterises her last words : " Now, my friends,
you may depart, and may that intellectual sphere, whose
centre is everywhere, and circumference nowhere, whom we
call GOD, keep you in his almighty protection. When you
come into your world, do not fail to affirm and witness that the
greatest treasures, and most admirable things, are hidden
under ground "[2].

The *Fifth Book of Pantagruel* was no less successful than
the previous ones. In 1565, an edition of it was published,
without the name of the place or printer[3], more correct than
the 1564 edition. It contained, on a folded leaf, larger than
the size of the book itself, a drawing of the Holy Bottle, in
which was enclosed Panurge's prayer to it. Another edition
followed in the same year, published at Lyons " by Jean
Martin ", seemingly a fictitious name ; and, then, another,
at Lyons, without the printer's name.[4]

---

[1] *Third Book*, ch. X.   [2] Ch. XLVII.
[3] Cf. P. P. Plan, *op. cit.*, pp. 182–183.   [4] Cf. *Ibid.*, no. 99, p. 195.

PLATE VII

GROTESQUE FIGURES FROM THE SONGES DROLATIQUES DE PANTAGRUEL

At the same time, a Parisian publisher, Richard Breton, issued a collection of one hundred and twenty grotesque figures, engraved upon wood, without titles or explanations, under the following title : *Les Songes drolatiques de Pantagruel, où sont contenues plusieurs figures de l'invention de maistre François Rabelais et dernière œuvre d'iceluy pour la récréation des beaux espritz*[1].

The publisher claims to have received from Rabelais himself, with whom he is supposed to have been on very intimate terms, " this last of his works ". As a matter of fact, these strange figures—a monk clothed with a bell, a man-at-arms in a dribbler, a saucepan armed with a spoon, figures who are all head or all stomach—seem rather the work of an artist who had allowed himself to be carried away by his comic *verve* to the most extravagant eccentricities, without, in general, basing himself on the reading of Rabelais.

This was not destined to be the last work of Rabelais' then " brought to light ". In 1567, an edition of the five books, published at Lyons, contained in addition the *Pantagrueline prognostication*, the Island of the Apedefts (withdrawn since 1562 from *Ringing Island*), and two further facetious pieces— the *Cresme philosophale des questions enciclopédiques de Pantagruel, lesquelles seront disputées sorbonicolificabilitudinissement es escholes de Decret pres S. Denis de la chartre à Paris*—a list of ridiculous theses which is a parody on Scholastic disputations in the manner of the Repertory of the Library of St. Victor,— and an epistle in decasyllabic verses, in the style of the Limousin Scholar—*Épistre du Lymosin de Pantagruel grand excoriateur de la lingue latiale, envoyée à un sien amicissime, résident en l'inclite et famosissime urbe de Lugdune*.

Clearly, Rabelais was not the author of these two compositions. It may have been their inclusion in the body of his works, where they were henceforth to figure, which aroused the first suspicions as to the genuineness of the *Fifth Book*.

In 1572, Estienne Tabourot, in his *Bigarrures* (ch. XX), mentions the *Fifth Book*, as " *attributed* to the inimitable Rabelais". Elsewhere, it is true (folio 49, *recto*), having occasion to refer to the episode of the Furred Law-cats, he writes without reservations : " Has not Rabelais well described the *Entend trois* of Raminagrobis [*leg.* Grippeminault] who invited his guests by the words : *or ça ?* "

---

[1] Reprinted by Tross, Paris, 1869.

In 1604, a compilator, Antoine du Verdier, in his *Prosopographie*[1], wrote in his article on Rabelais : " His misfortune is that everybody wished to put his hand to Pantagruelising, and many books have appeared in his name, and have been added to his works, which are not his, like *Ringing Island*, composed by a student of Valence, and others ". What value has this testimony ? Du Verdier, born in 1544, was eighteen when *l'Isle Sonante* appeared ; he belonged for some time to the Du Bellay household and may have been well informed on Rabelais[2].

In the same year, Louis Guyon, " Consellor of the King in his Finances of Limousin ", in a defence of those doctors who were unjustly calumniated (contained in his *Diverses Leçons*) denied that Rabelais had ever attacked what concerned the Roman and Apostolic Church. " As to the last book which is included amongst his works ", he added, " called *Ringing Island*, which seems really to blame and make ridicule of the servants and officers of the Catholic Church, I protest that he did not write it, for it was composed a long time after his death ; I was at Paris when it was written, and I well know who was the author of it, and he was not a doctor ".

The majority of commentators, critics and readers continued, nevertheless, to include the *Fifth Book* among Rabelais' writings. The question of its authenticity became the object of study only in the middle of the 19th century. In 1840, Paul Lacroix discovered in the Bibliothèque Nationale a manuscript of the *Fifth Book* (*fonds français*, no. 2156) in which three chapters—the Apedefts, ch. XVI, and the Ball in the manner of a Tournament, chs. XXIV-XXV—are missing, but which, on the other hand, gives an additional chapter to the Lantern-land episode—*Comment furent les dames Lanternes servies à souper*—made up of a double enumeration of imaginary dishes and dancing tunes[3]. From this date, the controversy was re-opened. Paulin Paris proved that this manuscript was not in Rabelais' own hand[4], but a copy dating from the 16th century, and he added : " I do not think that the fifth book is Rabelais ' ;

[1] Lyons, Frelon, 1604, vol. III, p. 2452.
[2] Although Du Verdier names expressly *l'Isle Sonante*, Le Duchat is of the opinion that the book he has in mind is *Fanfreluche et Gaudichon* which Guillaume des Autels wrote while studying law at Valence. Such a confusion is not likely.
[3] Given in Marty-Laveaux, *op. cit.*, vol. III, p. 217.
[4] *Journal des débats*, March 19th, 1847.

it has neither the gaiety nor the stylistic characteristics of the others "[1].

Paulin Paris' doubts were, thus, based mainly on questions of taste. The same is true for those of Guy Patin and Le Duchat, who had, on the contrary, considered that the style and the spirit of the *Fifth Book* were Rabelais'[2]. Hence, the criterion of personal taste has been abandoned and an attempt made to find more solid grounds for accepting or rejecting the authenticity of this book. With what result ?

In connection with the reprinting of *l'Isle Sonante* by MM. Abel Lefranc and Jacques Boulenger, the relationship of this partial edition to the manuscript in the Bibliothèque Nationale and the complete edition of 1564 has been examined. The conclusion of this enquiry, carried out simultaneously by M. Boulenger[3], Mr. Smith[4], and Mr. Tilley[5], is that the manuscript and *l'Isle Sonante* are taken from the same archetype, which was badly written, often crude in style, seldom polished, and offering numerous *lacunæ*, of which only a part have been filled by the publisher. From this unfinished state of the archetype, some critics conclude that it was Rabelais' own text.

However, as Mr. Villey[6] has pointed out, this unfinished state of the archetype and the inaccuracies of the printed version of *l'Isle Sonante* admit equally of other hypotheses, for example, the theory that the sixteen chapters are an anti-Catholic pamphlet, hastily put together and thrown into the controversy at the height of the first Civil War, perhaps while the author was far away and unable to correct his proofs. The arguments afforded by textual criticism are not, then, decisive in favour of the attribution of the *Fifth Book* to Rabelais.

Those advanced by M. Sainéan[7] from the philological examination of the text, and particularly of those chapters which

---

[1] A German professor, Birch-Hirschfeld, comparing the style of this book with that of the preceding ones, arrives at the same conclusion as Paulin Paris. Cf. *Das fünfte Buch des Pantagruel und sein Verhältniss zu den authentischen Büchern des Romans*, Leipsic, 1906.

[2] Their opinions are given in Marty-Laveaux, vol. IV, p. 311.

[3] Introduction to the critical edition of *l'Isle Sonante* (Paris, H. Champion, 1905).

[4] W. F. Smith, *Rabelais in his writings* (Cambridge, The University Press, 8vo, 1910, p. 99).

[5] Arthur Tilley, *Studies in the French Renaissance* (Cambridge, The University Press, 1922, p. 85).

[6] P. Villey, *Marot et Rabelais* (Paris, É. Champion, 1923), p. 297.

[7] L. Sainéan, *Problèmes littéraires du seizième siècle* (Paris, E. de Boccard, 1927).

abound in terms of Scholastic Philosophy and of Medicine, in Greek, Latin and Hebrew words, are no more conclusive. A forger, or even a mere remodeller, desirous of accentuating the Rabelaisian character of these chapters, would naturally have thought of cramming into his text borrowings from the ancient tongues and sciences of which Rabelais had displayed such a wide and varied knowledge in his previous books[1].

We might mention the considerable number of allusions to places and persons known to Rabelais which are found in this *Fifth Book*. They are, indeed, numerous. It even contains a reference to a work of Scaliger's[2], which did not appear till after Rabelais' death, and attributes to Roberval, Viceroy of Canada, a voyage to Africa which he never made[3]! All that might be the work of a mediocre imitator who, in order to write in Rabelais' manner, would certainly have sought out the books which he habitually quoted, the persons and places with which he was familiar[4].

We must, then, conclude that, in a question of this nature, there can be no irrefutable proof ; neither textual criticism, nor philology, nor the determination of its sources[5], nor the

---

[1] Cf. L. Sainéan, *La langue de Rabelais* (Paris, E. de Boccard, 1922), 2 vols., 8vo.

[2] Scaliger is mentioned (ch.XIX) among the *diables de sages folz* who have written on *Entelechia*. However, he mentions it only in the 307th of his *Exercitationes adversus Cardanum* which appeared in 1557. And he adds, " Hæc quidem risui sunt atque contemptui novis Lucianis atque Diagoriis culinariis ". He seemingly includes Rabelais among these " new Kitchen Lucians and Diagorases ". This accounts for the above rejoinder in the *Fifth Book*, which answers Scaliger by ranking him with the inept defenders of Aristotle. Cf. Dr. de Santi's two articles on Rabelais and J. C. Scaliger, *R.É.R.*, III, 12–44, and IV, 29–44.

[3] If, indeed, Roberval is really intended by Robert Valbringue, in ch. III.

[4] Chinon is not mentioned in any of the preceding books as often as in the *Fifth Book*.

[5] The study of the sources has shown that ch. IX, *The Island of Tools*, and ch. XXXII*a*, of the manuscript, *Comment furent les dames Lanternes servies à souper*, are taken for a great part from the *Disciple de Pantagruel*, published in 1538, from which Rabelais had taken for his *Fourth Book* the story of Bringuenarilles, and the idea of Wild Island and of the Chitterlings' episode. Can we conclude from this that Rabelais alone was capable of drawing on this source for the composition of the *Fifth Book* ? Likewise, does the fact that he knew and quoted in *Gargantua* (ch. IX) and in the *Brièfve déclaration d'aucunes dictions plus obscures contenues dans le Quart Livre*, appended to some copies of the 1552 edition, Francesco Colonna's work *Hypnerotomachia Polyphili* (Venice, 1489), constitute an argument for his authorship of chs. XXIV–XXV (The Ball in the manner of a Tournament) and chs. XXXVII–XLIV (Description of the Temple of the Holy Bottle) of which a great part is taken from this work of Colonna's ? On the connections between the *Songe de Polyphile* and the *Fifth Book*, cf. Sölftoft-Jansen, *Revue d'histoire littéraire de la France*, 1896, p. 608 ; Louis Thuasne, *Études sur Rabelais*, Paris, 1904 ; and

study of the elements of contemporary reality contained in the work, furnish decisive arguments for attributing the *Fifth Book* to Rabelais. All the doubts which arise both from our uncertainty as to the fate of Rabelais' manuscripts after his death, and from the statements of Tabourot des Accords, Antoine du Verdier and Louis Guyon, remain.

Under these circumstances is it not allowable that impressionistic criticism should claim its rights and point out, at least, what it considers as absolutely foreign to Rabelais and what he might have acknowledged as his own work, in the extremely likely hypothesis that his manuscripts have been retouched, added to and published by a clever adapter[1]. We must not, of course, hide the fact that these conjectures are fragile, varying as they do with the individual's taste. Would it, however, be rash to exclude from Rabelais' work those episodes which

---

Sainéan, *Problèmes littéraires du seizième siècle*. The last-named author has given in an appendix the parts of Colonna's work which are translated in the *Fifth Book*.

[1] Attempts have, naturally, been made to identify this adapter or forgerer. The 1564 edition concludes with this epigram :

> Rabelais est-il mort ? Voicy encore un livre,
> Non, sa meilleure part a repris ses esprits
> Pour nous faire présent de l'un de ses Escrits,
> Qui le rend entre tous immortel et fait vivre.
>
> NATURE QUITE.

This signature has greatly perplexed the critics. M. Cons took it to be an anagram of Jean Quentin and attempted to prove that he was the author of the book. I refuted this theory (*Rev. XVIᵉ siècle*, 1914, pp. 259–282). It is inadmissible that Jean Quentin, who was spokesman for the clergy at the *États généraux* of Orleans in 1566, could have written the satire of *Ringing Island*, which the Protestants could use as a weapon against Catholicism.

Besides, as M. A. Dupont has shown (*Rev. XVIᵉ siècle*, 1925, pp. 403–408), *Nature Quite* was the anagram of the physician, Jean de Mayerne, called *Jean Turquet*. Paul Lacroix attributed the *Fifth Book* to him, but M. A. Dupont considers this ascription as improbable. It is, moreover, incompatible with Guyon's assertion, who expressly states that the author was not a doctor.

The writer whose learning and wit would have best qualified him for re-handling Rabelais and writing the *Fifth Book* was, perhaps, the author of the *Apologie pour Hérodote*, Henri Estienne. But we know that he had no love for Rabelais, on account of his Lucianism. He would hardly have completed a work which he judged to be harmful to the Christian Faith.

It may be remarked that an edition of the *Fifth Book*, unknown before 1900, had appeared, probably at Lyons, in 1549, i.e. before the complete edition of the *Fourth Book*, under the title : *Le cinquiesme livre des faictz et dicts du noble Pantagruel auquelz sont compris les grans Abuz et desordonnée vie de Plusieurs Estatz de ce monde.*

M. Lefranc has shown (*R.É.R.*, I, 29–54 and 122–142) that this supposed fifth book was apocryphal, and that it was really a compilation made up of various chapters of Sebastian Brandt's *Nef des Folz* and of Jean Bouchet's *Regnars traversants les voies périlleuses des folles fiances du monde* (1504).

have neither style, nor wit, nor humour, like Grippeminault's riddle (ch. XII), the stiff and lifeless developments like the Chamber of the Apedefts (ch. XVI), or the Tournament of Quintessence (chs. XXIV-XXV), the impassioned invectives against the Furred Law-cats (ch. XI), the tiresome allegory of the priest-birds in *l'Isle Sonante* (chs. II–V). Not that everything in these episodes is suspect—the apologue of the horse and the ass (ch. VII), the discourse of " the hospice wretch " (ch. XI) have a real Rabelaisian flavour ; but too many features are foreign to Rabelais' manner. On the other hand, we meet it again, almost without interruption, in certain episodes, such as the Island of Odes, and the landings at the land of Satin and at Lantern-land.

Is the conclusion of the work in the Rabelaisian spirit ? It seems rather disappointing to those who expect from the author of *Pantagruel* a disclosure " of dreadful Mysteries, as well in what concerneth our Religion, as matters of the public State and Life œconomical ". And the glossarists usually do not hesitate to attribute a hidden meaning to the Oracle's word, " *Trinch* ! Drink ".—Drink what ? Cool wine and of the best, think Panurge and Friar Jean ; but should not true Pantagruelists understand—" Drink at the fountain of knowledge " ? There is nothing against this interpretation ; nor is there anything to authorise it. The explanation of the Oracle as formulated by the priestess Bacbuc, is, in fact, of an entirely different nature—Seek the truth in wine, she says, and " be yourself the expounder of your undertaking ". Let Panurge, then, take a decision on the question of his marriage, glass in hand, if needs be ; but let him decide for himself—a practical piece of advice and a very ordinary recommendation ! But is it the first time that Rabelais has constructed a picturesque setting, organised a consultation on a large scale, and quoted profound maxims[1] to give eventually to a grave problem an ordinary common-sense solution ?

---

[1] Cf., along with those quoted above, the maxims at the end of ch. XXXVI : *Ducunt volentem fata, nolentem trahunt*—(" Fate leads the willing, and the unwilling draws ".)—" All things tend to their end ".

CHAPTER XVIII

RABELAIS IN FRENCH AND IN FOREIGN LITERATURES

A STUDY on Rabelais which made no mention of the fate of his works through the ages would be incomplete. The reputation of, and the influence exercised by his ideas, are varied, the literary imitations many. Few French books have been reprinted more often : there were ninety-eight editions of it in the 16th century, twenty in the 17th, twenty-six in the 18th, and about sixty in the 19th[1].

They have made popular the persons of Pantagruel, Gargantua and Panurge ; episodes like the holding of Picrochole's Council, the Abbey of Thélème, the drowning of Dindenault's sheep ; names like those of Perrin Dendin, the Catchpoles, Messer Gaster, the Furred Law-cats, and Grippeminault. Not only have they inspired story-tellers in prose and verse, pamphleteers, comic and satiric poets, but they have furnished scenarios for ballets[2], and comic operas[3], decorative motifs for fans[4] or printed cloths[5]. A vessel of a squadron, as we have said[6], has even had the name of Pantagruel.

A list of those famous in Literature, Art, Science and Politics, who delighted in reading Rabelais would be a long one. It would include poets like Du Bellay, Régnier, La Fontaine,

---

[1] The old Gargantuan Chronicles which had given Rabelais the idea of *Pantagruel* and *Gargantua* benefited by the success of his works, and were subsequently reprinted frequently, with alterations.

[2] M. Clouzot (*R.É.R.*, V, 90–97) enumerates ten *ballets-mascarades*, within the period 1626–1645, of which the subjects are taken from Rabelais—*La Naissance de Pantagruel*, a ballet performed at Blois during the Carnival of 1626 ; the ballet *Quolibets* by the poet Sigongnes, danced at the Louvre by Monseigneur, the King's brother ; the ballet of the *Pantagruélites*, taken from the *Third Book* (1638) ; the ballet of the Oracle of the *Sibile de Panzoust*, performed at the Palais Royal in 1645.

[3] *Panurge dans l'isle des Lanternes*, a comic opera in three acts, by M. Morel, music by Grétry (1785) ; *Les Noces de Panurge*, by Eugène and Édouard Adenis. Cf. *R.É.R.*, VII, 113 and VIII, 377.

[4] Cf. *R.É.R.*, VI, 279.

[5] Morel and Grétry's comic opera, *Panurge dans l'isle des Lanternes*, furnished the subject for a cloth design by Jouy. Cf. *R.É.R.*, VII, 113.

[6] *Vide supra*, p. 269.

Having no accurate information upon his life, their conception of it was based upon this formula and the new Democritus was credited with jests worthy of the cynic, Diogenes. De Thou, the historian, visiting his house at Chinon in 1598, and finding it transformed into an inn " where debauch was continually practised ", composed some humorous verses on this theme, and wrote gravely in his *Mémoires* : " François Rabelais, the celebrated physician, learned in the Greek and Latin tongues and highly proficient in his profession, had totally abandoned his studies towards the end of his days and abandoned himself to libertinism and the joys of the table. He held that joyousness was the distinguishing characteristic of man, and, in pursuance thereof, *giving full play to his temperament*, he had composed a very ingenious work in which, with a freedom worthy of Democritus and a spirit of mockery, often low and clownish, he amuses his readers, under fictitious names, by his ridicule of all the estates of life and all classes in the Kingdom "[1].

For a half-century the legend of the *joyeux curé de Meudon* is continually enriched with ridiculous anecdotes, the most famous being that of " Rabelais' quarter of an hour ". A professor of philosophy at the Collège d'Harcourt, Antoine Le Roy, priest and canon, author of a dictionary of philosophical terms[2], brought them together in a huge work, still unpublished[3].

The same general idea inspired the artists who drew, engraved or painted portraits of Rabelais. No picture of him

> Qui sic nugatur tractantem ut seria vincat,
> Seria quum faciet, dic, rogo, quantus erit !

Pœmata, ed. of 1548, p. 16, suppressed in subsequent editions. Tahureau du Mans renders it as follows :

> Puisqu'il surpasse en riant
> Ceux qui à bon esciant
> Traictent choses d'importance :
> Combien sera-il plus grand
> (Je te pry, dy moy) s'il prend
> Un œuvre de conséquence ?

Les premières poésies de Jaques Tahureau, Poitiers, 1554.
The same note is struck in an epigram by Estienne Pasquier (*Icones*, 1586) :

> Ille ego Gallorum Gallus Democritus illo
> Gratius aut si quid Gallia progenuit,
> Sic homines, sic et cœlestia numina lusi
> Vix homines, vix ut numina læsa putes.

[1] *Mémoires*, book VI.

[2] *Floretum philosophicum, seu ludus Meudonianus*, composed in the presbytery at Meudon, where Le Roy had betaken himself during the Fronde.

[3] *Elogia Rabelæsiana*, no. 8704 of the Latin MSS. in the Bibliothèque Nationale.

PLATE VIII

CHAPITRE XLI.

COMMENT LE MOYNE FEIST DORMIR GARGANTUA, ET DE SES HEURES ET BREVIAIRE.

E souper achevé, consulterent sus l'affaire instant, et feut conclud que environ la minuict ilz sortiroient à l'escarmouche pour sçavoir quel guet et diligence faisoient leurs ennemys; en ce pendent, qu'il se reposeroient quelque peu pour estre plus frais. Mais Gargantua ne povoit dormir en quelque façon qu'il se mist. Dont luy dist le moyne :

« Je ne dors jamais bien à mon aise, sinon quand je suis au sermon ou quand je prie Dieu. Je vous supplye, commençons, vous et moy, les sept pseaulmes, pour veoir si tantost ne serez endormy. »

L'invention pleut tres bien à Gargantua, et, commenceant le premier pseaulme, sus le poinct de *Beati quorum* s'endormirent

WAR

An illustration for *Gargantua*, by Hermann Paul (pub. L. Pichon)

[*face p.* 294

executed previous to his death is known to exist. The first
in date is a medallion, inserted as frontispiece to the edition
by Jean Martin (1569) : with its round head, thick black beard,
and short turned-up nose, it recalls the traditional portrait
of Marot. It is not considered by experts to be genuine. On
the other hand, they attribute great documentary value to
a portrait engraved in 1601, from an earlier model now lost—
it is that inserted by Léonard Gaultier, between the physicians
Dubois and Rondelet, in his collection of the hundred and forty-
four "*portraits of several famous men who figured in France
from* 1500 *to the present day* "[1]. It is a three-quarter bust of
Rabelais, from the left side, his head thrown slightly back
and wearing the four-lobed Doctor's cap. The nose is long[2],
thick and rounded at the end, the moustache and beard are
scant, the expression in his look and on his lips is caustic.
His bare neck issues from a loose garment, embroidered with
fur, showing some white linen. This face denotes decision,
irony and gravity. It is the archetype of all the engravings
and paintings executed in the 17th century, including that in
the Museum of Versailles, which dates from the last quarter
of the century.[3]

Some artists, however, considering probably that there was
too much doctoral gravity in this representation of the author
of *Gargantua*, wished to brighten it up—one of them, for
example, placed on a table in front of the Doctor, a glass
filled to the brim. Next, early in the 18th century, a new effigy
appeared, which emphasises this bacchanalian character—
Rabelais becomes a gay Silenus, with a short turned-up nose,
laughing heartily. A whole series of portraits of this type
take the place of the portrait of the Doctor.

The interpretation of his work has likewise varied between
two conceptions corresponding to these two different types.
But even those who were struck with and charmed by his
witticisms and drolleries were not satisfied with simply enjoying
them. They assigned to them various allegorical or moral

[1] Usually referred to as the *Chronologie collée*. On Rabelais' iconography,
cf. a study by H. Clouzot in Jacques Boulenger's volume *Rabelais à travers
les âges* (Paris, Le Divan, 1925).

[2] M. Abel Lefranc, struck both by the importance Rabelais assigns to the
nose in his personal descriptions, and by the admiration which he expresses
for long noses, conjectures that the nose was the most striking feature of his
physiognomy. Cf. *Le visage de Rabelais*, in *Rev. XVIᵉ siècle*, 1926, p. 112.

[3] See plate I.

U

meanings, which the author had no more thought of than Ovid of " the gospel sacraments " which the " gulligut friar " Lubin had discovered in his *Metamorphoses*[1]. Because the final books contain clear allegories in the episodes of Papimany, of Messer Gaster, of the Catchpoles, of the Furred Law-cats, of Ringing Island, many generalising minds came to the conclusion that all Rabelais' jokes were satirical allegories. They could not understand how a deep mind, a Democritus, could amuse itself with puns, plays upon words and obscene buffooneries. And, especially, they were disconcerted by them according as their taste became more refined. La Bruyère, who found in Rabelais " a monstrous assemblage of keen and ingenious moral observations and of filthy corruption ", considered him to be an inexplicable riddle[2]. Historical criticism would have given him the key to it. But even the scholars of the time did not possess it, just as Voltaire in the following century was lacking in it. He pitied the Regent for his fondness for Rabelais—assuredly this Prince must have " a corrupted taste " and " be associating with bad company " ! He later reverses this judgment. Having found among the " absurd buffooneries " and " terrible obscenities " a " slashing satire on the Pope, the Church and all the happenings of the time ", he concluded that all the fictions in Rabelais were merely historical events in disguise : " It is clear that Gargantua is François I, that Louis XII, although he was not François' father, is Grandgousier, and that Henri II is Pantagruel. Gargantua's education and the chapter on the ' wipe-breeches ' is a satire on the education which was then given to young princes ; the colours white and blue clearly stand for the livery of the French Kings. . . . The war over a cartload of cakes is the war between Charles V and François I. One cannot fail to recognise Charles V in the portrait of Picrochole, etc. "[3].

This method of interpretation, due to the advice given in a jocose way in the *Prologue* to *Gargantua* and to the desire for finding a hidden meaning in the creations of Rabelais' fancy, long remained in favour. During the Revolution,

---

[1] Prologue to *Gargantua*.

[2] He compares him to one of those " monsters " which he may have seen in the " Gothic " decoration of old churches : " A beautiful woman's face, with the *feet* and tail *of a serpent* . . . ".

[3] *Lettres à S. A. R., Monseigneur le Prince de . . . sur Rabelais et sur d'autres auteurs accusés d'avoir mal parlé de la religion chrétienne.* 1767. Ed. Moland, vol. XXVI, p. 469 *seq.*

Rabelais was enrolled among the precursors of the Philosophers who fought against " prejudice " for the " advancement of light ". In 1791, Ginguené disserted upon the *influence of Rabelais in the present revolution and in the civil constitution of the clergy;* he discovered in *Gargantua* and *Pantagruel* " royal, political and ecclesiastical institutions "[1].

Early in the 19th century this mania for historical interpretation led finally to the astounding commentary of the *Variorum* edition by Esmengart and Johanneau. There is not a paragraph, however clear it may be, which is not a cryptogram for these editors, in which they discover allusions either to political affairs or scandals of Court life. Following their example, commentators identified the grotesque figures of the *Dream of Pantagruel* with the captains, prelates, prominent men and favourites of François I's and Henri II's reigns.

Meanwhile, a new phase in the exegesis of Rabelais' work had begun with the Romantics. The scruples of *le goût*, which made Rabelais' style hard to understand for the Classics, were disappearing. Chateaubriand ranked the author of *Gargantua* among " the five or six writers who sufficed for the needs and sustenance of the mind ", among these " parentminds which seem to have given birth and nourishment to all others ". Pointing to those minds which are his descendants in the *gaulois* and naturalistic tradition—Montaigne, La Fontaine, Molière—he calls him the creator of French literature[2]. With an enthusiasm, which betrays his hostility to Voltaire, who had little appreciation except for the " impieties " of Rabelais, he extols his " great style ", his " profound satire of society and of man " and his " high philosophy ".

Victor Hugo, in his turn, frequently sounds the praises of this philosophy, and notably in a poem in the *Contemplations* (1856) where Rabelais is placed among the seers (*mages*) who represent the different aspects of man's genius.

> Et voici les prêtres du rire . . .
> Rabelais que nul ne comprit.
> Il berce Adam pour qu'il s'endorme,
> Et son éclat de rire énorme
> Est un des gouffres de l'esprit.

[1] His book is issued from Utopia, from the Presses of the Abbey of Thélème (on sale in Paris, in Gattez', at the Palais-Royal).
[2] *Essai sur la littérature anglaise* (1836), ed. Garnier, vol. XI, p. 614. He repeats this opinion in Book IX of *Les Mémoires d'Outre-Tombe* (ed. Biré, pp. 192-193).

In truth, if Victor Hugo frequently mentions Rabelais, he does not seem to have been a great reader of him. His references to his work are practically limited to the names of the Giants ; he makes no allusions to any particular scene, says nothing definite in his judgments on his language and style. The impression left with him is that of a chaotic, monstrous and enormous work. Now, these are precisely the signs by which he recognises genius, which is necessarily " out of all proportion (*outré*) " by reason " of the amount of the infinite which is in it ". That is why the author of *Gargantua* is worthy of a place among the fourteen literary geniuses who are the personification of mankind : with Cervantes, he is the " mocker who closes the Middle Ages "[1].

Contemporary criticism no longer regards Rabelais as " an abyss of the mind " or a prodigious thinker. Based upon the methods of the historical sciences, its tendency is to examine his work in the light of the different circumstances which influenced its conception and development. It finds out the materials on which the writer has worked, either in conforming to certain rules and traditions or in following his own taste. It would seem to place a lesser value on Rabelais' thought, which is not always original, than on his qualities as an artist.

Some of these had, from the time his work appeared, inspired imitators. Even in our author's lifetime a story-teller, Noël du Fail[2], had imitated some of the tricks of his style—the art of conveying an impression of reality by using real personal or place names, or by giving a familiar colour and easy turn to his conversations. Imitations of this nature are to be met with commonly in almost all the story-tellers of the end of the century—Guillaume Bouchet, Tabourot des Accords, Béroald de Verville.

Satirists and pamphleteers imitated some of his fictions. The episodes of Papimany and of Ringing Island were popular among the Huguenots. A Pamphleteer from the Low Countries, Marnix de Sainte-Aldegonde, copied it. In his *Tableau des*

---

[1] *William Shakespeare*. Jacques Boulenger gives—in his *Rabelais à travers les ages*, already referred to—a searching analysis of Hugo's judgments on Rabelais ; he concludes " that it is impossible to find in Hugo a single precise judgment on *Gargantua* and *Pantagruel* ".

[2] Cf. E. Philippot's thesis on Noël du Fail (Paris, É. Champion, 1914).

différends de la Religion, he " turned religion into *Rabelaiserie* "[1] as De Thou put it.

Janotus de Bragmardo's harangue served as a model to the authors of the *Satyre Menippée* for the speech of the Cardinal of Pelvé. The latter, like the Sorbonne theologian, " when everybody had sonorously and theologically coughed, and spit again and again" , exposes in his emphatic style, mingled with macaronic Latin, proverbs and popular sayings, the Pope's views on France, including the ingenuous confession of the minor profits which the orator hopes to receive as a result of them. Agrippa d'Aubigné, in his satire *La Confession de Sancy,* has imitated the learned comic elements used by Maître Alcofrybas, his litanies of words, his paradoxes supported with grave quotations.

His jokes, popular sayings, and *mots de gueule* are found in the authors of comedies—Jean-Antoine de Baïf, Odet de Turnèbe, François d'Amboise, and Captain Lasphrise.

He has supplied D'Assoucy, " the Emperor of burlesque ", and Scarron with comic themes, Molière with the outline of a scene in the *Mariage forcé* and more than one idea in *l'École des femmes,* La Fontaine with proper names, like Gaster and Raminagrobis, and sayings and anecdotes for his tales. Voltaire is indebted to the Picrocholian war for some points in his heroi-comical poem *La Pucelle*—for instance, the minutely technical descriptions of impossible wounds.

It is not only in France, but also beyond its frontiers that Rabelais found admirers and imitators. A German, born in 1550, at Strasbourg, Doctor of Law of Bâle University, Jean Fischart[2], published, as early as 1575, a considerably amplified translation of *Gargantua.* He adapted it to suit the German taste, including in his paraphrase scenes taken from their national history or satirical allusions to the customs of their country. As regards style, his principal aim was to reproduce the exuberance, the plays upon words, the changes in their form which he found in his model[3]. Another very free paraphrase,

---

[1] Cf. H. Pirenne, *Rabelais dans les Pays-Bas, R.É.R.,* IV, 224, and G. Cohen, *Rabelais et Marnix de Sainte-Aldegonde, R.É.R.,* VI, 64.

[2] On Fischart as an imitator of Rabelais, cf. M. Hœpffner, Professor of the University of Strasbourg, in *Rev. XVIᵉ siècle,* 1926, pp. 160–165.

[3] This is clear from the title of the work : *Affenteurliche und Ungeheurliche Geschichtschrift von Leben, Rhaten und Thaten der vorlangen Weilen vollenwohlbeschraiten Helden und Herren Grandgusier, Gargantua und Pantagruel, Königen in Utopien und Nieneureich. Etwan von M. Francisco Rabelais*

based upon Rabelais and Fischart[1], was published in the late 18th century about the same time. Goethe conceived the idea of composing a sequel to Pantagruel's travels, the *Voyage of Megaprazon*[2], which he left unfinished, and which was published after the author's death, in 1837.

Germany produced, in the first half of the 19th century, yet another translator of Rabelais, Gottlob Regis, who accompanied his translation with two volumes of commentaries, of which the second, in particular, abounds in information as to the sources on which our author drew[3]. In our own time some of her scholars, like Birch-Hirschfeld, Heinrich Morf, not to mention those still living, have displayed great interest in the study of Rabelais.

The name of Gargantua occurs frequently in the English writers from the last third of the 16th century onwards. The influence of Rabelais can be seen in Shakespeare's plays. The lexicographer, Cotgrave, has taken a host of obscure words from the text of *Pantagruel* and *Gargantua* for his French-English dictionary, so that, even to-day, he remains the main authority for the explanation of certain obscure terms in Rabelais[4]. His work was utilised by the first translator of Rabelais into English, Sir Thomas Urquhart, the Scot. He was a Doctor who had travelled extensively in France, Italy and Spain. His translation is a real masterpiece[5]. He left it unfinished. A French refugee, Le Motteux, translated the last two books, but with less flavour[6]. These translations inspired two eighteenth century writers, Nash and Sterne, who respectively rendered in their own language, the brilliance of Rabelais'

Französisch entworfen : nun aber uberschrecklich lustig auf den Teutschen Meridian visirt, und ungefärlich oben hin, wie man den Grindigen lausst, vertirt, durch Huldrich Elloposcheron Reznem. Si premes erumpit : si laxes effugit.

[1] *Gargantua und Pantagruel, ungearbeitet nach Rabelais und Fischart.* Von Dr. Eckstein (C. L. Sauder), Hamburg, 1785–1787, 3 vols.

[2] *Vide* Sainéan, *Les interprètes de Rabelais en Angleterre et en Allemagne,* R.É.R., VII, 206–238.

[3] *Meister Franz Rabelais der Arzenei Doctoren Gargantua und Pantagruel,* aus dem Französischen verdeutscht, mit Einleitung und Anmerkungen . . . herausgegeben durch Gottlob Regis (1832). Reprinted at Berlin in 1906 by Max Hurwitz.

[4] *Dictionarie of the French and English Tongues,* London, 1611.

[5] Title : *The first Book of the Works of Mr. Francis Rabelais, Doctor in Physick, containing five Books of the Lives, heroïck Deeds and Sayings of Gargantua and his sonne Pantagruel, all done by M. Francis Rabelais in the French Tongue and now faithfully translated into English,* 1653.

[6] In 1693–1694. Cf. R.É.R., VI, 123–126.

CHAPTER XVIII

RABELAIS IN FRENCH AND IN FOREIGN LITERATURES

A STUDY on Rabelais which made no mention of the fate of his works through the ages would be incomplete. The reputation of, and the influence exercised by his ideas, are varied, the literary imitations many. Few French books have been reprinted more often : there were ninety-eight editions of it in the 16th century, twenty in the 17th, twenty-six in the 18th, and about sixty in the 19th[1].

They have made popular the persons of Pantagruel, Gargantua and Panurge ; episodes like the holding of Picrochole's Council, the Abbey of Thélème, the drowning of Dindenault's sheep ; names like those of Perrin Dendin, the Catchpoles, Messer Gaster, the Furred Law-cats, and Grippeminault. Not only have they inspired story-tellers in prose and verse, pamphleteers, comic and satiric poets, but they have furnished scenarios for ballets[2], and comic operas[3], decorative motifs for fans[4] or printed cloths[5]. A vessel of a squadron, as we have said[6], has even had the name of Pantagruel.

A list of those famous in Literature, Art, Science and Politics, who delighted in reading Rabelais would be a long one. It would include poets like Du Bellay, Régnier, La Fontaine,

---

[1] The old Gargantuan Chronicles which had given Rabelais the idea of *Pantagruel* and *Gargantua* benefited by the success of his works, and were subsequently reprinted frequently, with alterations.

[2] M. Clouzot (*R.É.R.*, V, 90–97) enumerates ten *ballets-mascarades*, within the period 1626–1645, of which the subjects are taken from Rabelais—*La Naissance de Pantagruel*, a ballet performed at Blois during the Carnival of 1626 ; the ballet *Quolibets* by the poet Sigongnes, danced at the Louvre by Monseigneur, the King's brother ; the ballet of the *Pantagruélites*, taken from the *Third Book* (1638) ; the ballet of the Oracle of the *Sibile de Panzoust*, performed at the Palais Royal in 1645.

[3] *Panurge dans l'isle des Lanternes*, a comic opera in three acts, by M. Morel, music by Grétry (1785) ; *Les Noces de Panurge*, by Eugène and Édouard Adenis. Cf. *R.É.R.*, VII, 113 and VIII, 377.

[4] Cf. *R.É.R.*, VI, 279.

[5] Morel and Grétry's comic opera, *Panurge dans l'isle des Lanternes*, furnished the subject for a cloth design by Jouy. Cf. *R.É.R.*, VII, 113.

[6] *Vide supra*, p. 269.

Molière, Racine, Chénier, Victor Hugo, Alfred de Musset, Théophile Gautier ; thinkers and philosophers like Montaigne, Fontenelle, Diderot, Voltaire, Anatole France ; novelists like Scarron, Charles Sorel, Honoré de Balzac, Flaubert ; scholars like Étienne Pasquier and Huet, Bishop of Avranches ; historians like Michelet ; the classical Boileau and the romantic Chateaubriand ; the Protestants La Noue and Agrippa d'Aubigné ; the freethinker Théophile de Viau ; statesmen like Gambetta, Jaurès, and Clémenceau ; a noble lady, the Marquise de Sévigné ; a prince, the Regent ; a king, Henry IV.

His admirers are far in excess of his detractors. These latter are few in number : they comprise either Christians who are alarmed at the rehabilitation of Nature in Rabelais' work, or idealists who are shocked by the crudity of his expressions. Gabriel de Puits-Herbault, " the raging Putherbe ", is typical of the former category. Another religious, a Jesuit, went further in his anathemas at the beginning of the 17th century— Fr. Garasse. He confessed that he had never opened either *Pantagruel* or *Gargantua*[1], but the extracts from them which he had read in Estienne Pasquier had convinced him that Rabelais is " an accursed and pernicious writer " who " sucks piety away gradually " and " who has done more damage in France by his buffooneries than Calvin by his new-fangled doctrines "[2]. He then denounced him as the breviary of libertines, " the enchiridion of libertinism ".

It is for the same reasons that St. Francis de Sales advised a garrison-officer on holiday not to read, among other romances, that of " the infamous Rabelais ".

The same century saw another religious, a Franciscan, less severe on the unfrocked Cordelier of the Puy-Saint-Martin— Wadding, author of the *Annales Minorum*[3], a sort of catalogue of all the Friars Minor who had shed lustre on their Order by their learning or their writings. He had no hesitation in including Rabelais therein, and repeating the eulogy on him formerly made by Scévole de Sainte-Marthe. So there was at

---

[1] Cf. Abel Lefranc, *Garasse et Rabelais*, in *R.É.R.*, VII, 492–499.

[2] *La doctrine curieuse des beaux esprits de ce temps ou prétendus tels. Contenant plusieurs maximes pernicieuses à la Religion, à l'Estat et aux bonnes mœurs. Combattue et renversée par le P. François Garassus, de la compagnie de Jésus.* Paris, 1623, 4to. *Vide*, Book VIII, section 10.

[3] Rome, 1650.

least one monk who did not call the author of *Gargantua* an Epicurean swine ! " Capable of writing seriously and learnedly on Medicine, . . . he preferred to imitate Lucian. Like this author, he wrote amusing books in his mother-tongue, which, although they are mere fooleries, are none the less attractive for every learned reader, and fill him with unbelievable pleasure "[1].

The repugnance experienced by idealistic minds at the filth contained in Rabelais' works has found no more eloquent expression than through Lamartine. For him Rabelais is " the mudheap of humanity "—to the sewers with the feast he offers us ! he exclaims. Such vehement indignation is not surprising on the part of a poet who was shocked at La Fontaine's looseness and who feared lest the reading of the *Lutrin* might corrupt the taste of young people.

What a chorus of eulogy one could set against these few hostile or deprecatory references ! But the reasons for this admiration have varied with the times, and all parts of Rabelais' work have not always been equally appreciated.

The opinion on the man and on his work held by the generation of the end of the 16th century is fairly well represented by the judgment of Scévole de Sainte-Marthe, already mentioned, or again in the " epithets " suggested to writers in Maurice de la Porte's dictionary to describe Maître François—" Facétieux, mordant, utile-doux, raillard, second Épicure, gausseur ou gaudisseur, Lucian françois, docte gabeur, ventre épicurien, plaisant moqueur, pantagruélite "[2]. He is the French Lucian, or better still, the French Democritus, that is to say, the scholar or the philosopher whose reflections led him to see in life only a comedy to be laughed at[3].

---

[1] As has been pointed out by M. Gilson (*Rabelais franciscain*, in the *Revue d'histoire franciscaine*, 1924), this judgment is translated from the Latin of Scévole de Sainte-Marthe, *Elogia* (Paris, 1606). " Franciscus Rabelæsus. —Cum enim pro ea qua pollebat linguarum et medicinæ scientia multa graviter et erudite posset scribere, quod et Hippocratis aphorismi ab illo casta fide traducti et aliquot epistolæ nitido stylo conscriptæ satis indicant, Lucianum tamen æmulare maluit, ad cujus exemplum ea sermone patrio finxit, quæ meræ quidem nugæ sunt, sed ejusmodi tamen sunt ut lectorem quemlibet eruditum capiant et incredibili quadam voluptate perfundant ".

[2] *Les Épithètes de M. de la Porte, parisien, livre non seulement utile à ceux qui font profession de la Poésie, mais fort propre aussi pour illustrer toute autre composition Françoise* (Paris, 1571). Cf. Abel Lefranc, *Les épithètes de Maurice de la Porte et la légende de Rabelais*, Rev. XVIe siècle, 1915.

[3] *Vide* Théodore de Bèze's distich, often quoted by contemporary writers :

style and his humour. A revival of interest in Rabelais, in the second half of the nineteenth century, gave rise to a new translation, accompanied with notes, by W. F. Smith[1].

No period, perhaps, has been more fertile in imitations of Rabelais than that in which the French Romantic school flourished. The Romantics are infatuated with everything concerning the Middle Ages, and Rabelais benefits by this vogue. Is he not the inheritor of old regionalistic traditions ? Did he not preserve in his style that raciness of which Malherbe and the Classics subsequently robbed the French language ? Charles Nodier and Mérimée praise him and quietly imitate him. Alfred de Vigny himself, in a passage of his *Stello*, parodies the exuberance of his style. Honoré de Balzac is deeply indebted to *Gargantua* and *Pantagruel*. His *Contes drolatiques colligez ez abbayes de Touraine et mis en lumière pour l'esbattement des Pantagruelistes et non aultres* (1831) are direct imitations of the great Tourangeau, " prince of all wisdom and of all comedy," before whom he orders us all in his *Prologue*, to " take off our caps as a sign of reverence and honour ". Rabelais would have recognised in them his themes, his humour, and above all his picturesque speech. But he might, perhaps, have thought that those " fooleries " had the odour of oil rather than wine[2], and he would, doubtless, have preferred to these somewhat laboured imitations some passages of *Le Capitaine Fracasse* in which Théophile Gautier, a true disciple of Rabelais, has rendered not only Maître Alcofrybas' truculence and verbal juggling, but the very spirit of his works[3].

Thus Rabelais' book has often happily inspired writers who wished to lend an archaic flavour to their style, or impart to it an easy conversational tone, or a richness which leaves the impression of facility, fertility and abundance of invention[4].

---

[1] *Rabelais. The five books and minor writings together with letters and documents illustrating his life, a new translation with notes,* by W. F. Smith, 1893, 2 vols.

[2] Rabelais employs this expression in the *Prologue* to *Gargantua*.

[3] Cf. Jaques Boulenger, *op. cit.,* pp. 143–144.

[4] Among contemporary writers we must mention M. Léon Daudet, who professes a great admiration for Rabelais, " the giant of French prose literature ". He has, at times, imitated in his polemics Rabelais' satirical allegories. He seems, now, to recognize that this form is out of date. *Vide* his essay on Rabelais, in the second *Courrier des Pays-Bas,* entitled *Les Horreurs de la guerre* (Paris, 1928), and an article in the *Action Française,* 28th April, 1928.

Rabelais has also inspired numerous artists. The majority of them, like Gustave Doré, have gone in for the exaggerated representation on a gigantic scale of the portraits of his characters. Others have aimed at rendering the

But the very fantasy of their model escapes his imitators—his imaginative power in the creation of myths, the poetic gift of thinking in images, the unexpected turns of his humour.

The "joyous narrations" of *Gargantua* and *Pantagruel*, which have afforded so much amusement for close on four centuries, will always find readers. The artistic qualities of Rabelais' prose have never been the object of so much study, nor so highly appreciated as at the present day[1]. Are his general ideas capable of stimulating further thought ? Or are they played out ? It would be rash to prophesy. In any event, *Gargantua* and *Pantagruel* will always be an object of special study for those who wish to understand the spirit of our Renaissance at the period of François I. There is no writer who reflects more faithfully all its aspects. He has the merit of having been the first to give expression in French to some of the religious and scientific ideas of the Humanists. He has expressed in popular form their criticisms on wars of conquest, on popular superstitions, on the abuses of the Catholic Church at the eve of the Reformation, and their theories on the necessity for abandoning the "Gothic disciplines" and returning to the direct study of Greek and Latin antiquity. He represents not only the ideas, but also the feelings of his generation. His whole book is vibrant with the effervescence of creative forces, with that light-hearted trust in Nature and in man, with that forward surge which characterise the movement of the Renaissance in all the Western nations.

exuberance and life which are among the characteristics of Rabelais' work ; others, again, have made it a theme for grotesque and obscene figures (*Vide, Les Songes drolatiques de Pantagruel*). Finally, some have taken as the themes of their compositions the more broadly human aspects of his narratives or descriptions. Among these last is Hermann Paul, in the *Gargantua* published by L. Pichon. Cf. the specimen, Plate VIII.

[1] *Vide* Brunetière's *Histoire de la littérature française classique* (Delagrave, 1905), vol. I, pp. 142–148 ; Lanson's *Art de la prose* (Libraire des Annales, 1907), ch. II, entitled *The first of the great French artists, Rabelais* ; Faguet, *Seizième siècle, études littéraires* (Lecène, Oudin et Cie., 1894), pp. 118–122 ; Villey, *Marot et Rabelais*, ch. XIII ; Jacques Boulenger, *Rabelais à travers les âges*, p. 168 ; Pierre d'Espezel, *Les œuvres de M. François Rabelais* (La Cité des Livres, 1927), vol. I, *Introduction*, p. xvi, etc.

BIBLIOGRAPHY

By the Same Author

I. LITERARY HISTORY

L'Œuvre de Rabelais (Sources, invention et composition.) 1 vol., 8vo. Paris, H. Champion, 1910. (Ouvrage couronné par l'Académie française.)

Histoire de la Littérature française illustrée, publiée sous la direction de MM. Joseph Bédier, de l'Académie française, et Paul Hazard. Paris, Larousse, 1923. *Le seizième siècle, de Louis XII à la mort de François Ier.*

Guillaume Budé (1468–1540) et les origines de l'humanisme français. 1 vol., 8vo. Paris, Les Belles-Lettres, 1923.

L'Adolescence de Rabelais en Poitou. 1 vol., 8vo., illustr. Paris, Les Belles-Lettres, 1923.

La vie et l'œuvre de Scévole de Sainte-Marthe, officier de finances et humaniste (1536–1623). Paris, Éd. Champion, 1924.

La Renaissance des Lettres en France de Louis XII à Henri IV. (Collection Armand Colin.) 1 vol., small 8vo. Paris, A. Colin, 1925.

État présent des études rabelaisiennes. (Douzième cahier des *Études françaises*, avril 1927.) Paris, Les Belles-Lettres, 1927.

Appearing shortly

À propos du tricentenaire de la mort d'Agrippa d'Aubigné. Portrait et études. 1 vol., 8vo. Paris, Boivin, 1930.

II. EDITOR OF

Le quart livre de Pantagruel (Édition dite partielle, Lyon 1540). Texte critique avec une introduction. 1 vol., 8vo. Paris, H. Champion, 1909.

Œuvres de François Rabelais. Édition critique publiée sous la direction d'Abel Lefranc, Membre de l'Institut, professeur au Collège de France. Commentaire: sources antiques et mediévales. 5 vol., 8vo. Paris, Éd. Champion, 1912–1930.

La Muse de Ronsard. 1 vol., 8vo., avec vignettes sur bois par Carlègle. Paris, Léon Pichon, 1924.

Agrippa d'Aubigné. Supplément inédit à *l'Histoire universelle,* avec introduction et commentaire. Collection de la *Société de l'Histoire de France.* 1 vol., 8vo.   Paris, Éd. Champion, 1925.

Anthologie du XVIᵉ siècle français. (Nelson's " Modern Studies " Series.)   1 vol., 8vo.   London, Thomas Nelson and Sons, 1927.

Œuvres complètes de Rabelais. (Collection des Universités de France, publiée sous les auspices de l'Association Guillaume Budé.)   5 vols., 8vo.   Éd. Fernand Roches, Paris, 1929.

Œuvres de Mathurin Régnier. (Collection des Universités de France.)   1 vol., 8vo.   Éd. Fernand Roches, Paris, 1930.

Œuvres complètes de Montaigne.   7 vols., 8vo.   (*In preparation for the same collection.*)

Œuvres de Clément Marot (Édition Georges Guiffrey), Tome IV, *Épigrammes, Estrennes, Épitaphes, Cimetières, Complainctes, Oraisons.*   Paris, Schemit, 1930.

By the Translator

Claude Chappuys (?–1575), *poète de la Cour de François Iᵉʳ.*   1 vol., 8vo.   Paris, Les Belles-Lettres, 1929.

INDEX